Fighting the Retreat from
Arabia and the Gulf

J. B. Kelly being greeted by Sheikh Rashid of Ajman in 1957

Fighting the Retreat from Arabia and the Gulf

The Collected Essays and Reviews of J.B. Kelly Vol. 1.

edited by S.B. Kelly

Copyright © J.B & S.B. Kelly, 2013

All rights reserved. No part of this book may be reproduced in any form or by any means, electronic or mechanical, without permission in writing from the publisher except by reviewers who may quote brief passages in their reviews.

Published by New English Review Press
a subsidiary of World Encounter Institute
PO Box 158397
Nashville, Tennessee 37215
&
27 Old Gloucester Street
London, England, WC1N 3AX

Cover Design by Kendra Adams

ISBN: 978-0-9884778-3-4

First Edition

NEW ENGLISH REVIEW PRESS
newenglishreview.org

To Valda
1925 - 2013

Acknowledgements

It would not have been possible to put this this collection together without the help and co-operation of a number of people and organisations. I am grateful to the following publishers and their editors for permission to reprint my late father's articles, letters and book reviews: John Wiley & Sons (for Chapters 2-3,5,10,12,14-15,17-19, 21), *The Middle East Journal* (for Chapter 7), Indiana University Press (for Chapter 8), Taylor & Francis (for Chapters 11,13,16, and 28), Longman Pearson (for Chapter 20), Cambridge University Press (for Chapter 23,25 and 26), Oxford University Press (for Chapter 24), and the University of Chicago Press (for Chapter 27).

I owe a debt of gratitude to Karen Crouch and my wife, Sara, for so willingly giving of their time to type up several of the longer chapters. The Graphics team, under Graham Ford at the JSCSC (especially Aaron Cripps) have done wonders digitalising old articles for me. My thanks to Professor Edmund Bosworth, John O'Sullivan and David Pryce-Jones, who all knew my father, for reading and commenting on the manuscript. Above all, Hugh Fitzgerald and Rebecca Bynum have been the moving forces behind this book. It was Hugh, an old friend of my father, who put me in touch with Rebecca, the finest of editors, at the New English Review Press. I had been a fan of the *New English Review* for some years, one of the few remaining outlets of intellectual sanity in our darkening world. I recognised that its contributors were of the same stripe as my father, and me, and thought it entirely appropriate that my father's collected essays and reviews should be published by the NER Press. He would have approved. He has found his spiritual home.

Contents

Introduction: Macaulay's New Zealander   11

1 - The British Position in the Persian Gulf   17

2 - The Buraimi Oasis Dispute   30

3 - The Persian Claim to Bahrain   40

4 - A Nice Little Aggression   65

5 - Sovereignty and Jurisdiction in Eastern Arabia   67

6 - Sultanate and Imamate in Oman   77

7 - The Bahrain Question   101

8 - Britain in the Red Sea and Palestine   106

9 - The Persian Gulf   113

10 - The Kurds and Iraq   115

11 - Mehemet 'Ali's Expedition to the Persian Gulf 1837-1840   118

12 - The Economy of Kuwait   180

13 - Aden   182

14 - Arab Nationalism   190

15 - The USA in the Arab World   195

16 - Saudi Arabia in the Nineteenth Century 198

17 - The Future in Arabia   209

18 - An Arab View of T.E. Lawrence   231

19 - Southern Arabia   234

20 - Salisbury, Curzon and the Kuwait Agreement of 1899   240

21 - Saudi Arabia and Islam   280

22 - T.E. Lawrence and His Friends   282

23 - Eastern Arabia in the Eighteenth Century   303

24 - The European Empires and Islam 306

25 - Religion and Rebellion in Iran   310

26 - Islam and Imperialism   312

27 - Britain and Russia in Persia and the Gulf 316

28 - Oman   327

About the Author   343

Index   349

Introduction:
Macaulay's New Zealander

J B. Kelly was compared on a number of occasions by reviewers of his works (especially his last book, *Arabia, the Gulf and the West*, 1980) as having the prose style of the great nineteenth century Whig historian, Thomas Babington Macaulay, or his eighteenth century predecessor, Edward Gibbon, the author of *The Decline and Fall of the Roman Empire*. My father was amused, and not a little flattered, by these comparisons. He prided himself on his ability, as he put it, to write 'The King's English' as laid out by those estimable brothers, H.W. and E.G. Fowler, indefatigable lexicographers of the English language.[1] His love of language was learned at an early age in New Zealand, the only son of what would today be described as 'a one-parent family'. He never knew his father, Jack (a second-generation New Zealand Irishman), who had died on the operating table in 1927, of complications to wounds suffered whilst fighting with the ANZACs at Gallipoli in 1915 (his father had volunteered for war, even though he knew he was a haemophiliac, a 'bleeder'). Raised by nuns and aunts, whilst his mother Maud, worked as a hotel receptionist, he whiled away the long, lonely hours of the pre-television age by reading anything he could get his hands on, from Billy Bunter to *Aesops Fables* (always a favourite). A precocious lad, he entered Sacred Heart School in Ponsonby, Auckland at the age of eleven, where the Marist Brothers instilled in him a love of learning and languages, for he thrived at Latin, Greek and French. Like Macaulay, he won prizes for his Latin and English compositions. They were similar as well in the fact that they excelled at mathematics and science, and yet later revolted against them at university. My father had entered the University College of Auckland (later the Uni-

---

1 We had at all times a full set of Fowler's works in the house for perusal by all and sundry when engaged in the craft of composition.

versity of Auckland) at the early age of sixteen in 1941, set on becoming a geologist. But in his second year he 'bombed' as he put it. He was not to be a mining engineer. Instead he restarted his degree and 'majored', as the Americans term it, in history and English literature, just like Macaulay. They were both interested in education. In the practice of it, however, they followed different professions: Macaulay as an administrator in India, and later in the British Cabinet; my father as a school teacher and later as an academic historian in Britain and the United States. However, both wrote serious journalism to the end of their lives.

There is also a symbolic connection between Macaulay and my father. In a sonorous passage in his notice in *The Edinburgh Review* of *The History of the Popes* by the great German historian, Leopold Von Ranke, Macaulay had warned his largely Whig readership not to take for granted the apparent triumph of the English Protestant settlement embodied in the English Reformation, the Civil War and the Glorious Revolution of 1688. For the Church of Rome had endured for ages and might well continue to do so:

> She was great and respected before the Saxon had set foot in Britain, before the Frank had passed the Rhine, when Grecian eloquence still flourished at Antioch, when idols were still worshipped in Mecca. And she may still exist in undiminished vigour when some traveller from New Zealand shall, in the midst of vast solitude, take his stand on a broken arch of London bridge to sketch the ruins of St Paul's.[2]

Although my father in his later years was a lapsed Catholic, he retained a profound respect for the Church of Rome. This, and the fact that he was a New Zealander, made him an outsider in a largely decayed Protestant Britain, when he fetched up on her shores in 1949, to gaze upon

---

2 'Von Ranke.' (October,1840) in *Critical and Historical Essays* contributed to the *Edinburgh Review* by Lord Macaulay. New Edition in Three Volumes, Vol. III (London, Longmans, Green, and Co. and New York, 1891), p.101. Macaulay derived his idea of the New Zealander from a comment by Gibbon in *Decline and Fall* about the Picts: 'If, in the neighbourhood of the commercial and literary town of Glasgow, a race of cannibals has really existed, we may contemplate, in the period of Scottish history, the opposite extremes of savage and civilised life. Such reflections tend to enlarge the circle of our ideas; and to encourage the pleasing hope, that New Zealand may produce, in some future age, the Hume of the Southern Hemisphere.' Edward Gibbon, *The History of the Decline and Fall of the Roman Empire* (London,Allen Lane,1994), ed. David Wormersley, Vol.1, p.101.

Introduction: Macaulay's New Zealander

its wartime ruins and to observe the antics of its war-weary inhabitants. A time of great austerity, used by the post-war Socialist government to impose their levelling vision of the Welfare State, my father experienced at first hand the reality of the 'New Jerusalem', as he tried to pass on a love of literature to his unruly, ignorant, yet cocky, working class pupils at the run-down and smoke-begrimed Haverstock Hill School in London (later the alma mater of the scions of the 'trendy Hampstead intellectual', of a leftwards bent, and those twin hopes of the current British Labour Party, the Milliband brothers). A hard winter season teaching in a Leicestershire coal-mining village convinced him to go East in search of sun, warmth and a job teaching at the British Boys School in Alexandria, Egypt. The city was as Lawrence Durrell described it in his interminable sequence of novels and the British expatriate community spent much time at cocktail parties trying to identify the real-life models for his louche characters. My father met and married my mother, Valda Pitt, a teacher at the English Girls' College, and the daughter of a retired Royal Navy officer. They savoured the last years of King Farouk's misrule, when the playboy of the Eastern world spent much of his time cruising up and down Alexandria harbour in his flashy speedboat, bedecked by various European bathing beauties. They experienced the terror of an Egyptian riot, as the angry mob trashed European hotels, bars and businesses at the instigation of Muslim Brothers, the nationalists or even the royalists, as they competed for power in a decaying Egypt. They experienced the corruption of the effendi class as they tried, and succeeded, in taking their silver wedding presents out of the country without paying the expected *bakshish*, in this case my mother's virtue! They left the country just before the fall of Farouk in a coup at the hands of Colonel Nasser and his cohorts in 1952.

The antics of Nasser in the Middle East dominated the years from the Suez Crisis in 1956 to his death in 1970. Coincidently, they defined the period of my father's formal career as an academic at various British and American universities and provided the context for his ruminations in print on Arabia, the Gulf and the wider region, both in the past and the present. As such they represent a neat package and provide an obvious span and coverage for this volume. The early articles (Nos. 1-5) were for the house journal (*International Affairs*) of the Royal Institute of International Affairs, at Chatham House in St James's Square, London, and were the result of his association with the University of Oxford and the Foreign Office. After receiving a PhD in 1956 from the University of London (for a thesis on *Britain and the Persian Gulf, 1813-1843*) he was appointed a research fellow of Oxford's Institute of Colonial Studies, whose director was the retired British diplomat Sir Reader Bullard. The latter acted as mentor to my father introducing him not only to the Oxford milieu but to the scholars *manqué* of the Foreign Office. He did not take to the would-be don's life, with its equal measures of pretension and poverty, but he was impressed by the quality of the officials he worked with in the Arabian Department of the Foreign Office. He had been called in as an area specialist to help the mandarins in making the legal case for defensible boundaries for the British-protected Trucial shaikhdoms in the Gulf, threatened as they were by large Saudi territorial claims, aided and abetted by the Arabian-American Oil Company (ARAMCO) and the U.S. State Department. The early articles for *International Affairs* reflect the work he was doing in the late 1950s for the Foreign Office, and can be seen as part of an effort to influence political opinion in the UK and abroad on the related subjects of eastern Arabian frontiers, Buraimi, the Imamate rebellion in Oman and the Persian claim to Bahrain. It was all part of a concerted attempt in these years to defend the British position in the Gulf, upon which the British economy was so dependent for imports of sterling-denominated oil. As a loyal New Zealander, my father believed in the beneficent effects of Britain's long association with the Gulf, for both the rulers, their peoples and the British.

The British 'mission' in the Gulf was not readily understood in the United States, whence 'J.B.' (as the Americans called him) had decamped in the late 1950's and early 1960's in order to afford to bring up his young family (in Delaware, Ohio, and Ann Arbor, Michigan). This was a time of 'discovery' of the Middle East for many American universities, awash with U.S. government grant money for the study of Arab culture and politics. My father found an in-built distrust for the British position in Arabia and the Gulf which was regarded as an out-moded relic of empire by the anthropologists and political scientists who seemed to dominate the field, and were either enamoured by the 'beauties' of Arab nationalism, and their Hollywood idol Nasser, or were alert to the seemingly infinite possibilities of Arab oil money for academic study. During his American years, J.B. concentrated on the writing of his first book, *Eastern Arabian Frontiers* (Faber,1964) and produced relatively little in the way of other writing (see pieces 6-8). His return to England saw, however, a great spate of activity (see pieces 9-21). It was during the period from 1964-67 that the fateful decision was made by Harold Wilson's Labour governments to slash the defence budget and withdraw from all major British military bases east of Suez by 1971. The implications of this for Arabia and the Gulf were clear to my father, who realised that this would lead to the collapse of

Introduction: Macaulay's New Zealander

the Western position in the peninsula and the betrayal of Britain's solemn treaty promises of protection to the shaikhs, sultans and emirs of southern and eastern Arabia. More than that it would allow the traditional predators in the Gulf, Saudi Arabia, Iraq and Iran to vie for paramountcy in Britain's place. The result, he foresaw, would be the tribal caliban roaming the hills and wadis of South Yemen; an unfolding anarchy in the Gulf, as the contenders for power failed to achieve their ends and brought war and ruin to the area, and the West being held hostage by the now unrestrained oil-producing countries, greedy for revenue to fund their aggrandising schemes. J.B. was agog at the short-sightedness, complacency and ineptitude of British politicians. He could understand, if not sympathise with, the Labour Party's doctrinal hatred of the British Empire and all its trappings. But he failed to see why the Conservative Party under Edward Heath and Sir Alec Douglas-Home, who had done so much to defend the British position in south and eastern Arabia from 1951-64, and Kuwait in 1961, should not reverse Labour's disastrous policy of withdrawal from the Gulf in 1971. That they patently failed to do so he put down to the decision of the Foreign Office and the Tories to follow the path of least resistance and to embrace the Nixon Administration's misguided concept of handing over the security of the Gulf to those 'twin-pillars' of rectitude, Saudi Arabia and Iran, whose territorial designs on their neighbours was to cause such trouble in the region. There was also the cynical calculation that, by selling large quantities of highly sophisticated armaments to these two new 'policemen' of the Gulf, the British and Americans could recycle the great flow of money which was pouring east (like the 'river' of silver to China two centuries before), and underwrite British and American defence procurement programmes for the Cold War. This was the moment when J.B. parted company with the British Establishment, embodied in the Foreign Office and Chatham House, on Arabia and the Gulf. He saw the British scuttle from Aden and the abandonment of the Gulf as not only a betrayal of trust but a geo-strategic blunder of monumental proportions by the political pygmies who misgoverned Britain. It was to determine the thrust of his future writing, and his career.

J.B. returned to the United States in 1967 to take up a chair in British Imperial History at the University of Wisconsin-Madison (for what seems to have been his inaugural speech, see piece no 22). Although these were productive years, which saw the publication of his *magnum opus*, *Britain and the Persian Gulf, 1795-1880* (Clarendon Press, Oxford) and a slew of reviews (pieces 23-28), he was not happy at Madison. These were the years of the anti-Vietnam War protests on campus and the capitulation of faculties to the demands of lazy, draft-dodging students and faux political activists. This was not a fit and proper environment for academic endeavour and it was with regret mixed with some relief that he relinquished his chair and returned, perforce, to Britain in 1970. It was there, as an independent academic, that he was to chronicle the consequences of the British withdrawal from Arabia and the Gulf, which will be the subject of the next volume in this series of his collected essays and reviews. It was then that the symbolism of his role as Macaulay's New Zealander, a 'portent of doom' in much nineteenth century British political commentary, was to come fully to the fore.

S.B. Kelly
King's College, London.

1
The British Position in the Persian Gulf[1]

Britain in the Persian Gulf today occupies the dual position of residual legatee of the past and common trustee of the present. She has obligations to fulfil arising out of her historical connection with the Gulf, and vital interests to defend in the shape of large-scale oil investments, not only her own but those of Europe and the United States as well. Beyond that, her presence in the Gulf is part of the defensive strategy of the West and a contribution to the maintenance of peace and order in this part of the world. In playing these roles Britain has had to contend with pressures generated locally and outside, as the tide of nationalism and anti-colonialism in the Arab and Afro-Asian worlds races on. Together with Aden, the Gulf is the last place in the Middle East, and one of the last places on the continents of Asia and Africa, where Britain exercises direct authority. Inevitably, the Gulf and Britain's position there will come increasingly under scrutiny, and questions are already being asked as to how long that position, as it now stands, can be held, whether it should be held, or whether it should be modified to fit what are said to be the realities of the time. They are not questions that admit of facile answers.

Historically, the British connection with the Gulf goes back a long way, to the second decade of the seventeenth century, when the East India Company began trading with Persia through the Gulf. Political ascendancy in the Gulf, however, was not acquired until the nineteenth century, when it was considered essential to the defence of the north-western approaches to India and the protection of Indian sea-borne commerce. The granting of independence to India and Pakistan in 1947 destroyed the original

---

1 Source: *The World Today*, June 1964.

raison d'être of the British position in the Gulf, but there still remained the maintenance of Commonwealth communications through the Gulf, the protection of British commercial activities in the region, and the discharge of the obligations incurred in the past. This state of affairs did not last long. The policy of indirect expansion in the Middle East pursued by Russia in the 1950s, and the tremendous growth of the Gulf's oil industry in the same period, revitalized Britain's interest in the Gulf. From that time forward her overriding aim in the region became the protection and maintenance of Western oil interests there, not only for their significance for the well-being of Western Europe as a whole but also because of the implications for the defence of the Western world.

The Treaty Structure

Chief among the obligations remaining from the past are the preservation of maritime peace and the defence of the independence of the minor Gulf States. These obligations grew out of the campaigns to suppress piracy and maritime warfare in the first half of the nineteenth century. At the close of the second expedition to the Pirate Coast a General Treaty of Peace was concluded with the maritime sheikhs in January 1820 which declared: 'There shall be a cessation of plunder and piracy by land and sea on the part of the Arabs, who are parties to this contract, for ever.' Fifteen years later the first maritime truce was introduced, designed to reduce maritime warfare in the Gulf, and it was signed by all the sheikhs of the Pirate Coast from Ras al-Khaima to Abu Dhabi. The truce was renewed annually thereafter until 1843, when it was made valid for ten years, and at the end of that period a Treaty of Maritime Peace in Perpetuity was signed on 4 May 1853 by all the Trucial Sheikhs (as they were now called), who swore to observe 'a perfect maritime truce ... between ourselves and between our successors respectively, for evermore', to be watched over and enforced by the British Government.

In the years between 1820 and 1853 engagements were also taken by the British Government from the Trucial Sheikhs for the suppression of the slave trade from Africa. The most important of these engagements was concluded in the spring of 1847, when each sheikh undertook to 'prohibit the exportation of slaves from the coasts of Africa and elsewhere on board of my vessels and those belonging to my subjects or dependants', and granted rights of search and seizure to the British Government. By a supplementary agreement in May 1856 the sheikhs engaged to hand over to the British authorities in the Gulf any slaves landed in their territories. The adherence of the sheikhs to these engagements was confirmed in 1873. Similar engagements were taken from the Sheikh of Bahrein in 1847 and 1856. Successive Sultans of Muscat also made concessions to the British Government regarding the slave trade in their dominions between 1822 and 1873. By a treaty concluded in the latter year the ruling Sultan abolished the slave trade at Muscat and throughout the Sultanate, declared the importation of slaves to be illegal, and granted the British Government rights of search and seizure of Muscat vessels engaged in the trade. Arms traffic agreements were concluded with the Trucial Sheikhs, the Sheikh of Bahrein, and the Sheikh of Kuwait between 1898 and 1902. Agreements of a similar type concluded with the Sultan of Muscat at this time were later superseded by Muscat's adherence in 1921 to the Arms Traffic Convention of 1919.

The realization of Britain's objects in the Gulf in the nineteenth century was closely bound up with the maintenance of the independence of the maritime principalities. This was threatened periodically by Persia, the Ottoman Empire, and Egypt, but most consistently by the Saudi, or Wahhabi, Amirate of Najd. The British Indian authorities believed, as a result of the experience of the early decades of the century, that the extension of Saudi authority to the Trucial Sheikhdoms, Bahrein, and the Sultanate of Muscat would lead to a renewal of disturbances at sea. At the same time, they were averse to giving formal guarantees of territorial independence to these States lest they should lead to military intervention in the Arabian peninsula. They relied, therefore, upon naval means to defend the maritime States. Thus, what might have been expected to develop as a corollary to the evolution of the Trucial System, that is, the formal recognition of the independence of the Trucial Sheikhdoms and an explicit undertaking to defend them against outside aggression, never came to pass.

The same was true with respect to the Sultanate of Muscat and Oman. Muscat had been the first State on the Arabian side of the Gulf with which Britain had entered into a political relationship, when, in 1798, a *qaulnamah*, or written agreement, had been obtained from its ruler to exclude the French from his territories for the duration of the war with France. To avoid being committed in any way to the defence of Oman, the British Government did not ask the Al Bu Said Sultans to subscribe to the Trucial System, and the only engagements of any consequence taken from them up to the last decade of the century were the slave-trade agreements. Nevertheless, political and naval support was afforded the Sultans on occasions to help them resist the Wahhabis and to overcome their enemies in Oman, so that the upholding of the Sultanate's integrity and of the rule of the main Al Bu Said line became as fully established a principle of British policy in the Gulf as the maintenance of the independence of the Trucial Sheikhdoms and Bahrein.

Bahrein provides the only instance in the century of a departure from the policy of avoiding the grant of formal guarantees of independence and protection to the maritime States. Although Bahrein had signed the General Treaty of 1820, she had been left out of the Trucial System because Britain had no wish to assume the burden of defending her against the various contenders for her sovereignty—Muscatis, Saudis, Persians, Turks, and Egyptians. A conjunction of Saudi, Turkish, and Persian bids for the archipelago's sovereignty in 1859-60 led the British Government finally to make a formal avowal of its determination to preserve Bahrein's independence. By a Convention concluded on 31 May 1861, the Sheikh of Bahrein subscribed to 'a perpetual Treaty of peace and friendship with the British Government', and in return he was assured of 'the support of the British Government in the maintenance of the security of... [his] possessions against ... aggressions directed against them by the Chiefs and tribes of this Gulf'. Such a guarantee could be given to Bahrein and not to the Trucial Sheikhdoms because the island could be defended by naval means alone.

Exclusive Agreements

The second tier in the treaty structure was erected in the last quarter of the nineteenth century as a consequence of the intrusion of other European Powers, and of the Ottoman Empire, into the Gulf. Turkish activities in Bahrein led the British Government in December 1880 to obtain from the ruling Al Khalifah sheikh an agreement, binding on himself and his successors, 'to abstain from entering into negotiations or making treaties of any sort with any State or Government other than the British without the consent of the said British Government', and not to allow other governments to establish diplomatic or consular representation in Bahrein, or coaling depots, without the British Government's permission. This prohibition did not apply to customary friendly intercourse with neighbouring States. Seven years later assurances of a similar nature were obtained from the Trucial Sheikhs, following Turkish and Persian activities along the Trucial Coast. These were the first of the so-called 'Exclusive Agreements'. They were confirmed in March 1892, when an additional clause was inserted, requiring the Trucial Sheikhs and the Sheikh of Bahrein not to 'cede, sell, mortgage or otherwise give for occupation' any part of their territories, except to the British Government. Such an undertaking had already been given by the Sultan of Muscat the previous year, as a consequence of reports that the French were endeavouring to establish a coaling depot at Muscat. A new Treaty of Friendship, Commerce, and Navigation was concluded with Muscat in March 1891, and advantage was taken of the occasion of its signing to obtain from the Sultan a bond not to alienate any portion of the dominions of Muscat and Oman to anyone except the British Government. The bond was terminated in 1958 when the present Sultan negotiated the sale of Gwadar, on the Makran coast, to Pakistan.

No relationship comparable with that with Bahrein and the Trucial States had evolved during the century with Kuwait, Qatar, and the Saudi Amirate of Najd. Kuwait's inhabitants were not given to piracy, nor had they taken a conspicuous part in the slave trade. The sheikhdom's status vis-a-vis the Ottoman Empire, moreover, was rather vague. The ruling Al Sabah sheikh applied in 1896 to be admitted to the Trucial System, but his application was rejected. Three years later, in January 1899, the possibility that Germany might fix upon Kuwait as the terminus of the Berlin-Baghdad railway led the British Government to obtain the sheikh's agreement not to alienate any portion of his territory to another Power without the previous consent of the British Government, or to receive the agents or representatives of any other government. On the outbreak of war with the Ottoman Empire, the sheikhdom was formally recognized as 'an independent Government under British protection'. Kuwait remained a British-protected State until June 1961, when the 1899 agreement was terminated 'as being inconsistent with the sovereignty and independence of Kuwait'.

Qatar and the Saudi Amirate of Najd were both subject to varying degrees of Turkish control from 1871 onwards, and it was not until after the outbreak of war in 1914 that they contracted engagements with the British Government. By a treaty concluded in November 1916 the ruling Al Thani sheikh of Qatar subscribed to all the agreements previously entered into by the Trucial Sheikhs, and in return he was guaranteed protection 'from all aggression by sea' and the 'good offices' of the British Government in the event of aggression by land, so long as such aggression was not provoked by him or his subjects. A somewhat similar treaty had been concluded with the Amir of Najd, Ibn Saud, in December 1915, which accorded him recognition as independent ruler of Najd and Hasa. This treaty was replaced in May 1927 by the Treaty of Jeddah, which acknowledged the great changes that had taken place in Ibn Saud's power in the intervening years by recognizing him as 'King of the Hijaz and of Najd, and its Dependencies', as well as the 'complete and absolute independence of his dominions'. For his part, Ibn Saud promised 'to maintain friendly and peaceful relations' with the Gulf States in special treaty relations with the British Government. The treaty has not been terminated.

Concessionary Agreements

The last engagements that Britain took from the maritime States concerned concessions. The first concessionary agreement was made with Kuwait, Bahrein, and the Trucial States in 1911. It covered pearls and was designed to protect the inhabitants of these States by requiring their rulers not to grant pearling concessions without first consulting the Political Resident in the Gulf. In October 1913 the Sheikh of Kuwait entered into an oil concessionary agreement not to give a concession 'to anyone except a person appointed from the British Government'. A similar undertaking was obtained from the Sheikh of Bahrein in 1914, and the Sheikh of Qatar assumed a comparable obligation in his treaty of November 1916. The Trucial Sheikhs did not subscribe to oil concessionary agreements until after the first World War, when, in February and May 1922, they agreed 'not to grant any concession in this connection to anyone except to the person appointed by the High British Government'. Finally, the Sultan of Muscat signed an undertaking in January 1923 not to grant permission for the exploitation of oil in his territories without consulting the British Government. This undertaking proved binding upon the then Sultan only. His son and successor granted a concession to an American oil company in 1950 for his province of Dhufar. In practice, the concessionary agreements have not been applied to the exclusive benefit of British oil companies. American companies, for example, have a 100 per cent interest in Bahrein, 50 per cent in Kuwait, and a share in oil operations in Qatar, the Sultanate of Muscat and Oman, and the Trucial States. Their total share of the Gulf's oil, in fact, is greater than that of British companies. Dutch, French, and Japanese companies also have interests in concessions in the Gulf.

Upper and Lower Gulfs

The relevance of this treaty structure to the present situation in the Gulf is now being called into question, especially as it was erected at a time when Britain's interest in the region was primarily maritime whereas today it is predominantly territorial. There is no doubt that some of the old engagements have been rendered obsolete by the passing of the conditions they were designed to remedy; but any attempt to determine whether or not the remainder of the structure is equally antiquated must take into account the fact that there are, as it were, two Gulfs, the upper and the lower, which differ from each other to a considerable degree. The upper Gulf is made up of the wealthy and sophisticated States of Kuwait and Bahrein, the former's wealth, of course, being much greater than that of the latter. Both owe much of their good fortune to the energy and commercial acumen of their ruling families, the Al Sabah and Al Khalifah, who were the principal carriers and entrepreneurs of the Gulf's trade. Kuwait had the added advantage of remaining outside the numerous conflicts that distracted the States of the lower Gulf, while Bahrein, although embroiled in a series of disputes throughout the nineteenth century, was bolstered by her situation as the entrepôt of the Gulf and by having the lion's share of the pearl fishery. In this century both States have been saved by the discovery of oil from the decline that faced them in the decay of the pearling industry and the loss of the carrying trade to European shipping.

The States of the lower Gulf are, by comparison, poor and backward. Qatar has been rescued by the discovery of oil, and the location of on-shore and off-shore deposits in Abu Dhabi promises to redeem that sheikhdom's economy. Politically and socially, however, these States do not differ essentially from the other Trucial States and the Sultanate of Muscat and Oman. It is here, in the lower Gulf, that the contrast with the rest of the Arab world is most marked. The landscape is wild and harsh, a mixture of mountains, steppe, sand-dune, and salt-flat. The populations are riven by tribal feuds, political factionalism, and religious particularism. The carrying of personal arms is the rule, not the exception. Piracies still occur at sea, clandestine slave-trading and gun-running still go on. Perhaps the hardest hit by the caprices of fortune has been the Sultanate of Muscat. Once the most powerful State in the Gulf, the centre of its politics and commerce, Muscat in the second half of the nineteenth century became a backwater. Zanzibar and the East African possessions had been lost, the slave trade had been destroyed, Oman was rent by tribal strife, and the axis of commerce had moved north. The Al Bu Said Sultans, once the most forward-looking and cosmopolitan of the Gulf's rulers, withdrew to contemplate the world through their window at Muscat and, like the Lady of Shalott, to brood upon their own mischance.

The contrast between Kuwait and the lower Gulf has been made more evident in the last three years by the change in Kuwait's political status. Kuwait's startling economic growth in the 1950s, her increasing contacts with the Arab capitals to the north and west, and her emerging prominence internationally, all pointed to the need for such a change. The change was effected by the agreement of June 1961 which accorded Kuwait formal recognition as a sovereign independent State. Henceforth, Kuwait was free to conduct what political and economic relations she would with whomsoever she wished. The only shred of the old relationship with Britain that remained was a provision in the exchange of Notes that 'nothing in these conclusions shall affect the readiness of Her Majesty's Government to assist the Government of Kuwait if the latter request such assistance.' The value of this provision was demonstrated when Iraq put forward her sudden claim to sovereignty over Kuwait.

Such a stage has not yet been reached in Britain's relations with Bahrein. The Convention of 1861 and the Exclusive and Concessionary Agreements remain in force, but the real importance of the relationship for Bahrein lies not so much in the restrictions imposed upon her by these agreements as in the guarantee of the independence and security of the sheikhdom contained in the 1861 Convention. One factor that facilitated the change in Kuwait's status was that, alone among the States under British protection, her frontiers had been defined some time ago—with the Saudi Amirate of Najd in December 1922 and with Iraq in April 1923, when Britain was the protecting Power over Kuwait and Najd and the mandatory Power in Iraq. (What obligations, if any, may still devolve upon Britain regarding these frontiers is not clear, but it is probable that these were subsumed in the 1961 agreement.) Bahrein's frontiers, notwithstanding her claim to northern Qatar and Persia's claim upon her, are essentially maritime, which has simplified the problem of their lack of definition. The problem has been further reduced lately by the settlement of her maritime frontier with Saudi Arabia.

Britain's Defence Responsibilities

The bearing that the absence of defined frontiers has upon the political development of the Gulf States and on Britain's relations with them becomes clearer when one contemplates the situation in the lower Gulf. At the heart of the Trucial System is an understanding that Britain is responsible for the defence, independence, and territorial integrity of the States belonging to that system. The understanding may be explicit as in Bahrein's case, conditional as in Qatar's, or implicit as in the case of the Trucial Sheikhdoms. (An exception is the Sheikhdom of Fujairah, to whose ruler a formal pledge of protection was given in March 1952.) It is an understanding that is vital to the Trucial Sheikhdoms, whose territorial frontiers with Saudi Arabia have yet to be agreed, and only slightly less so to Qatar, which has long enjoyed amicable relations with Saudi Arabia and which has recently entered into negotiations with the Saudi Government on their common border. The Sultanate of Muscat and Oman is faced also by problems of defence and frontier definition, but it does not stand in the same relationship to Britain as do the Trucial States. The only extant engagements of any consequence between Britain and the Sultanate are a Treaty of Friendship, Commerce, and Navigation, concluded in 1951, and a secondary agreement entered into in July 1958 for the provision of financial, technical, and military aid, and for the extension of the arrangements regarding the use of facilities at Salalah and Masirah by the Royal Air Force. Nevertheless, although there is no formal obligation upon Britain to defend the Sultanate, there is a long tradition of friendship with the Al Bu Said Sultans, extending back over a century and a half, and a record of assisting them in their difficulties, external and internal.

The importance of the understanding on defence is underlined by the prevalence of territorial disputes in the Gulf and by the fact that every major crisis that has arisen on the Arabian shore since 1945 has been caused by such disputes. Persia exerts a claim to Bahrein, Bahrein to northern Qatar, Qatar and Abu Dhabi contest the sovereignty of Khaur al-Udaid, where the jurisdictions of their respective rulers meet. Iraq has put forward a claim to Kuwait, although she would appear to have withdrawn it in April 1963, when Kuwait made her a 'soft' loan of £30 m. Most important of all, Saudi Arabia maintains claims to the hinterlands of Qatar, Abu Dhabi, the Sultanate of Muscat, and the Eastern Aden Protectorates. Within Oman there is, or was, a separatist movement, directed towards the establishment of an 'Imamate of Oman' independent of the Sultanate, which has been supported at one time or another by Saudi Arabia, Egypt, and Iraq. Though the crisis caused by Iraq's claim to Kuwait in the summer of 1961 was more spectacular, the most serious and sustained territorial dispute in the Gulf has been that caused by Saudi Arabia's claim in 1949 to the coast-line and hinterland of the lower Gulf, from Qatar almost to Abu Dhabi town, which has become known as the Buraimi Oasis dispute. The dispute may now be on the way towards a *de facto*, if not an agreed, solution (the recent renunciation by the Arabian-American Oil Company of its concessionary rights beyond the modified Riyadh Line, the frontier declared by the British Government in October 1955, is a straw in the wind), but it is doubtful whether the outcome for the littoral States would have been so favourable if Britain had not supported them.

There is a disposition in some quarters to view with complacency, indeed to advocate, the eventual absorption of these States by Saudi Arabia, a tidying-up of the map, as it were, and to justify it by reference not so much to compatibility as to the apparently ineluctable tendency of the modern world towards coalescence into larger political units. To advocate this is to ignore the very real differences and animosities that divide, say, a State like Abu Dhabi from Saudi Arabia. It is, in effect, to arrogate to oneself the right to dispose of the territory, not to say the destiny, of another State, a point which was made time and again by the British Government during the course of the frontier dispute from 1949 onwards. These territories are not Britain's to bargain away. Again, it has been suggested that some kind of regional pact of mutual security among the major Gulf States might replace Britain's present commitment to the defence of the minor ones. It is not uncharitable to question the value of a pact by Saudi Arabia, Iraq, and Persia to preserve a status quo in the Gulf which they are all committed, or say they are committed, to changing.

Changes in the *status quo*, however, are thought more likely to result from internal developments in the protected States than from external causes. Britain's position within these States is an anomalous one, and depends as much, as it does in the Gulf as a whole, upon precedent and policy as upon legal formulas. It has normally been official policy not to interfere with the domestic institutions and customs of these States, particularly those which fall within the scope of the Shariah, or Islamic law. In some cases interference seems unavoidable, and in others the security of the State and the maintenance of good relations with the ruler might be held to justify impolitic acts, such as the removal of the political prisoners from Bahrein to St Helena. On the Trucial Coast the duties of British political agents go well beyond their diplomatic and consular functions, and resemble more those of colonial district officers, especially in the implementation of the plan to improve the economy, agriculture, and health of the Trucial States, to which Britain has allocated £500,000 so far.

One of the more popular current speculations is that, in the event of political upheaval in one of the protected States, Britain might find herself in the position of having to support the ruler against his own people, and that such upheavals must be expected if the present regime in Saudi Arabia is replaced by a revolutionary and more liberal one. The argument smacks more of predilection than prediction. It is predicated upon a number of assumptions that have yet to be verified, for instance, that sheikhly rule is *ipso facto* arbitrary and oppressive, that an attempted *coup d'état* will have wide popular support and will not be merely the work of a clique, that Saudi Arabia will survive intact the overthrow of the Al Saud and that a revolutionary regime will be a liberal one, and that the demise of autocratic and sheikhly rule will automatically be followed by the birth of broadly based and libertarian governments in a region where no libertarian traditions exist. It can be said with certainty that in Oman, for example, the alternative to Al Bu Said rule is tribal anarchy. At the other end of the scale, it might be noted that no such upheaval has so far taken place in Kuwait, which, with the access of wealth, the spread of education among its inhabitants, and the influx of thousands of politically more advanced immigrants from other Arab States, would seem the most likely candidate for transformation along these lines.

International Interest in the Gulf

Britain, of course, is far from being the only Power concerned in what happens in the Gulf. The Gulf is, after all, 'the Persian Gulf', despite attempts in recent years to rename it 'the Arabian Gulf' (the Arabian Gulf' is the old name for the Red Sea), and the Shah is known to be particularly sensitive to events in this maritime highway which is Persia's only unencumbered outlet to the rest of the world. The United States has almost as great an interest in the Gulf as Britain. In terms of participation in the oil industry her interest is even greater. She is committed to supporting Persia against Russia, and to preventing that Power from breaking through to the Gulf and dominating its oil reserves to the detriment of Europe and the West. Although the United States has not always seen eye to eye with Britain on Gulf questions—a decade ago, for instance, she was inclined to view with equanimity Saudi Arabia's expansionist ambitions in the direction of Trucial Oman—she nevertheless regards the area as one of primarily British responsibility, and she is fully appreciative of the security afforded it and the operations of American oil companies by the British presence. She herself keeps watch on events there through a small naval flotilla and an officer of flag rank who resides on Bahrein. It is reasonable to assume, therefore, that the United States would view with apprehension any serious diminution of Britain's responsibility for maintaining peace in the Gulf.

Such would not be the reaction of the other two outside Powers most interested in the Gulf, Russia and Egypt. Russia has not displayed much direct interest in the area in this century, apart from a short-lived attempt in the 1930s to push Russian trade with the Gulf. The volume of Russian publications on the Gulf has been very limited, which is usually the case with areas where there is no Russian diplomatic representation. Now that a Russian Ambassador has been appointed to Kuwait, an increase in publications may be expected, and the recent speeches of Mr Khrushchev on his visit to Egypt may herald a reawakening of political interest. Egypt's ultimate ambition in Arabia is control of the peninsula's oil resources: the foray into the Yemen would not make sense unless it were designed to exert pressure upon Britain to withdraw from Aden and open the road to the Gulf. Yet the premature eviction of Britain from the Gulf would not work to Egypt's advantage but rather to that of Saudi Arabia. It is this consideration that has led Egypt to play a waiting game in the area; its countries are not yet sufficiently evolved for a revolution on the Egyptian pattern to have much chance of success. It may be, too, that this consideration was the reason for the withdrawal of the Egyptian contingent from the Arab League force sent to Kuwait in 1961. So long as Kuwait remains independent of Saudi Arabia and Iraq, Egypt may feel that her long-term strategy is not jeopardized. At the same time, however, Egypt is under a compulsion to sustain the fervour of the Arab nationalist movement if she is to retain its leadership. So the campaign for the 'liberation' of the Arab South goes on, leading Egypt into the curious position of simultaneously contriving the overthrow of the Zaidi Imamate of the Yemen and supporting the revival of the Ibadi Imamate in Oman—and doing both in the name of progress and revolution.

There is a side other than the opportunist one to Egyptian activities in the Gulf region, and that is the work there of Egyptian teachers and technicians. Some are obviously little more than agents and agitators; others are virtual refugees from Nasserism. Some are incompetent timeservers; others are able and devoted men. The best of them are performing a mission that is truly *civilisatrice*. In contrast, India and Pakistan show scarcely a flicker of interest in the Gulf, which is all the more surprising when one recalls not only that the prime motive for the British presence in the Gulf was once the defence of the Indian Empire but also that there are thousands of Indian and Pakistani nationals working in the Gulf, and that the outside links of many of the Gulf States are as much with India and Pakistan as they are with the rest of the Middle East. Pakistan, in particular, as a member of CENTO, might have been expected to show more concern over what occurs in the Gulf.

Much that may occur in the future to affect Britain's role and position there will arise from events outside her ability to influence or control. The unpredictable is always happening in the Middle East, and international alignments nowadays seem to be subject to more vagaries than usual. Within the Gulf Britain still has power and room to manoeuvre, both in protecting her interests and in fulfilling her obligations. Of all her interests the economic is the most powerful, even the overriding, one. Access to the Gulf's oil, the security of operations, the return on investment, all are vital, not only to Britain but to the West in general, and in this sense Britain is the trustee of the West's stake in the Gulf. She is no less bound by the responsibilities laid upon her by the past, in particular the defence of the minor principalities against their enemies and, what is sometimes obscured, a duty to ensure their emergence into the modern world as credible States and not as medieval anachronisms. These obligations cannot be shrugged off because they may be uncomfortable or because they may expose Britain to criticism. Still less can Britain evade her responsibility to herself, to her allies, and to the world at large to continue to contribute to the upholding of peace, order, and the rule of law in an area to which she, and she alone, brought all three.

2
The Buraimi Oasis Dispute[1]

Recent happenings of a rather spectacular nature in Cyprus and Jordan and the constant attention paid to the perennial Arab-Israel deadlock have tended to overshadow another unresolved problem of Middle Eastern politics, the dispute between Britain and Saudi Arabia over the future status of the Buraimi oasis. Although of lesser magnitude than the Cyprus, Jordan, and Israel questions, the Buraimi issue possesses considerable significance and was one of the subjects discussed at the Washington conference in January 1956 and at the recent meeting of Arab heads of State in Cairo. Indeed, the issue is seen in some quarters as a crucial test for the future of British influence and prestige not only in the Persian Gulf region but along the whole littoral of Arabia.[2]

Briefly speaking, the dispute concerns the ownership of a group of villages situated in the south-eastern corner of Arabia, on the frontier of the Sultanate of Muscat and Oman[3] and the Trucial Shaikhdom of Abu Dhabi. The Saudi Arabian Government has asserted a claim to the sovereignty of these villages—collectively known as the Buraimi oasis—but this claim has been resisted by the Sultan of Muscat and Oman and by the Shaikh of Abu Dhabi, who contend that the oasis has long been under their joint jurisdiction. By virtue of its special treaty relationship with

---

1 Source: *International Affairs* (*Royal Institute of International Affairs* 1944-), Vol. 32, No. 3 (July, 1956), pp. 318-326.

2 See *The Egyptian Economic and Political Review*, September, October, and November, 1955.

3 The modern title 'Sultanate of Muscat and Oman' is often abbreviated to 'Sultanate of Muscat'. For the purposes of this article, however, the more accurate abbreviation, 'Sultanate of Oman', has been adopted throughout.

30

the Shaikh, and at the specific request of the Sultan, the British Government has represented their case both in direct negotiations with the Saudi Government and before an international tribunal. The dispute has been aggravated by the reported discovery of oil in the region, but it would now appear that this aspect of the case has been unduly emphasized, since there is no reason to suppose that there is any oil at Buraimi. What is, perhaps, of greater significance is that the Saudi Arabian claim to Buraimi, when placed in its historical context and related to other Saudi activities in Jordan, southern Arabia, and along the Yemen-Aden border, may be seen as one particular manifestation of a new phase in the long history of Saudi Arabian expansion, an expansion which has been going on, albeit with frequent interruptions, since the late eighteenth century. Not infrequently in the past the territorial and political ambitions of the Saudi dynasty have clashed with Egyptian efforts to dominate the Arab world, so that the recent report from Cairo that Colonel Nasser has pledged Egyptian support to King Saud in his bid to gain control of Buraimi—and with it the southern shores of the Persian Gulf—makes strange reading at a time when Egyptian propagandists are apparently hard at work in Bahrain and Kuwait.

Traditionally, Buraimi has always been considered to lie within the historical Province of Oman, but more strictly speaking, it is situated on the edge of al Dhahirah, the western district of Oman, and al Shamal (or al Sir), the northern district, otherwise known as Trucial Oman.[4] To the westward the frontier with Saudi Arabia has never been defined. The oasis derives its importance, in the main, from being the only well-watered locality in northern Oman and, as such, the natural resort of all travellers crossing the great desert to the west. As the crossroads of the principal routes from the west and from the Gulf coast into Oman proper, Buraimi possesses a particular strategic value: whoever holds the oasis can dominate the Trucial Shaikhdoms to the north and the Sultanate of Oman to the east and, conversely, no invading force from the west, bent on the subjection of those principalities, could afford to bypass Buraimi and leave its lines of communication exposed. Though doubtless owing much to the rumoured existence of large oil deposits in the region, the present Saudi bid for possession of the oasis is but the latest in a long series of attempts, which began as early as 1800, to dominate the south-eastern corner of Arabia. Conversely, the opposition of the British Government to the Saudi move is not motivated primarily by considerations of oil concessions, but is a natural reaffirmation of the policy it has pursued in the Persian Gulf region since the early nineteenth century, of safeguarding the independence and territorial integrity of these shaikhdoms and principalities along the western littoral of the Gulf from encroachment by others, whether they be Turks, Persians, Egyptians, or Saudi Arabians. Arbitration by an independent international tribunal as a means of determining the sovereignty of the Buraimi oasis has been tried and has failed, principally because the Saudi Government attempted to tamper with the impartiality of the tribunal, and to bribe the inhabitants of the oasis into declaring in favour of Saudi Arabia. That the Saudi Government apparently felt it necessary to resort to such means strongly suggests that it feared its case was basically weak and, indeed, on historical and legal grounds, such a fear is well justified.

The Saudi claim would appear to rest upon a threefold basis:

(i) that the Saudi Government exercised authority in the disputed area for the greater part of the nineteenth century;

(2) that the tribes of the area have willingly acknowledged Saudi suzerainty by paying *zakat*, or religious tribute, to Riyadh

---

[4] 'Trucial Oman' or the 'Trucial Coast' is the name generally given to the half-dozen independent maritime shaikhdoms along the southern shore of the Persian Gulf, all of which enjoy a degree of protection from the British Government. The name derives from the last century when the shaikhdoms undertook to observe an annual, and later a permanent, truce at sea.

for many years;

(3) that many tribes have become converts to Wahhabi doctrines and acknowledge the spiritual authority of the Saudi ruler.

The first seizure of the oasis by a Saudi force took place in 1800, as part of the first great Wahhabi expansion which eventually brought most of Arabia under the rule of Abdul Aziz I ibn Saud, Amir of Daraiya in central Arabia. Religious zeal was the principal motivating force behind this first phase of Saudi expansion, a zeal inspired by the teachings of one of the great reformers of Islam, Muhammad ibn Abdul Wahhab. But by the time of Ibn Abdul Wahhab's death towards the close of the eighteenth century what had begun as an attempt to purge Islam of its inconsistencies and idolatries had degenerated into the wholesale aggrandizement of the Wahhabi Amir—who now combined in his person the dual functions of temporal ruler and spiritual leader (or Imam)—at the expense of his neighbours in Arabia. Even by its mildest critics the Wahhabi Empire of the early nineteenth century has been labelled 'a politico-religious confederacy which legalized the indiscriminate thraldom of all peoples beyond its own pale', and which was sustained by 'constant aggression and expansion at the expense of those who did not share the great idea'. Among the Wahhabis' early victims were the maritime shaikhdoms of the Trucial Coast (or Pirate Coast, as it was then known) and the Sultanate of Oman further south.

Soon after the seizure of Buraimi in 1800 the maritime tribes of the Pirate Coast made their submission, and some of them, notably the Qawasim of Sharjah and Ras-al-Khaima, who were pirates by vocation, readily subscribed to the Wahhabi doctrines of proselytism and plunder. In the Sultanate of Oman the Wahhabis' progress was less rapid, although they found many adherents among the northern tribes, who had for some years been virtually independent of the authority of the Sultan residing at Muscat. The declining power of the Al Bu Said Sultans of Oman in their northern dominions was an important factor in the Wahhabis' progress in south-eastern Arabia. Fundamentally this decline was due, on the one hand, to the tendency of the Al Bu Said family to place increasing reliance on their maritime rather than their territorial resources and, on the other, to their having renounced the spiritual leadership of their people, whose dominant religion was *Ibadhiya*, a dissident branch of Islam, and who looked to their rulers for spiritual as well as temporal guidance. It was this separateness of religious beliefs that exposed the inhabitants of Oman to the wrath of the Wahhabi Amir, and for more than a decade after 1800 his forces struck again and again at the Sultanate, pausing in their attacks only when events elsewhere in the Arabian peninsula claimed Ibn Saud's attention.

Buraimi became the base for the Wahhabis' raids into Oman, and a strong fort was raised there by Mutlaq al Mutairi, the *naib*, or lieutenant, appointed by Ibn Saud to command his forces in Oman. Mutlaq's raids were marked by excessive violence and savagery: whole villages were put to the sword, a terror-stricken populace was forced to subscribe to Wahhabi tenets, and *zakat*, or religious tribute, was constantly exacted for the Wahhabi treasury at Daraiya. His way was made easy for him by the absence of a strong ruler at Muscat, the former Sultan having been killed fighting at sea against the Qawasim of the Trucial Coast, and the succession being bitterly disputed between his sons and kinsmen. The *naib's* attacks reached a climax in 1812, when, in concert with two of the Wahhabi Amir's sons, he is said to have cut 'a swathe of blood and destruction' through eastern Oman as far as the port of Sur. To all intents and purposes this was to be the last Wahhabi onslaught on Oman for some time to come: the previous year the campaign of Muhammad Ali Pasha of Egypt against the Saudi dynasty had opened, and did not close until Ibrahim Pasha had razed Daraiya to the ground in 1818 and the Wahhabi Amir had been executed at Constantinople. The Wahhabi garrison withdrew from Buraimi, Mutlaq al Mutairi had long since been slain by tribesmen of the Dhahirah, and a new and strong ruler had emerged in Oman, Saiyid Said ibn Sultan, who was destined to become the greatest of the Al Bu Said rulers.

Despite the apparently crushing defeat inflicted by Ibrahim Pasha the power of the Wahhabis was restored in central and eastern Arabia within a few years by the efforts of a new Amir, Turki ibn Abdullah. Making Riyadh the capital of his new kingdom Turki set out to win back the territories lost to his family in 1818. A Wahhabi force was dispatched to Buraimi in the mid-eighteen-twenties under the command of Saad ibn Mutlaq, the son of the former *naib*, who soon forced the submission of the Naim tribe inhabiting the oasis and established the Wahhabi occupation on its old footing: *zakat* was levied upon the surrounding countryside, recalcitrant tribes were summarily dealt with, and a fresh series of raids was launched on the Oman Sultanate. Internal rebellions within Oman weakened the resistance of the Al Bu Said ruler, Saiyid Said, to the invaders, and in 1833 he was forced to come to terms with the Amir Turki: in return for *zakat* of $5,000 (about £1,100) annually the latter agreed to respect the frontiers of Oman.

The settlement found little favour with Saad ibn Mutlaq, and when, a year later, Turki was assassinated, he resumed his threats and extortions. Help came to Oman once again through the agency of Muhammad Ali of Egypt, who launched a new campaign against the Wahhabis in 1837. By the close of the following year the Egyptian Army under Khurshid Pasha had overrun central Arabia and taken the new Amir, Faisal ibn Turki, prisoner. Emboldened by the Wahhabis' defeat, the Naim, Shuwamis, and Dhawahir tribes dwelling around Buraimi drove out Saad ibn Mutlaq and his garrison and declared they would never allow them to return. Saad appealed in vain to those tribes of al Dhahirah and Trucial Oman who had been converted to Wahhabism to aid him against the Naim and their allies; but he had so disgusted the tribes by his extortions and cruelties that even the Qawasim, once the Wahhabis' staunchest supporters, now turned against him, and he was forced to flee to central Arabia.

There he took service with the Egyptian commander, Khurshid Pasha, who sent him back to Trucial Oman with a force to take possession of Buraimi in the name of the Pasha of Egypt. The Naim and their allies stoutly maintained their opposition to his return, and appealed to the British Resident in the Persian Gulf for aid against him. The Resident obtained the expulsion of the *naib* from Trucial Oman, and an officer of the Bombay Army was dispatched to Buraimi to assist in the defence of the forts, and to assure the Naim and other shaikhs of the support of the Government of India in resisting the efforts of both Saad ibn Mutlaq and the Egyptians to establish themselves at the oasis. Unfortunately, the tribes of Buraimi were not destined to enjoy their independence for long: largely at the instance of the British Government the Egyptian Army was forced to withdraw from eastern Arabia in the summer of 1840, and within three years the Wahhabi Amir, Faisal ibn Turki, was back at Riyadh. One of his first acts was to dispatch Saad ibn Mutlaq into Trucial Oman at the head of an imposing force. The Naim, Shuwamis, and Dhawahir were overwhelmed and punished, and Saad set forth upon a new career of oppression and extortion among the tribes of al Dhahirah. As in the past his violence and cruelty eventually brought retribution: tribe after tribe in al Dhahirah and al Shamal refused to pay *zakat* or acknowledge his authority; the British Resident in the Gulf sent cruisers to patrol the Batinah coast of Oman and warned Saad against trying to impose his demands for *zakat* on the Sultan by force; and in May 1848 the Al Bu Falah Shaikh of Abu Dhabi, in league with the Naim and the Regent of Oman, stormed and took the forts of Buraimi. It required the intercession of the Sharif of Mecca before the Al Bu Falah Shaikh could finally be persuaded to relinquish control of the forts to the *naib* in February 1849. A year later the Abu Dhabi ruler returned to the attack in concert with the Naim and the Qawasim of Sharjah, but their efforts to retake the forts were unavailing. They were not, however, entirely without result, for Saad was recalled to Riyadh shortly afterwards and never returned to Trucial Oman.

What was destined to be the last full-scale Wahhabi attempt to overrun south-eastern Arabia began at the close of 1852 when Abdullah, the son of the Amir Faisal, appeared at Buraimi in great force, with instructions from his father to extend his authority over Oman and the Trucial Shaikhdoms. Demands of an impossible nature were preferred upon the Regent of Oman, clearly with the intention of provoking him to war, but on the advice of the British Resident at Muscat the Regent stood firm. A compromise resulted, Abdullah undertaking in the name of his father to respect the frontiers of Oman on condition that *zakat* of $12,000 (about £2,700) was paid annually to Riyadh. As in the past a Wahhabi *naib* was left at Buraimi to collect this *zakat* and that from the surrounding tribes, but his position was far less secure than in bygone days. Wahhabi rule in eastern Arabia was drawing to a close, and with the death of the Amir Faisal early in 1866 the 'Puritans of Islam' rapidly lost their hold over their neighbours. One sign of the changed times was the dispatch in April of that year of a mission from the new Amir, Abdullah ibn Faisal, to the British Resident in the Gulf, Colonel (later Sir Lewis) Pelly, with an offer to respect the independence of those principalities in eastern Arabia in friendly relationship with the British Government, provided that the Resident would guarantee the payment of the yearly *zakat* from them. Although Pelly refused to commit the British Government to such a guarantee, the Wahhabi emissaries gave him a written promise that the Amir Abdullah would not 'injure or attack the territories of the Arab tribes in alliance with the British Government, especially in the Kingdom of Muscat, further than in receiving the *zakat* that has been customary of old'. Three years later the Wahhabi *naib* at Buraimi was slain on a visit to Sharjah on the Trucial Coast. No time was lost by the Naim at the oasis in calling on the Sultan of Oman for aid in expelling the Wahhabi garrison from the forts. The Sultan marched on the oasis in June 1869 and on 18 June the Wahhabi garrison surrendered. The Al Bu Falah Shaikh of Abu Dhabi, a close ally of the Omani ruler, was entrusted by him with the defence of Buraimi, and a short time afterwards the Qasimi Shaikh of Sharjah joined the compact to defend the western frontier of Oman. Meanwhile, the Saudi dynasty, rent by a fratricidal struggle for succession, was rapidly crumbling, and within a few years Turkish sovereignty had been extended

The Buraimi Oasis Dispute

over the Gulf coast as far south as the Qatar peninsula

For more than eighty years now the tribes of Buraimi have been free of Saudi rule. These years have seen the Shaikh of Abu Dhabi consolidate his position in the oasis, chiefly at the expense of the Dhawahir, who have shown less inclination than the Naim to view the extension of Al Bu Falah power with complacency. The ruling family of Abu Dhabi have become considerable landowners of villages and districts around the oasis, although Buraimi itself and Mutlaq al Mutairi's forts are still in the hands of the Naim, and the Shuwamis still hold the village of Hamasa. Saudi Arabian claims to the sovereignty of the oasis are of very recent date: in 1935, when the government of Abdul Aziz II ibn Saud put forward proposals for the delineation of the southern and eastern frontiers of Saudi Arabia, it claimed territory only up to a point 150 miles west of Buraimi. No agreement on frontiers was reached in the negotiations that took place at Riyadh in that year between the British and Saudi Governments, and the matter was allowed to rest until 1949, when, following upon reports that there might be oil deposits located in the Buraimi region, the Saudi Government put forward a fresh demand for the delineation of the frontier with Abu Dhabi and the Sultanate of Oman, this time along a line passing some miles to the north and east of Buraimi. Talks were held in London and at Dammam between the two governments in 1951 and the early part of 1952 but, as in 1935, no agreed solution of the frontier problem was found. Then, at the end of August 1952, a Saudi official by the name of Turki ibn Ataishan arrived at Buraimi with a number of armed followers and installed himself in the village of Hamasa. Stung by this challenge to his authority, the Sultan of Oman resolved to eject the interlopers by force, and tribesmen from all parts of Oman were gathering to his support when the British Government intervened to dissuade the Sultan from resorting to arms to preserve his rights in the oasis. Instead, a blockade was imposed upon Turki and his followers: they managed, however, to maintain themselves in Buraimi until July 1954, when it was agreed between the British and Saudi Governments to submit the frontier dispute and the question of the sovereignty of Buraimi to 'a just and impartial arbitration'.[5] Under the terms of this same agreement Turki ibn Ataishan was to withdraw from Buraimi immediately: a neutral zone was established around the oasis to a depth of about twelve miles, and the forces of the contending parties were forbidden access to this zone. When the international arbitration tribunal

---

5 *Arbitration Agreement between the Government of the United Kingdom (acting on behalf of the Ruler of Abu Dhabi and His Highness the Sultan Said bin Taimur) and the Government of Saudi Arabia, Jedda, 30 July 1954* (H.M.S.O. Cmd. 9272, 1954).

broke down in the autumn of 1955 the Sultan of Oman and the Shaikh of Abu Dhabi, on the advice of the British Government, stationed forces in the oasis to forestall any sudden *coup* by the Saudis after the fashion of those of the last century.

It seems fairly clear, from what has been said earlier, that the Saudi claim to Buraimi based on the previous exercise of authority in the region cannot be supported, for the various Wahhabi occupations of the oasis in the nineteenth century were little more than hostile incursions for purposes of plunder. Nor are the Saudi arguments based on the payment of *zakat* by tribes in the area and their conversion to Wahhabism any more substantial. Originally the payment of *zakat* was a recognition of the authority of the Wahhabi ruler in his spiritual capacity of *Imam*: later the religious significance of *zakat* was lost sight of, and the Wahhabi Amir demanded its payment from all, whether Wahhabi or not, and the independent rulers of eastern Arabia, like the Sultan of Oman, the Shaikh of Bahrain, and the Trucial Shaikhs, came to regard it as a sort of *Danegeld*, paid to the Amir to restrain him from molesting their possessions. These rulers were far from regarding such payments as an admission of Saudi sovereignty over their territories, and whenever they could, as their history clearly shows, they refused demands for *zakat* and strenuously resisted Saudi attempts to enforce such demands. The Saudi interpretation of *zakat* as tribute from a subject people and an acknowledgement of sovereignty is hardly compatible with the agreements of 1833 and 1853 concluded between the Sultan of Oman and the Wahhabi Amir, whereby the latter agreed to respect the Sultan's dominions in return for a stipulated amount of *zakat* annually. Nor is it compatible with the offer made to Colonel Pelly by Saudi emissaries in 1866 to respect the territorial integrity of the independent principalities along the eastern littoral of Arabia, provided they paid *zakat*. What is more, some of the Arab tribes dwelling on the Persian coast of the Gulf, in particular the branch of the Qawasim dwelling at Lingah, who were converted to Wahhabism early in the nineteenth century, occasionally paid *zakat* to the Wahhabi Amir. Plainly, this could be regarded only as a religious offering, without any reference to temporal authority, and not as an admission of Saudi authority over the Persian coast.

Objections of a similar nature may be raised to the Saudi argument based on the conversion of tribes in the Buraimi area to Wahhabi practices. Several of the maritime tribes of the Gulf embraced the Wahhabi creed in the nineteenth century, especially—and this applies particularly to the Qawasim of the Trucial Coast—for the licence it gave them to plunder. There is little doubt that these tribes would regard as absurd any suggestion that in adopting Wahhabi beliefs they were signifying their willingness to be governed from Riyadh. It would be equally absurd to argue that the Naim of Buraimi, or the Dhawahir or the Shuwamis, with their long record of struggle against Saudi rule, have, by subscribing to the teachings of Ibn Abdul Wahhab, voluntarily surrendered their independence to the government of Saud ibn Abdul Aziz.

It might justly be objected that no attempt has been made in the foregoing account of the historical origins of the Buraimi dispute to subject to equally close examination the rights of the Sultan of Oman and the Shaikh of Abu Dhabi in the oasis. A fair answer to such an objection might be found in the undoubted historical location of Buraimi within the Sultanate of Oman and in the uninterrupted administration of the oasis by the Al Bu Falah Shaikh since 1869: it is the Saudi Arabian Government, after all, which has put forward a claim to the sovereignty of the oasis and which must furnish the burden of proof. Whether the issue can eventually be resolved 'through friendly discussion', as President Eisenhower and Sir Anthony Eden hopefully suggested at the close of their conference in Washington, would seem to depend largely upon whether the Saudi Government curbs its present expansionist tendencies. So long as these are maintained Britain will continue to be involved in difficulties in eastern Arabia and the Persian Gulf, as a consequence of defending her own interests and those of States like Kuwait, Bahrain, Qatar, and the Trucial Shaikhdoms, whose independence she has guaranteed. Inevitably British efforts to fulfil long-standing obligations to these States will be made by Arab nationalists to appear as attempts to maintain an outmoded political hegemony in defiance of Arab aspirations. Yet issues like the Buraimi dispute, as has been seen, are not in origin the result of a conflict of Western and Arab interests: if this point is not appreciated both within and beyond the Middle East the fault would seem to lie partly with the British Government for not making the history of the case more widely known.

3

The Persian Claim to Bahrain[1]

During the past year reports from Tehran have indicated that the Persian Government is contemplating raising once again the question of Persia's claim to ownership of the Bahrain Islands. These reports have followed closely upon the publication by a Persian scholar, Dr Fereydoun Adamiyat, of a book entitled *Bahrein Islands, A Legal and Diplomatic Study of the British-Iranian Controversy* (New York, 1955), which is a detailed exposition of the legal and historical grounds upon which the Persian claim to sovereignty over Bahrain is based. Twice before in this century, in 1906 and in 1927, this claim has been put forward in earnest by Persia, and in both cases it has been made in the form of a protest against some action of the British Government which has allegedly violated Persia's sovereign rights in Bahrain: in 1906 it was the protection of Bahrain subjects in Persia by the British Government; in 1927 it was the designation of Bahrain in the treaty signed at Jidda in May of that year between the British Government and King Abdul Aziz as a State 'in special treaty relations with His Britannic Majesty's Government'. The result of such protests—and of others before them in the nineteenth century—has been to make the Persian claim a matter for dispute between Persia and Britain (for that reason notice of the 1927 protest was given to the Secretary-General of the League of Nations), for Bahrain's independence has in the past been the subject of engagements between the British Government and the island's rulers. The substance of the Persian case, as set forth in the documents presented to the League in 1927 and 1928, and recently in an expanded form

---

[1] Source: *International Affairs* (Royal Institute of International Affairs 1944-), Vol. 33, No. 1 (Jan., 1957), pp. 51-70.

by Dr Adamiyat, is that Persia has never recognized the independent status of Bahrain, that the bulk of historical evidence points to the continued sovereignty of Persia over the island and to the acknowledgement of that sovereignty by successive rulers of Bahrain, and that the British Government has on former occasions admitted the validity of the Persian claim.

On Persia's own admission the claim must stand or fall on its historical merits.

> A territory belonging to a sovereign State [the acting Persian Foreign Minister contended in 1928] cannot be lawfully detached so long as the right of ownership has not been transferred by this State to another State in virtue of an official act, in this case a treaty, or so long as its annexation by another State or its independence have not been officially recognized by the lawful owner of the territory. As a matter of historical truth, it is beyond question that the Bahrein Islands belong to Persia.[2]

Persia's case, as Sir Austen Chamberlain, the British Foreign Secretary, pointed out in reply, depended upon her affording proof 'that she is, or ever has been, the lawful owner of Bahrain'. Moreover, the contention advanced by the Persian Foreign Minister, that the consent of a dispossessed State was invariably required to validate a change of sovereignty, was, as Chamberlain explained, contradicted by both history and international practice.

> . . .the effective establishment by the territory of its independence is the deciding factor in the question of international title, and, in the case of Bahrein, His Majesty's Government regard as wholly untenable the proposition that effective possession and administration by the present ruling family for one hundred and forty-five years, during which these rulers have been independent of Persia, and during which no Persian authority has been exercised in their dominions, can be affected by the mere consideration that the Persian Government have not set their signature to a document formally recognizing the fact of their independence.[3]

---

[2] *Official Journal of the League of Nations*, September 1928, p. 1360, F. Pakrevan to R. C. Parr (British chargé d'affaires at Tehran), 2 August 1928.

[3] *Off. Journal of League*, May 1929, pp. 790-3, Chamberlain to Hovhannes Khan Mossaed (Persian Minister in London), 18 February 1929.

A noted Iraqi scholar, Professor Majid Khadduri, has endorsed Chamberlain's view of the juridical value of the Persian case in an article published in the *American Journal of International Law* in 1951:[4] 'International practice . . .', says Professor Khadduri, 'could hardly support this rule, and its validity would actually permit any state to advance a claim to territory on the ground that its loss in the past had not been confirmed by an express approval of the owner.'

Essentially, then, the Persian case depends upon its historical evidence, as the Persian Government have admitted in their previous protests, and as Dr Adamiyat now admits in his present work, by placing the weight of their argument upon the history of Bahrain over the past century and a half, during which time, they contend, the rulers of the island on several occasions recognized Persian sovereignty and paid tribute to the Shah's government. A degree of scepticism is necessary in assessing the value of such recognitions—if, indeed, they were ever made—for, as Sir Austen Chamberlain observed in 1929,

> [His Majesty's Government] have always been well aware that the unfortunate rulers of the islands, surrounded by warlike and more powerful States which menaced their independence, professed on various occasions during the first sixty or seventy years of the nineteenth century an unwilling allegiance to Muscat, to Persia, to Turkey, to the rulers of the mainland of Arabia, even to Egypt—to any Power, in short, who would agree to offer them protection and seemed at the time in a strong enough position to do so; and that at different times for short periods they paid tribute to Muscat, Egypt, or the Wahabi Arabs of the mainland. Any argument based on payment of tribute would therefore be available in support of a claim to sovereignty over Bahrein by any of the States to which tribute was in fact paid....[5]

The modern history of Bahrain as an independent principality dates from the year 1783, when the Atabi Arabs from the Arabian mainland expelled the Persian garrison from the islands. Persian rule over the Bahrain archipelago, exercised through the medium of the Shaikh of Bushire on the Persian mainland, dated, for all practical purposes, from 1600 when the Portuguese, who had occupied the islands since 1522, were driven

---

4 'Iran's Claim to the Sovereignty of Bahrayn', Vol. 45, pp. 631-47.
5 *Loc. cit.*, Chamberlain to Hovhannes Khan Mossaed, 18 February 1929.

out. The authority of the Shah, however, had not gone unchallenged in the years between 1600 and 1783. In 1718 the Imam of Muscat, Sultan ibn Saif II, seized Bahrain and held it for a short time. Towards the middle of the century effective rule in Bahrain seems to have passed from the Persians to the Huwailah Arabs, for in 1753 a Persian expedition under Shaikh Nasir of Bushire was despatched across the Gulf to reconquer the island. For the next thirty years the Shaikh and his family were entrusted with the government of the island and with the transmission of its revenues to the Persian provincial government at Shiraz.

The final loss of the island by Persia in 1783 was largely the result of Shaikh Nasir's imprudence earlier that year in attacking the settlement of Atabi Arabs at Zubarah on the Qatar peninsula. The Atabi were comparative newcomers to the Gulf's shores, having migrated to Kuwait—some say from southern Iraq, others from northern central Arabia where they were an off-shoot of the Anaizah—in the second decade of the eighteenth century. Of the three principal divisions in the tribe—Al Sabah, Al Khalifah, and Al Jalahimah—the Al Sabah had remained at Kuwait while the other two had moved on, in or about 1766, to found settlements at Zubarah and elsewhere on the western side of the Qatar peninsula. Late in 1782 the Al Khalifah had raided Bahrain, plundered Manamah, its principal town, and retired with a great quantity of loot. Shaikh Nasir of Bushire was despatched by the Prince of Shiraz, Governor of the Persian province of Fars, to destroy Zubarah and chastise the Al Khalifah, but was himself defeated and compelled to withdraw. Fired by their success, the Al Khalifah crossed over to Bahrain and, with the help of the Al Sabah, their kinsmen from Kuwait, overcame the Persian garrison and made themselves masters of the island.[6]

Although the provincial government at Shiraz refused to reconcile itself to the loss of Bahrain, events within Persia and without conspired to render the recovery of the island virtually impossible in the years immediately following 1783. Good use was made of these years by the Al Khalifah to consolidate their hold on the Bahrain archipelago: within a short time they acquired almost complete control of the pearl fisheries around Bah-

---

6 'Historical Sketch of the Uttoobee Tribe of Arabs, 1716-1817' by F. Warden (Chief Secretary to Govt. of Bombay, 1819), *Selections from Bombay Govt. Records* xxiv (Bombay, i856), pp. 362-5; [Public Record Office] Adm. I/189, 'Short Sketch of the Atabi Arabs' by Lieut. Wm. Bruce (British Resident at Bushire), 26 October 1816, enclosed in Rear-Adm. Sir R. King (C. in C. East Indies) to J. W. Croker (Secy. to Admiralty), Trincomali, 5 March 1817 (No. 6). This report was handed to the commander of H.M.S. Challenger on the occasion of his proceeding to the Gulf to cruise against the Qasimi pirates late in 1816.

rain; their ships, together with those of the Al Sabah of Kuwait, became the chief carriers of the traffic between Muscat and Basra; while Bahrain itself became the chief emporium for the trade of the north-western shores of the Gulf. Yet what served even more than the Atabi's mercantile success to prevent a Persian reoccupation of Bahrain after 1783 was a shift in the political balance of the Gulf from the Persian to the Arabian shore. The close of the eighteenth century saw the religio-military empire of the Wahhabis under the leadership of the Saudi dynasty of Daraiya established as the dominant political force in central and eastern Arabia, threatening the precarious independence of the small coastal principalities. Almost as great an obstacle as the Wahhabi Empire to the exertion of Persia's influence in Gulf politics and to the execution of her designs on Bahrain was the lack of Persian naval power. Without this the conquest of the island was impossible, and so it was that the first blow against the new Atabi State was struck, not by Persia, but by the only Gulf State possessed at that time of strong naval resources, the Sultanate of Muscat and Oman. For several years the wealth of Bahrain had excited the cupidity of the ambitious ruler of that principality, Saiyid Sultan ibn Ahmad, and in the autumn of 1800 an expedition was despatched from Muscat which quickly overran the island and forced the Al Khalifah rulers to flee for safety to Kuwait. A year later they managed to expel the Omani forces but Saiyid Sultan returned to the attack in 1802. On this occasion the Al Khalifah turned for help to the Wahhabi Amir, Abdul Aziz I ibn Muhammad, and, as the Wahhabis were already menacing the landward *frontiers* of Oman, Saiyid Sultan was forced to retire to defend his own country.

From 1802 onwards Bahrain seesawed between the Wahhabis and Oman, siding now with one, now with the other, as their respective fortunes rose and fell, striving to maintain some semblance of independence and prosperity. A price was paid in the form of submission and the payment of tribute to Daraiya, on the one hand, and invasion by Omani forces, on the other, but by 1818, when the Wahhabi Empire was brought to its knees by the army of Ibrahim Pasha, son of Muhammad Ali Pasha of Egypt, the Atabi of Bahrain were still masters of the archipelago.

Throughout these troubled years Persia had played practically no part in the history of the Gulf, the attention of Fath Ali Shah being primarily directed towards the protection of his northern dominions against the encroachment of Russia. So far as Bahrain was concerned Persian interest in its fate was limited to affording encouragement to the Sultan of Oman in his efforts to conquer the island. Yet the claim has often been made, most recently by Dr Adamiyat in his book, that Bahrain did not cease to be part of the Persian dominions after 1783, and the Al Khalifah Shaikhs are reputed to have made acknowledgement of this fact on more than one occasion, notably in 1817, when they solicited aid from the Shah against the Wahhabis.[7] As the latter were then on the threshold of defeat by the Egyptians, and as an envoy from the Sultan of Oman was then at Tehran asking for Persian military aid for yet another attack on the island, it would appear that the Shaikhs' motive in acknowledging Persian suzerainty—if, in fact, they did so—was to avert yet another assault from Oman. All the extant contemporary authorities are agreed on the fact of Bahrain's independence at this period. Lieutenant William Bruce, the East India Company's acting Resident at Bushire in 1816, who visited Bahrain in the summer of that year, describes the Al Khalifah Shaikhs as being the 'sole and undisputed rulers' of the island which they had won from Persia by right of conquest.[8] Captain Robert Taylor, the assistant Resident at Basra, noted in a report delivered to the Government of Bombay in 1812 that, after their conquest of Bahrain in 1783, 'the Uttoobees paid a trifling tribute to the Persians only four times, and then discontinued it altogether.'[9] A year later, Francis Warden, Chief Secretary to the Government of Bombay, advised the Governor that the records of government clearly showed that the Atabi of Bahrain regarded themselves, and were regarded on the Arabian coast, as independent.[10] Ten years later, the officer in charge of the Bombay Marine's survey of the Persian Gulf found Bahrain to be under the sole authority of the Al Khalifah, and was told by the inhabitants that it had been so since 1790, 'when the Persian yoke was entirely thrown off, and they have been independent of Persia ever since'.[11]

The awakening of British interest in Bahrain in the early nineteenth

---

7 *Bahrein Islands*, pp. 35, 63-4. It may be worthy of note that this is one of the few occasions on which Dr Adamiyat has had recourse to Persian sources: for the greater part of his original material he has drawn on the British records, which, as he acknowledges, are practically the sole source for the history of the Gulf in the early nineteenth century.

8 [India Office Records] Bombay Secret Proceedings, Vol. 41, Secret Consultation 29 of 2I July 1819, Bruce to Chief Secy. Bombay, 31 July 1816.

9 Taylor's report is published in *Selections from Bombay Govt. Records*, xxiv, pp. 1-40. Dr Adamiyat has somehow managed to twist Taylor's statement into a surprising form: 'The taxes of Bahrein again went to the Persian Treasury' (*Bahrein Islands*, p. 35).

10 Warden's report, together with several others on the Arab tribes of the Gulf, was delivered to the Governor-in-Council on 12 August 1819 (Sec. Consultn. 37 of 20 September 1819, [I.O.] Bombay Sec. Proc., Vol. 41). They were later published in the volume of Selections already cited.

11 'Memoir descriptive of the Navigation of the Gulf of Persia' by Lieut. G. B. Brucks, 21 August 1829, reprinted in *Selections from Bombay Govt. Records*, XXIV, p. 565.

century was a direct consequence of the resolution of the Indian Government to put an end to the large-scale piracies committed by the maritime tribes of the Arabian coast on seaborne commerce between India and the Gulf. In November 1819 an expedition was despatched from Bombay under the command of Major-General Sir William Grant Keir to attack the ports of the piratical tribes on the inner coast of the Gulf, particularly Ras-al-Khaima on the Pirate Coast, the stronghold of the Qawasim, the most notorious and formidable of the freebooters, to destroy their shipping, and to exact from them an undertaking to refrain from piratical activities in the future. Bahrain was suspected of being a frequent resort of the Qawasim and a clearing-house for their plunder, but as the Atabis' complicity in piracy seemed the result rather of their cupidity as merchants than of any vicious propensity, the Governor-General of India, the Marquis Hastings, was not prepared to sanction their punishment.[12] There was, however, another more difficult decision to be taken: the expedition against the Gulf pirates was being actively supported by the Sultan of Oman, Saiyid Said ibn Sultan, who expected in return to receive positive encouragement from the British Government for his plans to make good his claim to Bahrain, based on the conquest of the island by his father in 1800. Against this claim the British authorities in India had to weigh the pretensions of Persia: whatever step they took towards recognition of either claim, one of the claimants was bound to be offended. So the Governor of Bombay, the Hon. Mountstuart Elphinstone, whom the Governor-General had entrusted with the direction of British policy in the Gulf, at the close of 1819 made the only possible decision:

> ... We should abstain from all interference in the pretensions which are advanced to the occupation of Bahrain, under a distinct explanation to the Shaik of that Island that so long as he restrains his tribe from the prosecution of acts of aggression on the high seas . . . he may rely on experiencing from the British Government every degree of encouragement and of friendly intercourse...[13]

Yet Elphinstone did not completely repudiate the Persian claim to the island: on the contrary, he was quite prepared to mediate between the

---

12 [I.O.] Bombay Sec. Proc., Vol. 40, Sec. Consultn. 17 of 14 April 1819, J. Adams (Secy. to Gov.-Gen.) to F. Warden (Chief Secy. to Govt., Bombay), 2 January 1819.

13 [I.O.] Bombay Sec. Proc., Vol. 43, Sec. Consultn. 53 of 15 December 1819, Gov.-in-Council, Bombay, to Gov.-Gen.-in-Council, 15 December 1819.

Al Khalifah Shaikhs and the Persian Government to secure for the latter an acknowledgement of sovereignty and the payment of an annual tribute. But this offer was contingent upon two conditions: first, that the Al Khalifah Shaikhs should express a desire to acknowledge Persian suzerainty (which Elphinstone conceived they might do from fear of the Sultan of Oman) and, secondly, that Persian suzerainty would be exercised in name only, the Atabi being left in undisturbed possession of Bahrain.[14]

Events in the Gulf, however, overtook Elphinstone's offer before it was put to the Persian Government. On 23 February 1820, Sir William Keir admitted the Shaikhs of Bahrain to the General Treaty of Peace he had concluded with the tribes of the Pirate Coast (later known as the Trucial Coast). A few days later Saiyid Said of Oman informed Keir that the Al Khalifah had made submission to him, promising to pay an annual tribute of 30,000 dollars (about £6,500). Though Elphinstone refused to regard the accession of the Al Khalifah to the General Treaty as involving the British Government in a pledge to uphold the independence of Bahrain against future aggressors, he could no longer hold out his offer of mediation to Persia, especially in view of the Al Khalifah's submission to the Sultan of Oman. Accordingly he instructed Sir William Keir to observe the strictest neutrality towards Bahrain, and to make it quite clear to the Shaikhs that the British Government would play no part in any attempts that might be made by Persia or Oman to conquer the island.

> ... It is equally important [he wrote] to convince the Courts of Tehran and Muscat of our entertaining no views of our own on Bahrain, and having no motive for arguing against their attacks on that Island, except the apprehension that such a measure may prevent the complete pacification which we are desirous to introduce among all the States in the Gulf of Persia.[15]

Little support for the oft-made Persian contention that the British Government has in the past recognized the Persian claim to Bahrain can be derived from Elphinstone's sentiments on the subject, or from those uttered by other members of the Bombay Government during the policy-making discussions of 1819 and 1820. Yet Dr Adamiyat, in his account

---

14 [I.O.] Bombay Sec. Proc., Vol. 43, Sec. Consultn. 53 of 15 December 1819, Elphinstone to Henry Willock (Br. charge d'affaires at Tehran), 15 December 1819.
15 [I.O.] Bombay Sec. Proc., Vol. 46, Sec. Consultn. 10 of 5 April 1820, F. Warden to Keir, 1 April 1820.

of the events of these years,[16] has, by a process of selection and omission, contrived to produce the contrary impression. It is to be regretted that his examination of British official records in the compilation of his account did not extend to the Secret and Political Proceedings of the Government of Bombay for these years, which give a much fuller account than do other series in the India Office and Foreign Office Records. Nowhere in these Proceedings can be found any positive recognition of the validity of the Persian claim to Bahrain; and it is difficult to detect, in the information placed at the disposal of the Bombay Government, any support for the contention that Persia had continued to exercise sovereignty over the island since 1783. Despite this, it was the Bombay Government's unfortunate lot, in the autumn of 1822, to be placed in an embarrassing position over Bahrain, vis-a-vis Persia, through an extraordinary indiscretion on the part of their Political Resident at Bushire, Captain William Bruce. On 8 August 1822 Captain Bruce concluded a completely unauthorized agreement with the Persian authorities at Shiraz, the second article of which stated that Bahrain had 'always been subordinate to the Province of Fars', while the fifth article stipulated that British cruisers should be loaned to the Prince of Shiraz should he require them for the reconquest of Bahrain.[17] To this day Bruce's motives in concluding an agreement which outraged all the principles of policy by which his government had acted in the Persian Gulf remain unexplained. He never attempted to justify his conduct to his superiors, but the lines along which such an explanation might have proceeded may be easily discerned. Bruce was himself *persona non grata* with the Persian authorities—his recall had been asked for more than once but had been refused by the Bombay Government—he may have thought to contribute to the amelioration of Anglo-Persian relations, then in a strained condition, and he may well have believed, as he told Elphinstone, that the reversion of Bahrain to Persian authority 'will tend more to the tranquillity of the Arabian side of the Gulf than almost any other act'— though he was careful to add that it was very unlikely that the Prince of Shiraz would venture to assert that authority.[18]

Whatever the reasons for his action, however, Bruce's conduct was indefensible: every aspect of his proceedings was condemned by the Government of Bombay and he was abruptly dismissed from his post. Mount-

---

16 *Bahrein Islands*, Chapter III.
17 [I.O.] Enclosures to Bombay Sec. Letters Recd., Vol. 7, enclosures to Sec. Letter 3 of 9 November 1822, Bruce to Elphinstone, Shiraz, 3 September 1822 (No. 35 Political Dept.).
18 *Ibid.*

Stuart Elphinstone was particularly concerned to denounce the admission of 'the sovereignty of Persia over Bahrain, of which there is not a shadow of proof, to the prejudice . . . of the independence of the Uttoobees with whom we are bound by a treaty of friendship'.[19] Letters were despatched to the Prince of Shiraz and to the Al Khalifah Shaikhs, disowning Bruce's action and reaffirming British neutrality in the Perso-Bahrain controversy. Nor was Elphinstone alone in condemning the Resident's action: Fath Ali Shah refused to acknowledge the existence of the agreement and soundly rated the Prince of Shiraz for entering upon negotiations without his prior knowledge and consent.[20] This last point has subsequently been made light of by the Persian Government, which has not scrupled in the years since 1822 to bring forward Bruce's discredited agreement as proof both of Persian sovereignty over Bahrain and of British recognition of the claim. Nor does Dr Adamiyat in his book scruple to make use of it, even while admitting that the document has neither value nor validity. What he fails to mention—and it may well be that he does not know—is that Bruce was given to the practice of making unauthorized agreements and that, in July 1816, he had concluded an agreement with the Shaikhs of Bahrain designed to guarantee the Al Khalifah against external aggression.[21] Taken in conjunction with his testimony in the same year—as mentioned earlier—to the independent status of Bahrain, this earlier agreement makes his pact of 1822 with the Prince of Shiraz all the more mystifying. Unhappily for the Prince he derived no benefit from Bruce's conduct: without naval means of his own and unable to persuade the maritime Powers of the Gulf to lend him ships, he was powerless to make good his claim to Bahrain. As time went by, the project of conquering the island came to assume the appearance of an annual attraction staged by the Prince for the edification of the Court of Tehran. Nor were these displays without purpose, as the British Resident at Bushire in 1824 noted:

> These annual demonstrations against the Uttoobees [have] become a regular and essential part of the policy of the Shiraz Government, as not only holding forth a plea for deductions

---

19 [I.O.] Enclosures to Bombay Sec. Letters Recd., Vol. 7, enclos. to Sec. Letter 3 of 9 November 1822, F. Warden (Secy. with Gov.) to J. Farish (acting Chief Secy.), 27 October 1822).
20 [I.O.] Persia and Persian Gulf Series, Vol. 35, Geo. Willock (charge d'affaires Tabriz), to Secret Committee of the E.I. Company, 25 January 1823.
21 [I.O.] Bombay Sec. Proc., Vol. 41, Sec. Consultn. 29 of 21 July 1819, Bruce to Chief Secy., Bombay, 31 July 1816.

from the usual remittances to Tehran, but also affording a pretence for extortions from its own dependencies.[22]

More than twenty years were to elapse after the conclusion of Bruce's agreement before the Shah's government put forward another serious claim to ownership over the Bahrain Islands. A half-hearted move was made in 1839 to take advantage of the crisis caused in the Gulf by the arrival of an Egyptian army on its shores to persuade the Al Khalifah to acknowledge Persian suzerainty. Dr Adamiyat's version of this incident is, to put the most charitable construction upon it, quite unreal. According to him, a *vakil* or emissary was sent from Shiraz early in 1839, when the first rumours of an impending Egyptian attack on Bahrain reached the Government of Fars, to reside on the island 'in the capacity of an official of the Government of Shiraz and was in charge of receiving and transmitting the annual tribute of Bahrein to the treasury of Fars'.[23] One of the sources from which Dr Adamiyat derives this statement is an account of Bahrain by Lieutenant A. B. Kemball, the Assistant Resident in the Gulf in 1844, published in *Selections from Bombay Government Records*, XXIV (1856). The relevant passage runs:

> He [the Persian *vakil*] was under directions to remain at Bahrein as Persian Agent, and to be the medium of receiving and transmitting the annual tribute, which the Persian authorities vainly flattered themselves the Bahrein Chief was disposed to pay for their countenance and protection.[24]

Not only does Dr Adamiyat omit the latter part of this sentence, but he fails to mention that Bahrain received no protection whatever from Persia, and was shielded from Egyptian attack only by the ships of the Royal and Indian Navies. For obvious reasons he has also chosen to remain silent on two further incidents which contradict the argument of continued Persian sovereignty over Bahrain. One is the offer made by the Al Khalifah Shaikhs, in February 1839, to place the island under the permanent protection of the British Government;[25] the other is the submission, after this offer

---

22 [I.O.] Bombay Political Letters Recd., Vol. 9, Gov.-in-Council, Bombay, to Court of Directors of E.I. Co., 2 July 1825 (No. 6 Polit. Dept.), citing a report from Lt.-Col. E. G. Stannus.
23 *Bahrein Islands*, p. 125.
24 *Selections*, p. 388.
25 [I.O.] Enclosures to Bombay Sec. Letters, Vol. 12, enclosures to Sec. Letter 41 of 13

The Persian Claim to Bahrain

had been rejected, of the Al Khalifah to the Egyptian commander in eastern Arabia and the payment of a tribute of 3,000 dollars to the Pasha of Egypt.[26]

The renewal of Persian pretensions in the eighteen-forties was a more serious affair. Rebellion and civil strife in Bahrain had resulted in 1843 in the expulsion of the ruling Shaikh, Abdullah ibn Ahmad, and his replacement as ruler by his grand-nephew, Muhammad ibn Khalifah. Shaikh Abdullah found refuge at first at Bushire where he was soon in negotiation with the Persian authorities for aid in recovering his position, on the understanding that should he do so he would henceforth hold Bahrain as a fief of Persia. The prospect thus raised, of a naval war between Shaikh Abdullah and his nephew, posed a serious threat to the maritime trade of the Gulf and to the peace which the British Government in India had laboured for thirty years to establish. Already the previous year the Government of India had been moved by reports of maritime disorders in the Gulf to issue instructions to its Resident there that

> In the event . . . of the Persian Government sending out any force of armed vessels, or vessels carrying armed men, such vessels should be watched, and any actual attempt to possess themselves of territory belonging to Arab Chiefs in friendly alliance with the British Government should first be remonstrated against, and then, if persevered in, resisted.[27]

A similar warning was given to the Persian Government in May 1844, by Lord Aberdeen, the Foreign Secretary, as a result of the ex-Shaikh's intrigues with the Persian Government:

> ... Unless Persia can show that she has a clear and indisputable right to the sovereignty of Bahrein, that she has exercised it without interruption under the dynasty of the Kajar family, and that consequently her present policy is directed to the

---

April 1839, Capt. S. Hennell (Res. in Gulf) to J. P. Willoughby (Chief Secy., Bombay), 22 February 1839 (No. 13 Sec. Dept.).

26 [I.O.] Enclosures to Bombay Sec. Letters, Vol. 14, enclosures to Sec. Letter 87 of 16 July 1839, Khurshid Pasha (Egyptian commander) to Hennell, 18 Muharram, A.H.1255 (4 April 1839).

27 [I.O.] Bombay Sec. Proc., Vol. 192, Sec. Consultn. 38 of 7 September 1842, T. H. Maddock (Secy. with Gov.-Gen.) to L. R. Reid (Chief Secy. to Govt., Bombay), 13 August 1842 (No. 679 Sec. Dept.).

maintenance of her lawful claims, and not to the assertion of a pretension not founded in law, Persia must be prepared to encounter in any scheme of this kind the active opposition of the British Government in India.[28]

In an effort to furnish the proof demanded by Aberdeen, the Persian Prime Minister, Haji Mirza Aghasi, in March 1845, presented the British envoy at Tehran, Colonel Sheil, with a lengthy exposition of the Persian case which, it may be noted, has formed the basis for practically every subsequent Persian protest over Bahrain. The calibre of the Prime Minister's arguments may be gauged from his opening sentence:

> In the first place the sentiments of all governments, far and near, are in accordance with those of Persia that the Persian Gulf from the commencement of the Shatt-al-Arab to Muscat belongs to Persia, and that all the islands of that sea, without exception and without the partnership of any other Government, belong entirely to Persia, as indeed, in Your Excellency's language, you call that sea 'the Persian Gulf'.[29]

Bahrain, the Prime Minister continued, had been in the possession of the Government of Fars since the fourteenth century; all European and Turkish books of geography described Bahrain as Persian; the British Government had warned the Pasha of Egypt against seizing the island on the grounds that it did not form part of the mainland of Arabia, and it therefore followed—the Prime Minister argued—that it must form part of Persia: the British Government had 'repeatedly' asked for permission to rent the island from Persia; and Bruce's agreement of 1822 explicitly admitted Persian sovereignty over Bahrain. As a final piece of proof Haji Mirza Aghasi handed Colonel Sheil a gold coin which, he said, had been struck in Bahrain in 1817 in the name of Fath Ali Shah, Qajar.[30] Most of the points raised in the Haji's argument have been dealt with previously, but the use made of Bruce's agreement is interesting. The reference to British requests to lease Bahrain from Persia was probably a confused account of

---

28 [I.O.] Board's Drafts: Sec. Letters to India, Vol. 18, Draft to Gov.-Gen., 2 May 1844, enclosing Aberdeen to J. Sheil (Min. at Tehran), 1 May 1844 (No. 23).
29 [I.O.] Enclosures to Bombay Sec. Letters, Vol. 76, enclos. to Sec. Letter 42 of 10 June 1845, Sheil to Aberdeen, 18 March 1845 (No. 28); enclosing Haji Mirza Aghasi to Sheil 6 Rabi-al-Awal, A.H. 1261 (15 March 1845).
30 *Ibid.*

The Persian Claim to Bahrain

Captain John Malcolm's proposal on his Persian mission in 1800 to lease the islands of Kharag and Qishm, and of the Bombay Government's efforts between 1820 and 1823 to use Qishm Island as a base against pirates. As for the gold coin reputedly struck at Bahrain in 1817, this was later found by Captain (later Major) Hennell, the Resident in the Gulf, to be a clumsy forgery.[31]

As the Persian Prime Minister, after delivering his note, did not appear inclined to pursue the question, Colonel Sheil, under instructions from London, let it drop. Apart from sporadic protests from Tehran over the next few years against British actions in the Gulf which supposedly prejudiced Persian rights in Bahrain, no practical step was taken by the Shah's government until 1860 to make good their claim. Bahrain, meanwhile, led a somewhat precarious existence, troubled within by civil disobedience and the oppressions of Shaikh Muhammad ibn Khalifah, and threatened from without by the powerful Wahhabi Amir, Faisal ibn Turki, and by the dispossessed sons of the ex-Shaikh. Shaikh Muhammad's efforts in these years to retain control of Bahrain led him successively in 1849 to offer the sovereignty of the island to the British Government,[32] in 1850 to open a correspondence with the Sharif of Mecca with a view to placing Bahrain under Ottoman jurisdiction,[33] and in 1851 to submit to the Amir Faisal and agree to pay *zakat* or tribute of 4,000 dollars per annum.[34] Before many years had passed Shaikh Muhammad was refusing to keep up the payment of this tribute, and he was saved from Faisal's wrath only by British intervention. Despite warnings from the Resident in the Gulf not to provoke the Amir, Muhammad continued to harass the Arabian mainland opposite Bahrain, blockading the Wahhabi ports of Dammam and Qatif, and even interfering with British-Indian trade to those ports. Faisal's patience ran out in 1859 and he began preparations to launch a

---

31 [I.O.] Persia and P. Gulf Series, Vol. 81, Sheil to Aberdeen, 23 April 1845 (No. 42). It is somewhat strange, to say the least, that Dr Adamiyat, who refers to this coin twice in his book (pp. 35 and 135) as proof of Persian sovereignty over Bahrain, and who claims to have used this series of records, should make no mention of Captain Hennell's testimony.

32 [I.O.] Enclos. to Bombay Sec. Letters, Vol. 99, enclos. to Sec. Letter 57 of 21 May 1849, Muhammad ibn Khalifah to Major Hennell, 15 Rabi-al-Awal, A.H. 1265 (9 February 1849).

33 [I.O.] Enclos. to Bombay Sec. Letters, Vol. 104, enclos. to Sec. Letter 69 of 2 December 1850, Hennell to A. Malet (Secy. to Govt., Bombay), 18 October 1850 (No. 389 Sec. Dept.).

34 [I.O.] Enclos. to Bombay Sec. Letters, Vol. 102, enclos. to Sec. Letter 73 of 2 October 1951, Hennell to Malet, 5 August 1851 (No. 257 Sec. Dept.).

full-scale attack on the island. Thoroughly alarmed now, especially as he had alienated British sympathy by the commission of maritime irregularities, Shaikh Muhammad appealed for aid to the Persian Governor of Fars and the Turkish Pasha of Baghdad. His appeal was answered with alacrity by the Shiraz authorities; within a short space of time a Persian agent had arrived in Bahrain where he lost no time in proclaiming Persian sovereignty over the island and raising the Persian flag. Scarcely had he done so when an emissary from the Pasha of Baghdad reached the island, where he was effusively welcomed by Shaikh Muhammad. The Persian flag was hauled down and the Turkish ensign run up in its place. To complete the absurdity of the situation the Persian agent refused to leave the island or to surrender his imaginary authority there.[35] This piece of *opéra-bouffe* is taken seriously by Dr Adamiyat,[36] who adduces it as further proof of Persian sovereignty over Bahrain. For his own purposes, however, he has seen fit to avoid all mention of the arrival of the Turkish emissary, of Shaikh Muhammad's submission to the Ottoman Sultan, and of the swift exchange of ensigns. A more realistic view of the affair was taken at the time by Sir Henry Rawlinson, then British Minister at Tehran:

> It seems to have been the normal condition of Bahrein for some years past that three rival authorities, the Pasha of Baghdad, the Wahhabi Amir and the Prince Governor of Fars, should lay claim to the allegiance of the island, and endeavour either by intimidation or intrigue to supersede the independence of the Sheikh.... Hostilities against Bahrein from any quarter are to be repelled by us by force of arms; whilst the voluntary tender of the Sheikh's allegiance to any other power, so long as it is not followed up by military occupation, is to be ignored as of no practical importance.[37]

British policy towards Bahrain in the eighteen-sixties, to which Rawlinson made allusion in the above letter, was influenced by one overriding consideration, the need to keep down the incidence of maritime warfare in

---

35 [I.O.] Enclos. to Bombay Sec. Letters, Vol. 142, enclos. to Sec. Letter 25 of 22 June 1860, Capt. F. Jones (Res. in Gulf) to H. L. Anderson (Secy. to Govt., Bombay), 7 May 1860 (No. 2A Sec. Dept.); Enclos. to Bombay Sec. Letters, Vol. 143, enclos. to Sec. Letter 37 of 11 September 1860, Jones to Anderson, 2 July 1860.
36 *Bahrein Islands*, pp. 155-63.
37 [I.O.] Enclos. to Bombay Sec. Letters, Vol. 143, enclos. to Sec. Letter 37 of 11 September 1860, Rawlinson to Jones, 4 May 1860.

the Gulf, which was only too apt to degenerate into indiscriminate piracy and to upset the system of maritime truces which the Government of India had been at pains to build up over a long period. The execution of this policy had led that government at various times to discourage or actively oppose the despatch of expeditions against Bahrain by the Persians, the Sultan of Oman, the Trucial Shaikhs, the Egyptians, and the Wahhabis. Dr Adamiyat apparently refuses to accept that British policy was as much opposed to Wahhabi as to Persian attacks on Bahrain (cf. Chapter V of his book), or that on several occasions, notably in the eighteen-fifties, the island was saved from Wahhabi conquest only by the timely intervention of British naval forces. So it was again in 1860, after Shaikh Muhammad had failed to secure concrete help from Shiraz or Baghdad, but the British authorities in India were fast coming to the conclusion that the independent position of Bahrain must soon be regularized: a recommendation to this effect was made to the Secretary of State for India by the Government of Bombay in September 1860, and was approved by him the following February.[38] Not only the island's status but also the responsibilities of its inhabitants towards the maintenance of the peace at sea awaited definition, for the Atabi of Bahrain, whose first line of defence lay in their ships, had not been required, as had the tribes of the Trucial Coast, to subscribe to the trucial system at sea or to the treaty of permanent maritime peace drawn up in 1853. The behaviour of the Atabi at sea, on the other hand, and more particularly that of their ruler, had not been irreproachable. When, therefore, in the early months of 1861 Shaikh Muhammad began once again to harry the Wahhabi ports of Dammam and Qatif, the Government of India decided to bring him to task. The Resident in the Gulf sailed for Bahrain with the Gulf Squadron and at his insistence the Shaikh signed a convention on 31 May 1861 whereby he undertook to refrain from 'the prosecution of war, piracy and slavery by sea': in return he received a guarantee of British protection against all external aggression.[39]

The normal protests against British interference in the affairs of Bahrain were made at the time by the Persian Government, but it was not until 1868-9 that these protests assumed a serious form. If for no other reason, this next attempt to revive the near moribund Persian claim to Bahrain—the last noteworthy one of the nineteenth century—merits examination,

---

38 [I.O.] Bombay Sec. Letters Recd., Vol. 35, Gov.-in-Council, Bombay to Secy. of State, 11 November 1860 (No. 37 Sec. Dept.); Sec. Letters to India, Vol. I (1859-69), Secy. of State to Gov.-in-Council, Bombay, 18 February 1861 (No. 2).
39 C. U. Aitchison, *A Collection of Treaties, Engagements and Sanads relating to India and Neighbouring Countries* (4th edn., 12 vols., Calcutta, 1909), XII, 159-60.

because it produced what the Persians still claim to be a decisive British admission of Persian sovereignty over the island, the oft-quoted Clarendon despatch of 29 April 1869. Shaikh Muhammad ibn Khalifah, far from mending his ways in the years after 1861, had continued to misbehave at sea, and in revenge, apparently, for his chastisement by the British authorities he had so oppressed the Indian community on Bahrain that they fled *en masse* to Bushire. The Resident in the Gulf, having failed by remonstrance to induce the Shaikh to settle various claims outstanding against him, seized one of his *baghlas* (sailing vessels) in December 1865. An immediate protest against the Resident's action was made by the Persian Government: Bahrain, they asserted, was a dependency of Persia, and to prove it they dusted off Bruce's almost forgotten agreement of 1822 and handed it to the British envoy at Tehran. He rejected both the claim and the document as worthless, and there for the time being the issue rested. Its revival three years later was again the consequence of Muhammad ibn Khalifah's misconduct: flagrantly violating the convention he had signed in 1861, Shaikh Muhammad in October 1867 plundered and destroyed two towns on the Qatar coast, forcibly expelling their inhabitants and driving them to seek refuge at various places on the Arabian and Persian coasts. The seriously depleted state of the Persian Gulf Squadron at the time prevented the Government of India from immediately bringing the Shaikh to account, but in September 1868 three warships were despatched to Bahrain to exact reparation for his crimes. Shaikh Muhammad did not await their arrival but fled to Qatar, and an agreement was made with his brother, whom the British authorities recognized as his successor, to compensate those who had suffered from Muhammad's actions.[40]

A flurry of protests from the Persian Government followed: one was delivered to the British minister at Tehran, another to the Resident in the Gulf, and a third was lodged with the Foreign Office by the Persian *chargé d'affaires* in London. The principal grounds of complaint were those of interference with 'the Persian Governor' of Bahrain, and the failure of the British authorities to give the Persian Government prior notice of their intention of proceeding against Shaikh Muhammad. Colonel Lewis Pelly, the Resident in the Gulf, was asked by the Government of India for his

---

40 The correspondence connected with events in Bahrain between 1867 and 1869 may be found in [I.O.] Enclos. to Bombay Sec. Letters, Vol. 147. Nowhere in this volume can any evidence be found to support the contention advanced by Dr Adamiyat (*Bahrein Islands*, p. l65), in his highly tendentious account of these events, that Shaikh Muhammad was deposed by the British authorities because he asked for Persian aid against his enemies in Qatar.

opinion of the justice of these complaints: he replied in January 1869 that the claim to sovereignty over Bahrain, as the Shah's government had been informed on several previous occasions, was groundless, and that he failed to see why he, as British Resident, should give the Persian authorities advance notice of his actions in respect of his duties on the Arabian coast.[41]

The answer given to the Persian Government by the Foreign Secretary, the Earl of Clarendon, though less harsh was quite firm on the main issue in question, the British Government's determination to maintain the maritime police of the Gulf. He was ready to acknowledge that the Persian Government had protested against the Persian right of sovereignty over Bahrain being ignored by the British authorities in the Gulf, but he pointed out that the Shaikh of Bahrain had entered into direct contractual engagements with the British Government to keep the peace at sea, and that he would be held to those engagements for that purpose. If the Shah's government were prepared to maintain a naval force in the Gulf to keep the peace the British Government would be relieved of a troublesome and costly duty, but if the Shah's government were unwilling or unable to assume this responsibility then the British Government could not allow disorder and anarchy to reign in the Gulf. For the sake of Anglo-Persian friendship Clarendon was prepared to arrange that, in future, whenever it was practicable to do so, the Persian Government should be informed beforehand of any measures of coercion that the conduct of the Shaikh of Bahrain might call forth; but, he added, the British Government could not consent to debar its officers, to whom the superintendence of the police of the Gulf had been entrusted, from punishing promptly any violation by the Shaikh of his treaty obligations, when a reference to Tehran might entail delays which might endanger the peace of the Gulf.[42]

Some surprising assertions have been made by the Persian Government in the years since 1869 on the basis of this letter, and are made again in Dr Adamiyat's book. The letter delivered by the acting Persian Foreign Minister to the British *chargé d'affaires* in Tehran in August 1928 made these points:

(i) On the subject of Clarendon's acknowledgement of the Persian protests of 1868-9: 'Thus, after examining facts and documents, he states that he has given due consideration to the

---

41 [I.O.] Enclos. to Bombay Sec. Letters, Vol. 147, Pelly to C. Gonne (acting Chief Secy. to Govt., Bombay), 16 January 1869 (No. 1 Pol. Dept.).
42 [I.O.] Home Correspondence (Secret), Vol. 63 (1869), Clarendon to Haji Mohsin Khan (Persian *chargé d'affaires* in London), 29 April 1869.

protest by which the Imperial Government affirmed its right of sovereignty. We claim that it is impossible to read into the phraseology employed by the Secretary of State any meaning or interpretation other than the obvious one.'

(ii) On Clarendon's remarks concerning Persia's ability to maintain the police of the Gulf: 'The letter goes on to make the recognition of Persian sovereignty over Bahrein even more strikingly apparent.'

(iii) On Clarendon's offer to inform the Persian Government of coercive measures employed against the Shaikh of Bahrain: 'This passage can only be explained by the necessity of rendering account to the legitimate sovereign.'[43]

Dr Adamiyat has added to these arguments an original observation of his own:

... Lord Clarendon deliberately and significantly avoided any reference to the Sheikh of Bahrein as an 'independent ruler'. The Foreign Secretary went as far as to repudiate any significance in the engagements which Britain had concluded with Bahrein.[44]

These interpretations are deserving of examination, if only because they have been put forward by the Persian Government on several occasions: their ultimate value can be determined only by a close study of the circumstances in which Clarendon's letter was framed. Late in December 1868 the Foreign Secretary received through the British minister at Tehran a detailed complaint from the Persian Government against Colonel Pelly's proceedings at Bahrain in the summer. Almost simultaneously a formal complaint along the same lines was lodged with the Foreign Office by the Persian *chargé d'affaires* in London, General Haji Mohsin Khan. Clarendon passed the complaints to the India Office with a request for advice on the reply that should be returned to the Persian Government.[45] A little over

---

43 *Off. Journal of League*, September 1928, p. 1361, F. Pakrevan to R. C. Parr, 2 August 1928.
44 *Bahrein Islands*, p. 171.
45 [I.O.] Home Corresp. (Sec.), Vol. 62 (1868), E. Hammond (Under-Secy., F.O.) to H. Merivale (Under-Secy., I.O.), 29 December 1868.

a month later he again addressed the India Office with the suggestion that if, in the future, similar proceedings against Bahrain became necessary, it might be advisable to inform the Persian Government of them.[46] Clarendon's motive in making this suggestion was to avoid the embarrassing complications that could so easily arise from the system of divided control over British policy in the Persian Gulf, whereby the British Political Resident was responsible to the Indian authorities while the British minister at Tehran was responsible to the Foreign Office. Before the India Office's opinion could be obtained Clarendon was handed, on 11 February, a second complaint by the Persian *chargé d'affaires* about Pelly's actions against the Shaikh of Bahrain. The Shaikh was described in Mohsin Khan's note as the Persian Governor of the island, and the suggestion was put forward that any grievances the British authorities might have against him should be referred to the Persian Government who would afford redress.[47]

This suggestion also was passed to the India Office for comment. On 27 February the reply of the Secretary of State for India, the Duke of Argyll, was sent to the Foreign Office.

> ... His Grace, having fully considered the question, is of opinion that the attitude assumed by Persia in this instance is not warranted by the actual state of the relations of Bahrein with Persia and with the British Government. The Sheikh of Bahrein is an independent Chief, whose independence we have recognized by entering into treaty engagements with him. We have not only never recognized, but on the other hand have always denied the right of Persia to assert her sovereignty over that territory.... Under these circumstances the Duke of Argyll is of opinion that it would be advisable to abstain as far as possible from discussing the question, whether in London or in Teheran. It would be sufficient to state that the Sheikh of Bahrein is an independent Chief whom the British Government will hold strictly to the performance of the Treaty obligations into which we have entered with him.[48]

---

46 [I.O.] Home Corresp. (Sec.), Vol. 63 (1869), Hammond to Under-Secy. I.O., 1 February, 1869.

47 [I.O.] Home Corresp. (Sec.), Vol. 63 (1869), Mohsin Khan to Clarendon, 11 February 1869, enclos. in Hammond to Under-Secy. I.O., 15 February 1869,

48 [I.O.] Home Corresp. (Sec.), Vol. 63 (1869), Merivale to Hammond, 27 February 1869.

A brief letter incorporating these views was sent by Clarendon to Mohsin Khan on 5 March.[49] The reaction of the Persian *chargé d'affaires* to this note was immediate: he wrote to Clarendon on 6 March, asking for an interview, and was granted one on 9 March.[50] At this meeting Mohsin Khan revealed himself as very reluctant to pass on to his Government the short and unequivocal answer on the political status of Bahrain returned him by the Foreign Secretary. He had received further communications from Tehran on the subject, but before laying these before Clarendon he wished to discuss the question further. Clarendon replied that as Bahrain affairs closely concerned the Government of India Mohsin Khan might find it useful to seek an interview with the Duke of Argyll, a suggestion the Persian representative readily adopted.[51] He saw Argyll towards the end of March but derived scant comfort from the meeting: Argyll merely repeated to him the answer conveyed in Clarendon's letter of 5 March, that the British Government regarded the Shaikh of Bahrain as an independent ruler. As Dr Adamiyat sees the omission of any reference to the independence of Bahrain in Clarendon's later letter of 29 April as 'significant', perhaps the evidence of Mohsin Khan himself may clear up any doubts as to what was said to him, verbally and in writing, on this point:

> Aux réclamations que j'ai adressées par écrit, de la part de mon Gouvernement, à Son Excellence Lord Clarendon, au sujet des faits accomplis dans l'île de Bahrein, il m'a été repondu par Son Excellence, comme ensuite par Votre Grâce, dans l'entrevue qu'elle a daigné m'accorder à ce sujet, que si votre Gouvemement avait agi de la sorte c'est dans la ferme conviction: où il était d'avoir affaire, dans l'île de Bahrein, a un Gouvernement indépendant.[52]

The protests to which Mohsin Khan referred in the foregoing passage were not only those of 11 February but also a new set—those, in fact,

---

49 [I.O.] Home Corresp. (Sec.), Vol. 63 (1869), Hammond to Merivale, 3 March, enclosing Clarendon to Mohsin Khan; M. E. Grant Duff (Under-Secy. IO.) to Hammond, 5 March 1869. The phrasing of Clarendon's letter is very similar to that of Argyll's.
50 [Public Record Office] F.O. 60 (Persia) /323, Mohsin Khan to Clarendon, 6 March 1869.
51 The main features of the interview of 9 March are recapitulated by Mohsin Khan in a letter to Clarendon of 15 March, enclosed in Hammond to Merivale, 17 March 1869, [I.O.] Home Corresp. (Sec.), Vol. 63 (1869).
52 [I.O.] Home Corresp. (Sec.), Vol. 63 (1869), Mohsin Khan to Argyll, 15 April 1869, enclos. in Hammond to Under-Secy. I.O., 16 April 1869.

which he had mentioned to Clarendon earlier as having received from Tehran and which he eventually delivered to the Foreign Secretary on 13 April. They included two letters, purported to have been written by Shaikh Muhammad ibn Khalifah (possibly in 1859 or 1860), declaring his allegiance to the Shah.[53] It is very doubtful whether, in delivering this fresh protest, Mohsin Khan was doing other than merely carrying out the orders he had received the previous month; for he was well aware by this time that the British Government was quite decided on the question of Bahrain's independence. Indeed, by the latter half of April both Argyll and Clarendon had reached the conclusion that Bahrain's political status could not be profitably discussed further: what was of more immediate concern was the necessity of reaffirming the British Government's determination to retain its responsibility for the maritime peace of the Persian Gulf. An additional consideration, which troubled Clarendon more than Argyll, was how to rebuff the Shah's pretensions to dominion over all the Gulf's waters—implicit in Mohsin Khan's suggestion that British complaints against Bahrain be referred to Tehran—without causing undue irritation to that monarch. The compromise he found, and which he persuaded Argyll to agree to, was that the British authorities in the Gulf should notify the British Minister at Tehran, for the information of the Persian Government, whenever the Shaikh was to be called to account for a breach of his engagements. In accepting this arrangement, however, the Secretary of State for India took care to emphasize that it was to be regarded only 'as a matter of courtesy to the Persian Government', and that the British Government had never recognized, directly or indirectly, the validity of the Persian claim to suzerainty over Bahrain.[54]

On 29 April Clarendon wrote to Mohsin Khan, omitting, so as to avoid cause for dispute, any reference to Persian claims to Bahrain: instead, he confined himself to repeating, in an extended form, what he had said in his letter of 5 March about holding the Shaikh to the engagements he had contracted with the British Government, and to informing the Persian representative that his Government would be told, whenever practicable, of any action to be taken against the Shaikh in the future.[55] Mohsin Khan lost no time in letting Clarendon know that he was unhappy about his let-

---

53 [I.O.] Home Corresp. (Sec.), Vol. 63 (1869), Mohsin Khan to Clarendon, 13 April 1869, enclosed in Hammond to Under-Secy. I.O., 16 April 1869.
54 [I.O.] Home Corresp. (Sec.), Vol. 63 (1869), Grant Duff to Hammond, 21 April 1869.
55 [I.O.] Home Corresp. (Sec.), Vol. 63 (1869), Hammond to Under-Secy. I.O., 26 April 1869, enclosing Clarendon to Mohsin Khan.

ter of 29 April, and that it was what the letter left unsaid, rather than what it said, that was the cause of his unhappiness. He wrote to Clarendon on 30 April, seeking an interview, and was accorded one the following day.[56] The upshot of this meeting was that Mohsin Khan submitted to Clarendon on 8 May a memorandum containing two points which he would like to see inserted in the original letter of 29 April. These bear so directly on the conclusions drawn by the Persian Government in 1928 and by Dr Adamiyat recently that they warrant quotation in full:

> 1. On établit dans le début de cette note que si le Gouvt. Britannique a imposé des engagements aux Sheikhs de Bahrein, c'est que le Gouvt. Persan n'ayant pas de représentant officiel de son autorité dans les eaux du Golfe Persique, le Gouvt. Britannique a cru pouvoir considérer comme indépendants les Sheikhs de Bahrein. Ici il serait à désirer qu'on ajoutât que le Gouvt. Persan ayant protesté pour réserver ses droits de souveraineté, le Gouvt. Britannique voulant lui donner un nouveau témoignage de ses sentiments aillicaux prend cette protestation en considération.

> 2. Le Gouvt. Brit. serait heureux, est-il dit ensuite, de se voir délivré d'une surveillance pénible et onéreuse pour lui. Ici il est à désirer qu'on ajoutât que jusqu'à ce que le Gouvt. de S.M.I. le Shah ait les ressources suffisantes pour maintenir le bon ordre dans ces eaux, le Gouvt. Brit., dans le cas où il se commettrait quelque désordre grave exigeant une repression rigoureuse, ne prendrait aucune mesure sans en avoir préalablement référé au Gouvt. de S.M.I. le Shah comme d'ailleurs il est énoncé dans la lettre.[57]

In his covering letter Mohsin Khan assured Clarendon that the insertion of these two points would leave the sense of the original letter of 29 April exactly the same, and he expressed the hope that Clarendon would consent to their insertion, 'et donner ainsi au Gouvt. de mon auguste maître un nouveau témoignage des intentions amicales du Gouvt. de S.M. la Reine à son égard'. At the close of his memorandum he again assured Clarendon that the only object he had in mind was to 'elucidate' the points in ques-

---

56 [P.R.O.] F.O. 60/323, Mohsin Khan to Clarendon, 30 April 1869.
57 [I.O.] Home Corresp. (Sec.), Vol. 63 (1869), Memo. by Mohsin Khan, 8 May 1869, enclosed in Hammond to Under-Secy. I.O., 11 May 1869.

tion, which, he repeated, did not alter the sense of the original letter in the slightest.[58]

The desired changes seemed innocuous enough: Mohsin Khan was patently anxious to be able to report to his Government that the protests he made had received due consideration from the British Government—perhaps even more consideration than similar protests on previous occasions. As proof of this, and perhaps as a sop to the Shah's pride, he wanted to see his second point conceded: that until the Shah's Government should possess sufficient naval resources to maintain order in the Gulf's waters, the British authorities would always refer to the Persian Government before quelling disturbances. This was too much for Argyll at the India Office, to whom Clarendon referred the Persian envoy's requests: on 19 May Clarendon was informed that while Argyll saw no objection to an acknowledgement of the Persian protests, he saw every objection to the second request:

> ... His Grace cannot consent to debar the officers of the British Government, to whom the superintendence of the police of the Persian Gulf is entrusted, from the exercise of the right of punishing, by prompt measures, any violations of Treaty engagements by the Sheikh of Bahrein, when a reference to the Court of Teheran would be attended with embarrassing delays which might jeopardise the general peace of the Gulf.[59]

Clarendon's revised letter, still bearing the date '29 April', was delivered to Mohsin Khan early in June. As a mere acknowledgement of the fact that the Persian Government had entered a protest against their rights in Bahrain being ignored meant nothing more than it said, Clarendon had deferred to Mohsin Khan's wishes on this score. The *caveat* suggested by Argyll to the question of informing the Persian Government of any action to be taken against Bahrain was also added, but Clarendon promised that in the event of such action being taken a full communication concerning it should be made to Tehran.[60] Time and again in the years since 1869 the Persian Government have tried to construe the alterations made at the request of their representative in London in the sense of a British

---

58 [I.O.] Home Corresp. (Sec.), Vol. 63 (1869), Mohsin Khan to Clarendon, 8 May 1869 (confidential), and memo.
59 [I.O.] Home Corresp. (Sec.), Vol. 63 (1869), J. C. Melvill (Under-Secy., I.O.) to Hammond, 19 May 1869.
60 [I.O.] Home Corresp. (Sec.), Vol. 63 (1869), Clarendon to Mohsin Khan, 29 April 1869 (second version), enclos. in Hammond to Under-Secy. I.O., 24 May 1869.

'recognition' of Persian sovereignty over Bahrain, and Dr Adamiyat does not hesitate to do so in his book. There is no need to point up the irony inherent in their attempts to interpret Mohsin Khan's alterations, made, as he himself put it, 'so as to give the Government of my august master fresh evidence of the friendly intentions of Her Majesty's Government', in the sense of 'admissions' by Clarendon. Nor does any further comment appear necessary on the Persian attempt in 1928 to transmute the offer to inform the Court of Tehran, 'as a matter of courtesy', of any action taken against the Shaikh of Bahrain into 'the necessity of rendering account to the legitimate sovereign'. What may, perhaps, be remarked is the threadbare nature of the Persian case, when efforts are made to admit as historical evidence of British recognition of Persian sovereignty over Bahrain a letter written with the purpose of restating the British Government's determination to maintain the maritime police of the Gulf, including Bahrain, and in terms designed, in consultation with the representative of the Persian Government, to soften the rebuff to the Shah's pretensions.

The actual fact of Bahrain's independence has been established now for more than a century and a half, not by arguments, agreements, or official recognitions but by the events of the island's history, by the uninterrupted rule of the Al Khalifah Shaikhs since 1783, and by the long and finally successful struggle of their subjects against various would-be conquerors. Virtually no State which conducts political or commercial relations with Bahrain regards the island as other than independent, least of all Great Britain, which stands as protecting Power to the island and its dependencies. Whether or not Persia is serious in her latest bid to assert her claim to sovereignty cannot be foreseen, but it is doubtful whether such a claim would have any more success today than it had in 1927-9. It is to be regretted that Dr Adamiyat in his book has forsaken a valuable opportunity of presenting what might have been the first adequate account of the history of Bahrain, written largely from original sources, by adopting a markedly partisan approach to his subject; it is to be hoped that the Persian Government will not be misled by the distorted picture he has painted into trying to revive an issue which can only be regarded nowadays as dead and buried.

4
A Nice Little Aggression[1]

Sir, - "A nice little aggression" is Mr. Crossman's considered verdict, in his review of James Morris's *Sultan in Oman* (February 2), on the events which took place in Oman at the close of 1955. "... the Sultan of Muscat (a British protege) was given an army," writes Mr. Crossman, "and told to make war against the Imam of Oman (a. Saudi American protege)." From this, and from similar statements in Mr. Crossman's review (*e.g.* "... the armies which invaded Oman from the north..."), one might be led to suppose that Oman was a separate, independent, and wholly foreign state from Muscat, with a well-defined international frontier between them, and that the Sultan was encouraged to violate this frontier and invade Oman by a British government anxious to acquire control over the supposed oil resources of the region. Was this really the case, or was the Sultan in fact reasserting his authority over an area to which he had legitimate title? The most cursory reading of the history of south-eastern Arabia is bound to lead, I believe, to the formation of the latter view.

Many of the tribes of the Sultanate of Muscat and Oman are of the Ibadhiya sect of Islam, who for centuries were accustomed to being ruled by an *imam* who combined in his person the dual roles of spiritual leader and temporal sovereign. From the middle of the eighteenth century Muscat and Oman have been ruled by members of the Al Bu Said dynasty (the family of the present Sultan), who were at first *imams* but later resigned the spiritual duties of the imamate, retaining only temporal authority over Oman. A movement for the revival of the imamate in its religious aspect

---

[1] Letter to the Editor of the *New Statesman and Nation*, 23 February 1957.

arose in the interior of Oman at the close of the nineteenth century, and only acquired political significance as the Sultan's authority waned in the districts beyond the Hajar mountains. What happened in Oman at the close of 1955 was a reassertion of rightful Al Bu Said authority in these districts and the overthrow of the *soi-disant* Imam. Mr. Morris's book makes it plain that 'the tribesmen shed no tears over the Imam's eclipse and gave the Sultan a cordial welcome'.

How, then, does the exercise of the Sultan's legitimate rights in Oman become, in Mr. Crossman's phrase, "a nice little aggression"? Because it was directed against a self-styled "independent" Imam, supported, for their own obvious purposes, by the Saudi Arabians? Because the Sultan was determined to ensure that whatever oil resources might be discovered in the area should benefit his subjects in Muscat and Oman and not the Saudi-Arabians?

Or, because the British government applauded the reassertion of his rights in Oman? "Mr. Morris," avers Mr. Crossman, "makes it clear that the legal basis of the Sultan's claim to Oman was very dubious." Mr. Morris does no such thing; in rhe whole length of his book I can find no informed or reasoned e:xamination of the Sultan's claim. Mr. Morris is not an historian and does not profess to be one; his book is not, nor does he claim it to be, a political history of south-eastern Arabia, but, as Mr. Crossman so aptly describes it, is "a travelogue," "an elegant trifle." As such, it is a very slim peg on which to hang such opinions as Mr. Crossman expresses with respect to British policy in the area. He speaks of the British government having given the Sultan an "army" with which to carry out his *coup*; I, for one, should like to hear more from Mr. Crossman on this "army." "Indirect colonialism" is the label Mr. Crossman tries to affix to British support of the Sultan. What of support for the Imam by the Saudi-Americans (to employ Mr. Crossman's quaint term) for the purpose of bringing western Oman under Saudi control and within the sphere of operations of the Arabian-American Oil Company? Was this not an attempt at "colonialism," or is "colonialism" merely a British or European vice to which non-Europeans or Americans are not addicted? "Colonialism" as an epithet of abuse may hold good in other parts of the world: I wonder whether Mr. Crossman, if he examined the history of Saudi Arabian expansion in south-eastern Arabia, with its record of bloodshed, terrorism and extortion, would really apply it to the British government's efforts to preserve the independence of Muscat, Oman and the Trucial Sheikdoms since the early nineteenth century.

5
Sovereignty and Jurisdiction in Eastern Arabia[1]

A reminder of the difficulties and complications that can arise from the absence of any agreed frontiers in Eastern and South-Eastern Arabia has recently been afforded by the struggle in Oman between the Sultan of Muscat and the *soi-disant* Imam, Ghalib ibn Ali. To some observers at the time the gravest implication of the struggle appeared to lie in the opportunity it offered Saudi Arabia to resume the pursuit of her long-standing ambition to gain control of South-Eastern Arabia by giving the Imam and his followers material and moral backing; it was even suspected that the Saudi Arabian Government might have actively instigated the Imam to raise the standard of revolt. While there is a danger, in so emphasizing the external influences that may have contributed to the uprising, of under-estimating its more relevant internal causes, it is nevertheless true to say, as some commentators have said, that the opportunities for Saudi Arabia to exploit a disturbed situation of this kind might have been considerably fewer if the frontiers in this part of Arabia had been delineated. So long as these remain vague and unfixed King Saud will continue to feel free to challenge the authority of the Sultan of Muscat and Oman and that of the rulers of the Trucial Shaikhdoms in the western marches of their dominions, as he did five years ago when he despatched a force to seize the Buraimi Oasis.

Unfortunately, the demarcation of the frontiers of Eastern Arabia is a task of far greater complexity than the readiness with which the sugges-

---
[1] Source: *International Affairs (Royal Institute of International Affairs* 1944-), Vol. 34, No. 1(Jan., 1958), pp. 16-24.

tions were put forward during the Oman troubles would indicate, and the opposition of Saudi Arabia, now as in the past, to any boundary settlement not based upon the complete acceptance of her claims is far from being the only difficulty in the way of such a settlement. Sovereignty and jurisdiction, the essential accompaniments of frontier delineation, are not subjects that admit of easy discussion in the context of the desert border-lands of Eastern Arabia; nor has the political evolution of the countries of the region yet reached a stage where these concepts might be expected to possess easily recognizable force and meaning.

The only frontiers in existence in Eastern Arabia, defined by treaty and internationally recognized, are those of Kuwait with Saudi Arabia and the frontiers of both with the neutral zone lying between them on the Persian Gulf coast. Elsewhere in Eastern Arabia there are what might be termed *frontieres de convenance* which have not yet received the sanction of written recognition. Only the sea, one might say, provides the countries of the Arabian littoral with the semblance of frontiers, and even here there is uncertainty over maritime rights and the extent of territorial waters, not to mention the ownership of islands in the Gulf. All the principal States of Eastern Arabia—Saudi Arabia, Bahrain, Qatar, Abu Dhabi, and the Sultanate of Muscat and Oman—are involved in frontier disputes and some of them are at loggerheads with two or more of their neighbours. Oil exploitation and discovery have exacerbated these disputes, but it would be a mistake to assume that oil is the sole or even the prime motive behind the disputes or that the removal of this element from the frontier questions would automatically contribute to their settlement. What makes their settlement problematical is the tribal nature of Arabian society and politics and the fact that the areas concerned are, in the main, desert wastes peopled only by nomad tribes. There is no concept of territorial sovereignty in Arabian society and no grasp of the idea of political sovereignty vested in a people or in a ruler. A shaikh exercises *sultah* or authority over a tribe, the members of which signify their loyalty to him and concede authority to him. He may exercise jurisdiction over several tribes in this fashion, and, by implication, over the land they inhabit. With nomad tribes the complications that may ensue are many, and further reference will be made to them later in connexion with the territorial disputes of Saudi Arabia and the Trucial Shaikhdom of Abu Dhabi.

Taken in what may be described as a descending order of acrimony, the more prominent disputes may be summarized as follows:

(i) the dispute between Saudi Arabia and Abu Dhabi over the

coast and hinter-land between Qatar and Abu Dhabi town and over the region to the south and west of the Buraimi Oasis, including the oasis itself;
(2) the dispute between Saudi Arabia and the Sultanate of Muscat and Oman over the Buraimi Oasis;
(3) the dispute between Abu Dhabi and Qatar over Khaur al Udaid, the large bay at the base of the Qatar peninsula on its eastern side;
(4) the dispute between Bahrain and Qatar over the ruined town and environs of Zubara in north-western Qatar;
(5) the dispute between Qatar and Saudi Arabia over their common frontier.

Generally speaking, the parties to these quarrels base their claims to the territories in dispute upon one or both of two grounds: past or present occupation and the previous or current exercise of jurisdiction. To take the last two disputes, which may be dealt with briefly: the historical grounds upon which the Shaikh of Bahrain bases his claim to Zubara are those of the continual occupation and administration of the town and its hinterland by the Al Khalifah Shaikhs of Bahrain, from the time of their settlement at Zubara in 1766, seventeen years before they conquered Bahrain from the Persians, until their relinquishment of the town in the last quarter of the nineteenth century, partly as a consequence of the Turkish occupation of Qatar and partly at the instigation of the British Government. Today Zubara is a deserted ruin, but the Shaikh of Bahrain still presses his claim to it and cites as supporting evidence the ownership of property there by the Al Khalifah family. He maintains, also, that certain of the tribes around

Zubara, particularly the Al Naim, acknowledge his authority, and he states that he wishes to exercise jurisdiction over them. It has been pointed out to him that he cannot expect to exercise jurisdiction over those he claims as subjects in the territory of another ruler unless a specific agreement has been made to this effect, but his contention is that the sea coast of Qatar cannot automatically be taken to constitute the maritime frontier of that State to the exclusion of his claim to Zubara, especially as the coast has not been explicitly recognized as such a frontier in any written agreement. In putting forward this argument, however, the Shaikh of Bahrain is relying rather upon European ideas of sovereignty and jurisdiction than upon those traditional to and understood by the inhabitants of Eastern Arabia.

There is no comparable inclination on the part of the Shaikh of Qatar to argue the case for Zubara: rather does he feel it to be unnecessary, since in his case the old adage about possession and the law works to his advantage. Nor does the unmarked state of his frontier with Saudi Arabia trouble him unduly, since relations between Qatar and Saudi Arabia are good, a circumstance due as much to the similarity in religious outlook of the two rulers—both adhering to the puritanical observance of Islam decreed by the eighteenth-century reformer, Muhammad ibn Abdul Wahhab—as to the fact that Saudi Arabia does not exert the same pressure upon the marches of Qatar as upon those of Abu Dhabi and Oman. Yet the elements of discord are present in the situation and could emerge into the open if relations between the two States should deteriorate. A *de facto* frontier exists along a line that runs across the lower half of the peninsula, roughly speaking, from the lower half of the Dauhat al Salwa, the long inlet that separates the western coast of Qatar from the Saudi Arabian mainland, to the vicinity of Khaur al Udaid. At the northern end of this line the Saudis maintain a customs and frontier post. Within Qatar the ruler of Saudi Arabia collects *zakat* (a payment, the nature of which will be described more fully later) from some sections of certain tribes and also pays them subsidies, notably to the Qatar branch of the Bani Hajir, a tribe of which the major portion resides in the Saudi Arabian province of Al Hasa. It is not impossible that one day this two-way flow of money may be cited in support of a Saudi Arabian claim to jurisdiction over parts of Qatar beyond the *de facto* frontier, a claim which might well be bolstered up by reference to previous Saudi jurisdiction over the area in the nineteenth century. There are, in addition, frequent crossings of wandering tribes into and out of Qatar, a consideration which complicates the question of jurisdiction and consequently of sovereignty, as will be seen later with reference to the rivalry of Saudi Arabia and Abu Dhabi.

The third of the disputes under consideration is that between the rulers of Qatar and Abu Dhabi over their common frontier in the vicinity of Khaur al Udaid. It would be fairly safe to say that the claims and counter-claims of the rulers concerned are by no means so important intrinsically as the animosity displayed would appear to indicate. Abu Dhabi's historical claim to Khaur al Udaid rests upon the sojourn there for several years in the nineteenth century of a branch of the Bani Yas, the principal tribe of Abu Dhabi, called the Qubaisat, who became estranged from the rest of the Bani Yas and removed to Khaur al Udaid at different times between 1835 and 1877. The settlement was abandoned in the latter year by the Qubaisat, most of whom eventually returned to Abu Dhabi, and the site has stood deserted to this day. Occasionally it is visited by wandering tribes like the Al Murra and the Al Manasir, or by Bani Yas fishermen, all of whom resort to the place for water. It is on the strength of past associations with the place, as well as upon the fact of its being frequented by his subjects, the Bani Yas and certain of the Al Manasir, that the Shaikh of Abu Dhabi rests his claim.

It is when one comes to consider that desolate and unmarked tract of Arabia immediately to the south and east of Qatar that one finds oneself confronted with the more troublesome aspects of the question of sovereignty and jurisdiction in Eastern Arabia, aspects which have so far been only lightly touched upon in the account of the foregoing disputes. More than forty years ago, when Ottoman sovereignty extended over the Arabian shore of the Persian Gulf as far as the Qatar peninsula, an agreement was reached between the British and Ottoman Governments defining the limits of Turkish jurisdiction in the area. The British Government had never formally recognized Turkish suzerainty over Qatar, and by 1913 it had definitely set its face not only against any further Turkish penetration of the Persian Gulf but also against the continuance of Turkish rule in Qatar. On 29 July of that year the two Governments agreed to recognize as the limits of Turkish sovereignty in Eastern Arabia a line running due south from a point on the Arabian coast opposite Zakhnuniyah Island. By this so-called 'Blue Line' Agreement, which demarcated the eastern limits of the Turkish *sanjaq* of Najd, the Sublime Porte renounced all claim to Arabia east of that line, including the peninsula of Qatar. The agreement never, in fact, came into force for, although the instrument embodying it was supposed to be ratified within three months of its conclusion, ratification had not been effected by October 1914 when Britain and Turkey went to war. In any case, it is doubtful whether ratification would have averted future difficulties over frontiers in Eastern Arabia, for when the late Abdul Aziz ibn Saud, ruler of Najd, threw off the trappings of Turkish suzerainty and began to extend his sway over the coastal region, he refused to be bound by any agreements concerning this area, whether ratified or not, previously concluded by his former Turkish suzerain. Although the 'Blue Line' Agreement has been used as a basis for discussion in attempts made since 1913 to define the frontiers of Eastern Arabia, its validity has never been accepted by Saudi Arabia.

None of the parties to territorial disputes in Eastern Arabia is entirely unaware of the ideas implicit in the European conception of sovereignty, and, indeed, one of them, Saudi Arabia, has subscribed to the definition of its northern boundaries in a fashion and upon principles which are recognizable to a European observer. It has been seen, also, in the case of the Shaikh of Bahrain that some appreciation exists of the European view that unless an agreement on extra-territoriality has been concluded with a neighbouring country jurisdiction cannot be exercised over people residing in that country who are claimed as subjects. Without an agreement defining extra-territorial rights a claim to jurisdiction over subjects in another country amounts to a claim to sovereignty over the area they occupy. These instances notwithstanding, the territorial claims put forward by the various rulers of Eastern Arabia have been drawn up primarily with reference to the political and social composition of the region, which is overwhelmingly of a tribal nature. By and large, the claim of a ruler to jurisdiction over a certain area depends upon his claim to *sultah* or authority over all or most of the inhabitants of that area, whether settled or nomad. To substantiate his claim to authority the ruler concerned will generally point to his levying of taxes upon the inhabitants of the area, to his possession of property therein, movable or immovable, such as flocks or date trees, and to such other evidence of his exercise of authority as the settlement by him, either personally or through a deputy, of disputes between the inhabitants.

Saudi Arabia, in a sweeping demand put forward in 1949, claimed the entire area south and east of Khaur al Udaid up to a point several miles east of Mirfa, on the southern coast of the Persian Gulf, and beyond that up to and including the oasis of Al Buraimi. In justification of its claim the Saudi Arabian Government pointed to the acknowledgement of Saudi authority by most of the tribes of the region and to the previous occupation of the area by Saudi forces for long periods in the nineteenth century. To this the ruler of Abu Dhabi retorted that the area claimed included the Liwa Oasis, the ancestral home of his family and of most of the Bani Yas inhabitants of Abu Dhabi, many of whom still owned property there to which they returned every year, and where many of his subjects resided the year round; and he strongly denied the claim of the Saudi Arabian Government that its authority had been acknowledged by most of the tribes of the region.

The steps taken by the Saudi Arabian Government to substantiate its claim, steps which included the seizure by a Saudi force of the Buraimi Oasis in 1952, are sufficiently well known not to require repetition here.[2] What is interesting is the evidence put forward by both sides-notably before the international tribunal set up to arbitrate in the Buraimi dispute-to prove jurisdiction over the tribes dwelling in the disputed area. Apart from the Liwa area most of the country between Abu Dhabi and Qatar is desolate and barren: in the west there is the great salt flat of the Sabkhat Matti, in the east the desert wastes of the Dhafrah. South of the Dhafrah lie the burning sands of the Rub al Khali. What settlement exists is confined mainly to the Liwa Oasis and to a few fishing villages on the coast. Several nomad tribes roam the area, of which the better known are the Al Manasir, Al Awamir, and the nomad sections of the Bani Yas confederation. Two only of the three principal sections of the Al Manasir, the Al Bu Sha'ar and the Al Bu Rahmah, remain in the area today, most of the third section, the Al Bu Mundhir, having migrated to Saudi Arabia at some time within the last twenty years. The Al Bu Sha'ar and Al Bu Rahmah spend their summers in Liwa and their winters grazing their flocks. A dramatic change in grazing may alter this pattern of movement and cause some of them to wander north into Saudi Arabia in search of pasturage, but their loyalty remains constant to the Shaikh of Abu Dhabi. The branch of the Al Awamir that frequents the region—other branches dwell in Oman and the Hadhramaut—has been there only a few decades: over the last hundred years they have wandered in various parts of Eastern Arabia. They, too, regard themselves as subjects of the Shaikh of Abu Dhabi. The loyalty of the Bani Yas to him is unquestioned. It would appear, in fact, that the only indisputably Saudi tribes that visit the region are the Al Murra, Al Rashid, and Al Manahil. Of these the Al Rashid come only occasionally and the Al Manahil have not been seen there for ten years.

By demonstrating its jurisdiction over these nomad tribes each party to the dispute hopes to prove its ownership of the *dirah* or range over which each tribe roams, at certain times of the year, to graze its flocks. To buttress this argument additional evidence has been offered about the exclusive use of wells in the region by a particular tribe or section of a tribe. Exclusive use of a *dirah* by a tribe is not unknown—the Duru of south-western Oman, for instance, will not permit other tribesmen even

---

2 See Chapter 2: The Buraimi Oasis Dispute.

to cross their *dirah*—and the denial of the use of wells to others is not uncommon practice with some tribes such as the Al Manasir. It is far from clear, however, whether the use of a *dirah* by a tribe constitutes a claim to ownership of the land concerned, or anything approaching sovereign title in the European sense, either for the tribe or for the ruler it acknowledges as overlord. While this point remains unresolved the arguments over *dirahs* are bound to be somewhat sterile.

As evidence of their alleged jurisdiction over the tribes of the area both sides have instanced the payment of taxes or tribute by the tribes to the rulers concerned. The ruler of Abu Dhabi simply describes as taxes the payments made to him by the tribes over whom he claims jurisdiction, but in the case of Saudi Arabia the payments claimed are described as *zakat*. *Zakat* in the early days of Islam was held to constitute contributions paid by the faithful for the relief of the poor and needy, and its collection in Saudi Arabia today is still reckoned, in theory at least, to be directed towards this end. Yet, despite the fact that the ruler of Saudi Arabia is looked upon as the spiritual leader, or *imam*, of his people, as well as their temporal ruler, or *amir*, it is doubtful whether the levying of *zakat* in that country has ever been prompted purely by religious motives. If it is looked upon solely or even primarily as a religious offering, then it is difficult to see how any claim to jurisdiction, particularly of a territorial nature, can be based upon its payment in the same way as if it were a political tribute. That the precursors of the present Saudi Arabian Government did not view *zakat* solely as a religious offering is amply illustrated by numerous instances in the nineteenth century when *zakat* was levied upon tribes and rulers in Eastern Arabia, particularly in the cases of Oman, Bahrain, and the Trucial Shaikhdoms, who did not profess allegiance, spiritual or temporal, to the Saudi ruler. In their cases *zakat* was merely a tribute or a payment extorted under threat of attack by Saudi forces, a sort of *Danegeld*, in fact. *Zakat* has been collected from a few of the Al Manasir and Al Awamir on isolated occasions in the last thirty years but is not collected nowadays. How such payments were viewed by the contributors is not known. It is known, however, that the Bani Hajar of Qatar regard the *zakat* they pay to King Saud purely as a religious offering.

At the oasis of Al Buraimi the territorial dispute between Saudi Arabia and Abu Dhabi merges with that between Saudi Arabia and the Sultanate of Muscat and Oman, for the Saudis lay claim to the strategically valuable oasis in which jurisdiction is at present shared by the Shaikh of Abu Dhabi and the Sultan of Muscat. While little need be said of the complications, international as well as local, that have followed upon this dispute, it may be noted that all three parties trace their rights in the oasis to past or present occupation of the villages there, and to the acknowledgement of their jurisdiction by the present inhabitants, in the form of tribute or taxes or by submission to their authority. Three of the nine villages in the oasis are governed today by the Sultan, the remaining six by the Shaikh of Abu Dhabi. It is difficult to see what grounds exist for a Saudi claim to the oasis—except those of sporadic military occupation in the last century—since the Sultan of Muscat has long-standing historical rights in the oasis, while the family of the Shaikh of Abu Dhabi, the Al Bu Falah, has owned property and exercised authority there for more than eighty years.

To the south and east of Al Buraimi lies the region known as the Dhahirah, which stretches from the Hajar Mountains of Oman to the edges of the Rub al Khali. Here, the limits of territorial sovereignty are even more difficult to ascertain than elsewhere in Eastern Arabia. Traditionally regarded as one of the ancient provinces of Oman, the Dhahirah nowadays is claimed by the Sultan of Muscat and Oman as falling within his dominions. Discernible evidence of his actual jurisdiction, however, at least in the westernmost fringes of the province, is lacking. In the tense state of politics in Eastern Arabia today no ruler who wishes to retain title to his lands, particularly those remote from the seat of his power, can afford to allow his jurisdiction to become or to remain merely nominal. The Sultan of Muscat is particularly vulnerable in this respect. The political fulcrum of Oman lies in the mountainous centre of the country, around Nizwa: the Sultan's capital is at Muscat, away on the east coast. During the nineteenth century the Al Bu Said Sultans of Muscat exercised little authority beyond the Hajar Mountains, and in this century their rule in the Dhahirah has been of an intermittent character. A few of the tribes there were converted in the last century to the Wahhabi practice of Islam, and Saudi agents collected *zakat* from them between 1926 and 1931. While no legitimate foundation exists for a possible Saudi Arabian claim to the Dhahirah, the Sultan of Muscat cannot afford to take his own jurisdiction there for granted; for it is here, in the question of the substance as opposed to the shadow of a ruler's authority over the lands to which he lays claim, that the heart of the problem of territorial sovereignty in Eastern Arabia may well reside.

While the obstacles that stand in the way of frontier delineation in Eastern Arabia are many, their existence should not constitute the sole or even the principal criterion by which the desirability or otherwise of delineation should be judged. There was a tendency evident in the comments made at the time of the Oman crisis to view the frontier question in terms of expediency and practical convenience, especially so far as the subject of oil exploitation was involved, and this attitude is implicit in much of the comment made at other times. Whether demarcation of the boundaries is desirable, or even practicable, in the context of Arabian society and politics is not a question that normally receives adequate consideration. It is doubtful whether the rulers of the various countries of Eastern Arabia desire sovereignty over their territories in the complete European sense of the term; and even if they do, it is questionable whether they would find it practicable. It might be observed in this respect, at the risk of adding another complication—to the question of *dirahs* and their ownership, that nomad tribes sometimes alter allegiance to particular rulers, but continue to use the *dirahs* over which they have been accustomed to roam, unless, of course, they are driven from them. In settled areas, such as the Buraimi and Liwa Oases, or in the seaports of the Trucial Coast, the problem is less acute. Here, and especially in the coastal towns, dwell heterogeneous agglomerations of tribes paying allegiance to a ruling family, like the Qawasim in Sharjah and Ras-al-Khaima, or the Al Bu Falah in Abu Dhabi. A case may be made for defining the boundaries of the Trucial Shaikhdoms—indeed the British Political Resident in the Persian Gulf has lately been engaged in doing so—for practical reasons, such as the avoidance of quarrels over any oil deposits that may be discovered in the region; and it is true that these shaikhdoms have existed for long enough as separate entities for them to be recognized as States. Whether arguments of this nature can be applied equally to the whole of Eastern and South-Eastern Arabia is questionable. To the British Government, which stands in the relationship of protecting Power to the small countries of Eastern Arabia, the delineation of their frontiers might prove welcome by removing any doubts that may exist about their territorial limits. At Buraimi in 1955 the British Government gave proof that it intended to honour its responsibilities in this matter. But the Buraimi affair was fairly straightforward: on another occasion the situation may not be so clear-cut.

6
Sultanate and Imamate in Oman[1]

South-eastern Arabia has an existence apart from the rest of the Arabian peninsula. Enclosed on three sides by the sea—on the north by the Persian Gulf, on the east by the Gulf of Oman, and on the south by the Arabian Sea—it is cut off on the fourth from the bulk of the peninsula by the sand wastes of the Rub al-Khali, or Empty Quarter. The whole of the area thus circumscribed is known as Oman. Politically it is divided into the Sultanate of Muscat and Oman, comprising most of the land between the Rub al-Khali and the sea, and Trucial Oman, the northern strand on the Persian Gulf. Trucial Oman, or the Trucial Coast, consists of a chain of petty independent shaikhdoms, stretching from the peninsula of Qatar in the west to the promontory of Ruus al-Jibal in the north-east, at the entrance to the Persian Gulf. There are six such shaikhdoms facing the Gulf: a seventh, Fujaira, faces the Gulf of Oman. Ruus al-Jibal itself is part of the Sultanate of Muscat and Oman. The only recognized frontiers in this part of Arabia are those which separate Ruus al-Jibal from Fujaira and the south-western marches of the Sultanate from the Eastern Aden Protectorate. To the west, the limits of Saudi Arabian territory and those of Trucial Oman and the Sultanate of Muscat are undefined. Until the close of the Second World War the politics of the area was of little concern to anyone except the British Government in India, for long the guardian of the Gulf's waters and the reluctant arbiter of Eastern Arabia's political quarrels. No more than a handful of Europeans had set foot in the interior of Oman and few echoes of what went on there ever reached the outside world.

---

1 *Chatham House Memoranda* issued by the Royal Institute of International Affairs, December 1959.

Oman's isolation has been broken in the last decade by two disturbances in the region which have had international repercussions—the Buraimi Oasis dispute and the Imamate uprising of 1957. While the two disturbances are interrelated—they owe their inception, in varying degree, to the non-existence of defined frontiers in south-eastern Arabia and to the exploitation of this jurisdictional lacuna by Saudi Arabia[2]—their origins are dissimilar. The one originated in an attempt by Saudi Arabia to assert sovereignty over the Buraimi Oasis, lying in the north-western corner of Oman where the jurisdiction of the Sultan of Muscat overlaps that of the Trucial Shaikh of Abu Dhabi. The origins of the other are more complex, and may be determined only by a reference to the religious animosities, tribal rivalries, and contests for political ascendancy which are endemic to the soil of Oman.

Politics in Oman is dominated by geography. Those elements which isolate the country have already been mentioned—the desert and the sea. Within Oman the outstanding physical feature is the Hajar mountain range, which stretches in a great crescent south-eastwards from Ruus al-Jibal almost to the Arabian Sea. To the east of the range, lying between it and the sea, is a narrow plain, the Batinah, ten to twenty miles broad, which begins in the north near Fujaira and ends 150 miles farther south near Muscat, where the Hajar Mountains abut on the sea. On the inner side of the Hajar the land falls away to a bare and rock-strewn plain, crossed by numerous straggling *wadis* or stream-beds, and merging at length with gravel plains which stretch away to the Rub al-Khali, the great desert. Cutting through the Hajar at intervals are a number of *wadis* which allow access from the Batinah coast to the interior. The greatest of these, the Wadi Samail, splits the Hajar into two halves, the western Hajar and the eastern. Only a thin ridge separates the head of the Wadi Samail, running eastward to the Gulf of Oman, from the second greatest *wadi* in Oman, the Wadi Halfain, which runs due south almost to the Arabian Sea. Towering above the Samail gap is the Jabal Akhdhar, or Green Mountain, a formidable cluster of peaks 10,000 feet or more in height, the highest of the entire Hajar range. A few miles to the west lies the almost equally impressive height of Jabal Kaur. Eastern Oman, from Ras al-Hadd in the north-east to the province of Dhufar in the south-west, is bare and dreary, a succession of stony deserts, sand-dunes, and gravel plains. Dhufar, where the Sultan of Muscat has his summer residence, is thrice blest, by the south-west monsoon which touches it briefly every year, bringing rain; by the Jabal Qara which protects it from the hot winds which blow out of the Rub

---

2 See 'Sovereignty and Jurisdiction in Eastern Arabia' *International Affairs*, Jan. 1958.

al-Khali and by the presence of an American oil company, which invests it with an aura of prosperity. Northern Oman, or Trucial Oman, is a low, arid, sandy plain bordering on the Persian Gulf, its shoreline fretted with lagoons and shallow creeks. On the north-east it is terminated by the Ruus al-Jibal, a towering mass of mountains, an extension of the Hajar, which rises abruptly from the sea and is deeply fissured by narrow winding fjords.

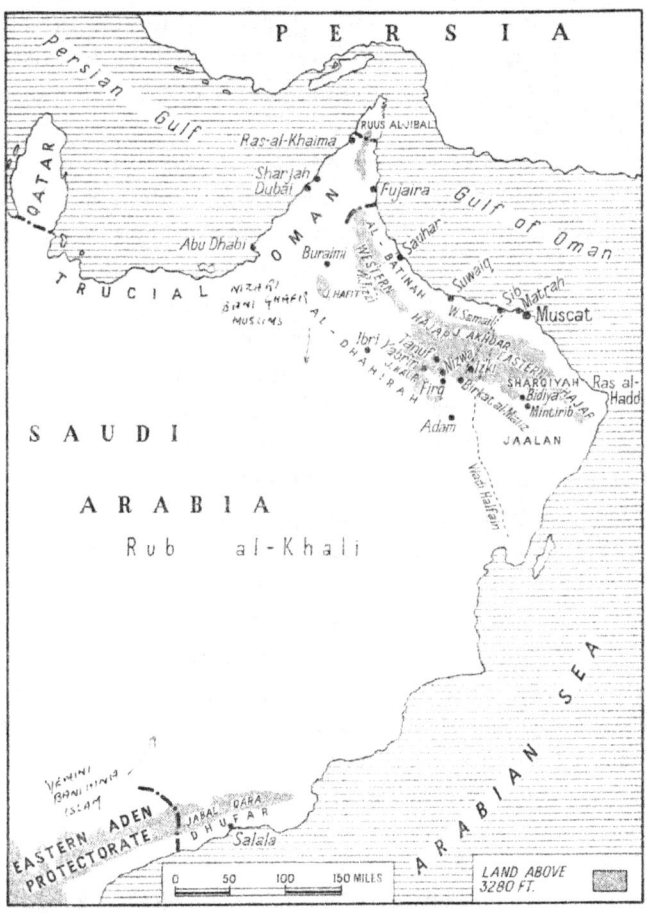

Traditionally, the whole of the area known as Oman is divided into a number of provinces, whose bounds cannot be defined with any exactness. Three of these have already been mentioned: Dhufar, al-Batinah, and Trucial Oman or al-Shamal, the 'northern' province. On the other side of the Hajar from the Batinah lies al-Dhahirah, a wide plain which extends from the Buraimi Oasis in the north to Jabal Kaur in the south. The province of Oman proper, or central Oman, lies directly south of al-Dhahirah, in the area around the Jabal Akhdhar, Jabal Kaur, and the upper reaches of the Wadi Halfain. The mountain complex to the east of the Samail Gap is known as al-Sharqiyah, the 'eastern' province. Immediately south and east of it is the province of Jaalan, bordering on the Arabian Sea. Its limits in the direction of Dhufar are uncertain.

The population of Oman, generally estimated to number about half a million, is organized on an almost exclusively tribal basis. There are more than 200 distinguishable tribes. Most of them dwell in the valleys of the Hajar, especially in the area around the Jabal Akhdhar, and in the plain of the Batinah.

Long isolation from the world outside and their own rancorous natures have made them suspicious, vengeful, factious; and highly individualistic. The manner of their lives is indicated by the appearance of their villages: clusters of squat, dark-grey houses of mud or stone huddle together amid groves of dark-green palms, guarded by grim stone *qasrs* or keeps. Life in Oman is harsh, its aspect medieval. The Omani tribesman, afflicted by ailments of a pulmonary or respiratory nature from a lifetime of working in the dank palm groves, beset by what seem to be the twin evils of Omani society, trachoma and hernia, ever brooding upon injuries suffered or wrongs endured, has a fatal disposition towards self-immolation. Slight of stature and small-boned, he is distinguished as a rule by fine fragile hands and features, the latter overlaid by a shadowed, not to say haunted, cast. His costume is a long white or dun-coloured shirt, reaching to mid-calf, a bright red, orange, or purple scarf of the Indian type wrapped turban-wise around his head, and a cartridge belt girdling his waist, into which is thrust a curved dagger, its handle chased with silver or gold. Nearly every man carries a rifle, slung from the shoulder and borne parallel to the ground at waist level. On the Batinah coast the population is mixed, the original Arab stock strongly infused with Negro, Indian, and Baluch blood. The Batinah people are fishermen and date cultivators, and are looked upon with contempt by the hillmen. Several nomad tribes roam the barren steppes between the Hajar and the Rub al-Khali, the most prominent of which are the Duru and, farther south, the Janabah and Wahiba.

As though their mutual rivalries and dislikes were not sufficient cause of dissension, the tribes of Oman are split into two distinct and opposing factions, the Hinawi and the Ghafiri. The origin of this factionalism is difficult to determine: some authorities find it in a series of civil wars which ravaged the country in the eighteenth century; others trace it back to the original settlement of the country by the Arabs. Immigration into Oman from south-west Arabia began as early as the ninth century B.C. and continued at intervals for at least ten centuries afterwards. These Yemeni tribes, as they were called, had the country very much to themselves until the fourth and fifth centuries A.D., when a fresh series of immigrations began, this time from the north, from central and eastern Arabia. The newcomers, collectively known as the Nizari tribes, settled, not without considerable opposition from the Yemenis, north of the Samail Gap and along the present-day Trucial Coast. As a general rule the tribes of Yemeni origin may be identified with the Hinawi faction, those of Nizari origin with the Ghafiri. The factions derive their names from two tribes, the Bani Hina and the Bani Ghafir, which furnished the chief protagonists in the eighteenth-century struggle already alluded to and which will be described presently. Apart from these differences of origin the Hinawi and Ghafiri tribes may be distinguished by their religious beliefs. While the Ghafiri tribes are mainly orthodox Sunni Muslim, the majority of the Hinawi tribes belong to an offshoot of Islam, Ibadiya. Ibadiya dates from the first century of the Muslim era when the first Ibadis, so named from their leader Abdullah ibn Ibad, dissociated themselves from the Khawarij(or 'Outsiders'), who had earlier rebelled against the Caliph Ali, because of their aversion to Kharijite extremism.

Driven by persecution in later years from their settlements near Basra, they found refuge in the mountains of Oman, where their doctrines quickly took root among the Yemeni tribes. Despite many setbacks in succeeding years—the most severe of which was the devastation of Oman in the ninth century by an army sent by the Abbasid Caliph of Baghdad in response to a plea for help from the Sunni Nizari tribes of northern Oman—Ibadiya never lost its hold in Oman and is still today a powerful force in the country.

'There are no Mahometans that I know', remarked the Danish traveller, Carsten Niebuhr, after his visit to Muscat in 1765, 'who display so little ostentation and live so soberly as these *Bijasi* [Ibadi]: they never smoke tobacco, they drink little coffee and even less of strong liquors. Persons of distinction do not dress more splendidly than those of lesser estate... they do not let themselves be easily upset by violent passions; they are polite towards foreigners...'[3] A strict adherence to the proscriptive tenets of Islam is what principally distinguishes the Ibadi from his co-religionist. Doctrinally, Ibadiya differs little from orthodox Sunni dogma, except in that the Ibadis, like the Khawarij from whom they sprang, reject

---

3 *Voyage en Arabie et en d'autres pays circonvoisins* (Utrecht, 1775-9), ii.67.

the convention that the Imamate or Caliphate of Islam should be vested in the family of the Prophet. At first, an Imam was not even considered necessary by them, although they acknowledged that his presence in the community was desirable. His primary duty was the proper discharge of his religious office—to guide the community in the way of the Koran, the sunna (or precepts) of the Prophet, and the four rightful caliphs. Later the office of Imam among the Ibadiya acquired a temporal significance almost equal to its spiritual importance, the result of the prolonged struggles of the sect from the ninth century A.D. onwards to remain in being. By the eleventh century the Ibadi Imam functioned as both temporal lord and spiritual leader of his people. The mode of his appointment was election by the principal shaikhs and confirmation by the acclamation of the tribes. Unpopular or incompetent Imams could be deposed and the office could even be left vacant for a time. With the passage of the years Imams came to be selected almost exclusively from the Yemeni tribes, and, later still, from a few prominent families, the succession normally passing from father to son, though not necessarily according to primogeniture.

The eighteenth-century conflict which split Oman irrevocably into two opposing camps arose out of a contest for the Imamate which began in 1723 and lasted for twenty years. At the outset the struggle was confined to the Bani Hina and Bani Ghafir tribes, whose respective shaikhs were competing for the office. As the struggle developed, more and more of the tribes of Oman were sucked into the melee, until barely one remained outside. The southern or Yemeni tribes as a whole supported the Bani Hina, the northern or Nizari tribes the Bani Ghafir. The original contenders were eventually killed in battle against each other, but the Hinawi-Ghafiri conflict continued and the alignment into the two factions endured. Oman was invaded by the Persians during the course of the conflict, when a pretender to the Imamate, a scion of the former ruling dynasty, the Yaariba, called them in as allies. They came in 1737 and remained to rule over the Batinah coast and Muscat until 1744, when they were ejected by Ahmad ibn Said of the Hinawi tribe of Al Bu Said, whose provenance is the small town of Adam, on the edge of the central Oman steppe. Exhausted by the wars that had raged for more than twenty years, and chastened by the Persian conquest, the Hinawi and Ghafiri tribes temporarily suspended their feud in 1749 to elect Ahmad ibn Said to the Imamate.

With the advent of the Al Bu Said to power a change took place in the nature of political power in Oman. Hitherto the Imams of Oman had derived their authority from their position as tribal leaders, from their influence with neighbouring tribes, and from their personal standing as territorial lords. Ahmed ibn Said was a merchant and ship owner. He derived his strength largely from his maritime resources and from his commercial ventures abroad, and his successors among the Al Bu Said followed in the same path. Unlike them, however, Ahmad ibn Said remained aware throughout his life of the need to retain the support of the inland tribes, and he was no less aware of the importance of the spiritual authority conferred by his office. To all outward appearances he remained during his lifetime a tribal chieftain, and the true nature of Al Bu Said's rule did not become evident until after his death in 1783. His eldest son, Said, succeeded him as Imam but exercised temporal authority for only a year, being supplanted as ruler of Oman by his own son, Hamad, who made his capital at Muscat, on the coast. The transfer of the capital from the interior to the coast—it had for centuries been located at the Ibadi strong-hold of Nizwa, in central Oman, hard by the Jabal Akhdhar—was symbolic of the change to come. Henceforth the power of the Al Bu Said was to rest upon the sea and not upon the land. Hamad's father, the Imam Said, continued to discharge the spiritual duties of his office from the inland town of Rastaq until his death c. 1821. During his lifetime four Al Bu Said rulers succeeded one another at Muscat. None of them attempted to appropriate the dignity or office of Imam to himself, apparently deeming it of little value. They preferred, instead, the title of *saiyid*, or lord, and later rulers were styled Sultan by Europeans. None of the Al Bu Said rulers of Muscat, with the exception of a member of the collateral branch later in the nineteenth century, ever again became Imam in Oman. Muscat remained the centre of their world and their attention and energies were directed outward, to conquests in Africa and the Persian Gulf, to commercial intercourse with Persia, India, Turkish Iraq, Africa, and the Red Sea, and to the manipulation of the lucrative slave trade from their dependency of Zanzibar.

The preoccupation of the Al Bu Said Sultans with maritime and external affairs deprived the inland tribes of leadership which was sorely needed in the nineteenth century. From 1800 onwards inner Oman was periodically ravaged and held to ransom by the Wahhabis of Najd in central Arabia, fanatical followers of the puritanical Muslim reformer of the eighteenth century, Muhammad ibn Abdul Wahhab, and adherents of the house of Al Saud of Dara'iya, and later of Riyadh. Regarding as apostates all who did not conform to their own rigorous and austere practice of Islam, the Wahhabis found in the schismatic Ibadiya of Oman peculiar targets for their intolerance. Oman was fortuitously saved on several occasions from complete subjugation by these sectaries by the campaigns of Muhammad Ali Pasha of Egypt, whose armies overran central Arabia in

1818 and again in 1838, and by the intervention of the British Government in India, who were concerned that the maritime states of Arabia, including Muscat, should not succumb to Wahhabi rule and their resources be diverted to piratical ends. As a consequence, the Wahhabis—or Saudis, to employ the more modern term—never took Muscat, but from their base in the Buraimi Oasis they held inner Oman, and particularly the Dhahirah, in thrall for long periods during the century.

Twice at least during this time the Ibadi tribes sought to elect an Imam to govern them and perhaps to unite them sufficiently to enable them to dislodge the Saudis from Buraimi. At the second attempt they succeeded; in 1868 Azzan ibn Qais, of the collateral branch of the Al Bu Said, overthrew the reigning Sultan at Muscat and shortly afterwards was elected Imam. His election was largely the work of the *mutawwa* or religious extremists among the Ibadi tribes, led by Said ibn Khalfan al-Khalili, and supported by the paramount shaikh or *tamima* of the Al Harb, Salih ibn Ali, the Amir of the Sharqiyah, whose descendents have played a major role in the politics of Oman up to the present day. A year after his election Azzan ibn Qais took advantage of the collapse of Saudi authority in central Arabia, brought about by an internecine struggle for succession, to march upon the Buraimi Oasis and drive out the Saudi garrison. From that date until 1952 the Saudis never reappeared in the oasis in force. Azzan's reign proved brief; in 1871 he was killed by a member of the main Al Bu Said line, Turki ibn Said, the great-grandfather of the present Sultan. Sultan Turki, however, never aspired to be Imam nor would the *mutawwa* and Salih ibn Ali al-Harithi have accepted him, even though, like every Sultan of Muscat up to the present day, he was a practising Ibadi.

By the close of the nineteenth century the power of the Al Bu Said was in decline. Zanzibar had been lost soon after the death of the greatest of the Al Bu Said rulers, Said ibn Sultan (1806-56), and with it the revenue from the slave trade. Muscat's share of the Persian Gulf's trade had dwindled to a mere fraction of its former size. Opportunities for conquest had vanished as the British Government brought the smaller states of the Gulf under their protection and actively discouraged the disturbance of the maritime peace. Within Oman the power of the Sultan was narrowly circumscribed. The Al Bu Said had alienated themselves from the Ibadi tribes of the interior and especially from the *mutawwa* elements who considered the family not only as lax in their observance of Ibadi precepts but also as contaminated by too frequent intermarriage with African, Abyssinian, and Baluch stock. Repugnant also to these ecclesiastical zealots was the tolerance accorded at Muscat to the followers of other religions, notably

Hindus, and cause for further offence was found in the Al Bu Said's long association with foreign governments, foreign trade, and foreign ways. Particularly irritating to the *mutawwa* was the suppression of the slave trade and the arms traffic at Muscat on the insistence of the British Government and with the compliance, albeit unwilling, of successive Sultans.

The tribes' resentment found active expression in 1895, when, led by Salih ibn Ali al-Harithi, they attacked and looted Muscat. The immediate cause of the attack was the imposition by the Sultan of heavier customs duties on goods passing through Muscat to and from the interior. A more significant manifestation of the tribes' discontent, however, was the growing agitation, especially among the *mutawwa*, for the revival of the Imamate. Religious inspiration was provided by the blind Ibadi historian, Abdullah ibn Humayyid al-Salimi, practical support by Salih ibn Ali, the ackmowledged leader of the Hinawi tribes. Shaikh Salih died in 1896 and was succeeded as *tamima* of the Al Harth by his son, Isa. Before long a formidable triumvirate had been established in central Oman of Abdullah al-Salimi, Isa ibn Salih, and Himyar ibn Nasir al-Nabhani, *tamima* of the Bani Hiyam of the Jabal Akhdhar and leader of the Ghafiri tribes. Here, in the region bounded by the Green Mountain, the Samail Gap, and the headwaters of the Wadi Halfain, lay the ancient centres of Ibadi piety and theology, Nizwa, Yabrin, Izki, and Firq, and it is from these towns that the Imamate movement has long drawn its strength. The movement begun by Abdullah al-Salimi reached its climax in May 1913 when Salim ibn Rashid al-Kharusi, nephew of the blind historian, was elected Imam. Not only did the election represent, as in 1749, the temporary healing of the Hinawi-Ghafiri breach, but more important still it was underwritten by the two most powerful men in inner Oman, Isa ibn Salih and Himyar ibn Nasir. In fact, the new Imam was a mere figure-head, a pawn in the struggle that the *tamimas* of the Al Harth and the Bani Riyam were waging for ultimate power in Oman.

An attempt to overthrow the Sultan of Muscat followed hard upon the heels of the election. In June and July 1913 the Sultan's garrisons were expelled from Nizwa and Izki and in August the fortress of Samail, commanding the road to the Batinah coast, was taken. Sultan Faisal ibn Turki died in October and his son and successor, Taimur, tried in vain to come to terms with the leaders of the revolt. At the end of 1914 the Imam's forces moved to attack Muscat. British-Indian troops had been landed to assist in the defence of the capital, and in January 1915 they beat off an assault by the rebels to the north of Muscat with heavy losses to the attackers. Sultan Taimur was strongly advised by the Government of India to seek an accommodation with the rebels, but the obstacles in the way of a settlement were very great. The rebellion had assumed something of the character of a *jihad*: the Imamate tribes resented the curtailment of the traffic in arms and slaves, the laxity of the Sultan in applying Sharia law in his administration of justice, his reliance on British support, his tolerance of the importation of liquor and tobacco at Muscat, and, particularly, his action in cutting off the normal flow of imports to the interior. A settlement was not reached until 25 September 1920 when, through the mediation of the British political agent at Muscat, an agreement was signed at Sib, on the Batinah coast, by the Sultan on the one side, and by the principal dissidents, headed by Isa ibn Salih, on the other. Its terms[4] provided for the establishment of peace between the inland tribes and the Sultan, for the free movement of persons between the interior and the coastal region (including Muscat), and for the imposition of customs duties of not more than 5 per cent *ad valorem* on goods coming from the interior to the coast. Perhaps the most important clause was that which has in recent years been read—as conceding virtual autonomy to the Imam. It runs: 'The Government of the Sultan shall not grant asylum to any criminal fleeing from the justice of the people of Oman. It shall return him to them if they request it to do so. It shall not interfere in their internal affairs.'[5]

Before proceeding to an account of the relative fortunes of Sultanate and Imamate since 1920, it would be as well to examine the British connection with Muscat and Oman which was so strongly manifested in 1915 and again in 1920. British political relations with Muscat date back to 1798, when the French expedition to Egypt aroused fears on the part of the British authorities in India that Muscat might be used by the French as a privateer base for attacks on British and Indian shipping or even as a staging-point for an invasion of India. A treaty was therefore concluded with the reigning Sultan by which he promised to exclude the French from his dominions for the duration of the war. The close of the Napoleonic Wars in the East might well have resulted in the complete lapsing of British interest in Muscat, had not events in Arabia and the Persian Gulf compelled the British authorities in India to view the fortunes of the Sultanate with concern. Mention had been made earlier of the large-scale piracy which broke out in the Gulf following upon the establishment of Wahhabi

---

[4] The terms of the so-called 'Treaty of Sib' have never been published officially, either by the Sultan of Muscat or by the British Government, but unofficial versions were published, during the Oman rebellion of 1957 by *The New York Times*, *The Observer*, and *The Manchester Guardian*.
[5] *New York Times*, 13 Aug. 1957.

or Saudi domination over the Arabian maritime tribes. A genuine fear existed in India that Muscat might easily fall to the Wahhabis' attacks and its shipping be turned to piratical purposes. Naval support was therefore afforded the Sultan on several occasions against the seafaring tribes of the Pirate (now Trucial) Coast, the Wahhabis' principal allies in south-eastern Arabia; and twice within a decade (in 1809 and again in 1819) military expeditions were dispatched to root out these pirates and to save Muscat from being overrun by the Wahhabis.

The success of the campaign against the pirates and the temporary withdrawal of the Wahhabis to central Arabia after 1818 brought to an end British military operations in eastern Arabia. A costly and unnecessary expedition into southern Oman in 1820-1 led to a resolve on the part of the British Government in India never again to become involved militarily in the domestic politics of Arabia, a resolve that became a cardinal principle of British policy in the Persian Gulf in the nineteenth century. Efforts by successive Al Bu Said Sultans to construe the anti-French treaty of 1798 in terms of a defensive alliance, by which the British were obliged to defend Oman against her enemies, were strongly resisted by the Government of India. However, as the co-operation of Muscat, especially in its capacity as the prime naval power among the Gulf states and as an entrepot of the trade of India, Arabia, and Persia, was deemed essential to the maintenance of maritime peace in the Gulf, it became an object of equal importance in British policy to preserve the strength and integrity of the Sultanate. Later in the nineteenth century the campaign for the suppression of the slave trade—and, later still, of the arms traffic—largely depended for its success upon the co-operation of the Sultan of Muscat. Not only, therefore, was support lent to him against his foes in Arabia but his rule in Oman was upheld against his enemies. A heightened sense of Muscat's strategic position in the last quarter of the century, due mainly to the activities of other powers, notably France, in the Gulf region, led the British Government in India to contemplate seriously the extension of a protectorate over Muscat and Oman, but the idea was ultimately rejected in London. Instead, an undertaking was obtained from the Sultan in 1891 'never to cede, to sell, to mortgage, or otherwise give for occupation, save to the British Government, the dominions of Muscat and Oman or any of their dependencies'.[6]

While it became an accepted principle of British policy in eastern Arabia to uphold the Sultan of Muscat against his enemies both within and without the borders of Oman, no specific or explicit obligation to

---

6 C.U. Aitchison, *A Collection of Treaties, Engagements and Sanads relating to India and Neighbouring Countries*, 5th ed., (Calcutta,1929-33), xi, 317-18.

do so was ever entered into by the British Government. On occasion, in the past, they have refused, for reasons of a wider policy or because of the traditional reluctance to become committed militarily on the Arabian mainland, to aid a Sultan in difficulties. But there exists, no less, a disposition on the part of the British Government to regard it as incumbent upon them to come to the Sultan's aid in times of serious trouble, both because of the friendship that has endured since 1798 and because of the sacrifices that the Al Bu Said have made in the past, particularly with respect to the slave trade, to meet British wishes. Again, the nature of British interests in the Gulf region, which has in this century undergone a change, may require the extension of such aid. Until the First World War British interests in the Persian Gulf and peripheral countries were predominantly maritime the protection of seaborne commerce, the suppression of piracy and the slave trade, and the maritime defence of India on the north-west. Nowadays British interests are largely territorial, especially with respect to oil investments in the Gulf region, which cannot be safeguarded by the policies and practices of former years. Nor can the Al Bu Said Sultans be upheld, as in the past, against their opponents in Oman or the Arabian peninsula by the simple expedient of a naval demonstration. Intervention today must largely take the form of military or aerial support, and the present international climate makes such intervention, as the example of 1957 has shown, undesirable if not impracticable.

For thirty years after the conclusion of the *modus vivendi* at Sib in 1920 relations between the Al Bu Said Sultan at Muscat and the inland tribes would appear to have been harmonious if somewhat distant. The Imam elected in 1913, Salim ibn Rashid, died in 1920, shortly before the agreement of Sib was signed. His successor was Muhammad ibn Abdullah al-Khalili of the Bani Ruwaihah, grandson of the prominent *mutawwa* leader, Said ibn Khalfan, who had been involved in the election of Azzan ibn Qais in 1868. For the greater part of his tenure of the Imamate—which lasted until his death in May 1954—the Imam Muhammad's authority was overshadowed by that of his powerful sponsors, the *tamimas* of the Bani Riyam and the Al Harth. The geographical limits of his authority were, on the east the watershed of the Wadi Samail, on the north the town of Ibri at the edge of the Dhahirah, and on the south Bidiya and the villages of the Wadi Batha, Westwards his authority was acknowledged by the fanatical Duru, the principal Badu tribe of the Oman steppes. From Ibri northwards to the Buraimi Oasis, in other words over the greater part of the Dhahirah, he exercised no influence whatever. Nearly all the tribes of this area are Sunni Muslims, who regard Ibadiya as heretical and who would strongly resist any attempt by an Ibadi Imam to control them. The only outside influence to which they have been amenable has been that of Wahhabism. Some of the tribes, notably the Naim, the leading tribe of the region, subscribe to Wahhabi tenets, mainly as a result of the Wahhabi occupation of the Buraimi Oasis for long periods during the nineteenth century. In 1925 emissaries of Ibn Saud appeared in the Dhahirah to collect *zakat*, or religious tribute, from the Sunni tribes for remission to Riyadh.[7]

Alarmed by this move, Shaikh Isa ibn Salih of the Al Harth gathered a force under the Imam's banner and advanced into the Dhafrah. The Naimi Shaikhs resident in the Buraimi Oasis sent an immediate call for aid to Ibn Saud's governor in Al Hasa. Before the latter could respond Shaikh Isa had a severe attack of dropsy and was forced to call off the advance and retire into central Oman. Once the danger was past the Naim quickly resumed their old posture of independence, of both the Imam and Ibn Saud.[8]

Over the next twenty years little occurred to disturb the political life of Muscat and Oman. The Sultan Taimur ibn Faisal abdicated in 1932 and was succeeded by his son, Said, the present Sultan. Isa ibn Salih died in 1946 and was succeeded as *tamima* of the Al Harth by his son, Salih. The new *tamima* seems to have wielded far less power in Oman than did his father, for much more is heard of the Imam's political influence after 1946 than during the lifetime of Shaikh Isa. A more formidable rival of the Imam in the post-war period was Sulaiman ibn Himyar, who had succeded his father, Himyar ibn Nasir, as *tamima* of the Bani Riyam of the Jabal Akhdhar. This chieftain, who was to play a leading role in the uprising of 1957, has been variously described as 'a powerful if not very congenial personality—without the narrow fanaticism of most Omani townsmen, interested in the inventions of the west and prepared to make use of them'[9] and more colourfully, as resembling 'some infinitely clever beast in Aesop, about to hoodwink a lion, goat or slow-witted bird'.[10] He stood in direct contrast to the Imam Muhammad ibn Abdullah, who was said to

---

7 Of the motives of Ibn Saud in dispatching these agents Sir Percy Cox later remarked: 'Practically he thinks that he is justified, in principle, in regaining any territory that his forefathers had a century ago, whether as territory or as a "sphere of influence". Oman was in their sphere of influence' (*Journal of the Central Asian Society*, xiv (1927), p. 40).

8 See Captain G. J. Eccles, 'The Sultanate of Muscat and Oman', ibid. p. 23; and Bertram Thomas, *Alarms and Excursions in Arabia* (London, 1931), pp. 174-5.

9 Wilfred Thesiger, 'Desert Borderlands of Oman', *Geographical Journal*, cxvi (1950), p. 159.

10 James Morris, *Sultan in Oman* (London, 1957), p. 107.

be 'fanatical, reactionary and hostile to the Sultan of Muscat and to all Europeans'.[11]

The politics of inner Oman, hitherto a recondite affair, was to become of international interest in the years following the Second World War. Sultan Said ibn Taimur granted a concession to Petroleum Development (Oman) Ltd., a subsidiary of the Iraq Petroleum Company, in 1937 to prospect for oil in Oman. The company did not begin active exploration beyond the Hajar until after 1945, when the appearance of prospecting parties excited unfavourable reactions on the part of the more fanatical tribes. At the same time another subsidiary of the Iraq Petroleum Company began exploration along the Trucial Coast, to the north. Whether or not it was inspired by the Iraq Petroleum Company's activities in Oman, a sweeping claim was put forward by the Saudi Arabian Government in 1949 to the sovereignty of the region extending from the base of the Qatar peninsula up to, and including, the Buraimi Oasis. A second concession for the province of Dhufar was granted by him to Cities Service, an American company, in 1951.

The Sultan of Muscat countered the claim by asserting his longstanding rights over the Dhahirah, while the ruler of the Trucial Shaikhdom of Abu Dhabi, whose territory was primarily affected by the Saudi claim and who not only owned considerable property in the Buraimi Oasis but exercised authority over the greater part of it, rejected it outright. A series of conferences ensued, at Dammam, on the Saudi Arabian coast, and in London, at which Britain represented the interests of the Sultan and the Shaikh, in an endeavour to reconcile the claims, but it proved of no avail. Then, in August 1952, an armed party from Saudi Arabia seized control of part of the oasis. The Shaikh of Abu Dhabi and the Sultan wanted to eject by force, but they were dissuaded from doing so by the British Government. Years of negotiations with Saudi Arabia followed, at the end of which time parties to the dispute agreed to submit their claims to the arbitration of an international tribunal.

The Buraimi Oasis dispute provoked mixed emotions among the tribes of inner Oman. Few partisans of the Saudis were to be found among the northern tribesmen—the Naimi shaikhs of Buraimi were the most prominent exceptions—while for the Ibadi tribes the Saudi foray awakened distasteful memories of sufferings endured in the previous century at the hands of the Wahhabis. On the other hand a certain uneasiness was felt at the prospect of firmer control being exercised over the Dhahirah by the Sultan of Muscat. The upshot was that the Imam held aloof from the

---
11 Thesiger, 'Desert Borderlands', p. 137.

Sultanate and Imamate in Oman

dispute, as also, apparently, did Sulaiman ibn Himyar and Salih ibn Isa.

In May 1954 the Imam Muhammad ibn Abdullah al-Khalili died. A good deal of the fire went out of the Imamate movement with his passing, for he had been revered for his piety and respected for his integrity throughout inner Oman. However bigoted or fanatical he might have appeared to Europeans, he was the embodiment in Omani eyes of the spirit of Ibadiya—exclusive, rigid, austere. No candidate of comparable qualities came forward to succeed him. The two arbiters of central Omani politics, Sulaiman ibn Himyar al-Nabhani and Salih ibn Isa al-Harithi, appear to have been indifferent to the question of whether or not a new Imam should be elected. In the event, a candidate did make his appearance, a little known and inconsiderable figure, Ghalib ibn Ali, a shaikh of the Bani Hina, the tribe that had originally given its name to the Hinawi faction. To this day hardly anything is known of Ghalib ibn Ali personally. His age, his appearance, his character, and, in particular, the manner of his assumption of the Imamate all are obscure or unknown.[12] There is certainly no record of his having been elected Imam according to the classic mode of Ibadiya —selection by the leading shaikhs and acclamation by the tribes—nor does he appear to have exercised, to any degree, the functions of the office. A more conspicuous figure politically speaking, than Ghalib has been his brother, Talib ibn Ali. While Ghalib is a mere shadow, content, apparently, with the dignity rather than the reality of his office, Talib is the vigorous opportunist, the astute promoter of schemes and canvasser of outside aid. Lacking support in inner Oman, where the tribes and the tribal leaders paid them scant heed, Talib and his brother had perforce to seek friends outside, and they found them readily enough in Riyadh and Cairo. Saudi Arabia, already contending for overlordship in the Buraimi area, was only too happy to support anyone who might embarrass the Sultan of Muscat in his own country. Revolutionary Egypt, ardent for the cause of Arab nationalism, even where the concept was unknown, had no difficulty in accepting Talib's thesis of an independent Imamate of Oman striving to maintain itself against the inimical designs of the pro-British Sultan of Muscat. To translate this theory into reality Talib and the Imam required money and arms. These they got primarily from Saudi Arabia in the latter half of 1954 and during 1955. An 'Imamate Office' was established in Cairo in 1955, and an application made for the Imamate's admission to the Arab League. Beyond furnishing grist for the propaganda mills of

---

12 The only known photograph of him appeared in a Cairo newspaper in 1957 and showed 'a slender dark-skinned Bedouin type, possibly about 30' (*New York Times*, 6 Aug. 1957).

Cairo, the application served little real purpose. Indeed, the delegates who considered it in formal session were said to have been in some doubt about the exact location of Oman.

One of the new Imam's first moves was to proclaim that the concession under which Petroleum Development (Oman) was operating in the interior of Oman was invalid, as it had been granted by the Sultan without the consent—perhaps even the knowledge at the time—of his predecessor. Later Ghalib began to issue his own passports—obligingly printed for him in Saudi Arabia - to Omanis leaving the country to work in the oil states of the upper Gulf. The assiduous activities of the two brothers would seem to have been viewed by Sulaiman ibn Himyar, Amir of the Jabal Akhdhar (who had no doubts about his own independence and who had once applied to the British Resident in the Persian Gulf for recognition as 'King of the Green Mountain'), with something of the amused detachment of the lion in Aesop's fable for the fox who decided to try his hand at hunting alone. However, Sulaiman was not above accepting an offering or two from Saudi Arabia, purveyed by the brothers, including, so it is said, an American motor car,

Gradually Ghalib gained ground in the old Ibadi centres—Nizwa, Firq, Izki, etc.—although as yet the only palpable responses he had awakened sprang from the tribesmen's hatred of foreign things and their bigotry in theological matters. At this juncture—which had barely moved past the preliminary stages—the Sultan of Muscat decided to move against the Imam Ghalib and his brother and to assert his sovereignty over Oman beyond the Hajar. His decision was prompted by developments farther north, at the Buraimi Oasis. The international arbitration tribunal which was to have decided the sovereignty of the oasis broke up in the autumn of 1955 when the British member resigned, after accusing the Saudi Arabian Government of conspiring to tamper with the impartiality of the tribunal and of attempting to bribe the inhabitants of the oasis to declare for Saudi Arabia. The resignations of the Belgian and Cuban members followed shortly afterwards. The British Government advised the Sultan and the Shaikh of Abu Dhabi in October 1955 to reoccupy the oasis, and lent them the support of a British-raised force, the Trucial Oman Scouts, to help them do so. The Sultan saw the chance to deal with Ghalib with one stroke and did so swiftly in December 1955. While one detachment of his armed forces advanced up the Wadi Samail from the Batinah coast, he himself advanced from Dhufar with a motorized column. Nizwa, Izki, and Firq fell without a fight. Ghalib and Talib fled, the Imam to his home village of Sait, where the Sultan afterwards allowed him to remain in peace, and Talib to Saudi Arabia where he found refuge. Sulaiman ibn Himyar came down out of his fastness in the Jabal Akhdhar to pay his respects to the Sultan.[13]

Whatever the Imam Ghalib may have thought about his defeat, his brother was far from regarding it as ending his own bid for power in Oman. At Dammam, in Saudi Arabia, where Talib lived for eighteen months as the guest of the Saudi Arabian Government, he began recruiting and training an Omani 'Liberation Army' from Omanis who had come north to work in the oilfields of Al Hasa. Talib's hosts betrayed a flattering interest in his activities. The Saudi Arabian Government were still determined to obtain access to the Oman steppes and to the possible oil resources that might lie there. They had employed the direct approach at Buraimi and had failed in their object. Now was the time to resort to indirect methods, to exploit Talib's and Ghalib's religio-political ambitions. Money and arms began to trickle through from Saudi Arabia to the mountains of central Oman in such quantities as to attract bigger fish to the lure. Sulaiman ibn Rimyar began to take a keener interest than he had in 1954-5 in the aspirations of the brothers Talib and Ghalib. Shaikh Salih ibn Isa al-Harithi, Amir of the Sharqiyah, followed his example, and two of his brothers, Sulaiman and Muhammad ibn Isa, journeyed to Cairo where; they took charge of the Imamate office. None of these moves seems to have troubled the Sultan Said ibn Taimur unduly, or if it did, he took no effective steps to arrest it. Not only did he not visit inner Oman again after December 1955 but he spent the greater part of his time in the pleasant surroundings of Salala, the capital of Dhufar on the south coast. It was left to an elderly cousin of the Sultan at several removes, Saiyid Ahmad ibn Ibrahim (grand-nephew of the Imam Azzan ibn Qais), as Minister of the Interior, and to his other male relatives to endeavour to make Al Bu Said rule effective beyond the Hajar. The methods they employed were those sanctioned by long usage in Oman, an admixture of persuasion and intimidation: gifts and 'sweeteners' for the more influential shaikhs, meaningful references to the Sultan's standing army for the ill-disposed or the recalcitrant. Neither type of gesture served much purpose. Saudi Arabia could furnish more splendid bribes, and the Sultan's army, recruited mainly from the heterogeneous population of the Batinah, ill equipped and short of officers (having only a handful of retired British officers), was scarcely of a calibre to frighten the inland tribes.

Signs of trouble in the interior began to manifest thenselves in the spring of 1957. Muhammad and Sulaiman ibn Isa al-Harithi, from the

---

13 Morris, *Sultan in Oman*, *passim*.

Imamate office in Cairo and with Egyptian collaboration, had been conducting a sustained campaign to invest the Imamate movement with significance and to undermine the Sultan Said ibn Taimur's position. Members of Talib ibn Ali's 'Liberation Army' in Saudi Arabia began leaving Dammam and drifting back to Oman with arms and money, mainly through the port of Dubai on the Trucial Coast. A minor revolt broke out in the Sharqiyah in April, led by Ibrahim ibn Isa al-Harithi and Muhammad ibn Abdullah Al-Salimi, son of the blind Ibadi historian, Abdullah ibn Humayid. His presence lent a tinge of religious fervour to what was essentially a secular affair. A half-hearted move was made against the dissidents by the Sultan's army, accomplishing little except the partial demoralization of the regiment concerned. Somewhat at a loss, it would seem, to know what to do, the Sultan invited Ibrahim ibn Isa and Sulaiman ibn Himyar to Muscat early in June. Surprisingly enough, Ibrahim came, and was immediately clapped into Fort Jalali, one of the two forts overlooking Muscat harbour, built by the Portuguese in the sixteenth century, and now used by the Sultan as a gaol. On practically the same day Talib ibn Ali slipped ashore from a *dhow* at a point on the Batinah coast, possibly Suwaiq, several miles north of Muscat. With him he brought a consignment of modern automatic weapons and small land mines. His arrival cannot have been unanticipated in Oman, for almost immediately Sulaiman ibn Himyar, who was sojourning in Muscat under the Sultan's eye, surreptitiously took his departure from the capital and headed for his home village of Tanuf, in the Jabal Akhdar. Talib, meanwhile, had made his way inland to the Jabal Kaur region, north-west of the Jabal Akhdhar. There he was joined by his brother Ghalib, who declared himself to have resumed the active functions of Imam. July saw the white flag of the Ibadi *mutawwa* breaking out all over central Oman—in Nizwa (where the brothers had now moved), Firq, Izki, Bahla, and Yabrin. Sulaiman ibn Himyar now declared openly for the Imam, bringing out the powerful Bani Riyam and the towns of Tanuf, Birkat al-Mauz, and Shabat Sait. Only the Sharqiyah lagged behind, presumably deprived of leadership by the incarceration of Ibrahim ibn Isa. The white *mutawwa* banner was seen in only one town, Mintirib in the Wadi Batha, during the revolt.

What followed is of sufficiently recent vintage as not to require lengthy reiteration here. Finding himself incapable of dealing with the uprising, the Sultan called upon the British Government for help late in July. His request was acceded to for a variety of reasons: because the Al Bu Said were allies of more than 150 years' standing; because the revolt had outgrown the character of a merely internal struggle through the interference of Saudi Arabia and Egypt; because the rulers of the other Gulf principalities were awaiting with anxiety the British reaction to the subversion of one of their number within his own country by Saudi Arabia; and because Britain had at major economic investment at stake in the oil-bearing principalities as well as a strategic interest in the Sultanate of Muscat and Oman, to which, one day, might be added an economic interest if oil should be found there in any quantity. Three weeks after the Sultan had asked for aid, the revolt had been crushed and the three leaders, Ghalib, Talib, and Sulaiman ibn Rimyar, were in flight. Royal Air Force aircraft had attacked their principal strongholds with cannon and rocket fire, while a small military column, composed of British troops, Trucial Oman Scouts, and elements of the Sultan's army, had advanced from the Trucial Coast into Inner Oman, where they were joined by contingents from tribes loyal to the Sultan. Most of the rebel centres capitulated after only a token resistance.

If the campaign itself was a minor affair, the political exploitation of it was on a grand scale. The Imamate office in Cairo worked feverishly to convince the world that the uprising was the brave struggle of an independent state against unprovoked aggression, and appeals for intervention were sent to the United States, the Soviet Union, the Bandung powers, and the Arab states. A ludicrous touch was lent by the efforts of Egyptian propagandists to portray the Imamate movement, at heart xenophobic, fanatical, and atavistic, as progressive and liberal, in contrast to the rule of the Sultan, who is at least, whatever his improvidence, modern in his outlook and ambitious for his country and his people. Such considerations, however, carried little weight in the Arab world after Suez, and on 20 August eleven of the Arab states lodged a complaint with the Security Council, charging that Britain had violated the United Nations Charter by aiding the Sultan of Muscat. The Council voted, by five votes to four, with one abstention (the United States) and one 'not participating' (Nationalist China), not to place the matter on its agenda. A curious and somewhat obscure outcome of the uprising was the fate of the so-called 'Treaty of Sib'. On 11 August, the same day that Nizwa, the chief stronghold of the Imamate, fell, the Sultan told a correspondent of *The Times* that he considered the treaty to be no longer valid as its terms had been breached by the other signatories. At the same time the correspondent was informed by the Sultan's English *wazir*, or minister, that the treaty had been binding only upon the Sultan's father and not upon his successors. A day later the Foreign Office stated that they shared the Sultan's view that the treaty was no longer valid. The diplomatic correspondent of *The Times* commented the following day, 13 August, that each side felt that the other had broken it—the Imam's supporters accused the Sultan of having done so in 1937 when he had granted the oil concession without consulting them; the Sultan accused the Imam of having done so in 1955 when he began issuing his own passports and asserting his independence in other ways—and that it could fairly be regarded as dead. The Foreign Office denied the charge that the Sultan had broken the treaty by his grant of an oil concession. The dispute, they said, hinged upon the interpretation of the phrase 'internal affairs' in the treaty.[14] If the previous Imam, Muhammad ibn Abdullah al-Khalili, had considered the Sultan to be breaking the treaty when he granted the oil concession he surely would have protested at the time. Suitably chastened, the diplomatic correspondent of *The Times* wrote on 14 August:

> There is good evidence to support the Foreign Office view that, in oil concessions as in other matters, the previous Imam acknowledged the Sultan's suzerainty. There appears to have been no definite denial of Omani independence in the Treaty—but a refusal to affirm it.

At the Security Council hearing six days later Sir Pierson Dixon, the British representative, stated that the treaty was simply an agreement, 'of a kind familiar in that area, between the sovereign and certain of his tribes, which did no more than allow the Omani tribes a measure of autonomy.'[15]

There seems to have been a plethora of elucidators. The assertion by the Sultan's *wazir* that the treaty was binding only upon the Sultan's father, though a correct evaluation of the normal practice with agreements in this part of Arabia, was given the lie by both the Sultan and the Foreign Office. They plainly regarded the treaty as continuing in force; after the death of the Sultan's father according to the Sultan himself it was broken by the Imam only in 1955. Again, if the *wazir's* interpretation were correct, then one must presume that the treaty was binding upon the other signatories also only during their lifetime and did not bind their successors. It is equally plain, however, that the Imamate supporters held the treaty still to be in force in 1955 when, they charged it was violated by the Sultan in co-operation with the British Government.[16] The charge,

---

14 See above, p. 74, footnotes 4 & 5.
15 *The Times*, 21 Aug. 1957.
16 The note delivered by the Imamate office to the United States Embassy in Cairo for transmission to Washington, read in part, 'We are not the aggressors. Rather the Sultan of Muscat is the aggressor with the help of the British who provoked us and violated

made by the Imamate office in Cairo during the crisis of August 1957, accords somewhat peculiarly with a simultaneous assertion by the same agency that the Sultan had broken the treaty in 1937 by his grant of an oil concession without consultation. Either the treaty was in force or it was not in force in 1955: if it was—and from their statements in 1957 both sides would have it so—then some substance is lent to the Foreign Office's contention that the previous Imam had not felt the Sultan to be breaking the treaty in granting the oil concession. Whether this implied, as the Foreign Office argued it did, the Imam's acceptance of the Sultan's suzerainty in such matters is another question. If anything at all emerges from this clash of views, it is that the dividing-line between the Sultan's and the Imam's spheres of authority, *de facto* or *de jure*, was obscure in the extreme. As for the conflict of views itself, all sides - Sultan, Imam, Foreign Office, and *The Times*—seem to have overlooked the origins of the treaty and what exactly it was intended to regulate: namely, customs duties on goods moving from and to the interior through Muscat and Matrah, and the application of the Sharia law in the trial and punishment of wrongdoers among the tribesmen. All discussion of the treaty, however, may now be of purely academic interest: the Sultan has declared it invalid and the Foreign Office has supported his view.

In the two years that have elapsed since the rebellion strenuous efforts have been made to render the Sultan of Muscat's hold on Oman more secure. An agreement was concluded by him with the British Government in January 1958, by which he was to receive material assistance and the help of regular British army officers in training his armed forces. What has been happening in Oman since September 1957 is not clear, for news from there has been sparse and cryptic.[17] The pacification of the interior has been accorded first preference, for the survey and drilling work of the oil company cannot be carried out (the principal site of the company's operations is at Fahud in the central Oman steppe[18]), or any economic and social progress made, until security has been established in the country. The Imam Ghalib ibn Ali, his brother, Talib, and Sulaiman ibn Hinwar all fled after the uprising of 1957 into the mountainous wilderness of the

---

treaties... They violated the pact between us and the Sultan...' (*New York Times*, 6 Aug. 1957).

17 *The Times* had occasion to complain editorially on 16 December 1958 of the reluctance of the Sultan and of the British Government to allow any news to come out of the country. The situation has not radically improved since then.

18 At the time of writing (September 1959), oil had not been discovered at Fahud; other sites were being explored.

Jabal Akhdar. From there they kept up a spasmodic running fight with the Sultan's forces which strove, with little success, to force them out of the mountains. In November 1958 Talib ibn Ali and Sulaiman ibn Himyar were reported to have sought peace on the basis of their forsaking the Imamate cause and recognizing the Sultan Said ibn Taimur as the sole ruler of Muscat and Oman. In return, they wanted the release of Omani rebels held prisoner at Muscat and permission for them to return home; a guarantee that Sulaiman would be allowed to continue as *tamima* of the Bani Riyam; and the restoration of his property confiscated in the village of Birkat al-Mauz. Saiyid Ahmad ibn Ibrahim, the Muscat Minister of the Interior, was reported to favour these terms, except, possibly, the return of Sulaiman to the chieftainship of the Bani Riyam. There was also the question of whether Talib ibn Ali would be allowed to remain in Oman.[19] The negotiations would appear to have broken down, for they were followed by an intensive effort, mainly by British arms, to force the rebel leaders out of the Jabal Akhdhar. Two squadrons of the 22nd Special Air Service Regiment were flown in from Malaya to form the core, of an assault force which could penetrate to the highest valley of the Green Mountain, where no European foot had trodden since Lieutenants J.R. Wellsted and H.H. Whitelock of the Indian Navy recklessly plunged into the heart of Oman in 1837. Supported by a dismounted troop of the Life Guards—from a squadron sent to Oman to keep open communications through the Wadi Samail—and elements of the Northern (Oman) Frontier Regiment, the S. A. S. squadrons forced their way to the top of the Jabal in the last week of January 1959. Dismayed by this rude violation of their supposedly unassailable sanctuary, the rebels capitulated.[20] Talib, Ghalib, and Sulaiman managed to evade capture and, later, to slip out of Oman, eventually to eat the bread of exile in Riyadh and Cairo. A new element has been introduced into Omani politics with the conclusion, on 20 December 1958, of a treaty of 'amity, economic relations and consular rights' between the United States and the Sultanate of Muscat and Oman. The purpose of the treaty, according to the State Department, is simply 'to regulate basic economic relations' between the two countries. It has, so they aver, no political significance.[21] Time will tell. Certainly, up to date American relations with the Sultanate, where they have existed at all, have been purely commercial and humanitarian (there is an American mission hospital at Matrah, near Muscat). Had they been otherwise they might have proved embarrassing

---

19 *The Times*, 21 Nov. 1958.
20 *Ibid.* 9 Apr. 1959.
21 *Ibid.* 23 Dec. 1958.

in the context of Arabian politics since 1945. The United States' commercial relations with the Sultanate had a purely fortuitous beginning. In the early decades of the nineteenth century a number of American merchants carried on a not inconsiderable trade with Zanzibar, at that time a dependency of the Sultanate. Owing primarily to their efforts a treaty was concluded between the United States and the Sultanate in 1833, providing for freedom of trade for American subjects in the Sultan's dominions. Article 9 of the treaty granted to the United States Government the right to appoint consuls at the principal ports where commerce was carried on. In practice, the right was exercised primarily at Zanzibar, where American trade was concentrated. After 1861 when Muscat and Zanzibar became separate sultanates, it became customary for a United States consular representative to be appointed to Muscat, but in 1915 the consulate was closed down following upon the death of the acting consul.

Unless there has been a startling increase in the volume of American trade with Muscat and Oman in recent years, the recently concluded treaty and the proposed appointment of a consul to Muscat is scarcely justifiable on commercial grounds alone. On the other hand if the move possesses any political signifioance—*pace* the State Department—it would be interesting to know what it portends. Once diplomatic relations are established, the United States Government can hardly avoid being drawn into Oman's politics. As has been seen above, the Sultan Said ibn Taimur is beset in his country by two overriding and interrelated problems: the consolidation of his authority over the inland tribes and the maintenance of his existing territorial rights. Twice in the last few years Saudi Arabia has challenged those rights: directly at the Buraimi Oasis, and indirectly through her support of the Imam Ghalib and his followers. For its part, the United States has a double commitment in Saudi Arabia. King Saud—and before him, his father—has been sedulously wooed as the principal friend of the United States in the Middle East. Further, the United States is heavily involved in the exploitation of Saudi Arabian oil through the agency of the Arabian American Oil Company—and Aramco has shown itself in the past to have been a ready, even eager, partisan of Saudi policy in eastern Arabia. But the United States, like Britain, also has interests at stake in the independent Gulf principalities through American participation in oil exploitation: a 50 per cent share in Kuwait, 100 per cent in Bahrain, and 2 per cent in the Iraq Petroleum Company's operations in Qatar, the Trucial Coast, and Muscat and Oman. Unlike Britain, however, the United States has no clear-cut political position in this area. Not only is there no British oil investment in Saudi Arabia but Britain has a long and steady record, extending over 150 years, of preserving the independence of the littoral shaikhdoms against Saudi encroachment. When the Security Council met in August 1957 to decide whether or not to hear the charge by the Arab states that Britain had violated the United Nations Charter by going to the aid of the Sultan of Muscat, the United States abstained from voting on the issue. As a propitiatory in the direction of Saudi Arabia the gesture was not only inexpensive but it sufficed for the occasion. Next time the price may be higher, if diplomatic relations have, by then, been established with the Sultanate of Muscat and Oman. For further trouble is bound to come. King Saud has made the resumption of relations with Britain contingent upon a settlement of the Buraimi dispute. An Omani 'Liberation Army' is again in training at Dammam; President Nasser clearly hopes that a renewal of the antics of Ghalib ibn Ali and Sulaiman ibn Himyar may open the way to him to the 'Arab South', from Aden to Bahrain. Adroit diplomacy will be needed if the United States is not to be forced, at some not distant date, to declare its hand in the contest for authority in south-eastern Arabia.

7
The Bahrain Question[1]

La Question des Iles Bahrein, by Gholam-Reza Tadjbakhche, (Publications de la Revue Generale de Droit International Public, nouvelle serie, numero 1) Paris: Eiditions A. Pedone, 1960, xvi + 389 pages. Preface, index, appendices. 3 maps.

Territorial claims are the stuff of life in the Persian Gulf, and none is more enduring than that of Persia to Bahrain. Two Persian scholars in recent years have made full-length studies of the Bahrain dispute: Dr. Ferydoun Adamiyat in his *Bahrein Islands, A Legal and Diplomatic Study of the British-Iranian Controversy* (N.Y.: Praeger, 1955) and now Dr. Tadjbakhche in his *La Question des Iles Bahrein.* Like Dr. Adamiyat, Dr. Tadjbakhche based his work largely on the Foreign Office Records in London, and to a lesser extent on the India Office Records. These, he says, so far as the Persian Gulf is concerned, "have, as a whole, escaped an impartial and minute examination" (p. 7). Unfortunately, it cannot be said that his examination of them was impartial and minute for, like Dr. Adamiyat, he seems less disposed to make an objective study of the Bahrain controversy than to deliver an exposition of his government's official case.

His book is divided into three parts: a description of the Bahrain Islands, an account of their history and a legal argument. While he professes himself to be more interested in the juridical aspects of the dispute-his book is, in essence, his doctoral thesis presented to the faculty of law of the University of Paris in 1956—the largest section in his book is the historical. This is understandable since the Persian case depends almost entirely

---

[1] Source: *The Middle East Journal,* Vol. 16, No.4 (Autumn 1962), pp. 543-545.

upon events in the nineteenth century.

According to the author, the Al Khalifah, after their conquest of Bahrain in 1783, undertook to pay tribute to Persia in 1799, 1817, 1839 and 1860. For its part, the Persian Government sent emissaries to Bahrain in 1816, 1839 and 1860 to receive the submission of the Al Khalifah. The continued subjection of Bahrain to Persia after 1783, he claims, is confirmed by contemporary British authorities "in various letters existing in the Foreign Office archives" (pp. 232-3), and "not a single document is to be found among those at the beginning of the nineteenth century to justify the conclusion that the British regarded the independence of Bahrain at this time as a *fait accompli*" (pp. 206-7). One may say to this that Dr. Tadjbakhche must have been singularly unobservant in his scrutiny of the records. There is an abundance of evidence in the India Office Records, which he does not appear to have used very much, and in the Foreign Office Records, that British political officers in the Gulf and their superiors in India during this period viewed Bahrain to be, in fact, independent. One volume of records alone contains statements from the British Resident at Bushire, after a visit to Bahrain in 1816, that the Al Khalifah were the "sole and undisputed rulers" of the island; from the assistant Resident at Basrah in 1818 that after 1783 the Al Khalifah "paid a trifling tribute to the Persians only four times, and then discontinued it altogether;" from the Chief Secretary of the Government of Bombay in 1819 that the records of his government showed that the Al Khalifah regarded themselves, and were regarded on the Arabian mainland, as independent; and from the naval officer in charge of the survey of the Gulf that in 1829 he found Bahrain to be under the sole authority of the Al Khalifah, and that it had been so since 1790, "when the Persian yoke was entirely thrown off, and they have been independent of Persia since," None of these reports is mentioned by Dr. Tadjbakhche, although he has made extensive use of the volume in which they occur.

The author fails to bring out fully that every one of the "submissions" to Persia was made at a time when Bahrain was threatened with invasion. Bahrain, in fact, only retained its independence for much of the nineteenth century through the skill of the Al Khalifah in playing off one pretender to its sovereignty against another, and through British naval intervention to defend the island when invasion threatened. Conversely, it was the lack of naval resources that in huge measure, particularly in the early part of the century, prevented Persia from making good her claim. Between 1800 and 1860 the Al Khalifah made various submissions to the Sultan of Muscat, the Saudi Amir of Najd, the Pasha of Egypt, and the

Sharif of Mecca, all of which Dr. Tadjbakhche brushes aside as in no way affecting the continuance of Persian sovereignty over Bahrain. For him the only submissions and payments that count are the half-a-dozen made to Persia between 1783 and 1860.

Dr. Tadjbakhche's apparent inability to notice evidence unfavorable to his thesis is most obvious in his handling of the origins and contents of the two documents by which, he says, the British Government recognized the validity of the Persian title to Bahrain in the last century, *viz.*, the so-called "Treaty of Shiraz" of 1822 and the Clarendon letter of 29 April 1869. The "Treaty of Shiraz" was an unofficial agreement concluded, without the knowledge or approval of his superiors, by the East India Company's Resident at Bushire, Captain William Bruce, with the Prince-Governor of Pars, Husain Ali Mirza, on 30 August 1822. Bruce, whose motive in negotiating the agreement was solely his personal desire to improve his standing with the Persian authorities, who more than once had demanded his recall, acknowledged in it that Bahrain "has always been subordinate to the Province of Pars."

When word of what he had done reached India he was immediately dismissed from his post and ordered home, and the Governor of Bombay wrote to Husain Ali Mirza, disavowing the agreement and saying that Bruce had not had the authority or the power to conclude it. Fath Ali Shah, too, when he learned of the "Treaty," refused to accept it, and reprimanded his son for having negotiated it without his knowledge or orders.

Dr. Tadjbakhche, although he reluctantly acknowledges that the "Treaty of Shiraz" has no legal validity, insists that it is "an historical document which fully proves the existence of the Persian title to the islands at this period." (p. 232) He also contrives (p. 69) to give the impression that the "Treaty" was concluded by Bruce on prior instructions from Bombay. Apart from the absurdity of this suggestion in the light of Bruce's subsequent fate, it may be remarked that Dr. Tadjbakhche's account of the events leading up to the "Treaty" is wrong in nearly every respect. Moreover, it is difficult to see how he could have made these errors if he had had full recourse to the monographs and records that he cites in his bibliography. It could hardly have escaped his notice also that Bruce was given to making unauthorized agreements. He made one, for instance, with the Al Khalifah in 1816, assuring them of the friendship and support of the British Government in their capacity as "sole and undisputed rulers" of Bahrain.

The Clarendon letter of 29 April 1869 was a reply given by the British Foreign Secretary, the Earl of Clarendon, to a protest made to him by the Persian *charge d'affaires* in London on the subject of the punitive action taken by the Political Resident in the Gulf the previous year against the Shaykh of Bahrain for piracy. In the letter Clarendon acknowledged the *charge d'affaires*' protest with the words,

> The British Government readily admit that the Government of the Shah has protested against the Persian right of sovereignty over Bahrein being ignored by the British authorities, and they have given due consideration to that protest.

This sentence Dr. Tadjbakhche construes, as the Persian Government has construed it for years, as an admission of Persian sovereignty over Bahrain. It would hardly appear to warrant so large a construction, particularly as it was inserted in the letter at the specific request of the Persian *charge d'affaires*. There were, in fact, two letters, both dated 29 April 1869, from Clarendon to the *charge d'affaires*. The first was withdrawn at the latter's request and altered slightly. A paragraph was also added to the original at the request the Secretary of State for India. While Dr. Tadjbakhche is aware that there were two letters he seems unable to distinguish correctly between them. This and the fact that he is prone to confuse what the *charge d'affaires* asked Clarendon to put in the letter with what the Foreign Secretary actually inserted largely vitiates his argument on its significance. His conclusion, *viz.*, "that by the communication of 29 April 1869 Persia's rights of sovereignty over Bahrain were fully recognized and affirmed by the British Secretary of State;" (p. 238), not only is reached by an argument which can most charitably called tortuous, but it is made possible solely by completely ignoring the convention concluded by the British Government with the Shaykh of Bahrain only eight years previously, recognizing him as an independent ruler and guaranteeing the security of his possessions.

The legal arguments adopted by Dr. Tadjhakhche in support of his general thesis are not impressive. They follow closely the argument advanced by the Persian Government in 1928, *viz.*, that a territory belonging to a sovereign state cannot be lawfully detached or its independence recognized except by the official consent of the sovereign state in question. The adoption of such a principle, as the British Foreign Secretary, Sir Austen Chamberlain, pointed out to the Persian Government in reply, would mean that any state would have the power "to advance a claim to a territory of which it had not for centuries been in effective possession, on the ground that its loss of possession in distant ages had not been confirmed by a subsequent treaty." Dr. Tadjbakhche's contribution to the debate is to invoke the doctrine of legitimacy propounded by the powers of the Holy Alliance at the Congress of Troppau in 1820, a rather odd doctrine, it would seem, to invoke at the present day.

As a whole, his work is marred by numerous errors of fact and by misspellings and misprints, both in the text and in the lengthy appendices of documents. There are three maps: one is an undistinguished sketch map of the Persian Gulf; and another is a map of Kuwait, the reason for whose inclusion is not clear; while the third is a poor reproduction of an early map of the Gulf, which is not identified but which may possibly be from Carsten Niebuhr's *Voyage en Arabie*.

8
Britain in the Red Sea and Palestine[1]

Britain's Imperial Role in the Red Sea Area, 1800-1878
by Thomas E. Marston; pp. 550.
Shoe String Press: Hamden, Conn., 1961.

British Interests in Palestine, 1800-1901: A Study of Religious and Educational Enterprise
by Abdul Latif Tibawi; pp. 280.
Oxford University Press: London and New York, 1961.

On 3 MAY 1799 a British expeditionary force from Bombay occupied the island of Perim at the mouth of the Red Sea. On 20 May Napoleon Bonaparte abandoned the siege of the fortress of Acre, on the coast of Palestine, in the face of a stubborn Anglo-Turkish defence, and began his retreat into Egypt. Both the seizure of Perim and the joint defence of Acre with the Turks were actions taken by the British Government to prevent Bonaparte from using Egypt, which he had occupied the previous summer, as a springboard for an attack, by land or sea, upon the British possessions in India. For the rest of the nineteenth century, and well into the twentieth, British policy in the Middle East was shaped, in large measure, by a determination to prevent any other European power from dominating either the "direct" route to India (by Syria and Iraq) or the "overland" route (by Egypt). If this policy found its primary expression, at least until the Congress of Berlin in 1878, in the preservation of the integrity of the Ottoman Empire and the opposing of a Russian ascendancy at Constantinople and the Straits, its secondary manifestation

---
[1] Source: *Victorian Studies*, Vol. 6, No. 4 (Jun., 1963), pp. 361-364.

was the insulation of both the "direct" and the "overland" routes from the absolute control of any one local ruler. Thus, in the 1830's Britain opposed the extension of Egyptian rule by Muhammad Ali to Syria and the Yemen. "The terms to be imposed upon the Pasha are good," observed Lord Palmerston, the British Foreign Secretary, in 1833, after Muhammad Ali had forced the Ottoman Sultan to grant him Palestine, "inasmuch as he does not get Damascus or Aleppo, and so has not the avenues of Mesopotamia." A few years later Palmerston himself closed the "avenues of Arabia"—to the Indian Ocean and Persian Gulf—to Muhammad Ali by forcing him to withdraw from the Yemen and Eastern Arabia. Echoes of the Pasha's grand design have been heard even down to our own times, in President Nasser's brief liaison with Syria and his recent foray into the Yemen. British opposition to Egyptian ambitions still lingers, too, although the security of India is no longer a British responsibility and the imperial shadow grows tenuous in the Arabian peninsula.

Perim Island was evacuated after only four months' occupation, and it was not until the development of steam communication between Britain and India in the 1830's and the Pasha's subsequent bid to control the passage of the Red Sea by subduing the Yemen that British interest in the region was again quickened. Aden was occupied by a force from Bombay in 1839, both to deny the port to the Egyptians and to make it available for use as a coal depot between Suez and Bombay. Barely had Aden been taken when the attention of the British Government was directed across the Straits of Bab al-Mandeb to Abyssinia, where French missionaries and adventurers were active at the courts of Shoa, Tigre, and Gondar. Since the French were not bothering at this time to conceal their approval of Muhammad Ali's bid for paramountcy in Syria and Arabia, or their resentment at British efforts to check him, it seemed to Palmerston and others a fairly safe assumption that the French were intriguing to gain a foothold in Abyssinia from which they could undermine the strategic value of Aden. The outcome of these suspicions was the despatch of a mission from Bombay to Shoa in 1841, and the conclusion of a commercial treaty of dubious value.

From this time forward the British were to maintain a fluctuating interest in the eastern and western littorals of the Red Sea and in what went on there. For most of the time what went on was petty warfare—civil and religious wars between the Turks and the tribes of the interior of the Yemen, tribal wars in the hinterland of Aden, raids by the Egyptians on the marches of Tigre and Gondar for Christian slaves, wars by the rulers of Tigre, Gondar, and Shoa on one another and on their rebellious feudatories. To cut one's way through these thickets of feudal and sectarian strife is a painful task, and Dr. Marston has made a brave essay at it. His book has the virtues and the faults of a pioneer work: he presents a large body of new material but has failed to shape or interpret it sufficiently. This may be the consequence of imperfect digestion of the material, but it seems more the fault of the mould into which the book has been fitted. It is one of a series of Foreign Area Studies produced at Yale University, and it bears an unhappy resemblance to those other "non-books" put out by the Human Relations Area Files at New Haven. Like them, Dr. Marston's volume is largely a work of compilation. Fact is piled upon fact at a dizzying speed, with little regard apparently being paid to their importance or inconsequence in relation to one another. The result is an unfortunate hybrid, which is neither gazetteer nor historical study.

It is surely not too much to ask that in a work 200,000 words long some attention should be paid to the reasons for the formulation or non-formulation of British policy in the Red Sea in the period under consideration, and that there should be informed discussion of the relationship of such policy to British policy in the Middle East and the western Indian Ocean in general in the nineteenth century. Although Dr. Marston has used the Secret and Political Proceedings of the Government of Bombay, he seems to have taken little notice of the deliberations of the Governor-in-Council. It is a truism, furthermore, that one cannot use the India Office records properly unless one understands the workings of the Indian administration. Dr. Marston is plainly not at ease in dealing with the relations of the Bombay Presidency with the Government of India, or of both with the East India Company (which he calls the "British" East India Company) and the India Board in London. Indeed he seems to understand little if anything of the purpose and function of the India Board, or Board of Control, for he writes: "The East India Company was an independent agency and communication between the Secretary of State for Foreign Affairs and the India Board was private and unofficial in nature. The chief effect of the establishment of the India Office was to provide a Cabinet seat for its Secretary of State and bring the vast governmental structure which had grown up under the Company under the direct control of the British government." The President of the India Board was normally a member of the Cabinet after 1784, when Pitt's India Act set up his office as a department of government to oversee the affairs of the Company, and the Crown's control over the Company's activities, especially outside India, was well established by the time of the Charter revision of 1833. The practical effect of Dr. Marston's unfamiliarity with these elementary matters has been to prevent him from finding his way to some of the pertinent series of records, and from making the best use of those he has found. His references to the latter leave much to be desired. "Bombay Secret Consultations 1852," for example, is not good enough to denote a volume in a series which may have as many as forty volumes for a single year.

When Dr. Marston permits himself an historical judgment, as he does all too infrequently, the result is not encouraging. Thus, speculating on the motives behind Captain W. C. Harris' mission to Shoa in 1841, he writes: "The reason unquestionably lies in Anglo-French rivalry in the Indian Ocean. The stakes were very high, the domination of the southern waters of the world from the Cape of Good Hope to the South Pacific islands, and the game was played in the Foreign Offices of Paris and London as a grand chess game played on a map. It was the last appearance of the old imperialism of the eighteenth century which, essentially mercantilist in character, depended on the establishment of a line of bases from which effective raids could be made on the shipping lanes of the potential enemy. The main French base for this plan was the island of Bourbon (present day Reunion) returned to France by England after the Napoleonic wars." Apart from the identification of Bourbon rather than Ile de France (Mauritius), which Britain kept after 1815, as the former principal French base in the Indian Ocean, can one properly speak of "imperialism" in the eighteenth century? If the word is not to be wholly robbed of its historical implications, should its use not be limited to that phase of European expansion in Asia and Africa which took place between, say, 1882 and 1914? If the Harris mission is to be related to some larger historical movement, either preceding or following it, would it not be more logical to see it as the harbinger of British imperialism in the 1880's, when considerations of Indian defence and Imperial communications prompted Britain's interest in the Red Sea and the Horn of Africa, rather than as the last flutter of eighteenth-century Anglo-French commercial and colonial rivalry?

Perhaps if Dr. Marston had kept his work within a narrower compass he might have been more successful. His book is really four books in one: a history of Abyssinia in the period covered, a history of the Yemen, a history of Aden, and a history of foreign activities in these countries. It cannot be said that he has managed to weld these stories into one, or to extract any theme common to all of them. On the other hand, as remarked earlier, this failure may be due to the way in which his study, and the series of which it is a part, was conceived. If so, then Dr. Marston has been badly served, for much of what he has to relate is highly interesting and he tells it well. This is especially true of his chapters on Abyssinia, that dark, bloody, and cruel land, and on the Yemen, its Muslim counterpart across the Red Sea. His comments upon the difficulties experienced by the Turks in holding on to the Yemeni lowlands after their occupation of Mocha and Hodeida in 1849 might well be pondered in Cairo today: "It is not hard to see the temptation which this rich land, without any organized defense, offered to an official with a small organized army. Military progress was easily made with a very small force against such disorganization, but when a certain point was reached, and the fanaticism of the Zaidi populace became aroused against the Sunnite Turks, the small force requisite for military conquest was little protection to the conquerors."

One of the more curious situations in which the British Government found itself in the Middle East in the middle of the nineteenth century was that of acting as the protector of the Abyssinian Church at Jerusalem. The protectorate was largely brought about by the zeal of Bishop Gobat, the second Anglican Bishop of Jerusalem, who had a penchant for converting, or attempting to convert, members of the Eastern or Orthodox Churches in Palestine, and who had begun his ministry as a Church Missionary Society agent in Abyssinia. Although Dr. Tibawi in his *British Interests in Palestine, 1800-1901* does not mention the Abyssinian protectorate or the complications it produced during the Abyssinian War of 1867, his account of British missionary activities in Palestine in the last century is the most complete, as well as the most judicious, yet attempted. It is taken up mainly with a history of the Anglican episcopate of Jerusalem, which was established as a joint venture by the Church of England and the Church of Prussia (or Lutheran Church) in 1841. The creation of the see received the secular blessing of Palmerston, who apparently saw in it a means of spreading British influence in the Levant. Such, at least, must have been the real reason for his support, for although Dr. Tibawi is inclined to ascribe it rather to the Foreign Secretary's evangelical inclinations, there were not enough Protestant Christians in Palestine to warrant the care of a priest, let alone of a bishop. Palmerston may also have been moved by a desire to accommodate the King of Prussia, from whom much of the initiative for the creation of the see came, particularly as the principal negotiations for its creation took place at the same time as the conclusion of the Straits Convention of 1841. Whether the later behaviour of the incumbents of the see was to Palmerston's taste is doubtful, for their energies seem primarily to have been engaged in controversies with the prelates and patriarchs of the Latin, Uniate, and Orthodox churches.

Perhaps the lay mind is unable to appreciate the fervour that animates the clerical breast, but it is difficult to escape the feeling that the

Protestant missionaries who went to Palestine in the early nineteenth century went to meddle in the spiritual affairs of others. The first to go, in the early 1820's, were sent by the London Society for Promoting Christianity amongst the Jews (the L.J.S.). Agents of the Church Missionary Society followed not long afterwards, although a permanent C.M.S. mission was not established at Jerusalem until 1851. What emerges clearly from Dr. Tibawi's carefully documented survey is that the aim of both societies was not the care of Protestant souls or the conversion of the heathen but proselytism, in the one case of the Palestine Jews, in the other, of Muslims and, more particularly, Oriental Christians. Hostility towards Islam on the part of the early missionaries went hand in hand with ignorance of Muslim laws and customs, and of Arab and Turkish life in general. From the moment of their arrival in Palestine the L.J.S. began agitating for the appointment of a British consul to Jerusalem to protect their interests, and for the grant of permission by the Sublime Porte for the erection of a Protestant church there. At a time when Franks were not even permitted to reside within the city walls, and the erection of new Christian churches had long been forbidden by the Turks, the campaign was irresponsible, not to say reckless of Britain's political interests in the Ottoman Empire. The Anglican missionaries, however, whether of the L.J.S. or the C.M.S., showed in Palestine a contemptuous disregard for the fact that the province was part of the Ottoman Empire, and for the Sultan's rule in general.

By the middle of the century the Anglican bishop and the C.M.S. missionaries were primarily occupied in winning converts among the congregations of the Eastern Churches, regardless of how disruptive this practice was of the millet system, whereby the head of each community was held responsible by the Porte for its members. Religion being almost identical with nationality in the Ottoman Empire, for an Orthodox Christian to embrace Anglicanism was, in Turkish eyes, tantamount to his becoming a British subject ("to be made English" was the term used for such conversions). The inducements held out by the missionaries to prospective converts were blatantly material—food, housing, employment, education, and medical attention. "The early annals of the mission," remarks Dr. Tibawi of the L.J.S., "reveal no converts who gave up position and wealth for their faith." His clear analysis of the motives and methods of the Anglican missionaries is perhaps the most valuable aspect of his book, for in a quiet but telling fashion he disposes of the myth that the Protestant missionaries in the Levant turned to educational and medical work only after their efforts at converting the Muslims had come to naught. Proselytism, not charity, was the original purpose of the Anglican missionaries, and it was never lost sight of throughout the century. Education, material help, and medical care were merely means to this end, and if more prominence was given to these aspects of their work, both in Europe and the Ottoman Empire, it was for reasons of policy and not of preference. Dr. Tibawi's valuable book may well prompt someone to make an equally scholarly and objective study of American missionary activity in the Levant in the last century. *That* should be an interesting story.

9
The Persian Gulf[1]

John Marlowe, *The Persian Gulf in the Twentieth Century*
New York, Frederick A. Praeger, 1962, viii+280 pp.
Appendices, notes, bibliography, maps, index.

Mr. Marlowe's book is disappointing. Though its title would lead one to expect it to be concerned largely, if not exclusively, with Kuwait, Bahrain, Qatar, the Trucial shaikhdoms, the Sultanate of Muscat and Oman and, to a lesser extent, Saudi Arabia—in other words, the countries that are normally meant by the term "the Persian Gulf"—it is, in fact, mainly taken up with the history of Persia and Iraq in this century. While these countries may be ranked among the Persian Gulf states by virtue of their having coastlines on the Gulf, they, and particularly Iraq, whether under Ottoman rule or since the achievement of independence, have played little part in its politics over the past century and a half. To the affairs of the Gulf states proper, Mr. Marlowe devotes only about one-quarter of his book.

The author's resume of the course of events in Persia and Iraq since 1900 calls for little comment. It contains nothing more, and a good deal less, than what is available in other general accounts, and it shows obvious signs of having been hastily assembled and inadequately edited. Mr. Marlowe would have done better to have spent more time on the history of the Arabian shore states in the nineteenth century, since it is a particular truism in their case that one cannot understand their politics in this century unless one knows their history in the last, the Gulf, at least until

---
1 Source: *Middle Eastern Affairs*, Vol.XIV, No 8, October 1963, pp. 238-9.

very recently, having changed little in the interval. The survey of the Gulf in the nineteenth century is studded, in the book under review, with errors and omissions. The author seems to think, for example, that a line of Ibadi Imams continued to exist in the interior of Oman throughout the century, whereas, with the exception of the brief reign of Azzan ibn Qais from 1868 to 1871, there was no Imam of the Ibadiya between the death of Sa'id ibn Ahmad, probably in 1821, and the election of Salim ibn Rashid al-Kharusi in 1913.

There is little doubt that the most important political questions that have arisen along the Arabian littoral of the Gulf in the last two decades have been the frontier dispute between Saudi Arabia and her neighbors and the contest in Oman between the reigning Sultan, Sa'id ibn Taimur, and the *ci-devant* Imam, Ghalib ibn Ali al-Hinawi: Mr. Marlowe's treatment of both questions is disappointingly brief. There are a number of topics to which he might have addressed himself with profit to his readers, not least the origins of the paradoxical situation in which the present government of Egypt now finds itself of supporting simultaneously the restoration of the Ibadi Imamate in Oman and the overthrow of the Zaidi Imamate in Yemen. Egyptian activities in the Gulf region, and in Arabia generally, in the last ten years well merit examination in a work of this nature. So, too, do the difficulties in which the British now find themselves. With their legal position in the Gulf resting upon a treaty system created in the last century to safeguard the peace at sea and to prevent the acquisition by any other power of a foothold in the Gulf from which to threaten the security of British India, the British find themselves faced, on the one hand, with the necessity to protect interests which are now primarily territorial and economic, and, on the other hand, with the obligation to maintain the maritime policing of the Gulf in an international atmosphere shrill with the cries of "colonialist" witchhunters.

What of the role of the United States in the Gulf, now and in the future? Though Mr. Marlowe has some pertinent comments to make in his history of oil concessions in Eastern Arabia—much the best part of his book—he does not go far enough. Some day, perhaps, someone will tell the tale of the Arabian American Oil Company's part in the politics of the region, since 1945. As Harry W. Hazard remarked a few years ago in a review of the Aramco Handbook for 1960 (*Middle East Journal*, Summer, 1961): "If the authors had only told us everything they know: that would indeed be a book!"

10
The Kurds and Iraq[1]

The Kurds and Kurdistan by Derk Kinnane. London, New York: Oxford University Press for the Institute of Race Relations, London. 1964. 86 pp. Bibliog.

The Kurdish War by David Adamson. London: Allen &: Unwin. 1964. 215 pp.

Iraq under General Nuri: My Recollections of Nuri al-said, 1954-1958 by Waldemar J. Gallman. Baltimore: Johns Hopkins Press; London: Oxford University Press. 1964. 241 pp. Bibliog. Index.

The National Income of Iraq 1953-1961 by K. Haseeb. Foreword by W. B. Reddaway. London, New York, Toronto: Oxford University Press for the Royal Institute of International Affairs. 1964. 184 pp. (Middle Eastern Monographs: 6.)

The Kurds are the Irish of the Middle East. Contentious, passionate, romantic and fatalistic, their literature abounds in sagas of love and war, the two faces of the coin of life. David Adamson, in his book, likens the Kurdish nationalists of Turkey to the Sinn Fein, and he quotes (p. 16) a European traveller among them early in this century who called them

---

1 Source: *International Affairs*, April 1965, Vol. 41, No. 2, pp. 345-347.

shedders of blood, raisers after strife, seekers after turmoil and uproar, robbers and brigands, ... but a brave race and fearless, of a hospitality grateful to the soul, in truth and in honour unequalled, of pleasing countenance and fair cheek, boasting all the goods of beauty and grace.

The Kurdish struggle for a national identity has been a long one, and Derk Kinnane summarises it admirably in his little book. A former lecturer at Baghdad University, he saw the beginnings of the latest phase in this struggle, and he has travelled in Iraqi Kurdistan. Because Iraq's oil lies mainly in the Kurdish districts, and because the water resources of their mountains hold a great potential for hydro-electric development, no Iraqi government can allow their lands to be detached from Iraq. Yet no Iraqi government has made a decent effort to reach a *modus vivendi* with the Kurds since the period immediately after the First World War, when the British, as the mandatory Power in Iraq, tried and failed to create an autonomous province within the kingdom. The shabby story of neglect, alternating with violence and treachery, that has been the policy of most Iraqi administrations ever since, clearly emerges from both Kinnane's and Adamson's accounts.

Adamson travelled to Persia and Iraq in the late autumn of 1962 to report on the Kurdish revolt for *The Sunday Telegraph*. He saw for himself what Qasim's army and air force had done to the Kurds and their villages, and he met the leaders of the revolt, Mullah Mustafa al-Barzani, Ibrahim Ahmad and Jalal Talabani. What he has written as a result of his journeys (he went to Kurdistan again late in 1963) is a moving and sensitive portrayal of the Kurds and their struggles, a small masterpiece of Eastern travel, evocative, witty and humane. Like Kinnane, Adamson emphasises that the nationalist movement, drawing its strength from the old tribal and feudal order, on the one hand, and from the more forward-looking Kurdish Democratic Party, on the other, far from being Communist, has no love for the Communists because of the support that they gave Qasim. The Kurds fared no better under the Ba'ath than they did under Qasim, for the Ba'ath were committed to advancing Arab interests, not moderating them, and to have acceded to the Kurds' demands for autonomy would have compromised those interests.

No one outside Iraq has helped the Kurds much. The Soviet Union's attitude towards them has been conditioned by her attitude to Qasim and his successors. Britain is supposed to have agreed early in 1963 to support the Ba'ath against them in return for the dropping of the Iraqi claim to

Kuwait. If this is true, then it was a bargain of little value and great callousness. The Iraqi Defence Minister in July 1962 had described the campaign against the Kurds, in which over 500 villages had been destroyed (by, among other things, rocket fire and napalm bombs), as 'a national picnic by the Army'.

There is a certain confusion in the Iraqi Kurds' demands, as both Kinnane and Adamson point out. While they emphasise that they do not want to break away from Iraq and form an independent Kurdistan with their fellows in Turkey, Persia and Syria, but only to realise their aspirations (a one-party Kurdish state, a 30 per cent share of Iraq's oil revenues, and a proportional share of posts in the army and in the national councils) without affecting the independence and integrity of the Republic of Iraq, they have also put forward, through an emissary sent to Egypt in the spring of 1963, the conception of a Kurdish national state within the framework of a greater U.A.R. It may be that the Kurds felt that they might hope for more sympathy and understanding from the Arabs than from anyone else. To judge from events since that date it is a desperate hope.

Fear that the Baghdad Pact might be used by Ankara and Tehran as an instrument against them had led the Kurds to applaud Iraq's withdrawal from the Pact in March 1959. A good portion of Waldemar J. Gallman's book is devoted to the formation of the Pact and its fortunes from 1954 to 1958. Gallman, who was U.S. Ambassador to Iraq during these years, deplores the failure of the U.S. to join the Pact as a full member from the beginning. The blame for that failure he lays at John Foster Dulles's door. If the United States, he says, had fully assumed the initiative in the Middle East from 1955 onwards, much that has occurred since then of an unhappy nature might have been avoided, including the destruction of Nuri's regime in Iraq. Nuri, with all his faults, Gallman asserts, was the leader that Iraq needed, and still needs. He may be right on both counts. Certainly the criticisms made before July 1958 of Nuri's repressive internal policies look silly nowadays when set alongside the record of his successors.

Nuri's economic legacy to Iraq is examined by K. Haseeb, the present Governor of the Bank of Iraq, in his book. It is primarily a work for economists, though the layman, if he perseveres can winkle out some interesting facts from its pages (and more from between its lines) about the comparative state of the Iraqi economy now and in its pre-revolutionary days.

11
Mehemet 'Ali's Expedition to the Persian Gulf 1837-1840[1]

Part I

H. W. V. Temperley, almost thirty years ago, remarked in his *England and the Near East: the Crimea* of H. H. Dodwell's biography of Mehemet 'Ali, published five years earlier,[2] "He sees, as no previous writer has done, that Mehemet Ali's threats to the Persian Gulf, Red Sea and Euphrates valley were the real cause of Palmerston's hostility."[3] The tribute was no more than deserved, and Dodwell's interpretation of the origins of the quarrel between the two men, that culminated in the Eastern Crisis of 1839-40, has come to be accepted as standard. What is perhaps surprising is that, in the years that have passed since Dodwell and Temperley pointed the way, little attention has been paid to Mehemet 'Ali's activities in Arabia and the Persian Gulf, both before and during the crisis of 1839-40. The account that follows of these activities by no means pretends to be a definitive. or even a full, description of the Egyptian expedition to central and eastern Arabia from 1837 to 1840. For an adequate disclosure of Mehemet 'Ali's motives in sending the expedition, and of its day-to-day fortunes, we must wait for a scholar who will make use of the records of Mehemet 'Ali's reign preserved in the Egyptian archives. Meanwhile it may serve some purpose to describe how the expedition was viewed at the time

---

1 Source: Part I - *Middle Eastern Studies*, Vol. 1, No. 4 (Jul., 1965), pp. 350-381
Part II - *Middle Eastern Studies*, Vol. 2, No. 1 (Oct., 1965), pp. 31-65.
2 *The Founder of Modern Egypt*, Cambridge, 1931.
3 *England and the Near East: the Crimea*, London, 1936, p. 416.

by the British Government, and what counter-activities it brought forth, on the part of that government, along the Arabian shore of the Persian Gulf.

That the primary purpose of Mehemet 'Ali's campaign against the Wahhabis of Najd and Hasa was to clear the approaches for an advance upon Turkish Iraq, or the Pashaliq of Baghdad, as it was then called, is in little doubt. After the Pashaliqs of Syria and Adana had been grudgingly conceded to him by the Sultan Mahmud II in 1833, Mehemet 'Ali had given several indications that his next goal was Baghdad.[4] At the close of 1833 he attempted, without success, to raise a levy of 60,000 men in Syria, and at the same time he despatched a confidential agent, Saiyid Khalid Effendi, to Baghdad by way of the Persian Gulf. At Bushire, on the Persian coast, where he called in March 1834, Saiyid Khalid told the British Political Resident in the Gulf that he was the bearer of letters from Mehemet 'Ali to the Sultan of Muscat, the Prince of Shiraz, and the shaikhs of the Muntafiq and Ka'ab tribes of lower Iraq and the Shatt al-Arab. Mehemet 'Ali, he said, had been invested by the Porte with the Pashaliq of Baghdad and "the coasts and islands of the Gulph originally appended thereto." from the end of A.H. 1250 (28 April, 1835). 'Ali Pasha, the vali of Baghdad, was aware of the arrangement and had fallen in with it.[5]

Colonel Patrick Campbell, the British Consul-General in Egypt, who learned of Saiyid Khalid's mission from the British Resident at Baghdad, Lieutenant-Colonel Robert Taylor, questioned Mehemet 'Ali about it and about his views on Baghdad in general in June 1834. The Viceroy re-

---

4 Temperley (The Crimea, pp. 419-22) rightly dismisses, as being of little significance,, the conversation held with Mehemet 'Ali in April 1833 by Colonel Prokesch von Osten, the Austrian commissioner sent to Cairo to help arrange the terms of peace between the Sultan and the Viceroy, on the subject of creating an Arab kingdom stretching from Nubia to the Euphrates and encompassing the whole of Arabia, an accomplishment which, von Osten declared, would cause Mehemet 'Ali to be hailed as *"le vengeur des Khalifs"*. Mehemet 'Ali was not in need of instruction as to the direction his ambitions should take. But, in view of some of his subsequent actions, which will be described presently, the following remarks of von Osten are of interest: *"Il faudra commencer par négocier avec les Primats de Bagdad et avec les Chefs des Tribus sur la rive droite de l'Euphrate. Les Anglais ne s'opposeront point à un rapprochement avec les Imams sur l'Océan et dans le Golphe Persique."* ([Public Record Office] F.O. 78/343, "Extrait d'une Note: datee Alexandrie, 17/5, 1833, in Col. P. Campbell to Palmerston, 1 October 1838 (No. 69 Confidential).
See also Temperley, *loc. cit.*

5 [India Office Records] Persia and Persian Gulf series, Vol. 50, Sir John Campbell (British Minister at Tehran) to Secret Committee of East India Company, 9 April 1834 (No. 22), citing reports of Residents at Bushire and Baghdad.

plied that it was well known that the people of Iraq were greatly dissatisfied with Turkish rule, and had approached his governor in Syria, Sharif Bey, with a request that he take possession of the province in Mehemet 'Ali's name. He, however, could not entertain the idea for the present. As for Saiyid Khalid, Mehemet 'Ali said, he was a dependant of Da'ud Pasha, the last of the Mamluk Pashas of Baghdad, who had been deposed by the Porte and exiled in 1831. He had applied to Mehemet 'Ali for employment, and to get rid of him the Viceroy had sent him to the Sultan of Muscat, Saiyid Sa'id ibn Sultan, with a letter of recommendation. Campbell treated the explanation with scepticism. Mehemet 'Ali was not in the habit of giving letters of recommendation to anyone without a definite purpose in mind. Besides, there was at that very moment an envoy from Saiyid Sa'id ibn Sultan at the Viceroy's court, and the Viceroy himself had told Campbell that Saiyid Sa'id had reproached him for having gone to the expense of purchasing vessels for his expedition to the Yemen when he, Sa'id, would gladly have loaned him the ships. Saiyid Khalid, Campbell believed, had been sent to Baghdad for a good reason, even if it were only to scout the lie of the land, since Mehemet 'Ali was well aware of the discontented state of the province.[6]

Though Palmerston had known since the beginning of 1833 that Mehemet 'Ali might have in contemplation some grand design of controlling the Persian Gulf and Red Sea routes to India through possession of Egypt, Syria, Iraq, the Hijaz, and the Yemen, and of engrossing their trade as he had that of Egypt,[7] he did not apparently think it necessary at this stage to curb the Viceroy further than to warn him, as he did in October 1834, against attempting to carry into effect the intention he had confided to the European consuls at Alexandria the previous month, of declaring his independence of the Porte. "Mehemet is an old man," Palmerston wrote to

---

6 [I.O.] Board's Secret and Political General Correspondence, Vol. 2 (series i), Campbell to Palmerston, 14 June 1834 (No. 28), enclosed in Palmerston to Charles Grant (President of India Board), 29 August 1834.

7 The possibility had first been pointed out to him by Henry Ellis, a member of the India Board, in a memorandum dated 9 January 1833 (see [P.R.O.] F.O. 78/233, and [1.O.] Persia and P. Gulf, Vol. 48). The memorandum might fairly be described as one of the most important, and at the same time one of the most neglected, documents in the formation of British policy in the Middle East in the nineteenth century. To the present writer's knowledge it has been cited only by Dr. G. H. Bolsover in his unpublished thesis, "Great Britain and Russia and the Eastern Question, 1832-41" (University of London, 1933), by Dr. M. Vereté in his article, "Palmerston and the Levant Crisis, 1832" [*Journal of Modern History*, XXIV], and by the writer himself in his unpublished thesis, "British Policy in the Persian Gulf, 1813-1843" (University of London, 1956), from which much of the material for the present article has been taken.

Lord Ponsonby, the British Ambassador at Constantinople in November, "and what remains to him of life is nothing when set against the duration of an Empire."[8] The following year the expedition under Colonel F. R. Chesney to survey the rivers Euphrates and Tigris impeded, as Palmerston intended it should, any effective move by Mehemet 'Ali on Baghdad from Syria. But the Viceroy was already looking to the Arabian peninsula, where more than twenty years previously he had laid the foundation of his later fortunes by subduing the Wahhabis of Najd, as an alternative sphere of operations.

His first venture into Arabia had taken place at the behest of the Porte for the purpose of wresting control of the Holy Cities of Mecca and Madinah from the Wahhabis. It began in 1811 and it ended seven years later with the destruction of Dara'iya, the Wahhabi capital, by Ibrahim Pasha, the execution of the Wahhabi Amir at Constantinople, and the investiture of Mehemet 'Ali with possession of the Hijaz and a shadowy authority over the Qasim, the district intermediate to Najd. But more important for the future, it had endowed the Viceroy with great prestige in the Muslim world at large. The Wahhabis recovered power in Najd in the eighteen-twenties under a new Amir of the Al Sa'ud family, Turki ibn 'Abdullah, who established a new capital at Riyad and went on to reassert Wahhabi rule over Hasa, the province lying along the Gulf coast, and to force the littoral states to pay tribute again to the Wahhabi state. But in May 1834 Turki was assassinated, and his son Faisal, who succeeded him, had great difficulty initially in making his authority felt in Najd and more particularly in Hasa. It was this situation in which Mehemet 'Ali now prepared to intervene.

The first sign of a revival of the Viceroy's interest in Arabia was manifested early in 1834, when Ahmad Pasha, the Governor of the Hijaz, moved against the elements of the Egyptian garrison in the Hijaz which had mutinied eighteen months previously and established themselves in the two principal ports of the Yemen, Mokha and Hodeida. By the late spring Ahmad Pasha had not only subdued the mutineers and occupied the coastal plain but had compelled the Imam of Sana'a to acknowledge Mehemet 'Ali's authority. He then turned his attention to eastern Arabia, where Faisal ibn Turki was contending not only with revolt in Hasa, led by the Al 'Arai'ar shaikhs of the Bani Khalid, but also with attack by the Al Khalifah ruler of Bahrain, 'Abdullah ibn Ahmad, who even before the Amir Turki's death had thrown off his submission to him and blockaded

---

8 Palmerston to Ponsonby, 16 November 1934, cited in Sir Charles Webster, *The Foreign Policy of Palmerston, 1830-41*, 2 vols., London, 1951, I, 341.

Qatif and 'Uqair on the Hasa coast.⁹ In the summer of 1835 Ahmad Pasha despatched an agent to Hasa. The agent, 'Abdullah ibn Mishari, a former merchant of Bahrain, travelled from the Hijaz by way of Muscat, where he was hospitably received by Sa'id ibn Sultan. On arrival at Qatif 'Abdullah ibn Mishari announced that he was assuming control of the government of the town in the name of Ahmad Pasha, who had farmed Qatif and its districts to him for the sum of $M.T. 20,000-24,000 per annum.¹⁰ 'Abdullahi bn Mishari's stay at Qatif was brief: a few days after his arrival he was ejected from the town by a body of troops sent by Faisal to assert his prior rights to the port.¹¹

Ibn Mishari's mission may have been designed, as was thought in the Gulf at the time, to distract Faisal's attention from the Yemen, where Ahmad Pasha was completing the subjection of the tribes of the 'Asir.¹² It might also have been intended as a reconnaissance, and, equally, to help concert a plan with Sa'id ibn Sultan for bringing Bahrain and the Hasa coast ultimately under Egyptian, or joint Muscati-Egyptian, control. Mehemet 'Ali's attention had been drawn to Bahrain's strategic position and to its rich entrepot trade and lion's share of the Gulf's pearling industry at the time of Ibrahim Pasha's campaign in Najd. Saiyid Sa'id, for his part, had been trying for twenty-five years to make himself master of the island. He had sounded out Mehemet 'Ali in 1831 on the possibility of a combined expedition against the Al Khalifah, but he had lost enthusiasm for the project when the Viceroy proposed in return to place not only Bahrain but Hasa also under Sa'id's authority, and to keep sufficient troops in both places as to enable him to govern them, on condition that Sa'id paid him an annual tribute of $M.T. 300,000.¹³ Possession of Bahrain, however, remained an *idée fixe* with Sa'id, and it also became one of the principal objects of the expedition that Mehemet 'Ali now decided to send into Najd.

Late in 1836 Mehemet 'Ali released from detention in Cairo and

---

9 'Abdullah ibn Ahmad was also largely responsible for Turki's murder. Although H. St. J. B. Philby is inclined (*Arabia*, London, 1930, p. 108) to place the blame on Isma'il Bey, the Egyptian commander at Madinah, opinion in the Gulf at the time was that 'Abdullah was the main instigator of the crime. (See [I.O.] Selections from the Records of the Bombay Government, new series, no. XXIV: the Persian Gulf, p. 442, Lieut. A. B. Kemball, "Historical Sketch of the Wahabee Tribe of Arabs, 1832-44".

10 The Maria Theresa thaler or dollar was worth, at this time, about four shillings.
11 [I.O.] *Bombay Selections* XXIV, pp. 442-3, Kemball, "Sketch of Wahabees".
12 *Ibid.*
13 [I.O.] Bombay Political Letters Received, Vol. 15, Gov.-in-Council to Court of Directors, 13 April 1832 (No. 10 Political Dept.).

sent to the Hijaz a member of the Sa'udi dynasty, Khalid ibn Sa'ud, who, along with his brother, the Amir 'Abdullah ibn Sa'ud, who was afterwards executed at Constantinople, and other relatives had been captured by Ibrahim Pasha on the fall of Dara'iya in 1818. Mehemet 'Ali's intention in releasing Khalid, who during his stay at Cairo had become largely Egyptian in sympathies and outlook, was to use him as an instrument for the overthrow of Faisal ibn Turki, and, afterwards, for the government of Najd and Hasa as Egyptian dependencies. He sent orders to Isma'il Pasha, the Governor of Madinah, to supply Khalid with troops and guns, and early in 1837 Khalid began his advance into the Qasim. Faisal tried at first to persuade Mehemet 'Ali to withdraw his support from the pretender by offering to submit to the Viceroy, but Mehemet 'Ali turned a deaf ear to the suggestion. By the latter part of April Khalid was drawing near to Riyad, and soon afterwards he met and defeated Faisal in battle. Faisal fell back on Hasa, abandoning his capital to the usurper.[14]

News of the fall of Riyad reached the acting Political Resident in the Gulf, Captain Samuel Hennell, in the second week of May, and with it rumours that the Egyptian force accompanying Khalid was larger than had at first been supposed. To test the force of the rumours Hennell despatched a cruiser of the Gulf squadron of the Indian Navy to Bahrain with letters for the ruler, 'Abdullah ibn Ahmad, and the Residency Agent on the island, asking for information on the numbers and movements of the Egyptians. 'Abdullah ibn Ahmad replied that the force comprised 1,000 horse and 1,000 foot, and was reported to be already seven or eight days' march past Riyad. The Residency Agent put the numbers at 1,500 horse and 500 foot, under the command of Isma'il Pasha himself. There were also twelve guns and four mortars, commanded by Rashid Pasha. A reserve of 8,000 cavalry, he had heard, was stationed at Khaif, between Mecca and Madinah, under Khurshid Pasha. At every town between Madinah and Riyad a garrison had been posted, which indicated that the occupation was intended to be permanent. Shaikh 'Abdullah, the Residency Agent added, was somewhat uneasy about the ultimate destination of the expedition, suspecting that an arrangement might have been entered into by Mehemet 'Ali and Saiyid Sa'id of Muscat to force the submission of Bahrain with the aid of Sa'id's fleet.[15]

---

14 [I.O.] Board's Collections, Vol. 1699, Colln. 68472, Capt. S. Hennell (Pol. Res. in Gulf) to J. P. Willoughby (Chief Secretary, Bombay), 25 February, 15 March, 8 May and 15 May, 1837; and *Bombay Selections* XXIV, p. 444, Kemball, "Sketch of Wahabees".
15 Same series, volume and collection, Hennell to Willoughby, 8 June 1837 (No. 48 Pol. Dept.). enclosing 'Abdullah ibn Ahmad to Hennll, 17 Safar 1253/23 May 1837, and

Hennell forwarded the reports to his superiors at Bombay and to Dr. John McNeill, the British Minister at Tehran. The copies to McNeill were sent on to London, where they reached the Foreign Office on 13 November, a fortnight before those forwarded from Bombay reached the India Board.[16] Palmerston did not act on the news at once, preferring to wait until he had a clearer picture of what was happening in Arabia.[17] On 1 December he received from Ponsonby at Constantinople a letter sent to the ambassador from Baghdad by Lieutenant H. B. Lynch, I.N., who had taken charge of the Euphrates Expedition from Chesney. Lynch's letter, written in August, was most alarming.

> It is difficult to describe the state of affairs here in so short a space as I feel entitled to occupy your Lordship's attention, but in a word, there is no force here that could for a day oppose that of Mehemed Ali or an effort of his through the Arab tribes on this Pashalic. The Arabs are either in open rebellion or divided and poor; the Chiefs of Mohumrah openly refuse to acknowledge the power of the Pasha, and the present state of things can only go on 'till opposed. The revenues are already but a slight resource to the Turkish Treasury. How far Mehemed Ali is connected with this state of things is best known to your Lordship, but his present open proceedings demand an immediate decision as to the integrity of the Turkish Empire, and as to how far our immediate Indian interests would be affected by his becoming possessed of the embouchure of the Mesopotamian rivers or the ports of the Persian Gulf, in addition to those of the Red Sea, which I regret to say he has been allowed to occupy. It is his interest to rest on the Nile and Tigris or the Red Sea and the Persian Gulf. It is indeed a vital question with him and thereby render his present vulnerable position one that would defy even the power of England unless put forth in a tedious and protracted war in the desert.
>
> . . . Masking any views he may have on this Pashalic, he is now

---

Mirza Muhammad 'Ali to Hennell, 18 Safar 1253/24 May 1837.

16 See [I.O.] Persia and P. Gulf, Vol. 57, McNeill to Palmerston, 31 August 1837 (No. 67), and Bombay Pol. Letters Recd., Vol. 20, Gov.-in-Council to Court, 12 August 1837 (No. 40 Pol. Dept.).

17 [I.O.] Board's Pol. and Sec. Gen. Corresp., Vol. 8 (i), J. Backhouse (Under-Secretary, F.O.) to Secy., India Board, 13 November 1837.

advancing through Arabia on a line to the south through Nejd. He has succeeded in dividing and partly establishing his power over the Wahabees by setting up a rival to the Sheikh and we hear (doubtful) that his nominee is now at Lahsah [Hasa], a fertile district of the Nejd, not far from the Persian Gulf.[18]

Three days after reading this, on 4 December, Palmerston heard from Campbell at Alexandria that Ibrahim Pasha had left for Syria on 25 October, after talking to Campbell at length about the Pasha of Baghdad's inability to subdue the Beduin tribes which were troubling the Syrian frontier.[19] The intimation seemed plain, and on 8 December Palmerston instructed Campbell "to represent in friendly but forcible terms to Mehemet Ali how much Her Majesty's Government would regret to see any steps taken on his part that should indicate an intention of pushing on his authority towards Bagdad".[20] Later that day Palmerston decided to make the warning even stronger. ". . . I have to instruct you," he wrote to Campbell in a second despatch, "to intimate to the Pasha of Egypt that reports have reached H.M. Government of movements of his troops in Syria and Arabia which seem to indicate intentions on his part to extend his authority towards the Persian Gulf and the Pashalic of Bagdad; and you will state frankly to the Pasha that the British Government could not see with indifference the execution of such intentions."[21]

Campbell delivered the warning at the beginning of February 1838. Mehemet 'Ali's reaction to it was to deny absolutely any designs on the Pashaliq of Baghdad. "As for the Persian Gulf, . . . it was hardly necessary for him to talk on the subject; that there, there is only one country, which is Muscat, the chief of which country he loved and esteemed, because he had declared himself the partizan of civilized reforms, and the conquest of that country (Muscat), even if possible, could not be of any advantage to him, since it was so well governed."[22] Such assurances were hardly sufficient to dispel Palmerston's suspicions, but he does not appear to have thought it worth while to question the Viceroy more closely about his activities in Arabia until something should arise to justify it. At the end of the third week in May Mehemet 'Ali informed Campbell that all Najd

---

18 [P.R.O.] F.O. 78/306, Lynch to Ponsonby, August 1837, enclosed in Ponsonby to Palmerston, Therapia, 30 October 1837 (No. 260).
19 [P.R.O.] F.O. 78/321, Campbell to Palmerston, 3 November 1837 (No. 71).
20 [P.R.O.] F.O. 78/3 18, Palmerston to Campbell, 8 December 1837 (No. 23)
21 Same series and volume, Palmerston to Campbell, 8 December 1837 (No. 25).
22 [P.R.O.] F.O. 78/342, Campbell to Palmerston, 7 February 1838 (No. 5).

had submitted to him and that the whole of Arabia, from Mecca and Madinah to the Persian Gulf, was obedient to his rule. Faisal ibn Turki had acknowledged his suzerainty and engaged to punish those who disobeyed him. He had also undertaken, if Mehemet 'Ali so desired it, both to help him against the tribes of the 'Asir and to secure Basra for him.[23] Four days after telling this to Campbell, on 25 May, the Viceroy announced his intention of declaring his independence of the Porte and of establishing his own dynasty in Egypt and Syria.[24]

This announcement naturally took precedence in Palmerston's mind over the news of the submission of Najd. It came, furthermore, at a time when the Foreign Secretary was occupied with a mounting crisis with Persia. Muhammad Shah had marched from Tehran in the late summer of 1837 to attack the mountain principality of Herat, on the eastern borders of his dominions. Herat, the westernmost of the three principal Afghan states, stood at the beginning of the routes to Kabul and Kandahar, and thence to the Indian frontier. Its conquest by Persia, it was believed in London and Calcutta, would be tantamount to giving Russia an outpost from which to conduct intrigues among the tribes and states adjacent to India; for the Russian envoy at Tehran had encouraged the Shah to make the attempt on Herat, and Russia had the right, granted in the Treaty of Gulistan in 1813 and confirmed in the Treaty of Turkmanchai in 1828, to station consuls or commercial agents wherever within the Persian dominions the good of commerce might require. It was a right that Britain did not possess. McNeill, the British Minister at the Persian court, followed the Shah to Herat in March 1838 to try to persuade him to abandon the siege of the town; but before he left Tehran he had warned both Palmerston and the Governor-General of India, Lord Auckland, that more active measures might have to be adopted to compel the Shah to heed his advice. Among them McNeill had suggested the seizure and occupation of the Persian island of Kharag, situated off Bushire, the principal port on the Persian side of the Gulf.

It was against this background that the news of Mehemet 'Ali's projected bid for independence was received in London. On 9 June Sir John Hobhouse, the President of the India Board and Palmerston's closest colleague in the Cabinet, wrote to the Governor-General Auckland:

We must take part with the Sultan, and assuredly have the

---

23 [P.R.O.] F.O. 78/342, Campbell to Palmerston, 21 May 1838 (No. 35), enclosing Faisal ibn Turki to Khurshid Pasha, 9 Dhu'l-Qadah 1253/ 4 February 1838.
24 Dodwell, *Founder of Modern Egypt*, p. 171.

power of doing so with more effect than any of the other great continental sovereigns. Not only the shores of the Red Sea, but the Pachalic of Bagdad is within reach of your Indian forces, and I think it by no means improbable that you may have to send troops both to one and the other. At any rate, you will, of course, occupy Aden at *once*. You have bargained for it, and it does not belong to Mahomet Ali, and, even before this letter reaches you, I trust either you or Sir Robert Grant [Governor of Bombay] will have taken measures to accomplish that object. I cannot help thinking that the necessity which this contemplated declaration of independence by Mahomet Ali might create, would justify also the occupation of Karrack [Kharag]. The Viceroy of Egypt will, doubtless, follow up his declaration by an attack on the Pachalic of Bagdad; and we shall want a position for British Troops in the Gulph of Persia, which may be found *conveniently* at Karrack. True that place belongs to the Shah,—but, considering his conduct—there is no need of much delicacy. We might occupy it first, and offer to buy it afterwards; and, in the meantime, that step, so decisive, might assist Macneill in his negotiations at Herat.

I say all this to you for your consideration—but, if the Pacha of Egypt should actually declare his independence, the government here must not leave these matters to your discretion, but give you positive directions how to act.[25]

Auckland had already decided to act. On 1 May he ordered Sir Robert Grant, the Governor of Bombay, to despatch as large a naval force as possible to the Gulf, together with a detachment of troops from the Bombay Army, and to hold them there in readiness for any service that McNeill might think desirable.[26] The expeditionary force, consisting of five hundred sepoys with two sixpounder guns, sailed on 4 June, accompanied by the steam frigate *Semiramis*, the armed steamer *Hugh Lindsay*, the brig *Tigris*, and the sloop *Coote*, all of the Indian Navy. Before it left,

---

25 [I.O.] Home Miscellaneous series, Vol. 838, Hobhouse to Auckland, 9 June 1838. Vols. 833-862 of the Home Miscellaneous series contain that portion of the Broughton (Hobhouse) Papers which is deposited with the India Office Library. The remainder of the Broughton Papers are in the British Museum (Add. Mss. 36467-36476).
26 Accounts and Papers, 1839, Vol. 40, Paper 131 IV (H. of C.), letter 2, W. H. Macnaghten (Secy. to Govt. of India) to J. P. Willoughby, 1 May 1838.

Grant, unwilling to have the troops cooped up on the ships in the Gulf for an indefinite period, sent orders to the Political Resident at Bushire to land them, on arrival, on Kharag Island.[27] On 7 June, having received no satisfactory answer from the Shah to his demand of three weeks previously that the siege of Herat be lifted, McNeill struck his flag in the Persian camp and set out for Tehran and the Turkish frontier.[28] On 13 June the expeditionary force from Bombay dropped anchor in Bushire Roads, and two days later the troops were put ashore on Kharag Island.[29]

Even before McNeill had left the Shah's camp Palmerston had sent him instructions to inform that monarch "that the British Government cannot view with indifference his project of conquering Afghanistan", that "the British Government must look upon his enterprise as undertaken in a spirit of hostility towards British India", and that "if this project be perservered in . . . Great Britain may take such steps as she may think best calculated to provide for the security of the possessions of the British Crown".[30] McNeill, who was at Tabriz when these instructions reached him, deputed Colonel Stoddart, a member of his mission, to convey Palmerston's warning to the Shah. Stoddart arrived in the Persian Camp in August to find the Shah in both a gloomier and a more reasonable frame of mind than he had been in two months earlier. A grand assault on Herat by the Persian forces in late June had been repulsed with heavy losses, and the presence of the British expeditionary force in the Gulf, and rumours of an army gathering in India to march against him through Afghanistan, had made him uneasy. After a show of reluctance he yielded to Stoddart's representations, and on 9 September the siege of Herat was raised.[31]

Before news of what had happened reached London the Cabinet had decided that whatever further action might prove necessary to save Herat and to provide for the future security of the Indian frontier would have to be taken in Afghanistan, and not by means of an attack upon Persia from the Gulf. The occupation of Kharag Island would continue, pending the adjustment of British differences with Persia, and the Shah might afterwards be asked to agree to its permanent retention as a base for the

---

27 A. and P. 1839, Vol 40, Paper 131 IV (H. of C., letter 4, Proceedings of an Extraordinary Council of the Bombay Govt., 19 May 1838.
28 [I.O.] Persia and P. Gulf, Vol. 60, McNeill to Palmerston, Meshed, 25 June 1838.
29 [I.O.] Enclosures to Bombay Secret Letters Recd., Vol. 10, enclos. to Sec. Letter 14 of 14 July 1838, Hennell to Secy, to Govt., Bombay, 20 June 1838 (No. 38 Pol. Dept.).
30 [P.R.O.] F.O. 60/55, Palmerston to McNeill, 21 May 1838 (No. 29).
31 A. and P., 1839, Vol. 40, Paper c. 171 (H. of C.), letters 98, 100, McNeill to Palmerston, 11 September, 6 October, 1838.

Indian Navy squadron maintained in the Gulf for the protection of seaborne commerce.[32] The preference for Afghanistan as the theatre of action had been Auckland's all along, and he had tended, from the start, to regard the expedition to the Gulf with disfavour. "I do not quite like this expedition," he wrote to Hobhouse barely a fortnight after it had sailed, "for I always dislike small armaments. or indefinite objects, and if it were to do again, I should be more precise in my instructions to the Government of Bombay, to have cruisers and steamers at Bushire, and otherwise only to keep a small body of troops in readiness."[33] This attitude soon hardened into a disposition to view anything that developed in the Gulf as an irritating distraction from the real business at hand in Afghanistan, which, in turn, led Auckland to underestimate, and then to react inadequately to, the threat to the British position in the Gulf that now developed from the Egyptian conquest of Najd.

Command of the Egyptian troops in Najd was transferred in May 1838 to Khurshid Pasha, who set up his headquarters at 'Anaiza, roughly two hundred miles to the north-west of Riyad.[34] He spent the summer there, consolidating the Egyptian hold on the country and building up a supply depot. Reinforcements of troops, numbering about 2,000, were sent to him, and with these he set out in late September for Riyad. There he joined forces with the Amir Khalid and shortly afterwards began to advance eastwards into Hasa. Ahead of him he sent messengers to the Shaikhs of Bahrain and Kuwait, informing them of his advance and asking them to provide supplies for his troops when they reached the Gulf coast. Faisal ibn Turki, who would appear to have relented of his earlier submission to Mehemet 'Ali, prepared to meet Khurshid in the vicinity of Riyad and to conduct a fighting retreat to Hasa, whose defence he had left in the hands of the province's governor, 'Umar ibn 'Ufaisan.[35] For two months Faisal managed, by skill and courage, to hold back the Egyptians and Khalid, but by early December Khurshid Pasha had shut him up in Dilam, about fifty miles south of Riyad, and Khalid had reached the Hasa coast at Qatif. Before the month was out Faisal was forced to surrender, and 'Umar

---

32 [I.O.] Board's Drafts: Secret Despatches to India, Vol. 10, Draft to Gov.-Gen.-in-Council, 24 October 1838 (Most Secret).

33 [British Museum] Add. Ms. 36473, Auckland to Hobhouse, Simla, 17 June 1838.

34 [P.R.O.] F.O. 78/343, Campbell to Palmerston, 2 July 1838 (No. 43), enclosing Khurshid Pasha to Husain Pasha (principal A.D.C. to Mehemet 'Ali), 'Anaiza. 4 Rabi' I, 1254/28 May 1838.

35 [I.O.] Persia and P. Gulf, Vol. 62, Hennell to Sec. Committee, Bushire, 26 October 1838; Lieut.-Col. R. Taylor to Sec. Committee, Baghdad, 11 November 1838 (No. 36 Sec. Dept.).

ibn 'Ufaisan gave up the fight in Hasa and escaped to Bahrain.[36]

The first word that reached Palmerston of Khurshid Pasha's advance from 'Anaiza came from Campbell at Cairo, but it was from Lieutenant-Colonel Taylor, the Resident at Baghdad, and not from Campbell, that he first learned that Khurshid's objective was probably the Gulf coast and possibly Bahrain. On 29 November he sent the following despatch to Campbell:

> Advices . . . which Her Majesty's Government have recently received from Bagdad represent the Egyptian forces as being about to cross the Peninsula of Arabia to Lahsa and Katif, with the ultimate purpose of taking possession of the Island of Bahrein in the Persian Gulf.
>
> I have to instruct you to ask Mehemet Ali whether the fact is so; and you will add that Her Majesty's Government hope and trust that he will upon full consideration abandon any intention of establishing himself on the Persian Gulf, because, as you have already declared to him, such a scheme on his part could not be viewed with indifference by the British Government.[37]

Palmerston was confident that the warning would suffice to deter the Viceroy from pursuing any further adventures in Arabia, not only on the eastern side of peninsula but also in the south-west. Writing to Hobhouse on 12 December to suggest that the troops on Kharag Island, if they were no longer needed there, might be employed in effecting an occupation of Aden, he declared:

> Auckland need make no ceremonies with Mahomet Ali, nor be under any apprehension about offending him. Mahomet Ali would not dare move his little finger in hostility to England, or in serious opposition to anything which we might do, with a view to our own interests; and the Karrack garrison would, no doubt, explain very clearly to the Sultan of Aden any point connected with the cession of that place, about which the Sul-

---

36 [I.O.] Persia and P. Gulf, Vol 63, Hennell to McNeill, 1 November 1838 to Sec. Committee, 18 December 1838; *Bombay Selections* XXIV, p. 445, Kemball, "Sketch of Wahabees".
37 [P.R.O.] F.O. 78/343, Palmerston to Campbell, 29 November 1838 (No. 30).

tan may, upon second thoughts, have felt any doubts.[38]

A month later, in January 1839, Aden was taken, against the opposition of the local Sultan, by an expeditionary force from Bombay. Earlier that month Campbell had delivered Palmerston's protest to the Egyptian Government. Mehemet 'Ali was then absent in the Sudan, and the only reply that Campbell could get from his minister, Boghos Bey, was an assurance that the message would be forwarded to the Viceroy, and a denial that the Viceroy had any designs on Bahrain. Boghos Bey, Campbell noted, made no reference to the Egyptian occupation of Hasa.[39] By the beginning of January Khurshid Pasha had garrisoned the principal ports along the Hasa coast, Qatif, 'Uqair and Saihat, with Egyptian troops, and had despatched agents to Kuwait and Bahrain, and to the shaikhs of the Muntafiq tribe, near Basra, to procure supplies. He himself set up camp at Sulaimiya, a few miles to the north of Dilam, on the route between Riyad and Hufuf. At the end of February his personal physician, Joseph Arton, arrived at Bushire with letters from the Pasha for the Political Resident, Captain Hennell, and the commander of the British garrison on Kharag Island. Arton, who described himself as a Frenchman but who was more probably a Syrian, said that he had come to procure brandy, wine and other necessities for the Pasha. In his letter to Hennell Khurshid dropped entirely the pretence which had hitherto been maintained, that the campaign in central and eastern Arabia had been fought on behalf of Khalid ibn Sa'ud. Najd, he declared, had been subdued and restored to the rightful authority of Mehemet 'Ali, and Bahrain, which for several years had been tributary to the Wahhabis, would likewise be forced to submit to the Viceroy of Egypt. Faisal ibn Turki had been captured and was on his way to Cairo. Those of his adherents who, like 'Umar ibn 'Ufaisan, had taken refuge on Bahrain would be captured, and the treasure that they had taken with them impounded. No harm would come to those inhabitants of Bahrain who had trading connexions with the British as a result of the occupation of the island by Egyptian troops.[40]

Khurshid had hoped, before he wrote to Hennell, to be able to present him with a *fait accompli*. In January he had sent an emissary, Muhammad Effendi, to Bahrain to demand from Shaikh 'Abdullah ibn Ahmad

---

38 [I.O.] Home Misc., Vol. 839, Palmerston to Hobhouse, 12 December 1838.
39 [P.R.O.] F.O. 78/373, Campbell to Palmerston, 21, 26 January 1839 (Nos. 2, 4).
40 [I.O.] Enclos. to Bombay Sec. Letters, Vol. 12, enclos. to Sec. Letter 41 of 13 April 1839, Hennell to Willoughby, 2 March 1839 (No. 14 Sec. Dept.), enclosing Khurshid Pasha to Hennell, 24 Dhu'l-Qadah 1254/9 February 1839.

the surrender of 'Umar ibn 'Ufaisan and the treasure he reputedly had with him. Shaikh 'Abdullah was also told that the attendance of his sons was required at the Pasha's camp, presumably to act as hostages, and that he was expected to resume payment of the tribute he had formerly paid to Riyad, plus arrears for the past few years. It was not clear at the time whether the last demand was being preferred in the name of the Amir Khalid ibn Sa'ud or in that of Mehemet 'Ali. 'Abdullah ibn Ahmad tried to buy off the Egyptian agent with the offer of $M.T. 13,000 in cash, and when this was refused he declared that he could not comply with Khurshid Pasha's demands because he was a Persian subject. This said, he promptly sent off a letter to the Prince-Governor of Fars, offering to place himself under Persian protection and to pay tribute.[41]

Two months earlier, when the Egyptians were pushing into Hasa and 'Abdullah ibn Ahmad was anxiously observing their progress, he had made a similar offer to Hennell. The Resident had passed the offer to Bombay without comment at the time, but later, when asked his opinion by the authorities there, he expressed the view that, while a British protectorate over Bahrain would be advantageous in counter-balancing the ascendancy that Mehemet 'Ali seemed likely to acquire over the Arabian maritime tribes as a result of his conquest of Najd and Hasa, the embarrassments to which a formal alliance with the Al Khalifah might give rise, especially if the British Government were to be committed to the defence of their possessions in Qatar, would outweigh any such advantage. Hennell considered the maintenance of Bahrain's independence essential to the peace of the Gulf, but he believed that Khurshid Pasha could be dissuaded from violating it by a warning to leave the island alone.[42] A few days after voicing this opinion Hennell was forced to revise it, or at least the last part of it, by the arrival of Joseph Arton with Khurshid's letter.

Arton told Hennell's assistant, Lieutenant T. Edmunds, that Khurshid was ready to invade Bahrain but was waiting to see what the British reaction to such a move might be. He was also waiting for transports from the Red Sea, which were expected to arrive shortly. Hennell was inclined to believe that Bahrain could hold out against Khurshid, at least until the transports arrived, but Edmunds was not so sure. "... An enterprising fellow like Koorshid Pasha, who has marched victoriously from the Red Sea to the Persian Gulf, and who now perfectly overawes the coast, can hardly

---

41 [I.O.] Persia and P. Gulf, Vol. 64, Hennell to Sec. Committee, 24 January, 17 February 1839; Taylor to Sec. Committee, 21 March 1839.
42 [1.0.] Enclos. to Bombay Sec. Letters, Vol. 12, enclos. to Sec. Letter 41 of 13 April 1839, Hennell to Willoughby, 22 February 1839 (No. 13 Sec. Dept.).

Mehemet 'Ali's Expedition to the Persian Gulf 1837-1840

find much difficulty in getting boats to carry his troops across the narrow sea that divides the Island from the main."[43] Nor did Edmunds think that the Egyptian commander would be restrained by any protests that the British authorities in the Gulf might make to him. ". . . This much is evident, that the Pasha and his troops are most impatient to get to Bharein on account of the Dollars innumerable and sacks of pearls which they flatter themselves will be found there. One item alone is quite enough to excite the cupidity of such forces as these, and that is the 400,000 Dollars which they say (but probably it is an immense exaggeration) Fysul's Wuzeer [wazir], who had taken refuge with the Sheikh of Bahrain, carried off with him."[44] Rather than make protests, Edmunds reflected, "surely it would be easier to arrange the affair by making Bharein give up the refugees, or at any rate the valuables they brought with them, than hereafter to have to eject this Pasha with three tails and his army. He must be a man of talent for the Arabs on the line between Medina and Bharein have been so well managed and conciliated (as well as thumped at first) that they alone garrison the different posts and keep open the communication with Egypt".[45] Despite the fact that he had been reporting Khurshid's progress towards the Gulf to his superiors in India for the past three months, Hennell was still without orders from them on the line of policy he should adopt towards the Pasha when he reached the Gulf. In replying to Khurshid, therefore, he had to limit himself to telling him that the British Government would probably view with concern any hostile move against Bahrain, which was a signatory of the General Treaty of Peace of 1820,[46] and to asking him to postpone his proposed attack on the island until he, Hennell, had had time to refer the matter to Bombay and to receive instructions. If Khurshid refused to wait, then he was to give Hennell sufficient warning before making his assault to allow the Resident to send the Gulf squadron to the island to protect the lives and property of British subjects there.[47] Hennell despatched his reply to Qatif with Edmunds in the brig *Tigris*, with orders to find out all he could about the disposition of Khurshid's troops and their future move-

---

43 [B.M.] Add. Ms. 36473, Edmunds to Willoughby, Bushire, 5 March 1839.

44 *Ibid.*

45 *Ibid.* Noting that Khurshid received his despatches in 21 days from Cairo, Edmunds drily suggested that the British Government might well make use of the same service.

46 The General Treaty was concluded after the expedition against the Piratical Shaikhdoms in 1819-20. The Al Khalifah, though not given to piracy, were admitted to the treaty at their own request. The treaty provided for a cessation of piracy by the maritime Arabian tribes, which was to be enforced by the British Government.

47 [I.O.] Enclos. to Bombay Sec. Letters, Vol. 12, enclos. to Sec. Letter 41 of 13 April 1839, Hennell to Khurshid Pasha, 28 February 1839.

ments. Edmunds reached Qatif on 24 March. The garrison commander, Muhammad Qashif, told him that Khurshid was still at Sulaimiya with the main body of his troops, numbering 3,000 men. He had asked for a reinforcement of 1,000 cavalry and 2,000 infantry from the reserve of 15,000 troops held at Madinah under Sulaiman Pasha, and these could be expected to reach Sulaimiya, by forced marches, within 25 days. It seemed reasonable to conclude, Edmunds reported to Hennell, that the Pasha would not attack Bahrain until the reinforcements had reached him.[48]

From Qatif Edmunds crossed to Bahrain to see 'Abdullah ibn Ahmad. He found the Al Khalifah ruler comparatively unperturbed by Khurshid's threats. Bahrain, he said, could hold out for a year against the Egyptians, but it would be useful if the British Government would forbid them to advance any further. Mehemet 'Ali, he believed, wanted Bahrain as a base from which to mount an expedition against Basra, using the Al Khalifah's ships for the purpose. Although he had no desire to ally himself with Mehemet 'Ali, 'Abdullah went on, he had offered to pay him a "trifling tribute of $ M.T. 3,000 *per annum* to placate him.[49] What 'Abdullah did not tell Edmunds was that he had been visited by an emissary from the Prince-Governor of Fars, whom the Prince had sent to Bahrain with a *khel'at*, or robe of honour, for the Shaikh, in the fond expectation that he would return to Shiraz with the tribute offered earlier by 'Abdullah.[50] Abdullah was simply hedging his bets. The Egyptians were close by in strength; the British had failed to respond to his overtures for a protectorate and had given him little encouragement to resist Khurshid Pasha; the Persians did not have the naval means to assist him, and, in any case, he had no wish to avoid Egyptian tutelage at the cost of submitting to that of Persia. There seemed, in addition, every chance that a new crisis was developing between Britain and Persia which might radically alter the distribution of power in the Gulf. Muhammad Shah, after his return to Tehran from Herat, had failed to redeem the pledge he had made to Stoddart in August 1838 to comply with the British Government's demands. At the beginning of 1839, therefore, McNeil withdrew the British mission from Tabriz, where it had been since the previous summer, to Erzerum, in Turkish territory,

---

48 [I.O.] Enclos. to Bombay Sec. Letters, Vol. 13, enclos. to Sec. Letter 67 of 18 May 1839, Edmunds to Hennell, n.d., enclosed in Hennell to Willoughby, 10 April 1839 (No. 22 Sec. Dept.).

49 *Ibid.*

50 [I.O.] Persia and P. Gulf, Vol. 64, Hennell to Sec. Committee, 15 March 1839. The emissary was a certain Haji Kassim, the former supercargo of a trading vessel. He came with an escort of ten *sirbaz*, or soldiers. (See [I.O.] *Bombay Selections* XXIV, p. 388, Lieut. A. B. Kemball, "Historical Sketch of Uttoobee Tribe of Arabs, 1832-44".)

Mehemet 'Ali's Expedition to the Persian Gulf 1837-1840

thus severing diplomatic relations with Persia. Earlier, Palmerston had decided that should such a step prove necessary, the Political Residency in the Gulf should not be withdrawn but should remain at Bushire and carry on its normal functions.[51] What Palmerston perhaps did not foresee was that the Resident, as the only British official representative remaining in Persia, would become a target for the Shah's hostility. Already several members of the Residency, or persons connected with it, had been involved in incidents at Bushire, and these increased in frequency and unpleasantness after the severance of diplomatic relations and the arrival of a new governor in the town early in 1839. So seriously did the authorities at Bombay view these incidents that in late February they asked the commander-in-chief on the East Indies station, Rear-Admiral Sir Frederick Maitland, who was then on a visit to Bombay, to sail for the Gulf and show the flag.

Maitland left Bombay on 23 February with H.M.S. *Wellesley* (74 guns) and H.M. brig *Algerine*, and arrived off Bushire on 20 March. In the next few days he found himself subjected, as Captain Hennell had been subjected for some time, to a sequence of deliberate insults by the Governor of Bushire, the *qadi* (or judge), and other officials. These culminated in his being forbidden to embark or disembark at the Residency landing stage, which faced the open sea on the outskirts of the town. Instead, he was told, he would have to land at the customs house, in the inner harbour, and make his way to the Residency through the town. As it had long been the practice for British political and naval officers to land directly at the Residency steps, Maitland refused to comply with the order. On 25 March, as he waited with Hennell at the Residency landing stage to board his gig, he and the Resident were fired upon by Persian soldiers who had been stationed nearby. Hennell demanded an apology for the incident from the governor and a guarantee that no further interference with communication between the Residency and the squadron would take place. When, by nightfall, it was apparent that neither apology nor guarantee was forthcoming, Hennell decided to strike his flag, and on 29 March he withdrew the Residency to Kharag Island.[52]

---

51 A precedent for such a step had been found in the retention of the Residency at Bushire in 1807-8, when diplomatic relations were broken off as a result of the Shah's reception of the French mission under General Gardane. (See [I.O.] Board's Sec. and Gen. Pol. Corresp., Vol. 8 (i). Backhouse to Gordon, 20 March 1838; Gordon to Backhouse, same date.)

52 [P.R.O.] Admiralty 1/219, Maitland to Chas. Wood (Secy. to Admiralty), 1, 7 April and 1 May 1839 (Nos. 33, 34 and 39); [I.O.] enclos. to Bombay Sec. Letters, Vol. 13, enclos. to Sec. Letter 55 o f 8 May 1839, Hennell to Willoughby, 30 March 1839 (No. 23 Pol. Dept.)

Palmerston, when he heard what had happened, was highly annoyed, and he expressed his annoyance in forcible terms to the Shah's ambassador who was then in London. "... Had the Admiral," he told him, "on arriving on board turned his guns upon the town and knocked it about their ears, in my opinion he would have been justified in so doing."[53] Auckland reacted differently, placing the blame for the withdrawal upon Maitland and Hennell for not having acted in a sufficiently conciliatory manner towards the Persians.[54] It was hardly a fair criticism to make since Hennell had been authorised by both the Bombay Government and McNeill to withdraw the Residency if conditions warranted it.[55] Furthermore, Auckland himself had failed to give the Resident any instructions at all on what his behaviour should be if the situation at Bushire became intolerable.[56] Wherever the blame for it, if any, may lie, the apparent rout of Maitland and Hennell by the "rabble of Bushire",[57] which was how the Gulf tribes saw it, reduced British prestige in the Gulf at a time when prestige was almost all that the British Government had to rely upon to meet the Egyptian challenge.

At the beginning of March 1839 Auckland had received a copy of Palmerston's instructions to Campbell of 29 November to warn Mehemet 'Ali against attempting to establish himself on the Gulf. On 13 March Auckland sent orders to Bombay that Hennell was to use his influence to check the further encroachments of the Egyptians on the Arabian coast. Maitland should be requested to support the Resident's efforts, particularly

---

53 [I.O.] Persia and P. Gulf, Vol. 65, "Memorandum of the Substance of a Conference between Lord Palmerston and Hoosein Khan held at Stanhope Street, 19 June 1839, by J. B. Fraser".

54 [1.0.1 Enclos. to Bombay Sec. Letters, Vol. 14, enclos. to Sec. Letter 76 of 12 June 1839, T. H. Maddock (Secy. to Govt. of India) to Willoughby, Simla, 9 May 1839.

55 [I.O.] Enclos. to Bombay Sec. Letters, Vol. 10, enclos. to Sec. Letter 30 of 24 October 1838, Willoughby to Hennell, 13 September 1838 (No. 232 Sec. Dept.); and Vol. 15, enclos. to Sec. Letter 103 of 10 September 1839, McNeill to Hennell, Tabriz, 28 December 1838.

56 Auckland also accused Maitland of having unduly influenced Hennell in reaching his decision to retire from Bushire, to which Maitland retorted that he was not in the habit of submitting to the kind of insults to which he had been subjected by the Persians. ([I.O.] Enclos. to Bombay Sec. Letters, Vol. 14, enclos. to Sec. Letter 92 of 31 July 1839, Maitland to Sir Jas. Carnac (Gov. of Bombay), Trincomali, 22 June 1839). Auckland later withdrew his criticism, conceding that the situation at Bushire had deteriorated to such a degree that Hennell must eventually have been compelled to withdraw. ([I.O.] Enclos. to Bombay Sec. Letters, Vol. 15, enclos. to Sec. Letter 103 of 10 September 1839, Madock to Willoughby, Simla, 1 August 1839.

57 [I.O.] Enclos. to Bombay Sec. Letters, Vol. 19, enclos. to Sec. Letter 10 of 28 February 1840, Edmunds to Willoughby, 22 January 1840 (No. 2 Sec. Dept.).

with respect to preserving the independence and integrity of Bahrain. He should afford the Shaikh of Bahrain "every encouragement to resistance and all support short of placing himself in actual collision with the Egyptian authorities".[58] There was no need at this stage, Auckland believed, to do anything more. Khurshid Pasha had not yet had time to receive from Cairo any instructions that Mehemet 'Ali might have issued to him, following the receipt of Palmerston's protest, and Auckland was fully confident both that such orders would be issued and that Khurshid would act upon them.[59]

The Governor-General's instructions were transmitted to Hennell by H.M. sloop *Cruiser*, which left Bombay on 2 April to reinforce Maitland's squadron in the Gulf. *Cruiser* also carried a second and more strongly worded set of instructions from James Farish, the acting Governor of Bombay, which Farish had drawn up after receiving from Hennell, a few days earlier, Khurshid Pasha's letter of 9 February, threatening to subdue Bahrain by force. Farish directed Hennell, in reply, to remonstrate firmly with Khurshid against his projected attack, and to warn him that if he persisted in it he would run the risk of disturbing friendly relations between Britain and Egypt.[60] Before these instructions reached him Hennell had decided to act. Maitland had warned him in the second week of April that the state of *Wellesley*'s supplies would not allow him to remain in the Gulf much longer but would compel him to return to Bombay before the month was out. It was essential, therefore, if Hennell wished to make a demonstration of British strength on the Arabian shore, that it be made without delay. The best way, Maitland suggested, would be for him to cruise along the Arabian coast on his way out of the Gulf, beginning at Bahrain. Hennell agreed, and addressed a letter to Khurshid Pasha, to be forwarded by Maitland, informing the Egyptian commander of Palmerston's protest of 29 November, a copy of which had just reached Hennell from London.[61]

Maitland sailed from Kharag in *Wellesley* on 17 April. With him went Edmunds, the Assistant Resident, and Commodore G. B. Brucks, the of-

---

58 [I.O.] Enclos. to Bombay Sec. Letters, Vol. 12, enclos. to Sec. Letter 41 of 13 April 1839, Maddock to Willoughby, Pinjore, 13 March 1839.
59 *Ibid.*
60 Same series, volume and collection, Minute by Farish, 1 April 1839, and Willoughby to Hennell, same date (No. 671 Sec. Dept.).
61 I.O.] Enclos. to Bombay Sec. Letters, Vol. 13, enclos. to Sec. Letter 67 of 18 May 1839, Hennell to Willoughby, 10 April 1839 (No. 22 Sec. Dept.), enclosing Hennell to Khurshid Pasha, same date.

ficer commanding the Gulf squadron, in H.C.C. *Elphinstone*. Bahrain was raised on 21 April, and the next day two of Shaikh 'Abdullah's sons came on board. Their father, they explained, was away in Qatar. He had received no further demands from Khurshid Pasha since Edmunds' visit the previous month, and he was not apprehensive of any imminent attack on the island. Certainly, as Maitland noticed, there seemed to have been no attempt to put it in a state of defence. On 23 April, as *Wellesley* was standing out from Bahrain, Shaikh Sultan ibn Shakhbut, brother of the ruler of Abu Dhabi, came aboard to assure Maitland of the firm friendship existing between Bahrain and Abu Dhabi. The next day, as *Wellesley* was crossing the Gulf to Lingah, on the Persian coast, she fell in with *Cruiser*. The receipt of Auckland's and Farish's instructions did not cause Maitland to change his plans: *Wellesley*'s provisions were too low and in any case he believed that the essence of the instructions had been acted upon by Hennell.

At Lingah Maitland was warmly received by the chief, Sa'id ibn Qadib, who told him that he did not fear the Egyptians himself but he was concerned for the safety of his kinsmen on the Arabian shore, the Qawasim of Sharjah and Ras al-Khaima. Maitland found that concern fully shared by the paramount chief of the Qawasim, Sultan ibn Saqr, when he saw him at Ras al-Khaima on 27 April. Shaikh Sultan declared that the Arabs alone were incapable of stopping Khurshid Pasha, and they looked to the British, therefore, for protection. Maitland informed him of Palmerston's protest and of the other measures taken to halt Khurshid, but he also expressed the belief that the maritime tribes were capable of resisting the Pasha if they were prepared to present a united front to him. Commodore Brucks had informed him that the tribes of the Qasimi confederacy[62] alone, which encompassed the shaikdoms of Rams, Ras al-Khaima, Umm al-Qaiwain, 'Ajman and Sharjah, could raise 11,000 fighting men. Sultan ibn Saqr was not encouraged by Maitland's argument: the mutual hatreds of the tribes, he said, would prevent them from uniting for their common defence, although there was a chance that they might do so, for a time at least, if they were led by Hennell. Privately Maitland was inclined to agree with him. "It is . . . lamentable to observe the total apathy shewn by all the chiefs to the approaching danger, and that, notwithstanding the fears they have expressed, no measures have been undertaken to meet it."[63] A

---

62 The term "Qawasim", and its singular, "Qasimi" strictly applies to the ruling family of Sharjah and Ras al-Khaima, but it is used loosely to denote the heterogeneous collection of tribes, sections, and individuals that inhabits those two ports.
63 "[P.R.O.] Adm. 1/220, Maitland to Wood, 2 May 1839 (No. 40), enclosing "Notes of a Conference between Rear-Admiral Sir F. L. Maitland, K.C.B., and . . . Shaikhs in the

visit from the Shaikh of Dubai on the morning of 30 April did nothing to alter Maitland's views. He sailed from Ras al-Khaima later that morning, and cleared the Gulf soon after noon.[64] Captain Edmunds stayed behind at Ras al-Khaima to arrange the maritime truce for the coming year, and on 1 May he received all the Trucial Shaikhs on board *Elphinstone*.[65] From them he learned that a party of about 150 armed men from Najd had landed at Sharjah in mid-April. They had come from Qatif by sea and were led by Sa'ad ibn Mutlaq, who had formerly been the Amir Faisal's *na'ib*, or lieutenant, at the Buraimi Oasis. Sa'ad ibn Mutlaq had left Buraimi two or three months earlier, after the surrender of Faisal, to return to Najd, and he was now representing himself as being in the service of Faisal's successor, Khalid ibn Sa'ud. In his absence, the Na'im, the dominant tribe in the Buraimi Oasis, had ejected the garrison he had left behind in the principal fort of the oasis, and, declaring that "they would rather bury themselves in its ruins than give it up",[66] they had appealed for aid to Saiyid Hamud ibn Azzan, the Al Bu Sa'id governor of Sauhar, on the Batinah coast of Oman. He had responded by sending his brother with 200 fighting men to the oasis. Sa'ad ibn Mutlaq, on his arrival at Sharjah, had informed Shaikh Sultan ibn Saqr that he had come to re-occupy the Buraimi forts in the name of Khalid ibn Sa'ud. Shaikh Sultan, or so he told Edmunds, was none too pleased by the news, but he was afraid not to welcome the *na'ib* lest he take offence and seek support from Sultan's powerful rival, Khalifah ibn Shakhbut of Abu Dhabi, the chief of the Bani Yas tribe. Edmunds

---

Persian Gulf, taken by Capt. Edmunds, Asst. Resident, between 22nd and 30th April, 1839". (Edmunds was promoted to captain and Hennell to major in the spring of 1839.)

64 *Ibid*. See also [P.R.O.] Adm. 50/214, Maitland's Journal, 17-30 April 1839, and [I.O.] Enclos. to Bombay Sec. Letters, Vol. 13, enclos. to Sec. Letter 67 of 18 May 1839, Maitland to Farish, 3 May 1839.

65 The Trucial System came into being in May 1835, when Captain Hennell, acting upon a suggestion put forward by Sir John Malcolm a few years earlier, when he was Governor of Bombay, persuaded the principal shaikhs of the Pirate Coast to agree to a truce at sea, to be watched over and enforced by the British Government, for the duration of the approaching pearling season. The truce was renewed every subsequent spring for the next seven years, its duration gradually being extended to a full year. In 1843 the Piratical Shaikhs agreed to a truce of ten years' duration, and in 1853 they signed the Treaty of Maritime Peace in Perpetuity. The Designation "Piratical Shaikhs" was replaced, in time, by that of "Trucial Shaikhs", and the Pirate Coast became known as the "Trucial Coast" or "Trucial Oman". The gathering on board *Elphinstone* on 1 May 1839 was an unusual one, inasmuch as it was the first occasion on which all the shaikhs had met together in the presence of the Resident or his assistant. Usually their various jealousies and rivalries had prevented them from doing so.

66 [I.O.] *Bombay Selections* XXIV, p. 466, Kemball, "Sketch of Wahabees".

advised him to get rid of Sa'ad ibn Mutlaq as quickly as possible, whatever his apprehensions, since it was highly likely that the *na'ib* was in the pay of Khurshid Pasha and not of Khalid ibn Sa'ud.[67]

The extension of Egyptian activities into south-eastern and north-eastern Arabia was what Hennell had been fearing for some time. Rumours had been seeping through, even before Edmunds' visit to Ras al-Khaima, that Egyptian agents were active in the Trucial Shaikhdoms and at the head of the Gulf. On 5 May Hennell decided to send the Residency surgeon, Dr. T. Mackenzie, in the schooner *Emily*, to Kuwait, Muhammarah and Basra, to discover what basis, if any, there was for the rumours. Two days later he also sent the cruiser *Clive* to Kuwait with a letter for Khurshid Pasha, which *Clive's* commander was to give to the ruler, Shaikh Jabir ibn 'Abdullah, for forwarding. The letter, under flying seal, was a duplicate of one which Hennell had addressed to the Pasha on 29 April and sent to Qatif, after receiving Auckland's and Farish's instructions of the previous month, and which passed on the warning contained in those instructions. Hennell was counting upon the fact that the tone of the letter would convince Shaikh Jabir that the British Government were determined to stop Khurshid Pasha from moving beyond Hasa.[68] At least, Hennell hoped it would, for it was becoming more and more obvious to him that he would have to rely as much, if not more, upon his own wits to halt the Egyptian commander as upon any help he might get from India. Maitland was gone, and the two sloops that he had left behind him, *Cruiser* and *Algerine*, were under orders to follow him without delay to Bombay and Trincomali. By mid-May all the forces that Hennell had at his disposal were the two Indian Navy sloops, *Elphinstone* and *Clive*. The chances of his seeing any Royal Navy ships again for some time were very small, ". . . The station over which my command reaches," Maitland explained in a letter to Farish at the beginning of June, in reply to a request from the Governor for the despatch of a squadron, or at least a man-o'-war, to the Gulf as soon as possible, "is so very extensive, and the demands for the few ships attached to it are so numerous and pressing, that I cannot see any prospect of my being able to furnish a squadron of H.M. ships occasionally to visit the

---

67 [I.O.] Enclos. to Bombay Sec. Letters, Vol. 14, enclos. to Sec. Letter 87 of 16 July 1839, Edmunds to Hennell, 4 May 1839, and Mullah Husain (Res. Agent, Sharjah) to Hennell, 3 Rabi' I, 1255/17 May 1839.

68 [I.O.] Enclos. to Bombay Sec. Letters, Vol. 14, enclos. to Sec. Letter 76 of 12 June 1839, Hennell to Willoughby, 29 April, 7 May 1839 (Nos. 37, 41 Sec. Dept.), enclosing Hennell to Khurshid Pasha, 29 April 1839.

Persian Gulf...."⁶⁹

Hennell was no more fortunate in the backing he received from Auckland. The Governor-General told Farish in the third week of April, in reply to an urgent request from the Governor for guidance on the policy to be adopted towards Khurshid Pasha should he disregard the warnings already given him, that he believed that Khurshid must by then have heard from Cairo about Palmerston's protest of 29 November, and that, as a consequence, "the prosecution of his conquests in Arabia would, in all probability, have either been carried on with redoubled vigour in order that his conquest might be rendered as extensive as possible before it could be arrested by the strong remonstrance of the British Government, or they would have been suspended by orders from his master, the Viceroy of Egypt".⁷⁰ The fate of Bahrain would be determined by Khurshid Pasha or by Maitland. ". . . The necessity of further interference on the part of this Government to save Bahrein from falling into the hands of the Egyptian general will have been obviated, either by his having attacked it successfully before the admiral's arrival, or by the admiral's presence and interference having rescued it from attack."⁷¹ If Maitland, merely by his presence, failed to deter Khurshid from attacking Bahrain, then he would have to "exercise his discretion as to the most expedient method to be adopted for the defence of Bahrain".⁷²

When Auckland wrote these orders he was well aware that they would not be executed because Maitland was on his way out of the Gulf. On 10 May he wrote to Hobhouse: "I framed for Sir Frederick Maitland directions such as I thought would meet with the least hazard the tendency of our foreign policy; but I have felt my responsibility in doing so, and should be sorry to see new quarrels spring up in new places. It seems probable, however, that my instructions will not reach Sir F. Maitland before his return to Bombay and that they will, at least, have done no harm, and, in the meantime, the tone of Koorshid Pacha is said to have become less aggressive."⁷³ A fortnight later, when he knew for certain that Maitland

---

69 [I.O.] Bombay Sec. Letters Recd., Vol. 9 (i), Gov.-in-Council to Sec. Committee, 4 July 1839 (No. 85 Sec. Dept.), enclosing Maitland to Farish, Trincomali, 3 June 1839. There were fourteen vessels on the East Indies station in 1839-one ship, four frigates, and nine sloops or brigs. (C. Lloyd, "The Rating and Distribution of British Warships in the Nineteenth Century", *Mariner's Mirror*, April 1948, p. 114.)

70 [I.O.] Enclos. to Bombay Sec. Letters, Vol. 13, enclos. to Sec. Letter 55 of 8 May 1839, Maddock to Willoughby, Simla, 18 April 1839.

71 *Ibid.*

72 *Ibid.*

73 [I.O.] Home Misc., Vol. 841.

had left the Gulf, he confessed to Hobhouse that he did not know what to do. "I wish that you had sent me instructions upon the conduct to be observed towards Koorshid Pasha and Bahrein. I am afraid of doing too much or too little, and in the meantime am glad to expect by the Admiral's last despatch that it will not be necessary to do anything."[74] The indecision persisted. "I am glad to learn that Koorshid Pasha is not likely to make aggressions upon Bahrein," he confided to Farish in mid-June, "and that the instructions which with some hesitation I ventured to give for the protection of that Island will have been superfluous."[75] To Hobhouse he wrote: "I am anxious for instructions from you upon all that is occurring on the eastern and western sides of the Persian Gulph, though under present circumstances and with our present means we must perforce rest quiet in regard to both, and our influence may in consequence be impaired for a time. I ventured to issue to our cruisers strong instructions for the protection of the Island of Bahrein against Koorshid Pacha, but he seems to meditate no attack in that direction, and whether right or wrong, I shall have done neither good nor harm by them."[76]

The want of action or positive decision on Auckland's part was not due to mere irresolution. The Government of India's military and financial resources were already strained by the preparations for the venture into Afghanistan. Troops and ships had to be maintained at Aden to defend the town against local attack, and, possibly, assault by the Egyptians in the Yemen; while the altercation with China threatened to require the deployment of still more troops and ships in the Far East. The prospect of a campaign in the Gulf, therefore, was something that Auckland did not want to contemplate. "Military operations in that quarter," he told Farish in June, "may become desirable, but they cannot be so without ten thousand men, half a dozen ships of war, and two or three crores of money, and I need not add how unfavourable the present moment is to them."[77] Yet Auckland cannot be wholly absolved of blame for fearing to do too much or too little, and thereby resolving "that it will not be necessary to do anything"; for by arguing thus he was placing in jeopardy the whole British position in the Gulf, a position which it had taken thirty years to build up and one which was deemed essential to the security of British India. As Captain

---

74 [B.M.] Add. Ms. 36474, Auckland to Hobhouse, Simla, 25 May 1839.
75 [B.M.] Add. Ms. 37696, Auckland to Farish, Simla, 16 June 1839. Add. Mss. 37689-37718 comprise the private papers of George Eden, second Baron and first Earl of Auckland for the years, 1836-42.
76 [B.M.] Add. Ms. 36474, Auckland to Hobhouse, Simla, 18 June 1839.
77 [B.M.] Add. Ms. 37696, Auckland to Farish, Simla, 16 June 1839.

Mehemet 'Ali's Expedition to the Persian Gulf 1837-1840

Edmunds put it in a letter to the Chief Secretary at Bombay in March: ". . . The time is not distant when we must either extend to them [i.e. the littoral shaikdoms] our avowed protection or withdraw from interfering with the affairs of the Gulf further than by keeping a cruizer or two on the station for the sole purpose of protecting our trade, and letting Sheiks, Pachas, Egyptians, and Persians fight it out amongst themselves."[78]

This was Farish's view, also, and at the beginning of April he had advised Auckland to reconsider the question of extending British protection to Bahrain, while at the same time he instructed Major Hennell to sound Shaikh 'Abdullah ibn Ahmad on his conditions for a permanent connexion with the British Government.[79] Auckland's reaction to this advice was to issue the directions of 18 April, already noticed, for Maitland to cover Bahrain with his squadron; but he refused to entertain the notion of formal protection, basing his opposition on the objections expressed by Hennell two months earlier.[80] It would hardly have profited him to have done otherwise, for by this time, as will be seen shortly, the chance of redeeming the situation at Bahrain by positive action had been lost.

If Auckland did not fully realise what was at stake in the Gulf, or, if he did, felt unable to act upon the realisation, Palmerston did not suffer from a similar disability. On 9 May he learned for the first time, by way of a despatch from Hennell, of Khurshid Pasha's threat to reduce Bahrain by force.[81] On the same day he received a report from Campbell of the substance of a talk the Consul-General had had with Mehemet 'Ali, now back from the Sudan, on 2 April.[82] Mehemet 'Ali, at the interview, was inclined to minimize the significance of the campaign in Arabia, saying that its prime objects had been to protect Mecca and Madinah from the Wahhabis and to procure camels for the army of the Hijaz. The forces of Khurshid Pasha would be withdrawn within a few months, after which the government of Najd would devolve upon Khalid ibn Sa'ud. When Campbell asked about Bahrain, Mehemet Ali replied that Bahrain, like Kuwait,

---

78 [B.M.] Add. Ms. 36473, Edmunds to Willoughby, 5 March 1839.

79 [I.O.] Enclos. to Bombay Sec. Letters, Vol. 12, enclos. to Sec. Letter 41 of 13 April 1839, Minute by Farish, 1 April 1839, and Willoughby to Hennell, same date (No. 671 Sec. Dept.).

80 See above, p. 132, paragraph beginning "Two months earlier, when the Egyptians were pushing..."

81 See [I.O.1 Persia and P. Gulf, Vol. 64, Hennell to Sec. Committee, 28 February 1839.

82 Campbell also reported the arrival of the Amnir Faisal in Cairo on 26 March and his confinement in the same house as that in which the Amir Abdullah had been imprisoned in 1818. (See [P.R.O.] F.O. 78/373, Campbell to Palmerston, 6 April 1839 (No. 20).)

was a dependency of Najd and had paid tribute to the Al Sa'ud for many years. It was clear throughout the conversation that the Viceroy considered himself legally entitled to the government of Najd and its dependencies, and Campbell wondered whether he might not be justified in thinking so, seeing that the original *firman* to him from the Ottoman Sultan, ordering him to subdue and govern Najd, had never been revoked.[83] It was this last possibility that restrained Palmerston from taking a harsher line towards Mehemet 'Ali at this time than he did. On 11 May he wrote to Ponsonby at Constantinople, asking him to enquire of the Porte whether the Viceroy's recent conquests in Arabia had the Sultan's sanction, and to point out to the Ottoman Government that the security of the Pashaliq of Baghdad would be seriously compromised if Egyptian military and naval power were to be established on the Gulf.[84] That same day Palmerston instructed Campbell to await the outcome of Ponsonby's enquiries, and if these revealed that the Porte was equally opposed to the extension of Mehemet 'Ali's authority over central and eastern Arabia, he was to tell the Viceroy that "the British Government cannot permit him to establish his naval and military power on the shores of the Persian Gulf, and that if he should persevere in such projects, he must expect that a British force will dispossess him from any naval station at which he may attempt to establish himself on the Persian Gulf".[85] A little more than three weeks later, on 6 June, Palmerston received a despatch from Taylor, the Resident at Baghdad, describing in alarming terms the disorganized and defenceless state of the Pashaliq. He learned also, from a despatch from Hennell, of the arrival of Maitland in the Gulf in H.M.S. *Wellesley*.[86] Although aware that by this time Maitland would in all probability have left the Gulf, Palmerston had the Admiralty send him orders to protect Bahrain in the event of an Egyptian attack on the island. He himself wrote to Campbell, instructing him to inform Mehemet 'Ali of the issuance of these orders and to warn the Viceroy that if Khurshid Pasha tried to march on Basra, Maitland might resort to armed intervention to stop him.[87] Slightly more cautious

---

83 *Ibid.*
84 [P.R.O.] F.O. 78/352, Palmerston to Ponsonby, 11 May 1839 (No. 64).
85 [P.R.O.] F.O. 78/372, Palmerston to Campbell, 11 May 1839 (No. 10).
86 See [I.O.] Persia and P. Gulf, Vol. 64, Taylor to Sec. Committee, 8 April 1839 (No. 21 Sec. Dept.); Hennell to Sec. Committee, 21 March 1839.
87 [P.R.O.] Adm. 2/1695, Chas. Adam and Wm. Parker (Lords Commissioners) to Maitland, 14 June 1839; F.O. 78/372, Palmerston to Campbell, 15 June 1839 (No. 17). It was at this time, in a letter to Lord Granville on 10 June, that Palmerston made his famous outburst against Mehemet 'Ali: "For my own part I hate Mehemet Ali . . . etc."

instructions were sent by Hobhouse to Taylor at Baghdad. If Khurshid Pasha marched on Basra and the Pasha of Baghdad asked Taylor for help, the Resident was to make no promises of aid since he had no means at his immediate disposal with which to fulfil such promises. If Khurshid actually occupied Basra, Taylor was to send a British officer to him with a letter of protest and a warning that naval action might be taken against him to compel him to evacuate the town.[88]

Prompt though Palmerston's actions had been, their effectiveness had already been reduced by the changed situation in the Gulf in June 1839, especially with regard to Bahrain. On 2 June Campbell gave Mehemet 'Ali a copy of Auckland's orders of 18 April to Maitland to defend Bahrain against Khurshid Pasha, which Campbell had just received from Bombay. Mehemet 'Ali protested that Khurshid's only object in threatening Bahrain had been to protect himself against intrigues by the refugee Wahhabis on the island. Campbell, in turn, insisted that Mehemet 'Ali send positive instructions to Khurshid to cease from menacing Bahrain, on any pretext whatever. On 12 June Boghos Bey handed Campbell a copy of an order sent to Khurshid that day to refain from interfering with Bahrain in any way until the British Government had had time to consider and reply to the explanation offered by Mehemet 'Ali to Campbell in April.[89] It was an easy gesture for the Viceroy to make, for, whatever display he might put on, for Campbell's benefit, of his reluctance to forgo his incontestable right to Bahrain, of his sense of grievance at being asked to forgo it, and, at the same time, of his earnest desire to meet the wishes of the British Government, it was no more than a gesture. Bahrain had submitted to him and acknowledged his suzerainty for three months past.

On 27 May, Muhammad Effendi, one of Khurshid Pasha's confidential emissaries, arrived at Kharag Island to see Hennell. He had come by way of Kuwait, where he had spent the previous three weeks, so the ruler, Shaikh Jabir, informed Hennell by letter, gathering supplies for the Egyptian forces in Najd. According both to Shaikh Jabir and to the commander of the cruiser *Clive*, whom Hennell had sent to the head of the Gulf at the

---

(See Temperley, *The Crimea*, p. 89.)

88 [I.O.] Board's Drafts: Sec. Desp. to India, Vol. 10, Draft to Taylor, 13 June 1839 (No. 67 Most Secret). Privately, Hobhouse wrote to Auckland: "If circumstances had allowed you to spare us 5 or 6,000 bayonets, half of them British, we should have been inclined to send them to Bagdad, or, at least, in that direction, but we know you want your whole force for Indian service." ([I.O.] Home Misc., Vol. 839, Hobhouse to Auckland, 15 June 1839).

89 [P.R.O.] F.O. 78/374, Campbell to Palmerston, 15 June 1839 (No. 42), enclosing Mehemet 'Ali to Khurshid Pasha, 29 Rabi' I, 1255/12 June 1839.

beginning of the month to enquire into the activities of Egyptian agents, Kuwait stood in no immediate danger from Khurshid, who was then reported to be at Riyad. Dr. Mackenzie, the Residency surgeon, however, after visiting Basra and Muhammarah, as Hennell had asked him to do, reported that at both places it was believed that Khurshid would shortly march on Basra.[90] Muhammad Effendi, when he saw Hennell, gave no indication that such a move was imminent. Nor was there any indication of it in the letter that he brought Hennell from Khurshid. On the contrary, the letter was taken up almost wholly with Bahrain, and what the Pasha had to say was most disconcerting.

Replying to Hennell's letter to him of 28 February, in which the Resident had said that, while he had no specific instructions concerning Bahrain, he was certain that the British Government would take a serious view of any attempt to invade it, Khurshid told him that there was no longer any need for him to concern himself with the island's safety since he, Khurshid, had, in the interval, taken possession of it in the name of Mehemet 'Ali to prevent it from being used as a sanctuary by rebels from Najd. Bahrain, the Pasha went on, had been and still was a tributary of Najd, and no other country, including Persia, had any right to it. Of course, Khurshid added blandly, if the Persians could recover all that they had lost of their former great empire, he would gladly restore Bahrain to them. To remove any doubts that Hennell might have of the truth of what he had told him, Khurshid enclosed a copy of an agreement concluded by 'Abdullah ibn Ahmad, in which the Shaikh recognized Mehemet 'Ali's suzerainty over Bahrain and agreed to pay him an annual tribute of $M.T. 3,000 ($M.T. 750 of which were to be kept by 'Abdullah for his services), as well as to aid Khurshid Pasha and Mehemet 'Ali whenever they might require it. In return, 'Abdullah was recognized as the sole ruler of Bahrain, and he was assured that his possessions in Qatar would not be interfered with.[91] The date on the agreement was 22 Safar 1255/7 May 1839, but this proved to be, as Hennell later discovered from 'Abdullah ibn Ahmad himself, the date of ratification. The agreement itself had been concluded at least three weeks before Maitland's visit to Bahrain on 22 April.[92]

---

90 [I.O.] Enclos. to Bombay Sec. Letters, Vol. 14, enclos. to Sec. Letter 87 of 16 July 1839, Hennell to Willoughby, 18 May 1839 (No. 53 Sec. Dept.), enclosing Jabir ibn 'Abdullah to Hennell, 25 Safar 1255/10 May 1839.

91 [I.O.] Enclos. to Bombay Sec. Letters, Vol. 14, enclos. to Sec. Letter 87 of 16 July 1839, Hennell to Willoughby, 30 May 1839 (No. 57 Sec. Dept.), enclosing Khurshid Pasha to Hennell, 18 Muharram 1255/3 April 1839, enclosing text of agreement.

92 [I.0.1 Enclos. to Bombay Sec. Letters, Vol. 14, enclos. to Sec. Letter 89 of 18 July 1839, Hennell to Willoughby, 10 July 1839. Auckland, when he learned of the agree-

It would seem, therefore, that when Mehemet 'Ali spoke to Campbell about Bahrain early in June, he was well aware that the island had submitted to him. Furthermore, he must have known also that his claim to the island's sovereignty on the ground of its being a dependency of Najd would not stand close examination. Since the beginning of the century, when Saiyid Sa'id's father, Saiyid Sultan ibn Ahmad of Muscat, had overrun the island, its rulers had made token submission, or offers of submission, to the Shah of Persia, the Sultan of Muscat, and the British Government, as well as to successive Wahhabi Amirs. They had, in addition, signed the General Treaty of Peace of 1820 with the British Government, without reference to any other power, and they had been treated by that government as an independent power since then. So far as the tribute paid to the Wahhabis was concerned, it had first been exacted under threat of force in 1803, it was paid only sporadically after that date, and it was discontinued at least three years before the Wahhabis' defeat by Ibrahim Pasha in 1818. Not until 1831 were the Al Khalifah again compelled to pay tribute, this time by Turki ibn 'Abdullah; but by 1834, when Turki died, 'Abdullah ibn Ahmad had ceased to pay it, and had imposed a blockade on the Hasa ports which Turki had been unable to break. Faisal ibn Turki was no more successful in this respect than his father had been, but in 1836 'Abdullah agreed to lift the blockade and to pay tribute of $M.T. 2,000 per annum in return for the promise of military aid against the Sultan of Muscat and the Prince-Governor of Fars, whom 'Abdullah suspected of conspiring to attack him. It is doubtful whether he ever paid a single instalment of the tribute,[93] and he discarded the agreement altogether in 1838 when it became obvious that Faisal was about to be defeated by the Egyptians.

Another factor which rendered dubious the validity of Mehemet 'Ali's claim to Bahrain on the basis of its having paid tribute to the Wahhabis in the past was the nature of the tribute in question. It was commonly given the name of *zakat*, or 'alms tax', but it bore little resemblance to the classical *zakat* of Islam (if it had, its payment could hardly have been held to constitute an acknowledgement of political or territorial sovereignty). Nor was it ordinary political tribute, like that paid by the provinces of the Ottoman Empire to Constantinople. Rather was its true character that of

---

ment, refused to believe that it had been concluded in March, but there is no doubt that it had been. Khurshid's letter to Hennell, informing him of the submission of Bahrain, was dated 18 Muharram 1255/3 April 1839, and 'Abdullah ibn Ahmad had spoken to Edmunds in the last week of March of his having offered to pay Mehemet 'Ali a "trifling" tribute of $M.T. 3,000.

93 [I.O.] Persia and P. Gulf, Vol. 65, Hennell to Sec. Committee, 25 July 1839.

Danegeld, and it was exacted by the Wahhabis from all the littoral states of eastern Arabia at one time or another in the nineteenth century. If Mehemet 'Ali was claiming Bahrain as a tributary of Najd because it had paid *zakat* to the Wahhabis, then he would have been equally justified in claiming the Trucial Shaikdoms and the Sultanate of Muscat as well.[94]

Finally, what of Mehemet 'Ali's claim to Najd itself? Did it depend, as Campbell suggested, upon the grant of authority to him by the Sultan nearly thirty years previously, when he first undertook to subdue the Wahhabis, or had that authority been confirmed more recently? Ponsonby, who had been asked by Palmerston to discover the answer to this question, never apparently had a chance to do so, for at the end of June the Turkish capital was thrown into confusion by the death of the Sultan and the defeat of the Turkish army by Ibrahim Pasha. Perhaps the safest thing for one to conclude is that Mehemet 'Ali regarded himself as entitled to Najd by right of conquest.

Part II

Sultan Mahmud II had decided in the spring of 1839, against the advice of Ponsonby, to take the offensive against Mehemet 'Ali, and in late April he despatched an army into Syria. Ibrahim Pasha did not take the field against the Turks until the middle of June, and then, on 24 June, he inflicted a terrible defeat upon them at Nezib, near Biridjik on the upper Euphrates. On 29 June Mahmud II died, leaving as his successor, Abdul Mejid, a boy of sixteen. A little more than a week later the Kapitan Pasha, the commander-in-chief of the Ottoman Navy, defected to Mehemet 'Ali, and sailed with the bulk of the fleet to Alexandria. The road to Constantinople lay open to the Viceroy but he hesitated to take it openly. Instead, he ordered Ibrahim to stand on the line of the Taurus and not to advance unless he were attacked, while he busied himself with trying to bring about a change of regime at Constantinople by means of a lavish distribution of bribes and equally extravagant promises of reform.

It was the most luminous moment yet for an advance upon Basra and Baghdad if Mehemet 'Ali was of a mind to seize it. At the beginning of June, Cochelet, the French Consul-General in Egypt, had asked

---

94 A partial attempt to exert a claim of this nature was, in fact, made about thirty years later by Midhat Pasha, the Ottoman *vali* of Baghdad, after his conquest of Hasa from the Wahhabis in 1871.

him whether the rumours reaching Cairo of Khurshid Pasha's troops being on the march for Basra were true. The Viceroy dismissed the reports as *'une plaisanterie'*. Khurshid Pasha, he said, was still at Riyadh at the time of writing the latest letter that had been received from him.[95] Cochelet brought the subject up again towards the end of June, after he had learned of Palmerston's instructions to Ponsonby of 11 May to assure the Porte that Britain would not tolerate the establishment of an Egyptian position on the Gulf. 'Méhemét Ali'; the Consul-General reported, *'m'a encore assuré hier, de la manière la plus positive et je dirai même la plus solennelle en se soumettant à perdre tous les états qu'il gouverne si le fait de l'envahissement de Bassora était prouvé, que Kourchid Pacha n'avait pas dépassé la limite du Nejd, et qu'il n'avait aucune instruction pour aller plus loin'*.[96] The Viceroy repeated this assurance to Campbell a fortnight later, when the British Consul-General, acting upon Palmerston's instructions of 15 June, asked him about his supposed designs on Basra and Baghdad. Mehemet Ali not only denied the existence of such designs but he also, despite Campbell's protests that it was unnecessary, put his denial in writing for transmission to Palmerston.[97] In so far as it concerned the immediate moment the denial could doubtless be taken at face value, for the turn of events in Syria and at Constantinople was now to absorb Mehemet 'Ali's attention. But this did not mean that Baghdad was forgotten or that Khurshid Pasha would remain completely idle in Najd. What it did seem to signify, at least in the Gulf, was that he would switch his attention, for the time being, from north-eastern to south-eastern Arabia.

Towards the close of June Hennell received a report from the Residency Agent at Sharjah that Sa'ad ibn Mutlaq and his band had refused a request made to them by Shaikh Sultan ibn Saqr, after Edmunds' departure from Ras al-Khaima at the beginning of May, to leave the Trucial Coast, and that Sa'ad, discarding the pretence that he was acting for Khalid ibn Sa'ud, had produced letters from Khurshid Pasha, appointing him Egyptian governor of Trucial Oman. He could only be forced to leave, he said, by a written order from the Political Resident himself. Sultan ibn Saqr

---

95 Edouard Driault, *L'Egypte et l'Europe: la Crise de 1839-41*, 5 vols., Cairo 1930-34, I, 45-6, Cochelet to Duc de Dalmatie, 5 June 1839.

96 Driault, I, 77-8, Cochelet to Dalmatie, 25 June 1839. Soult, when he received Cochelet's earlier report, instructed him to draw Mehemet 'Ali's attention to the dangers of complicating an already delicate situation by making aggressive gestures in the directions of Baghdad, or the Gulf, which could well provoke the British into occupying Basra or some other place. (Driault, I, 127-8, Dalmatie to Cochelet, 7 July 1839).

97 [P.R.O.] F.O. 78/374, Campbell to Palmerston, 11 July 1839 (No. 51), enclosing Boghos Bey to Campbell, 9 July 1839.

had hastened to assure him that, in view of these changed circumstances, he could stay as long as he liked.[98] If Sa'ad ibn Mutlaq remained at Sharjah, it seemed to Hennell, it would only be a matter of time before the Trucial Shaikhdoms submitted to Mehemet 'Ali in the same way as Bahrain had done. The armed steamer *Hugh Lindsay* was then at Kharag, on her way to Basra with the desert mail. Hennell had the mail transferred to the Residency schooner, and sailed for the Trucial Coast in *Hugh Lindsay* within twenty four hours of receiving the agent's report.

He arrived off Abu Dhabi on 1 July. Khalifah ibn Shakhbut, the ruler, came on board, and Hennell questioned him closely about correspondence he was said to have had with Sa'ad ibn Mutlaq. Shaikh Khalifah denied that he had ever encouraged the Egyptian agent, and he offered to give a written pledge to resist any move by Khurshid Pasha in the direction of Trucial Oman, and to look only to the British Government for support and guidance. Hennell accepted the pledge, though he placed little value on it, and sailed the same day for Dubai. There the ruler, Shaikh Maktum ibn Buti, told him that it was common knowledge up and down the coast that Khalifah ibn Shakhbut was in touch with Sa'ad ibn Mutlaq. He himself, he said, had had nothing to do with him, and he had refused even to visit him at Sharjah. The Shaikh of Umm al-Qaiwain, 'Abdullah ibn Rashid, told Hennell the same thing later that day. At Sharjah, where Hennell put in on his way from Dubai to Umm al-Qaiwain, he heard that a messenger had arrived from Khurshid Pasha three days earlier, to tell Sa'ad ibn Mutlaq that reinforcements would shortly be on their way to him. Hennell was also told that the Qasimi chieftain, Sultan ibn Saqr, was fully supporting Sa'ad. On 3 July Hennell saw Sultan ibn Saqr at Ras al-Khaima. The old shaikh swore that he was doing no more for the *na'ib* than he was forced to do. If he had made him leave Sharjah he would have gone to Abu Dhabi. Khalifah ibn Shakhbut, Shaikh Sultan asserted, was courting Sa'ad's favour, and to prove this he produced for Hennell a letter from the Bani Yas chief to the Egyptian agent, which he had intercepted, offering to place the resources of Abu Dhabi at Sa'ad's disposal. The offer surprised Hennell, as the Bani Yas had been consistent opponents of the Wahhabis for many years, but the reason for it probably lay in Khalifah ibn Shakhbut's ambition to wrest control of the Buraimi forts from the Na'im, which he hoped to do, apparently, with Sa'ad's help. He already exerted

---

98 [I.O.] Enclos. to Bombay Sec. Letters, Vol. 14, enclos. to Sec. Letter 87 of 16 July 1839, Mullah Husain to Hennell, 3 Rabi' I, 1255 / 17 May 1839. See also, same volume, enclos. to Sec. Letter 89 of 18 July 1839, Mullah Husain to Hennell, 7 Rabi' I, 1255/21 May 1839.

some influence over the Dhawahir tribe, but to control the oasis he would have to get possession of the forts.[99]

Sultan ibn Saqr told Hennell privately that if he were to give him a written order to expel Sa'ad ibn Mutlaq, he would do so. The Resident not only gave him the order but he also addressed a letter direct to the Egyptian agent, denying his right to assume the governorship of Trucial Oman and ordering him to leave the Trucial Coast forthwith. Furthermore, he informed Sa'ad, he intended to take the Na'im of Buraimi under British protection for as long as the dispute between Britain and Egypt persisted. Hennell repeated these statements in a letter he addressed to Khurshid Pasha the following day. Expressing surprise at Khurshid's action in appointing Sa'ad ibn Mutlaq his governor over Trucial Oman, in direct contravention of Mehemet 'Ali's assurances that he had no intention of expanding his influence in the Gulf region, Hennell asked for the agent's prompt withdrawal. From Sultan ibn Saqr Hennell obtained a written pledge, similar to the one he had got from Khalifah ibn Shakhbut, and which he had also obtained from the other Trucial Shaikhs, to co-operate with the British Government in resisting any advance by Khurshid Pasha towards Trucial Oman. In addition, Hennell undertook to supply Sultan with arms, should be become engaged in hostilities with the Egyptians, in return for a further written undertaking not to enter into negotiations or agreements with foreign powers, except with the consent of the British Government, and to regard the friends and enemies of that government in the same light. Finally, Hennell saw an emissary from the Na'im, who had been waiting to see him, and gave him supplies of rice and gunpowder, and told him that he would send an agent to reside at Buraimi.[100]

Hennell had done what he could, but he was not sanguine about the resulcs. A victory by Ibrahim Pasha over the Sultan's army in Syria (the news of Nezib had not yet reached the Gulf), the arrival of reinforcements from Khurshid Pasha for Sa'ad ibn Mutlaq, the *na'ib's* return, if he was expelled, with more troops—any of these eventualities, Hennell advised the Government of Bombay, could deal a serious blow to the tenuous influence he now wielded over the maritime tribes. He had little faith in the efficacy of remonstrances at Cairo to curb Khurshid Pasha. Mehemet 'Ali would not be deterred from pursuing whatever design he might have in south-eastern Arabia by anything less than a display of armed strength in that quarter by the Indian Government. The naval force in the Gulf,

---

99 [I.O.] Enclos. to Bombay Sec. Letters, Vol. 14, enclos. to Sec. Letter 89 of 18 July 1839, Hennell to Willoughby, 10 July 1839.
100 *Ibid.*

therefore, should be increased immediately, and if Khurshid Pasha tried to send back Sa'ad ibn Mutlaq to Trucial Oman with a larger force, a blockade should be imposed on Qatif, 'Uqair and Saihat. If Khurshid attacked the Buraimi Oasis—and possession of Buraimi was the key to mastery of the Trucial Coast and northern Oman—and if the Trucial Shaikhs joined him in such an attack, then, Hennell declared, they should be threatened with the destruction of their fortifications and fleets if they did not desist. Trucial Oman should not be lost, as Bahrain had been lost, for the want of decisive action. 'Abdullah ibn Ahmad had told Hennell, when the Resident called at Bahrain at the end of June on his way down the Gulf to Abu Dhabi, that he would have stood up to Khurshid Pasha had he not despaired of receiving any support from the British Government. Even now, if the British were prepared to protect him from the Pasha, he would disown his submission to Mehemet 'Ali. Although Hennell was not prepared to swallow this explanation whole—he was more inclined to attribute 'Abdullah's capitulation to his advanced age and his desire for a quiet life—yet he believed that it contained an element of truth. Khurshid's reputation stood high among the tribes of eastern Arabia, and if something were not done to diminish it he would be free to extend his conquests as far as he pleased. On the other hand, Hennell concluded, if Mehemet 'Ali were to be told that he would be held responsible for any damage or casualties that resulted from any further conquests, there was a good chance that he would quickly withdraw his troops and agents from the Gulf coast.[101]

From the Trucial Coast Hennell sailed to Muscat, to see what effects, if any, the Egyptian advance had had there. An emissary from Sa'ad ibn Mutlaq had arrived at Muscat in the first week of June with letters from him and Khurshid Pasha for Saiyid Sa'id. Khurshid, in his letter, merely said that he was sending Sa'ad to Buraimi to take charge of the government of Trucial Oman and asked the Sultan to lend him every assistance. Sa'ad's letter was more peremptory in tone: he complained that so far he had received no support from Saiyid Sa'id, and he demanded the immediate resumption of payment of the tribute of $M.T. 5,000 *per annum* formerly paid to Riyadh by Sa'id.[102] Sa'id was away at Zanzibar when Sa'ad's messenger arrived. His son, Thuwaini, and his nephew, Muhammad ibn Salim, who were acting as joint regents of Oman in his absence, told Hennell on

---
101 Ibid. See also, same series,V ol. 15, enclos. to Sec. Letter 103 of 10 September 1839, Hennell to Willoughby, 31 July 1839 (No. 72 Sec. Dept.).
102 [I.O.] Enclos. to Bombay Sec. Letters, Vol. 14, enclos. to Sec. Letter 87 of 16 July 1839, Reuben Aslam (E. I. Co. Agent, Muscat) to Hennell, 29 Rabi' I, 1255/10 June 1839

his arrival at Muscat that they had no intention of helping Khurshid Pasha. They were at one with the British Government in opposing his encroachments. However, when Hennell suggested that they translate their intention into action by backing up the Na'im of Buraimi in their resistance to Sa'ad ibn Mutlaq, the regents showed little enthusiasm for the idea. The reason lay, Hennell suspected, in their jealousy of their kinsman, Saiyid Hamud ibn 'Azzan of Sauhar, who had helped the Na'im in the spring after they had expelled the Wahhabi garrison from the forts.[103]

Hennell's recommendations were strongly endorsed by the new Governor of Bombay, Sir James Carnac. 'It appears to me that half-measures will be productive of mischief. We must either league with the Arab chiefs in resisting the encroachments of Kurshid Pasha, or make up our minds to the complete establishment of Egyptian supremacy on the Arabian coast in the Gulf of Persia.'[104] Auckland disagreed. Any measures to preserve British influence along the Arabian coast, he explained to Carnac at the beginning of August, must depend upon whatever line of policy the Home Government eventually decided to adopt towards Mehemet 'Ali, as well as upon the outcome of Campbell's representations at Cairo.

> For it is evident that no warlike demonstrations that the Indian Government has the means of making in support of those of the Arab chieftains who may hold out against Korshid Pasha would lead to such decisive results as the complete withdrawal of his army and his lately established authority by the orders of his master; nor could we feel assured from the fickle and faithless character of many of these chieftains that our efforts in their behalf would be cordially seconded by themselves. Korshid Pasha appears to exercise an extraordinary influence over them; and while they remain lukewarm or indifferent to our endeavour to excite them to the maintenance of their independence, it would require an extent of force to preserve our influence over them which it is not consistent with other political considerations for the Indian Government at present to afford for this object.[105]

---

103 Same series and volume, enclos. to Sec. Letter 89 of 18 July 1839, Hennell to Willoughby, Muscat, 10 July 1839.
104 Same series and volume, enclos. to Sec. Letter 92 of 31 July 1839, Minute by Carnac, 20 July 1839.
105 [I.O.] Enclos. to Bombay Sec. Letters, Vol. 15, enclos. to Sec. Letter 103 of 10 September 1839, Maddock to Willoughby, Simla, 1 August 1839.

The submission of Bahrain to the Egyptians was extremely annoying to Auckland, and he refused to accept the explantion given by 'Abdullah ibn Ahmad for his action. 'Abdullah, according to Auckland, like the Trucial Shaikhs, had contracted obligations towards the British Government by virtue of his participation in the General Treaty of 1820. The agreement he had concluded with Khurshid Pasha was subversive of that treaty. So, also, were the dealings of Sultan ibn Saqr and Khalifah ibn Shakhbut with Sa'ad ibn Mutlaq. These shaikhs, in Auckland's view, were only stopped from making further displays of their subservience to the Egyptians by the arrival of Hennell and by his exaction of written pledges from them. Auckland approved the taking of these pledges and he was prepared to sanction the grant of arms to those chiefs who were prepared to defend their independence against the Egyptians; but he was disturbed by Hennell's grant of protection to the Na'im of Buraimi because it seemed to him to go beyond the principle on which British relations with the Arab tribes had been based, *viz.*, abstention from interference, and especially military interference, in their territorial affairs. However, for the time being, he would approve the extension of protection to the Na'im. He would put Hennell's request for a naval demonstration to the commander-in-chief, East Indies, but there was little likelihood of its being complied with in the near future. The Bombay Government would have to see what ships could be spared from the Indian Navy for that purpose. If a cruiser could be spared, he was prepared to adopt Hennell's suggestion that it be stationed off Qatif to prevent armed parties of men from leaving that port for the Trucial Coast.[106]

Auckland was evading the issue, as he well knew. '...Koorshid Pasha is waiting for instructions from Cairo as I must wait for instructions from London', he wrote to Maitland in late July. 'The whole affair is mixed up with Egyptian, Turkish and European, as well as with Eastern, politics, and I have very imperfect information to guide me'.[107] He can hardly be blamed for not acting when the resources at his disposal were insufficient, but the arguments with which he sought to justify his evasion were of doubtful merit. Because he considered the only satisfactory end to Khurshid Pasha's threat to be a complete Egyptian withdrawal from the Gulf he would take no steps to counter it; because he doubted whether the 'fickle and faithless' shaikhs of the Trucial Coast would appreciate any British efforts on their behalf he would make no such efforts; and because Khur-

---

106 *Ibid.*, and same series, Vol. 18, enclos. to Sec. Letter 113 of 5 October 1839, Maddock to L. R. Reid (acting Chief Secy., Bombay), Simla, 16 September 1839.
107 [B.M.] Add. Ms. 37696, Auckland to Maitland, 29 July 1839.

shid Pasha exercised an 'extraordinary' influence over them he would not try to counteract that influence. Auckland was being less than just to the Trucial Shaikhs (the rulers of Dubai and Umm al-Qaiwain had refused to pay court to Sa'ad ibn Mutlaq) and to the Na'im of Buraimi. His invocation of the principle of non-intervention, especially by military means, in the affairs of the Arabian mainland was unrealistic. Certainly the principle had been operative since 1821, but it had been suspended by Auckland himself at the beginning of 1839 when he had sanctioned the occupation of Aden to forestall a possible Egyptian seizure of that place. The situation in eastern Arabia demanded a similar suspension of the principle. For the first time since the Gulf had become a British preserve British ascendancy there was being challenged by an outside power. Khurshid Pasha's reputation among the tribes, moreover, had been won by military successes, and the belief was gaining ground among the tribes that the British, whatever their supremacy at sea, could not match the Egyptians on land. A naval demonstration, even if the ships had been available, might not have sufficed to impress the tribes; the despatch of a military force to Bahrain, and possibly to Buraimi, might have. On the other hand, a sortie into Arabia might have proved as great a military folly as Auckland was about to commit in Afghanistan.

On 1 August the news of the defeat of the Turkish Army by Ibrahim Pasha reached Kharag, and shortly afterwards came reports of the death of the Sultan and the desertion of the Turkish fleet to Mehemet 'Ali. Within days the news had trickled down to the lower Gulf, but by then Sa'ad ibn Mutlaq and his followers had left the Trucial Coast for Najd. Sultan ibn Saqr, true to his word, had expelled the Egyptian agent, but before he left, it was reported, Sultan had secretly assured him that if he were to return with a larger force he could count upon the support of all the Qawasim.[108] Simultaneously with the reports of Ibrahim Pasha's victory came word from Najd that Khurshid Pasha had relinquished control of the government to the Amir Khalid ibn Sa'id, on the express orders of Mehemet 'Ali.[109] One ominous interpretation of this development was that

---

108 [I.O.] Enclos. to Bombay Sec. Letters, Vol. 15, enclos. to Sec. Letter 103 of 10 September 1839, Hennell to Willoughby, 1, 9 August 1839 (Nos. 73, 78 Sec. Dept.); and Vol. 16, enclos. to Sec. Letter 111 of 4 October 1839, Hennell to Reid, 26 August 1839 (No. 88 Sec. Dept.).
109 [I.O.] Enclos. to Bombay Sec. Letters, Vol. 15, enclos. to Sec. Letter 103 of 10 September 1839, Hennell to Willoughby, 29 July 1839 (No. 71 Sec. Dept.). See also, same series, Vol. 14, enclos. to Sec. Letter 92 of 31 July 1839, Khurshid Pasha to Boghos Bey, 23 Muharram 1255/8 April 1839, enclosed in Campbell to Willoughby, 16 June 1839: 'D'àpres l'ordre de S.A. le Viceroi lorsque j'aurais procuré les chameaux nécessaires

Khurshid was regrouping his forces for the long-expected march on Baghdad. The Pashaliq's security had been rendered even more precarious by the Egyptian victory in Syria and the death of the Sultan, and there was little doubt that Khurshid could, if he wished, subdue it with ease, especially if he were to be supported by the army of Ahmad Pasha in the Hijaz and by the powerful Muntafiq tribe of lower Iraq. Khurshid's force, according to Hennell's information, did not exceed 300 regular cavalry, 3,500 regular and irregular infantry, and 8-10 field guns, most of them stationed at Tharmidah, midway between Riyadh and 'Anaiza; but Ahmad Pasha had 4,000 men at Madinah, and a convenient junction for the two forces would be 'Anaiza, from which they could advance northwards into Iraq.[110]

Campbell, in Egypt, did not believe that Mehemet 'Ali intended to go back on the pledge he had given in July not to move in the direction of Basra or Baghdad. Nor did Campbell believe that Khurshid Pasha, with whom Campbell was, in his own words, 'intimately acquainted' and for whom he had a 'great regard', would go against Mehemet 'Ali's orders. Besides, Ibrahim Pasha, after his defeat of the Turks, had withdrawn to the left bank of the Euphrates, which did not indicate that he was contemplating operations against Baghdad.[111] The correctness of Campbell's belief seemed to be confirmed at the end of August when a letter arrived at Kharag for Hennell from Khurshid Pasha, saying that he did not intend to move from his base at Tharmidah until he had had further orders from Egypt. But the messenger who brought the letter told Hennell that Sa'ad ibn Mutlaq, who had landed at 'Uqair at the end of July, was on his way to Khurshid's camp, which seemed to Hennell to indicate that the Pasha still had designs on Buraimi.[112]

Weight was lent to this surmise by news that Khalifah ibn Shakhbut had attacked the forts at Buraimi in late July, and by the receipt of letters which the Residency Agent at Sharjah had intercepted, addressed by Khurshid and Khalid ibn Sa'ud to Sultan ibn Saqr and Sa'ad ibn Mutlaq, which showed quite clearly that Khurshid's intention in sending Sa'ad to Sharjah

---

pour l'expedition d'Assir je dois consigner le gouvernement de Nejde à Kalide Bey qui maintiendra l'ordre et la sûreté dans cette partie de l'Arabie'.

110 [I.O.] Enclos. to Bombay Sec. Letters, Vol. 15, enclos. to Sec. Letter 103 of 10 September 1839, Hennell to Willoughby, 1 August 1839 (No. 73 Sec. Dept.); and Vol. 16, enclos. to Sec. Letter 111 of 4 October 1839, Hennell to Willoughby, 30 July 1839 (No. 72 Sec. Dept.).

111 [I.O.] Enclos. to Bombay Sec. Letters, Vol. 16, enclos. to Sec. Letter 111 of 4 October 1839, Campbell to Reid, 27 August 1839.

112 Same series, volume and collection, Hennell to Reid, 28 August 1839 (No. 89 Sec. Dept.), enclosing Khurshid Pasha to Hennell, 17 Jumada I, 1255/29 July 1839.

had been to establish Egyptian authority over Trucial Oman. It seemed to Hennell equally clear that Khurshid would have to be shown that the British Government would not tolerate his interference in Trucial Oman, and that Khalifah ibn Shakhbut should be made to realise that he could not break the pledge he had given with impunity. He therefore recommended to the Bombay Government that the Bani Yas chief be compelled, by threat of destruction of his shipping and town, if necessary, to compensate the Na'im for his attack on them. Hennell also drew attention to the recommendation he had made at the end of July that if Sa'ad ibn Muttaq were known to be contemplating a return to Trucial Oman by sea with a larger force, a ship of war should be stationed off Qatif and a warning given to the Egyptian governor of that port that no vessel carrying armed men would be allowed to quit Qatif for the Trucial Coast.[113]

The sense of urgency present in Hennell's latest despatches moved Auckland to action. He agreed to all the Resident's recommendations, and he put the case for a naval demonstration in the Gulf to Maitland as a matter of urgent necessity. The naval commander-in-chief responded as quickly as possible, sailing from Trincomali for Madras in late September to revictual his squadron, and then heading for Bombay, where he arrived on 3 November with H.M.S. *Wellesley, Larne* and *Algerine*. Before he could leave for the Gulf, however, he had to await orders from England regarding the situation in China. Within a few days instructions arrived from the Admiralty which left him with no choice but to sail immediately for the Far East.[114]

With Maitland's departure all hope of a powerful naval demonstration in the Gulf in 1839 vanished. Even more immediately disturbing for the Indian authorities, however, was the critical state of the Gulf squadron in the second half of 1839. In late September the commanding officer, Commodore Brucks, informed Hennell that the two vessels at his disposal were wholly inadequate to the duties of the station, which could not be performed with fewer than four sailing vessels and one steamer (or two sailing vessels and two steamers)—one to guard Kharag, another to watch Bushire, a third to patrol the Arabian coast northwards to Kuwait at least

---

113 Same series, volume and collection, Hennell to Reid, 26, 28, 29 August 1839 (Nos. 88, 90, 91 Sec. Dept.). See also, same series, Vol. 15, enclos. to Sec. Letter 103 of 10 September 1839, Hennell to Willoughby, 31 July 1839 (No. 72 Sec. Dept.).

114 [I.O.] Bombay Sec. Letters Recd., Vol. 10 (i), Gov.-in-Council to Sec. Committee, 26 October, 28 November 1839 (Nos. 118, 127 Sec. Dept.). See also [P.R.O.] Adm. 1/220, Maitland to Wood, 15 September 1839 (No. 110), and [I.O.] Enclos. to Bombay Sec. Letters, Vol. 18, enclos. to Sec. Letter 113 of 5 October 1839, Maddock to Reid, Simla, 16 September 1839.

once a month, a fourth to patrol the Trucial Coast and the Persian shore, a duty that required a month's cruising, at least, and a fifth to maintain communication with Bombay. In addition, Brucks pointed out, a situation might arise in the upper or lower Gulf at any time which would require the presence of two or even three cruisers together. There was nothing that the Bombay Government could do to improve the situation. The steamer *Hugh Lindsay*, which had cruised in the Gulf in July, had had to be withdrawn to resume her normal duty of carrying the overland mail to Suez, and the only vessel then at Bombay was the sloop *Elphinstone*. She was being refitted and there was little chance that she would be ready for sea for some time.[115]

Fortunately for Hennell, Khurshid Pasha showed no sign during September of resuming the offensive in eastern Arabia. He was reported to have been angered by the Resident's expulsion of Sa'ad ibn Mutlaq from Trucial Oman and by the failure of Khalifah ibn Shakhbut's attack on Buraimi. Khalifah had grudgingly yielded to Hennell's demand that he compensate the Na'im, after protesting that they had provoked him into attacking them. In retaliation, it would seem, both for Khalifah's failure and Hennell's intervention, an Egyptian force from Qatif raided the northern branch of the Na'im in Qatar in September, after preferring a demand for tribute on them through 'Abdullah ibn Ahmad of Bahrain. When the Na'im refused to acknowledge the authority of either 'Abdullah or Mehemet 'Ali, the Egyptians ravaged their date groves and pasture lands, and they only withdrew when a rumour reached them early in October that the Governor of Qatif had been murdered.[116] On 27 October Joseph Arton, Khurshid's physician, arrived at Kharag with a letter from the Pasha for Hennell. The letter contained little mention either of Bahrain, which Khurshid now considered tributary to Egypt, or of Sa'ad ibn Mutlaq's expulsion from Trucial Oman. Instead, the Pasha dwelt mostly on Buraimi, which, he said, belonged to the Al Sa'ud, now as in the past. The implication seemed to be that Khurshid considered himself entitled to occupy the oasis if he wished to.[117]

It seemed to Hennell high time that he knew more about Buraimi,

---

115 [I.O.] Bombay Sec. Letters Recd., Vol. 10 (i), Gov.-in-Council to Sec. Committee, 28 November 1839 (No. 127 Sec. Dept.).

116 [I.O.] Enclos. to Bombay Sec. Letters, Vol. 17, enclos. to Sec. Letter 133 of 24 December 1839, Hennel to Acting Chief Secy., Bombay, 26, 27 October 1839 (Nos. 109 A, 110 Sec. Dept.).

117 Same series, volume and collection, Hennell to Reid, 28 October 1839 (No. 111 Sec. Dept.), enclosing Khurshid Pasha to Hennell, 16 Rajab 1255/25 September 1839

which no European had ever seen, and so in mid-November he despatched an officer from the Kharag Field Force, Captain Atkins Hamerton of the 15th Bombay Native Infantry, to Sharjah with orders to make his way inland from there to the oasis.[118] Hennell himself took ship shortly afterwards for Muscat to see Saiyid Sa'id, lately returned from Zanzibar, and to discover what, if anything, the Sultan was prepared to do to support the frontier chiefs of Oman against the Egyptians. Sa'id, as Hennell found, was prepared to do very little. He believed, or he affected to believe, that Khurshid Pasha could not be stopped by any force that could be put in the field against him by the maritime states. For this reason, he told Hennell, he would not take advantage of the offer made to him by the Resident of arms and other supplies for the defence of Oman. It was hopeless, he said, to try to unite the tribes of Trucial Oman against an outside enemy: they would never live up to their engagements. When Hennell pointed out that the Na'im still stood firm at Buraimi, Sa'id replied that theirs was a special case, as they had suffered greatly from the exactions of Sa'id ibn Mutlaq in the past. Sa'id's disinclination to help the Na'im was due, as his son's had been in July, to his jealousy of Saiyid Hamud ibn 'Azzan of Sauhar. The bitter rivalry between the two men was a dangerous weakness in Oman's defences, and Hennell therefore did his best to patch up their quarrels during his week at Muscat at the beginning of December. He succeeded to the extent of getting them to agree in writing to put aside their differences for the duration of the crisis in the Gulf. He failed, however, in the principal purpose of his visit, which was to convince Sa'id of the need for a display, at least, of resistance to Khurshid Pasha. The Sultan continued to insist that only the British Government could stop the Pasha, and they could best do this by occupying Bahrain and sending a military detachment to garrison Buraimi. When Hennell told him that neither course had seriously been contemplated, Sa'id was greatly astonished. Bahrain, he said, must be occupied, and if the British would not do it, he would.[119]

The contrast between Sa'id's languid regard for the safety of Oman and his eagerness to occupy Bahrain was noteworthy but scarcely surprising. For thirty years he had been trying to get possession of the island, and it had been his cumulative failures to achieve this ambition that had led him, in the early eighteen-thirties, virtually to retire to Zanzibar and to devote himself thenceforth to the cultivation of his East African posses-

---

118 [I.O.] Enclos. to Bombay Sec. Letters, Vol. 17, enclos. to Sec. Letter 135 of 31 December 1839, Hennell to Reid, 25 November 1839 (No. 121 Sec. Dept.).
119 Same series, volume, and collection, Hennell to Reid, 10 December 1839 (No. 127 Sec. Dept.).

sions. Whatever his motives were in advocating the occupation of Bahrain, however,—and they were well known to Hennell—the Resident thought the idea well worth entertaining. As he explained in his report to Bombay, not only would Bahrain be a valuable acquisition in itself but its annexation would secure to Britain a preponderating influence in Gulf politics. In conjunction with the garrisoning of Buraimi it would effectively limit Khurshid Pasha's activities. If the British did not occupy Bahrain, then Sa'id might well try to do so himself, in which case the Indian Government would have to decide whether or not to assist him in the project. Hennell doubted whether it would be wise to do so. He had, in fact, had serious doubts for some time of the desirability of keeping up the British connexion with Muscat, and he did not agree with those who lamented its attenuation in recent years. '... I do not myself consider it to be a subject of deep regret, as the very close connexion which has hitherto subsisted between our Government and that of Muscat has rather proved a source of embarrassment than otherwise, by tending to involve us in disputes and quarrels constantly occurring between the latter and the other Arabian Chiefs'.[120]

Hennell left Muscat in the last week of December and sailed for Sharjah. Arriving there on 6 January 1840, he found that Captain Harnerton had been unable to leave for the interior because of the intrigues of Sultan ibn Saqr and his son, the governor of Sharjah. The Trucial Coast was alive with rumours of the imminent arrival of the Egyptians in force, by land and sea, of France's having ranged herself on the side of Mehemet 'Ali, and of the impending overthrow of British power in the East. Sultan ibn Saqr had adopted a menacing tone towards Hamerton, and most of the other shaikhs had been unfriendly to him. A messenger whom he had despatched to Buraimi with letters for the Na'imi shaikhs had been set upon and robbed, on the track from Sharjah to Buraimi, by Bani Qitab tribesmen loyal to Sultan ibn Saqr. Since Hamerton could not come to them the Na'imi shaikhs had journeyed to the coast in the latter half of December—with an escort of 350 men—to meet him at 'Ajman, which was also ruled by a Na'imi family. Learning from Hamerton that the Resident was due on the coast in the first week of January, they decided to wait and see him.[121]

---

120 [I.O.] Enclos. to Bombay Sec. Letters, Vol. 19, enclos. to Sec. Letter 5 of 31 January 1840, Hennell to Willoughby, 10 November 1838 [sic] (No. 89 Pol. Dept.). See also, same series, Vol. 17, enclos. to Sec. Letter 135 of 31 December 1839, Hennell to Reid, 10 December 1839 (No. 127 Sec. Dept.).
121 [I.O.] Bombay Secret ProceedingsV, ol. 132, Consultation of 2 April 1840, Hennell to Willoughby, 30 January 1840, enclosing Hamerton's diary.

Hennell met the shaikhs soon after his arrival and congratulated them on their stand against Khurshid Pasha and Sa'ad ibn Mutlaq. The British Government, he said, while having no desire to establish their authority in the interior of Arabia, or to take under their protection tribes or places beyond the reach of their power to defend, were anxious to encourage the tribes to unite against the Egyptians. For this reason he would like to see the breach between the Na'im and their neighbours at Buraimi, the Dhawahir, healed, particularly as it endangered the security of the oasis. The Na'imi shaikhs, in reply, said that they were willing to conclude a defensive alliance with the Dhawahir against the Egyptians, provided that Khalifah ibn Shakhbut of Abu Dhabi was restrained from attacking them again. After talking to the Dhahiri shaikhs, who had come to Sharjah to meet him, Hennell succeeded in getting both tribes to agree to subordinate their differences and present a united front to their mutual enemies. To both he gave money, ammunition and rice, and before he left he arranged for Hamerton to travel to Buraimi under the protection of the Na'im.[122]

Hamerton did not get away from Sharjah until 21 January, again owing to the opposition of Sultan ibn Saqr. Four days later he reached Buraimi, and was the first European to set eyes on the oasis. Buraimi town, he found, was of considerable size but in a state of dilapidation,... and the wall around the whole of the town, a perfect ruin'.[123] The main fort, which stood on the south side of the town facing an open plain, was about 150 feet square, with walls 14 feet high and 5-6 feet through at the base and 1-2 feet at the top. Round towers stood at the four corners, rising 8-12 feet above the walls. Another wall, about 8 feet high, ran around the fort, at a distance of about 30 feet, and beyond this outer wall was a dry ditch, about 24 feet wide, which gave to the fort its name—Qasr al-Khandaq, or 'Castle of the Moat'. The entire fort was constructed of sun-dried brick and was in 'a sad state of repair'. '[It] could not...stand for an hour against an enemy provided with guns'.[124] Nevertheless, it was spoken of throughout Trucial Oman as impregnable. If supplied with a few guns—it had only 'a few wretched guns of small calibre, about 3-pounders, without carriages'—it could be defended, Hamerton thought, against a force without guns, provided that the ditch was held, also. There was a second, and smaller, fort about 300 yards to the north-west of the Qasr al-Khandaq guarding the

---

122 [I.O.] Enclos.to Bombay Sec. Letters, Vol. 19, enclos. to Sec. Letter 10 of 28 February 1840, Hennell to Willoughby, 12 January 1840 (No. 2 Sec. Dept.).
123 [I.O.] Bombay Sec. Proc., Vol. 135, Consultn. of 20 May 1840, Hamerton to Hennell, 27 March 1840.
124 *Ibid.*

adjacent village of Hamasa. It was about 125 feet square, with towers at the angles, and walls 15-16 feet high, 5 feet thick at the base, 1 1/2 feet at the top. Like the Qasr al-Khandaq it had several broken-down, carriageless guns, about whose origins no-one knew anything. '... When intended to be fired', Hamerton noted wryly, 'the people place a stone or block of wood so as to raise the muzzle a few inches from the ground. There is no shot for any of the guns, but the Schaikh has some round stones and lumps of wrought iron which were collected last year when Said bin Mutluk came to Shargah'.[125] Both forts, it was said, had been constructed by Sa'ad's father, Mutlaq al-Mutairi, when he was Wahhabi *na'ib* at Buraimi between 1808 and 1813.

Buraimi town and the Qasr al-Khandaq were under the control of Muhammad ibn 'Abdullah, Hamasa under that of Ahmad ibn Surur. Both were shaikhs of the Al Bu Shamis division of the Na'im. The *tamimah* or paramount chief, of the Na'im was 'Ali ibn Hamuda of the Al Bu Khuraiban division, who lived at Sunainah, several miles to the south of the oasis. 'The Naim tribe,' Hamerton observed, 'are now evidently much reduced in numbers, and sunk in consequence among the tribes of Oman. The Suamis [Al Bu Shamis] of Byreemee [Buraimi] formerly mustered four thousand men, and they do not now amount to more than eight hundred'. All three divisions of the Na'im,[126] he was told, could put into the field no more than 2,650 fighting men.[127]

Hamerton left Buraimi on 28 January, accompanied by Muhammad ibn 'Abdullah and his brother, and an escort of five tribesmen. He headed for Sauhar on the Gulf of Oman, where he was to be picked up by a cruiser. Halfway along the Wadi al-Jizzi, which cuts through the Hajar Mountains to the east of Buraimi, he came upon a fort, at Burj al-Shujairi, which had an 18-pounder gun in it. When he asked why it was there he was told that it had been sent by the Sultan, Saiyid Sa'id, for the main fort at Buraimi, but that it could not be dragged any further through the pass. When Saiyid Sa'id had sent it Hamerton could not discover. On the afternoon of 30 January he reached Sauhar. 'Had I been a wild beast such as never before was heard of, I could not have excited greater curiosity: everyone came to

---

125 *Ibid.*
126 The third division of the Na'im is the Khawatir. Generally speaking, the Al Bu Shamis are regarded as a separate tribe, the name 'Na'im' being reserved for the Al Bu Khuraiban and Khawatir together.
127 [I.O.] Bombay Sec. Proc., Vol. 135, Consultn. of 20 May 1840, Hamerton to Hennell, 27 March 1840.

see the Englishman who had been to Byreemee'.[128]

Hennell's visit to Muscat and the Trucial Coast, and Hamerton's reconnaissance of the Buraimi Oasis, raised several questions for the Indian Government's decision, chief among them being the possible occupation of Bahrain by a British force, the strengthening of the defences of Buraimi, and the defence of Oman against possible Egyptian invasion. A further question was raised by the receipt of a report from Captain Edmunds, who had been left in charge of the Residency during Hennell's absence, that a *baghlah*, or large *dhow*, believed to hail from Kuwait, had arrived in the Gulf from the Red Sea, bound for Qatif with arms and military stores for Khurshid Pasha. Edmunds wanted to know whether any action was to be taken to intercept the *baghlah*, and whether the transport of arms and supplies by sea to the Egyptians as a whole was to be interfered with. Carnac at Bombay was inclined to believe that while relations between Britain and Egypt remained normal no such interference could take place, but the matter was rather one, he thought, for the Governor-General's decision.[129] Auckland was somewhat at at loss to know what to do about any of the questions put to him. 'I have never seen my way clear upon Egyptian politics', he wrote to Palmerston in February 1840,

> and have thought that their settlement almost exclusively appertained to your side of the Isthmus of Suez. Still, however, I may remark that whilst the language held at Cairo is one of perfect moderation in regard to all the movements of Khoorshid Pasha towards the Persian Gulph, this leader seems to be not less bent upon firmly establishing himself in that quarter; and with little or no exertion on his part it is but too likely that his influence will become strong and gradually extended, for he has in his favour the reputation of power, and we have that of weakness in this quarter. But even in the event of his going on I am far from disposed to recommend our taking possession of the Island of Bahrein, for it is reported to be unhealthy, and is so large that it could not easily be held by a small force. I see indeed no means by which we could easily obtain a good base from whence we could act with any effect, otherwise than by

---

128 *Ibid.* A shortened version of Hamerton's report is to be found in [I.O.] *Bombay Selections* X XIV.
129 [I.O.] Enclos. to Bombay Sec. Letters, Vol. 17, enclos. to Sec. Letter 133 of 24 December 1839, Edmunds to Willoughby, 27 November 1839 (No. 120 Sec. Dept.), and Willoughby to Resident, 26 December 1839 (No. 1842 Sec. Dept.).

an offensive and defensive alliance with the Imaum of Muscat. But this would be a serious step, and one which is not to be taken without a grave weighing of consequences.[130]

He had voiced the same sentiments to Carnac the previous month, when he told him that it was the Home Government's duty to determine the policy to be adopted towards the Egyptians in the Gulf, and that they had so far issued no specific orders to him.[131] It was best, therefore, Auckland argued, to avoid a clash of arms with the Egyptians, especially as Mehemet 'Ali seemed anxious to do the same. Yet it was important not to convey any impression of a lessening of determination to oppose Khurshid Pasha's aggression, and this could best be achieved by means of a naval demonstration. The Governor of Bombay was to report to the Home authorities what ships could be spared for this purpose from the Indian Navy, and what might be needed from England. Only in the event of a rapid advance by Khurshid Pasha into south-eastern Arabia would Auckland be willing to supply the Sultan of Muscat and the Trucial Shaikhs with arms and naval protection, and he definitely would not sanction the loan of British officers to raise a force in Oman, as had been suggested, until much more was known both of the Sultan's resources and of the extent of the danger to him. '...The first step which his Lordship would take for the recovery of our influence on the coast and for effectually checking the encroachments of the Egyptians is the present establishment of a British officer at Muscat, to have the more immediate charge, though subject to the general superintendence of Captain Hennell, of our political relations there....'[132]

For the Na'im of Buraimi Auckland would do no more than had already been done. He had been uneasy for some time about the pledge of protection given by Hennell to the Na'imi emissary at Sharjah the previous July, which might have been construed as a formal pledge by the Na'imi shaikhs, and he was relieved to learn that, at his meeting with them at 'Ajman in January, the Resident had made it clear that the British Government were not extending their protection to them but were merely acting

---

130 [B.M.] Add. Ms. 37698, Auckland to Palmerston, Calcutta, 16 February 1840.
131 Hobhouse had, in fact, instructed him in July 1839: '... We leave it to your discretion to adopt such measures, in concert with Her Majesty's Naval Commander-in-Chief, from the means at your disposal, as may be effectual to secure the independence of the Arab Chiefs on the shores of the Persian Gulf.' ([I.O.] Board's Drafts: Sec. Desp. to India, Vol. 10, Draft to Gov.-Gen.-in-Council, 1 July 1839 (Most Secret).)
132 [I.O.] Encls. to Bombay Sec. Letters, Vol. 19, encls. to Sec. Letter 5 of 31 January 1840, Maddock to Willoughby, 13 January 1840.

towards them as allies, who were opposed also to the spread of Egyptian rule in Arabia.[133] As for Bahrain, Auckland considered that 'Abdullah ibn Ahmad, by his conduct, had forfeited all claim to British friendship, but he was not prepared to encourage the Sultan of Muscat to attack Bahrain lest this should bring him into collision with Khurshid Pasha. Finally, Auckland agreed with Carnac that while normal relations continued between Britain and Egypt, the supply of arms by sea to the Egyptian army in Najd could not be interfered with; but he thought, also, that the British Government, as general conservator of the maritime peace of the Gulf, would be justified in demanding of the Egyptian authorities in Arabia an explanation of the movement of ships and arms into the Gulf.[134]

While the Governor-General was debating whether or not to prefer such a demand Hennell had gone halfway towards imposing a prohibition on the supply of ams to Khurshid Pasha by sea. Acting on the authority given him by Auckland the previous September to prevent the movement of armed men by sea from Hasa to the Trucial Coast,[135] he had addressed a letter on 7 February to the Egyptian governor of Qatif, saying that any expedition attempting to leave that port for Oman would be stopped 'by any British force which may be on the coast'.[136] Carnac supported Hennell's action,[137] and so also, at first, did Hobhouse;[138] but later, when he learned that the Bombay Government were inclined to view the warning as a pledge 'to resist forcibly the invasion of Oman, or any other part of the Sultan's territories',[139] Hobhouse wrote in haste to Carnac to protest that 'such a pledge might involve the necessity of military operations, in which it would be injudicious to engage, and which we have before

---

133 *Ibid.* See also, [I.O.] Encos. to Bombay Sec. Letters, Vol. 20, enclos. to Sec. Letter 15 of 31 March 1840, Hennell to Willoughby, 1 February 1840 (No. 9 Sec. Dept.).

134 Same series, volume, and collection, Maddock to Willoughby, Fort William, 9 March 1840. See also, [I.O.] Enclos. to Bombay Sec. Letters, Vol. 19, enclos. to Sec. Letter 5 of 31 January 1840, Maddock to Willoughby, 13 January 1840.

135 See above, p. 154 Beginning paragraph: "The submission of Bahrain to the Egyptians..."

136 [I.O.] Enclos. to Bombay Sec. Letters, Vol. 20, enclos. to Sec. Letter 15 of 31 March 1840, Hennell to Willoughby, 8 February 1840 (No. 14 Sec. Dept.).

137 See same series and volume, enclos. to Sec. Letter 16 of 27 April 1 840, Reid to Maddock, 14 April 1840 (No. 567 Sec. Dept.).

138 A note by Hobhouse on Hennell's letter reads: 'Say we approve of this proceeding on the part of the Resident'.

139 [1.0.] Board's Drafts: Sec. Desp. to India, Vol. 13, Draft to Gov.-in-Council, Bombay, 2 July 1840 (No. 631).

deprecated'.[140] Hennell eventually had to explain what should have been obvious from that start, *viz.*, that his letter to the Governor of Qatif had done nothing more than convey the sense of the Governor-General's instructions of the previous September. How his action could have been interpreted as committing the British Government to the defence of Oman he was hard put to understand.[141]

While Khurshid Pasha had remained immobile in Najd in the last few months of 1839 Palmerston had taken little notice of him or of events in general in eastern Arabia. The Foreign Secretary's principal concern during this time had been to secure agreement with Russia and Austria over the measures to be adopted towards Mehemet 'Ali if he should take the offensive against the Porte. Palmerston's suspicions of the Viceroy's ultimate ambitions in the direction of the Gulf, however, had not abated, and they were given fresh stimulus in late February by the receipt of Edmunds' report on the supplying of Khurshid Pasha by sea. A second report from Edmunds, written in December, that Khurshid might have received orders from Cairo to subjugate not only the Trucial Shaikhdoms but the Sultanate of Muscat as well, reached Palmerston at the same time. The two reports, taken in conjunction with the continued occupation of Qatif, 'Uqair and Saihat by the Egyptians, seemed to indicate that Mehemet 'Ali had no intention of abiding by his repeated assurances that he was not seeking to establish himself permanently on the Gulf. The latest such assurance had been given by the Viceroy to Colonel G. L. Hodges—who had replaced Campbell as Consul-General the previous September—on 12 February.[142] It seemed to Palmerston that the Government of India would be fully justified in resorting to force, if necessary, to compel the Egyptians to withdraw from the Hasa ports, and from any other place they might have occupied on the Gulf coast. The least that the Indian authorities could do would be to adopt, without delay, Hennell's proposal that a blockade be clamped on Qatif, 'Uqair and Saihat. Palmerston was prepared to go further and prevent Mehemet 'Ali from supplying his troops in eastern Arabia by sea; and he would not permit him to obtain physical possession of Bahrain. 'If the troops of the East India Company could occupy it, even provisionally, it would seem that such a measure could not

---

140 *Ibid.*
141 [I.O.] Enclos. to Bombay Sec. Letters, Vol. 29, enclos. to Sec. Letter 7 of 31 January 1841, Hennell to Reid, 2 December 1840 (No. 114 Sec. Dept.).
142 [P.R.O.] F.O. 781404, Hodges to Palmerston Alexandria, 12 February 1840 (No. 24).

fail to be attended with advantage'.[143]

In transmitting these views to Auckland, Hobhouse used rather less forceful language. The Governor-General was not to conclude from what Palmerston had said that a military expedition to eject the Egyptians from the Hasa ports was what was desired. However, Hobhouse went on, 'although we may not be prepared for any movement of a land force upon the points now held by the Egyptians,' yet we are disposed to have recourse to whatever naval force we may be able to employ to blockade those stations, and to prevent all communication between the Red Sea and the shores of the Persian Gulf, which might provide munitions of war or assistance of any kind to the Egyptians.'[144] Mehemet 'Ali was not to be allowed to compete with Britain for influence in the Gulf. 'Such rivalry, however insignificant at the outset, with our maritime supremacy in those waters, might soon be highly injurious to British influence and interests; and we trust that it will be checked and put an end to at once'.[145] As for Bahrain, 'we should regard any attempt by the Egyptians to possess themselves of the Island by force as giving a clear right to occupy it ourselves, or to assist the Sultan of Muscat in a similar enterprise'.[146] The necessity to evacuate Kharag Island when normal relations were resumed with Persia 'makes it more necessary to keep our attention vigilantly fixed on Bahrein'. 'But', Hobhouse added, 'we do not interpret Lord Palmerston's expression as implying a desire that an expedition against the island should be undertaken on the part of the Indian Government, unless some opening should offer itself, or necessity arise, which would give you the opportunity or the right of taking possession of the place'.[147]

A similar caution was evident in the orders Hobhouse sent to Auckland in the next few weeks concerning the defence of Oman against possible Egyptian attack. A commercial treaty between Britain and the Sultanate had been concluded on 31 May 1839, and ratifications were now due to be exchanged. Provision had been made in the treaty for the stationing of a British consul in the Sultan's dominions, and the developments that

---

143 [I.O.] Board's Drafts: Sec. Desp. to India, Vol. 12, Palmerston to Hobhouse, 24 February 1840, enclosed in Draft to Gov.-Gen.-in-Council, 29 February 1840 (No. 575). See also [1.O.] Home Misc., Vol. 839, Palmerston to Hobhouse, 29 February 1840.
144 [I.O.] Board's Drafts: Sec. Desp. to India, Vol. 12, Draft to Gov.-Gen.-in-Courncil, 3 March 1840 (No. 579).
145 *Ibid.*
146 [1.O.] Board's Drafts: Sec. Desp. to India, Vol. 12, Draft to Gov.-Gen.-in-Council, 29 February 1840 (No. 575).
147 *Ibid.*

had taken place in Arabia since the signing of the treaty made such an appointment doubly desirable. It was only sensible that the office of consul should be filled by the political agent whom Auckland had decided to appoint to Saiyid Sa'id's court, and so, at the beginning of April, the officer who had been selected, Captain Hamerton, was invested with a consular commission.[148] Neither Palmerston nor Hobhouse intended that the appointment of a consul should be taken to signify the formation of a closer alliance with the Sultanate than had hitherto existed, and this was made clear in Hobhouse's instructions to the Governor of Bombay on the policy he should follow in the event of an Egyptian move against Oman. 'Should Mehemet Ali make any attempt against the territories now actually held by the Imaum of Muscat, he will do so in defiance of the repeated remonstrances of the British Government; but we know not in what way your resources could be employed in resisting such an aggression. Your operations would in that case be confined to the Gulf, and to those stations on the coast which are accessible to a naval force'.[149]

Before these instructions reached Bombay word arrived from Saiyid Sa'id that he had been visited at Muscat early in February by emissaries from Khurshid Pasha. They told him that Khurshid had no intention of moving against Basra, Bahrain or Buraimi, but Khurshid himself, in a letter to Sa'id, said that an expedition would shortly be sent against Buraimi. He had no intention of advancing beyond the oasis, but he was determined to bring under his control all the territories formerly held by the Al Sa'ud. He offered to help Sa'id in any attacks that he might wish to make against his enemies. Sa'id himself said that he had declined the offer, but Hennell discovered later that he had asked Khurshid's envoy to suggest to the Pasha that he demand from 'Abdullah ibn Ahmad the surrender of Dammam, on the Hasa coast, south of Qatif, which the Bahrain ruler had controlled for some time.[150] Whether Khurshid was in earnest when he spoke of the intended expedition to Buraimi is doubtful. Mehemet 'Ali told Hodges at

---

148 [I.O.] Board's Drafts: Sec. Desp. to India, Vol. 12, Draft to Gov.-in-Council, Bombay, 3 April 1840 (No. 598), enclosing Palmerston to Hobhouse, 2 April 1840. See also, Bombay Sec. Letters Recd., Vol. 11 (i), Gov.-in-Council to Sec. Committee, 28 February 1840 (No. 10 Sec. Dept.).
149 [I.O.] Board's Drafts: Sec. Desp. to India, Vol. 12, Draft to Gov.-in-Council, Bombay, 30 April 1840 (No. 608).
150 [I.O.] Enclos. to Bombay Sec. Letters, Vol. 20, enclos. to Sec. Letter 15 of 31 March 1840, Saiyid Sa'id to Carnac, 11 Dhu'l-Hijjah 1255/15 February 1840; enclos. to Sec. Letter 16 of 27 April 1840, Sa'id to Carnac, 2 Muharram 1256/6 March 1840; and Vol. 23, enclos. to Sec. Letter 37 of 22 June 1840, Hennell to Reid, 20 May 1840 (No. 46 See. Dept.).

Mehemet 'Ali's Expedition to the Persian Gulf 1837-1840

the end of March that he had never heard of Sa'ad ibn Mutlaq, who was supposed to be leading the expedition, and that he had nothing but the friendliest of feelings for Saiyid Sa'id and had never intrigued against him in any way.[151] There is no reason to suppose that the Viceroy was not telling the truth. If anything, Sa'id was probably more ardent in his courtship of Khurshid that Khurshid was in his of him, particularly as he saw in the Pasha's presence in eastern Arabia perhaps his last chance of getting the help he needed for the conquest of Bahrain.

A much more formidable contender for the island, however, was in the offing. Palmerston had not entirely abandoned the idea of occupying Bahrain, and at the end of January he had had a request sent to the Governor of Bombay to enquire into the island's resources and its fitness for occupation by British troops.[152] At the end of March he suggested to Hobhouse that, in view of the need eventually to withdraw the occupation force from Kharag, 'it might be desirable that some arrangements should be made with the chiefs of Bahrein by which the British detachment might, for a time at least, occupy some position in that Island, so as to place it in perfect safety against aggression from Mehemet Ali'.[153] What Palmerston was coming more and more to appreciate was that possession of a permanent base in the Gulf would not only strengthen the British position there but would enable the British Government to act with more effect in Persian and Arabian politics. To judge from the course of events in the Gulf before and after 1840, he was probably right. Hennell was of much the same opinion, and at the beginning of November 1839 he had had Edmunds and an officer from the Gulf squadron survey the island of Falaika, off the entrance to Kuwait harbour, to see whether it would be suitable as a naval and military station. Their findings were unfavourable: the main anchorage was exposed to both north-east and south-east winds, making it unfit for use by a naval force.[154]

Hennell's own preference was for Kharag, and in this he had the support of Auckland.[155] Both men, for their own reasons, were strongly

---

151 [P.R.O.] F.O. 78/404, Hodges to Palmerston, 31 March 1840 (No. 35).

152 [I.O.] Board's Drafts: Sec. Desp. to India, Vol. 12, Draft to Gov.-in-Council, Bombay, 29 January 1840 (No. 568).

153 Same series and volume, Draft to Gov.-in-Council, Bombay, 2 April 1840 (No. 595), enclosing Palmerston to Hobhouse, 31 March 1840.

154 [I.O.] Enclos. to Bombay Sec. Letters, Vol. 17, enclos. to Sec. Letter 135 of 31 December 1839, Hennell to Acting Chief Secy., Bombay, 11 November 1839 (No. 115 Sec. Dept.), enclosing reports by Edmunds and Lieut. J. T. Jones, 5 November 1839. Jones's report is reprinted in *Bombav Selections* XXIV.

155 See [B.M.] Add. Ms. 37698, Auckland to Palmerston, 16 February 1840.

opposed to the annexation of Bahrain; Auckland because he did not wish to incur the expense of an expedition to seize the island, Hennell because he thought its climate would prove unhealthy, even deadly, for Europeans. Admittedly, as he observed in his reply to Palmerston's initial enquiry of January 1840, Bahrain looked a valuable prize. Pearls to the value of $M.T. 350,000 were taken by Bahrain vessels from the banks off Qatar every season, and these, plus dates, bullion, and other items, accounted for an annual export trade of about $M.T. 800,000. Imports, mainly rice, cloths and spices from India, were valued at about $M.T. 600,000 *per annum*. Three-quarters of these goods were re-exported to other parts of the Gulf. If Bahrain were to be annexed it might produce a revenue of 3 lakhs of rupees *per annum*, and there was no doubt that the island's situation, commerce and harbour all commended it as the site of a British political and commercial centre. But its climate was, after that of Muscat and Basidu, the worst in the Gulf, and the numbers and fighting spirit of its 'Utub inhabitants would make its conquest and retention a difficult proposition.[156]

The real need of the moment, however, was not for a decision on the occupation of Bahrain but for ships with which to implement the proposed blockade of the Egyptian held ports on the Hasa coast, and to prevent supplies from getting through to Khurshid Pasha by sea. When Hennell learned that the Home Government had authorized the blockade he asked the senior naval officer of the Gulf squadron, Commodore A. H. Nott, how many vessels would be required to maintain it effectively. Nott estimated five, one each to watch Qatif, 'Uqair and Saihat, and another two to cruise. The normal duties of the station required the services of three vessels, so that the squadron would have to be increased to eight vessels, though he thought that six might prove enough. He had three vessels at his disposal: the sloop *Coote*, the brig *Tigris*, and the schooner *Royal Tiger*.[157] It was thus futile for Hennell to contemplate trying to impose the blockade. After all the suggestions he had made, and all the earnest debates that had taken place in India and England, he found himself at the close of May 1840 powerless to do anything against Khurshid Pasha. It was a fortunate turn of fate that at this very juncture word should reach him from the Arabian shore that the Egyptians were beginning a complete

---

156 [I.O.] Enclos. to Bombay Sec. Letters, Vol. 23, enclos. to Sec. Letter 37 of 22 June 1840, Hennell to Reid, 21 May 1840 (No. 48 Sec. Dept.), enclosing Hennell to Willoughby, 2 March 1839 (No. 15 Sec., Dept.).
157 [I.O.] Enclos. to Bombay Sec. Letters, Vol. 23, enclos. to Sec. Letter 37 of 22 June 1840, Hennell to Reid, 25 May 1840 (No. 49 Sec. Dept.), enclosing Nott to Hennell, 20 May 1840 (No. 510 Sec. Dept.).

withdrawal from Najd and Hasa.

A hint of Mehemet 'Ali's intentions had been given to Colonel Hodges by Boghos Bey at Alexandria in late February,[158] and a month later the Viceroy himself told Cochelet, the French Consul-General, that Khurshid Pasha was under orders to evacuate central and eastern Arabia.[159] He made no mention of the subject, however, at an interview Hodges had with him a few days later,[160] but reports had begun filtering through to Hennell from the Arabian coast at the end of February that the Egyptian troops had begun levying heavy demands upon the inhabitants of Hasa for taxes and supplies, a fairly certain sign that they were contemplating a withdrawal. In both Hasa and Najd many of the tribes were up in arms against Khurshid Pasha, and he was finding it increasingly difficult to keep open his communications both east and west. The reported deterioration of the Egyptian position in central and eastern Arabia was corroborated by Joseph Arton when he called at Kharag at the end of February on his way to Bombay with horses to sell for the Pasha.[161] Though Hennell heard more rumours of Khurshid's difficulties when he was on the Arabian coast in April, to renew the maritime truce, he could not obtain confirmation of their accuracy. Then, in the last week of May, he heard from the Residency Agent in Bahrain that Hasa was clear of Egyptians, and that the main body of Khurshid's army had also retired from Najd.[162]

As soon as he could spare her from Kharag Hennell sent the schooner *Royal Tiger* across to Qatif to see what could be learned at first hand. Her commander found that the reports were somewhat premature. Qatif was still under an Egyptian governor, Muhammad Effendi, the official who had visited Hennell the previous year. The Pasha's cavalry and irregular troops were still in Najd, although the bulk of the regular infantry had departed for the Hijaz. Muhammad Effendi said that Khurshid had been ordered by Mehemet 'Ali to fall back on Madinah, where he was to remain and exercise a general superintendence over central Arabian affairs. Khurshid, however, was said to be reluctant to abandon his conquests, at least

---

158 [I.O.] Persia and P. Gulf, Vol. 68, Hodges to Palmerston, 21 February 1840 (No. 25) - extract.

159 Driault, *L'Egypte et l'Europe*, II, 188-9, Cochelet to Thiers, Alexandria, 26 March 1840.

160 See above, p. 168 paragraph beginning "Before these instructions reached Bombay..."

161 [I.O.] Enclos. to Bombay Sec. Letters, Vol. 22, enclos. to Sec. Letter 26 of 20 May 1840, Hennell to Willoughby, 7 March 1840 (No. 22 Pol. Dept.).

162 [I.O.] Enclos. to Bombay Sec. Letters, Vol. 23, enclos. to Sec. Letter 37 of 22 June 1840, Hennell to Willoughby, 25 May 1840 (No. 49 Sec. Dept.).

before he had squeezed all he could from them in money and goods, and he had appealed to Mehemet 'Ali to allow him to remain longer in Najd. Meanwhile, he had suspended execution of the Viceroy's orders until the results of his appeal were known. Muhammad Effendi also stated that he was making over Qatif to a dependant of the Amir Khalid ibn Sa'ud, although he intended to remain in the neighbourhood of the port and keep a watch on its affairs. Whatever he might say, however, it was obvious that neither he nor his superior would be able to linger much longer in Najd or Hasa. The whole country seemed to be aflame with revolt, and the Egyptians' main problem was rapidly becoming that of getting out of it alive.[163]

This was obviously Mehemet 'Ali's view, too, and he had the added spur of needing his army for the probable defence of Syria and Egypt in the near future. By the end of June all thirteen regiments of regulars in Arabia were on the march for Cairo. Ibrahim Pasha the Younger had evacuated the Yemen and Khurshid Pasha was retiring from Najd. By the beginning of August Ibrahim was back in Cairo with two regiments, and Khurshid was not far behind him. Mecca and Madinah were left in the hands of irregular troops under the authority of the Sharif of Mecca, Muhammad ibn 'Aun, whom Mehemet 'Ali had appointed Governor of the Hijaz in succession to Ahmad Pasha.[164]

With the retirement of the Egyptians from central and eastern Arabia the need for the measures decided upon by Hobhouse and Palmerston disappeared. Hennell was ordered in mid-July not to act on the instructions issued to him to blockade the Hasa ports.[165] The Bombay Government had already decided, in May, to sever the tenuous link with the Na'im of Buraimi. Hennell's and Hamerton's recommendations that the tribe be given assistance to put their forts in a better state of defence were rejected, and Hennell was told that, 'beyond extending civilities to the Chiefs of that place, and occasionally sending them small presents with the view of securing their goodwill, and encouraging them to unite and resist any attempt which might be made to subjugate them, the British Government should not incur any further expense on their account'.[166]

---

163 [I.O.] Enclos. to Bombay Sec. Letters, Vol. 23, enclos. to Sec. Letter 56 of 22 August 1840, Hennell to Reid, 2, 4 July 1840 (Nos. 80, 82 Sec. Dept.), enclosing letters from Muhammad Effendi and Mirza Muhammad 'Ali (Res. Agent, Bahrain).
164 Driault, *L'Egypte et l'Europe*, II, 323-4, Cochelet to Thiers, 22 June 1840; III, 88-90, Cochelet to Thiers, 6 August 1840; and IV, 161-2, Cochelet to Guizot, 24 December 1840.
165 [I.O.] Enclos. to Bombay Sec. Letters, Vol. 23, enclos. to Sec. Letter 47 of 18 July 1840, Reid to Hennell, 14 July 1840 (No. 1162 Sec. Dept.).
166 [I.O.] Enclos. to Bombay Sec. Letters, Vol. 22, enclos. to Sec. Letter 26 of 20 May

A more awkward problem was that of Bahrain. Hennell's unfavourable reports on the island led Hobhouse in August 1840 to conclude that the island would be unsuitable as the site for a base, and that no further move should be made towards acquiring it.[167] But Hennell had also pointed out that the conduct of 'Abdullah ibn Ahmad had been such as to justify the British Government's supporting, if they so desired, the claims of the Sultan of Muscat to the island. The suggestion had been sympathetically received at Bombay, and Hennell was instructed in July to throw no impediment in the way of Sa'id's conquest of Bahrain.[168] The Resident saw Sa'id at Muscat at the beginning of August and discussed the matter with him. Sa'id said that he did not really want Bahrain for himself but would gladly see the British take possession of it. If they did not want it and were inclined to favour its acquisition by him, he was willing to expend both the effort and the resources required for its conquest. However, to be assured of success in this venture he would have to be given some help. If the garrison on Kharag Island were to be placed at his disposal, he could, with a further 4,000 men of his own, easily subdue the 'Utub and their Al Khalifah rulers. Hennell, obviously, could make Sa'id no promises on this head, but he did tell him that the British Government would not be displeased to see him in possession of Bahrain. Sa'id appeared to be considerably cheered by this news, and confided to Hennell that he had begun to despair of ever getting possession of Bahrain and had been preparing to return to Zanzibar. Now he was willing to remain at Muscat, if the slightest hope of support were to be held out to him.[169]

Though Hennell still had reservations about the value of the Muscat alliance in general, and the wisdom of helping Sa'id to conquer Bahrain in particular, he nevertheless made a strong plea on his behalf to the Bombay Government. By his past endeavours on their behalf, Hennell said, Sa'id had a claim on the British Government's support. It would be in their interest, furthermore, to restore his declining influence in Gulf politics. Possession of Bahrain would help considerably to achieve this object. Sa'id had more or less given up his ambition to possess Bahrain, in deference

---

1840, Reid to Resident, 15 May 1840 (No. 803 Sec. Dept.).

167 [I.O.] Board's Drafts: Sec. Desp. to India, Vol. 13, Draft to Gov. in-Council, Bombay, 15 August 1840 (No. 645).

168 [I.O.] Enclos. to Bombay Sec. Letters, Vol. 23, enclos. to Sec. Letter 47 of 18 July 1840, Hennell to Reid, 3 June 1840 (No. 62 Sec. Dept.); Reid to Hennell, 14 July 1840 (No. 1162 Sec. Dept.).

169 [I.O.] Enclos. to Bombay Sec. Letters, Vol.23, enclos. to Sec. Letter 56 of 22 August 1840, Hennell to Reid, 4 August 1840 (No. 97 Sec. Dept.).

to British wishes, by rejecting the offers undoubtedly made to him by Khurshid Pasha for a joint expedition to conquer the island. If it were now decided to help him to acquire it, a small force should suffice to assure his success, *viz.*, 500 European troops, a battalion of sepoys, and half-a-dozen field guns.[170] The Resident's arguments met with a considerable measure of agreement at Bombay. Carnac, however, did not feel that the forces available in the Presidency were sufficient to allow any of them to be spared for such a venture, especially as the situation in Afghanistan remained uncertain.[171] This was also Auckland's opinion. No hope of assistance, he said, should be held out to Sa'id until the British position in the Gulf had been strengthened by the arrival of one or more ships of war from England.[172] Hobhouse, although he admitted the force of much of what Hennell had said, agreed with Auckland. '... The present would be a very inopportune occasion of undertaking military or naval operations for the purpose of putting His Highness in possession of Bahrein. Any such expedition would be premature before we are acquainted with the results of the war in Syria, and with the manner in which the Egyptian question is likely to be settled'.[173] At the close of the year he quashed any further deliberation on the subject by sending positive orders to Bombay to discourage Sa'id from making any attempt to invade Bahrain, and to take no action regarding the island without obtaining the approval of the Home authorities.[174] Long before Hobhouse's decision was made known to him Sa'id had given up the project as hopeless and sailed for Zanzibar.

* * *

The defeat of the Egyptian army in Syria between September and November 1840 by combined Turkish, British and Austrian forces ended forever Mehemet 'Ali's design of Arabian expansion, and with it his vision of an Egyptian empire reaching from the Nile to the Tigris. By the conventions concluded at Alexandria in November and December 1840 the Vice-

---

170 *Ibid.*
171 [I.O.] Bombay Sec. Letters Recd., Vol. 11 (i), Gov.-in-Council to Sec. Committee, 22 August 1840 (No. 56 Sec. Dept.).
172 [I.O.] Enclos. to Bombay Sec. Letters, Vol. 26, enclos. to Sec. Letter 90 of 30 October 1840, H. Torrens (Officiating Secy. to Govt. of India) to W. R. Morris (Secy. to Govt., Bombay), 14 September 1840.
173 [I.O.] Board's Drafts: Sec. Desp. to India, Vol. 13, Draft to Gov.-in-Council, Bombay, 31 October 1840 (No. 674).
174 Same series and volume, Draft to Gov.-in-Council, Bombay, 28 December 1840 (No. 688).

roy agreed to renounce possession of Syria, Adana, Crete and Arabia, and to restore the Turkish fleet to the Sultan. In renouncing Arabia, Mehemet 'Ali not only abandoned Khurshid Pasha's conquests in the Qasim, Najd and Hasa, but he also gave up the Hijaz, the Holy Cities and the Yemen. Khalid ibn Sa'ud, whom Khurshid had left behind as Amir of Najd and Hasa, could doubtless be looked upon as an Egyptian puppet, but it was highly unlikely that he would be capable of taking up and pursuing the Pasha's designs on Bahrain and Oman. Nevertheless, Auckland thought it best, in late February 1841, in response to an enquiry from the Resident in the Gulf, to instruct the Government of Bombay to warn Khalid, should he display any inclination to extend his authority into south-eastern Arabia, that the despatch of armed forces by sea from Hasa to the Trucial Coast would be opposed by British ships of war.[175] The following June it was learned that Khalid had submitted to the Porte and been appointed *vali* of Najd, and in September he wrote to Hennell, expressing a desire to be on friendly terms with the British Government.[176]

Notwithstanding this assurance, Khalid was reported in November 1841 to be contemplating sending an armed expedition by land to occupy the Buraimi Oasis. The commander of the force was to be Sa'ad ibn Mutlaq. Immediately on receiving this news Hennell despatched an officer of the Kharag Field Force, Lieutenant Keith Jopp, to Hufuf in Hasa to see Khalid and to tell him not to make any move in the direction of Trucial Oman. Though Khalid, when Jopp saw him, was inclined to insist that he had every right to occupy Buraimi, he agreed to abandon the projected expedition to the oasis. He repeated the assurance in a letter to Hennell which he gave to Jopp to deliver. It was hardly necessary for him to do so. Jopp reported to Hennell that, from what he had seen and heard of the Amir's situation and resources, it was clear that he was in no position to undertake an expedition anywhere outside Hasa. His tribal support amounted to no more than 3,000 rifles, and the only other fighting men he had under his command were some 800 Egyptian irregulars, half of them cavalry, half infantry, who were poorly armed and mutinous over arrears of pay.[177]

---

175 [I.O.] Enclos. to Bombay Sec. Letters, Vol. 30, enclos. to Sec. Letter 18 of 26 March 1841, Maddock to Willoughby, Fort William, 22 February 1841 (No. 202 Sec. Dept.).
176 [I.O.] Enclos. to Bombay Sec. Letters, Vol. 35, enclos. to Sec. Letter 67 of 30 August 1841, Hennell to Willoughby, 30 June 1841 (No. 80 Sec. Dept.); Vol. 39, enclos.to Sec. Letter 107 of 31 December 1841, Hennell to Willoughby, 5 October 1841 (No. 112 Sec. Dept.).
177 [I.O.] Enclos. to Bombay Sec. Letters, Vol. 41, enclos. to Sec. Letter 17 of 28 Febru-

Khalid's overtures of friendship of the previous September were received by Auckland 'in a frank and cordial spirit', but the Governor-General would not commit himself to any further recognition of the Amir's authority than that to which his eventual power might entitle him.[178] Auckland never had need to consider the subject again. At the close of 1841 Khalid was expelled from Riyadh by another member of the Al Sa'ud, and not long afterwards he fled to Kuwait. In the spring of 1843 Faisal ibn Turki, released from surveillance in Cairo, returned to Najd and resumed authority as Amir.

* * *

Two questions naturally present themselves in any reconsideration of the crisis in the Gulf in 1839-40: firstly, how much of a threat did the Egyptian expedition to central and eastern Arabia constitute to the British position in the Gulf, and, secondly, how adequately was that threat met by the British Government in India and in England? So far as the actual danger presented by Khurshid Pasha and his army is concerned, this must be reckoned as insignificant. At no time did his army exceed 4,000 men, and it included in its ranks a fair proportion of irregular Bedouin troops. The fact that Khurshid chose to make his headquarters as far west as Sulaimiya, and later, further west still, at Tharmidah, pointed to the absence of any serious intention on his part to press his conquests beyond the limits they had reached by the early summer of 1839. Although it cannot be proved conclusively, it would be fairly safe to say that the initiative for Sa'ad ibn Mutlaq's expedition to the Trucial Coast came from that individual himself rather than from the Egyptian commander. Sa'ad had probably thrown in his lot with the usurper Khalid in the hope of being reinstated as Wahhabi *na'ib* at Buraimi, and of resuming his exactions from the frontier chiefs of Oman, the Trucial Shaikhs, and the Sultan of Muscat. Khurshid Pasha, who had shown by his rapacious conduct in Najd that he was not indifferent to the spoils of war, may also have entertained hopes of benefiting from Sa'ad's extortions in Oman; but it is fairly certain that he was incapable, through lack of sufficient troops and adequate transport, of embarking

---

ary 1842, Jopp to Hennell, n.d. [December 1841]. The Comte de Rohan-Chabot, who succeeded Cochelet as French Consul-General in Egypt, had reported in May 1841 that all the irregular troops had by then returned from Arabia. (Driault, L'Agypte et l'Europe, V, 65, Rohan-Chabot to Guizot, 3 May 1841).

178 [I.O.] Enclos. to Bombay Sec. Letters, Vol. 40, enclos. to Sec. Letter 6 of 29 January 1842, Maddock to Willoughby, 27 December 1841 (No. 3709 Pol. Dept.).

upon a serious campaign in south-eastern Arabia.

If Khurshid's objects did not include the conquest of the Trucial Shaikhdoms and Oman, what was the purpose of his campaign? Certainly not the permanent subjection of Bahrain, however tempting its riches, which the Egyptians believed to include the Amir Faisal's treasure. Mehemet 'Ali's intention seems rather to have been to probe the southern approaches to the Pashaliq of Baghdad, while the attention of the Ottoman Sultan and of the European powers was directed primarily to his activiities in Syria. It was a leisurely investigation, inasmuch as it began in 1837 and was only completed by the early months of 1839. The part that Khalid ibn Sa'ud was to play in the scheme was that of a client, amenable to Egyptian control, behind whose nominal rule Mehemet 'Ali might conceal his true purposes in eastern Arabia. The opposition aroused by Khurshid Pasha's movements in England and India destroyed any hopes that Mehemet 'Ali might have had of a quiet descent upon Baghdad and Basra; and by the middle of 1839 he would appear to have abandoned the project as no longer feasible. The Egyptian army remained in Najd, partly to recoup the cost of the venture and partly to serve as a bargaining counter in any crisis that might later develop with the British. Some allowance must also be made for the fact that Khurshid Pasha found his stay profitable.

Whatever the motives for the Egyptian campaign against the Wahhabis may have been, its success not only provoked anxiety on the British Government's part for the safety of the Gulf route to India but it also challenged the British ascendancy over the maritime principalities of the Arabian shore. For, in defeating Faisal ibn Turki and assuming the government of Najd and Hasa, Khurshid Pasha also assumed, in British eyes, the traditional Wahhabi roles of ally of the piratical tribes of the Trucial Coast, in particular, the Qawasim of Sharjah and Ras al-Khaima, and enemy of the Al Bu Sa'id Sultans of Muscat. The Government of India, which, for the sake of maritime peace in the Gulf, had been competing with the Al Sa'ud for thirty years for influence over the Trucial Shaikhs, was not now prepared to yield the ascendancy to the new masters of Najd; and the intrigues of Sa'ad ibn Mutlaq with the Trucial Shaikhs lent substance to the suspicion that Khurshid Pasha was bent on acquiring such an ascendancy. Sa'ad's attempts to dislodge the Na'im from the Buraimi forts aroused the further suspicion that Khurshid might be contemplating an invasion of Oman, in conformity with the usual pattern of Wahhabi expansion in south-eastern Arabia. The appearance of Egyptian troops on the Gulf, moreover, coincided with a period of tension in Anglo-Persian relations, when the British Government were already concerned for the safety of the north-western approaches to India. This is why Khurshid's first intervention in Gulf politics, his demand for the submission of Bahrain, provoked the reaction it did, not so much because he threatened the independence of Bahrain (this had been threatened several times, by the Wahhabis, the Persians, and the Sultan of Muscat), but because his appearance in the Gulf at this critical juncture was taken for something of far greater moment than it actually was.

When the magnitude of Khurshid's threat is correctly assessed Auckland's reluctance to act swiftly and forcibly to meet it does not seem exceptionable; but when it is remembered that the Government of Bombay, Palmerston, Hobhouse, and even, to some extent, Auckland himself, regarded the danger as real, then his hesitancy is open to criticism. Even when due allowance is made for the widespread commitments and shortages of naval and military resources of the Government of India at this time, the fact remains that something more could have been done, and should have been done, than was done in the Gulf. As it was, the apparent inability of the Indian authorities to confront the Egyptians with a show of armed strength induced in the maritime tribes a contempt for British power. That they were forced to revise this opinion, though rather belatedly, was due primarily to the efforts of the British political and naval officers in the Gulf, supported by the Bombay authorities, who were better able to assess the significance of events in that quarter than the authorities at Calcutta. Had Auckland been more familiar with Gulf politics he would have been less surprised and chagrined than he was at the fickleness and faithlessness of the maritime shaikhs, and, consequently, less ready to reach the pessimistic conclusions that he did about the value of supporting them. Since the British Government, in their eyes, stood for little more than a tiresome interference in their enjoyment of their favourite pursuits, piracy and maritime warfare, it should have been expected that they would act with circumspection on the appearance of a rival power in the Gulf. Certainly the conduct of the Na'im of Buraimi, who had had little previous contact with the British, was deserving of better recognition than that accorded it by Auckland.

A deeper appreciation of what was at stake in the Gulf was shown by Palmerston and by the Political Resident, Samuel Hennell. Though Palmerston does not loom large in this particular episode of the great Eastern crisis of 1839-41, his influence, especially at the India Board, is often apparent. If Auckland was not perspicacious enough to see that the Egyptian drive through Arabia constituted as great a potential menace to the approaches to India from the north-west as did the Shah's attack on Herat,

Palmerston was fully aware of the danger, and he was prepared to sanction armed intervention on the Arabian littoral to contain it, whatever the limitations of British naval and military resources in the East. To Hennell must go the credit of halting the drift of the maritime tribes into the Egyptian camp after the capitulation of Bahrain. His achievement was all the greater because it owed little to the material power at his disposal but depended almost wholly upon his personal standing with the maritime shaikhs. In the final measure, it was upon the personal influence of their officers with the Arabian tribes that the British Government depended for their ascendancy in the Gulf.

12
The Economy of Kuwait[1]

The Economic Development of Kuwait: Report of Missions organised by the International Bank for Reconstruction and Development at the request of the Government of Kuwait. Baltimore: Johns Hopkins Press for the International Bank for Reconstruction and Development. London: Oxford University Press. 1965. 194 pp. Index.

At the request of the Kuwait Government the International Bank for Reconstruction and Development sent two missions to Kuwait in 1961 and 1963. The report of the 1963 mission, which includes and brings up to date the greater part of the 1961 mission's report, is perhaps the most informative and useful book on Kuwait that has yet appeared. The task of both missions was to advise the Kuwait Government on the best direction which the economic development of Kuwait might take, after the initial rush had ended, to acquire goods and amenities with which to enliven the Kuwaitis' hitherto austere existence. How best, in other words, to assure a stable economy for the future? The International Bank has no doubts about the answer: it lies in adequate investment, public and private, within Kuwait itself. Overseas investment can be left to take care of itself. Kuwait, with the highest per capita income in the world, 40-50 per cent. of which is saved, in both the public and the private sector, is in the fortunate position of being able to expand its domestic economy while exporting capital for investment abroad. Not enough has been done

---

1 Source: *International Affairs* (Royal Institute of International Affairs 1944-), Vol. 42, No. 1 (Jan.,1966), pp. 141-143.

The Economy of Kuwait

by the Kuwait Government, however, in the view of the International Bank's mission, either in public works or in making capital available for the development of the private sector of the economy. Two areas of public expenditure which the mission singles out as requiring special attention are low-cost housing and adequate water supplies. To stimulate private industrial growth, the Kuwait Government should either impose high tariffs and import restrictions, or make low-interest capital and technical assistance available to those who desire them. The mission rejects the first alternative and plumps for the second, as being both more relevant and more fruitful. It sees great possibilities for the petro-chemical industry in Kuwait, and more limited potentialities for such smaller industries as tyre-manufacturing and glass-making. There is as much value in the criticisms, often sharp, which the mission makes of government policy and organisation in Kuwait, as there is in its careful presentation of the facts which were made available to it—which were not always those which it wanted to know. It considers that the government's policy of distributing the wealth from oil revenues by the device of buying land at highly inflated prices, for development or resale later to private buyers, has resulted in the indiscriminate and inequitable disbursement of that wealth. Moreover, the investment of the money abroad by the recipients has stultified the object of the policy, which was to invigorate Kuwait's economy. The mission is roundly critical of (though it has largely ignored the political reasons for) the Kuwait Government's attitude towards non-Kuwaitis who make up half, at least, of the population, and whose skills are vital to the running of the country. By stipulating that only Kuwaitis may be appointed to senior posts in local government, the civil service and education, while at the same time they have made naturalisation a difficult and tedious process, the Kuwait Government have deprived these people of any long-term security. The mission paints a depressing picture (p. 40) of the civil service. '... Less than 1 per cent of the Kuwaitis in the classified civil service are college graduates, less than 5 per cent have graduated from secondary school and only 13 per cent from primary school. Three thousand, or nearly 30 per cent, were rated as illiterates. These data perhaps are less a gauge of inefficiency than of the redundancy in the government work force.' 'Redundancy' is hardly the word: with a civil service of 36,000 for a population of 350,000, Kuwait seems to be well on the way towards achieving that happy synthesis of Eastern tradition and Western progress which the Bank's mission confidently predicts for it.

13
Aden[1]

The View From Steamer Point, Being an Account of Three Years in Aden by Charles Hepburn Johnston, 224 pp., illustrated, index, end paper maps. Collins.

Imperial Outpost - Aden: Its Place in British Strategic Policy by Gillian King, Chatham House Essays, 95 pp., maps, Oxford University Press for Royal Institute of International Affairs.

Sir Charles Johnston went to Aden as Governor and Commander-in-Chief in 1960 and left there three years later as High Commissioner for Aden and the Federation of South Arabia. His prime task in those three years had been to accomplish the merger of Aden Colony with the Federation of Arab Amirates of the South, begun in 1959 with the joining together of six of the states of the Western Protectorate, and to take the Colony a further step along the road to self-government. The choice of Johnston, a member of the Foreign Service who from 1956 to 1960 had been Ambassador in Jordan, as successor to Sir William Luce (who left Aden to become Political Resident in the Persian Gulf) was a plain indication that the implementation of the proposed merger was regarded as calling more for diplomacy than direction. The View from Steamer Point is Johnston's account of his three years in Aden and how the merger and constitutional advance in the Colony were brought about.

It is a pleasant and good-humoured book, with none of the waspishness and asperity that characterize so much writing on the contemporary

---

[1] Source: *Middle Eastern Studies*, Vol. 2, No. 2 (Jan., 1966), pp. 164-170.

Aden

Middle East. The author has no blade to hone, except in the cause of good sense, honesty, and firmness of purpose. He emerges as a good-natured and urbane man, not without a few foibles, among which are a sometimes misplaced candour and a slight disposition to under-estimate other people's sensibilities. Some of his comments about Aden's politicians, though delivered without malice and with the best of intentions, may not be received in the same spirit. These, however, are momentary lapses. They do not detract from the man or from the value of his book as a record of the negotiations leading to the Federation.

The basic problem facing Britain in South Arabia in 1960 was how to advance Aden Colony and the Protectorate towards independence while at the same time providing for the maintenance and protection of British interests in the area. These interests were bound up with the retention of the Aden base in British hands, which was deemed essential for three main reasons: 1) Aden is a staging post on the routes to Malaysia and Australia and a dispersal point for V-bombers; 2) it is an operational base and acclimatization area for the defence of the Persian Gulf oilfields; and 3) it is necessary to the defence of Aden Colony and Protectorate. The solution devised to meet this situation was the merger of the Colony with the Protectorate into one political unit, having a special relationship with Britain which would secure to her the strategic facilities at Aden that she needed.

The difficulty with this plan was that there was a sizable opposition within Aden Colony itself to the merger on the grounds that Federation would drag the Colony down to the level of the Protectorate, and permanently retard its progress. For obvious and historical reasons the Colony was far more advanced than the Protectorate, and a number of Adenis believed that they would be submerged, and the Colony's prosperity along with them, in the proposed Federation. The proper course for the Colony, they argued, was to develop separately towards self-government and independence. How strong this opposition was, and still is, and how widely based, it is difficult to say, because there are so many interested parties involved in making a case for or against the Federation.

Johnston believes that at the time that Federation was carried out a majority of Adenis were in favour of it, and that after it came into effect the number increased. The principal opponents of Federation have been the People's Socialist Party, the political arm of the Aden T.U.C., and the South Arabian League, and their sympathizers abroad. With them, and with others in Aden, it is not merely a question of the Colony's future as part of the Federation, but also a question of Arab nationalism, Arab unity, and Arab socialism, especially as propounded from Cairo. Any British sponsored plan is anathema to them, and they regard, or profess to regard, the Federation as a device to frustrate union with the Yemeni Republic and the rest of the Arab world.

A focal point of the opposition to the Federation was the British Government's refusal to allow elections to precede the merger. This has been interpreted, and particularly by the Federation's critics in England, as a denial of democratic procedure and a refusal to allow the wishes of the Colony's inhabitants to prevail. But, as Johnston points out, the merger meant life or death to the Protectorate States. If Aden had refused to merge with them, they would have been cut off from the sea and forced into the arms of the Yemen—'a gloomy enough prospect under the Imam, and a desperate one under the distraught Republic' (p. 195). 'It would have been a strange application of our principles', he goes on, 'to insist that the Adenese, being urban and relatively sophisticated, should be allowed to decide the question of merger by their own vote, while the inhabitants of the original Federation, although five times as numerous and no less vitally concerned, should not be consulted at all—presumably on the theory that as illiterate rifle-carrying tribesmen they somehow counted as second class human beings'. (Pp. 195-6). According to the leaders of the Aden T.U.C., who had been showing their devotion to the idea of free elections by boycotting every one that had taken place since 1959, the proper course would have been to scrap all the arrangements made since 1958, when the Aden Constitution was introduced, and to start again with elections based on a franchise which would include all the Yemenis resident in Aden, 70,000 - 80,000 of them, which was rather more than there were Arabs born in the Colony. To have acquiesced in this demand, says Johnston, would have been to put Aden's future in the hands of 'transient Yemeni labourers who enjoyed no freedom of political expression under the regime then existing in their own country' (p. 120). The situation has not changed.

Democratic procedures, adult suffrage, and free elections are mere cant phrases in the Arab world today. The demand for free elections in Aden, as Harold Ingrams has recently observed, is merely so as to be able to use them as a form of plebiscite in favour of nationalism, to attract outside support, and to end colonial rule.[2] Once independence is attained, free elections disappear into a limbo from which they rarely re-appear. The fear of the young, anti-Federation politicians of Aden—and they are young, and ambitious, and ill-informed—is that their own political futures will be blighted by the absorption of Aden into the Federation. But as Johnston points out time and again in his book, Aden is the natural leader

---

2 See *The Yemen* London: John Murray, 1963, p. 149.

of the Federation, it has half the seats in the new Federal Council, and its influence, and the careers of its politicians, will inevitably expand. The city always controls the countryside in the end. Aden is the head of the Federation's body, and is already on the way to commanding it.

It is doubtful, however, if the Aden nationalists want to share power with the sultans and shaikhs of the Protectorate. What they want is to rule the Protectorate. If the sultans and shaikhs object, then they are prepared to 'do a Yemen,' even to the extent of calling in the Egyptians. Their real hostility to the Federation springs from this calculation, and from the further consideration that the Federation thwarts, if it does not entirely preclude, union with the Yemen. Johnston accepts that such a union will come about one day, but if it came now, he thinks, it would be disastrous for Aden. 'From its present proud status as a great international communications centre and as the biggest bunkering port in the world, it would be brought down to the level of a sleepy provincial harbour in an underdeveloped country, a sort of poor man's Hodeida. All the prosperity built up since the British occupation of Aden in 1839 would be lost, and the present easygoing internatonal cooperation would be replaced by Arab nationalism in its narrowest form'. (Pp. 152-3).

In his closing chapters Johnston allows himself some reflections on the nature of colonial rule and of gubernatorial power, on the differences in *esprit* and personnel beween the Colonial and Foreign Services, and on British aims in South Arabia and the peninsula generally. He has some sensible and trenchant things to say about the foolishness of recoiling in such confusion from 'gunboat diplomacy' as to 'fall flat on our faces before some imaginary "wave of the future"' (p. 193); about the need to reject the guidance of dogma and lean more heavily upon that of experience; and about the school of thought which insists that Britain must totally disengage herself from the Arab world, and reject any overture for assistance 'with virtuous horror on the grounds that any such relationship is very bad for the Arabs' (p. 202). About the future of the South Arabian Federation he is reasonably optimistic, provided that the British Government know what they want to do in Aden and are prepared to carry out a consistent policy there. 'Frankly', he concludes, 'the main question-marks as I saw them were not in Aden but in London'.

* * *

Imperial Outpost-Aden is a fairly blatant attempt to influence the answers that may be given to some of the current questions being asked about

Aden and its base. Its author is a former assistant at Chatham House, and the book itself is one of the series of *Chatham House Essays*, designed to provide background information on contemporary international problems. Contrary to its title, only half the book is concerned with Aden: the remainder is taken up with a review of British strategic policy, defensive commitments, and political and economic interests east of Suez and particularly in the Persian Gulf region.

The conclusions reached by Mrs. King with respect to Aden are that Federation was a mistake, that it was forced upon the Colony against its wishes, and that it ran counter to the desires of the leaders of the Aden T.U.C., whose aims, she says, included 'the expulsion of the British from Aden, the overthrow of the existing constitution, the destruction of the Federation of Arab Amirates of the South, and the formation of a single state made up of the Colony, the Western Protectorate, and the Yemen, either as part of the UAR, or in close association with it' (p. 53). These aims Mrs. King seems to approve, or, at least, to regard their achievement as inevitable. *Chacun a son gout*, but it is strange, as Sir Charles Johnston observes in his book, that the most vociferous opponents of the unification of Aden with the Protectorate under British auspices are also the most strenuous proponents of unity elsewhere in the Arab world, by force of arms, if necessary. It is all of a piece with the U.N.'s Anti-Colonialism Committee's characterization of the months of patient negotiation to persuade the Aden and Federal Minsters to unite as a policy of 'divide and rule'.

Au fond, Mrs. King is advocating a policy of retreat, not only from Aden but from the Persian Gulf as well. Her advocacy might be more convincing if it proceeded from a basis of established fact rather than from ideological inclination. Her arguments bear a close resemblance to those put forward by the Director-General of Chatham House, Mr. Kenneth Younger, in the supplement on defence issued by the *Financial Times* in March 1964, and by Miss Elizabeth Monroe at various times and more particularly in her article, 'Kuwayt and Aden: a Contrast in British Policies', in the Winter 1964 issue of the *Middle East Journal*. Oddly enough, Mrs. King makes no mention of either in her book, although her debt to Miss Monroe is particularly apparent. For instance, she writes (p. 21) of Britain's treaty arrangements with the Gulf states that 'some... had, with the complacency of the time, been labelled "perpetual"'. Miss Monroe wrote (p. 68) about 'agreements which the Victorians, with the complacency of their age, negotiated as "perpetual"'. Not only is the sneer unwarranted but it also betrays a profound lack of understanding of the conditions in which the treaties were negotiated. The political officers responsible for them were far from complacent men, as the slightest acquaintance with them would show. The term 'perpetual' is a technical one in treatymaking. How long would Mrs. King have preferred the treaties suppressing piracy, the slave trade, and maritime warfare to have run? For five years, ten years, twenty years—or 'in perpetuity'?

There are several examples like this, distributed through the pages on the Gulf, all of them marked by a superficiality of treatment and a subordination of fact to the dictates of dogma. To take one of them (p. 24): 'At the time when the treaties were made, the British obligation was conceived as a purely maritime operation. The inland frontiers were in deserts so remote and arid that several opportunities to define them were missed. From the mid-twentieth century, however, the possibility of discovering oil vested them with a new and sharp significance, and saddled the United Kingdom with awkward and embarrassing obligations in disputes between Arab and Arab'. These statements are simply absurd. What opportunities to define the inland frontiers of the Gulf states were missed in the nineteenth century? The answer is 'None': the question never arose. As for 'awkward and embarrassing obligations' regarding Arab disputes, Britain was saddled with these long before the internal combustion engine was invented.

The rest of Mrs. King's remarks about the Gulf, like her observations on strategy, are of the same order. According to her, the arguments advanced for retaining the Aden base do not stand up under examination. The chances of another Kuwait operation are remote: the Kuwaitis will not call on the British again. The protection at present afforded the Trucial States will become unnecessary because they will federate, or because they will be unable to resist the magnetic attraction exerted by a new regime in Saudi Arabia after the longed-for revolution has taken place. British oil interests in the Gulf do not need, nor can they be secured by, military protection. Aden, and islands like Gan, are not needed as stepping stones to Singapore and Malaysia: we can always fly by the 'westabout' route, presumably by Canada and the U.S. And, finally, the ultimate defence of Western interests in the Indian Ocean lies with the United States anyway.

There is a surface plausibility about such arguments but Mrs. King contrives to rob them of even that. Of course, the chances of another Kuwait operation, in the sense of meeting an overt military threat, are slender. The threat is far more likely to come from internal subversion in one of the Gulf states, aided by an outside power. In this case, the Oman operation of 1957 is a better guide to the future. Then, a few troops with air cover suppressed the Saudi and Egyptian-inspired rebellion against the Sultan with relative ease. Mrs. King does not even mention the operation or the uprising. Her prognostications about political developments in the Gulf are merely fancies. Her section on oil contains such statements as: 'Certainly British experience at Suez was that the use of force at one point provoked stoppages at others—a display of Arab unity that has seldom, if ever, been paralleled'. Did Kuwait cut off her oil? Did Qatar? Were oil prospectors in the Trucial Coast and Oman molested? Turning to Aden's place on the sea and air routes to the East, Mrs. King writes: 'For the navy the Suez Canal is the one possible hazard, but if the Egyptians tried to use the threat of a closure as a weapon against the United Kingdom, for example over Aden or the Yemen, which so far they have shown no tendency to do, ships could always go round the Cape.' (P. 34). The statement has a familiar ring to it. Mr. Dulles and the Canal Users' Association? 'What would American ships do if they were denied passage through the Canal'? Although Mrs. King quotes Article I of the 1888 Convention elsewhere, she does not seems perturbed about the legal aspects of closure.

Finally, there is the argument based on the needs of Western defence. Among the reasons that Mrs. King says are those given in support of retaining the Aden base there is one that she omits to mention, *viz.*, the maintenance of international law and order. In one of her excursions into the past she says that the chain of British bases east of Suez, together with the Royal Navy, used to provide for the defence of India and other possessions. But the prime function of the bases and the Navy, as Mrs. King would have discovered had she investigated further, was not so much the positive defence of India and other possessions against aggression as the preservation of peace and security around the Indian Ocean. For it is in the preservation of international peace and order, and respect for law, that the only true defence of national interests lies. The logical extension of the arguments set out in Mrs King's book is that Britain should abandon responsibility for maintaining order and security in the western Indian Ocean, and around the shores of Arabia, because the Americans are in a better position to do it. She does not appear to have consulted the Americans in the matter.

Apparently the Americans, according to Mrs. King, are not satisfied with the existing arrangements. They are building a powerful naval radio station on the north-western coast of Australia, of the type needed to control Polaris submarines. 'This recent development', Mrs. King goes on, 'implies that the United States will shortly be able to patrol the Indian Ocean with nuclear powered submarines controlled from western Australia. The whole strategic *apparat* will then have been removed far beyond the scale of effort on which this country's resources enable her to plan.' (P.

40). Does this mean that the British shall then sit on their hands while American nuclear submarines threaten, from a thousand miles away, to drop a Polaris missile on groups of tribesmen fighting on the Gulf's pearl banks or taking pot-shots at oil surveyors in the Oman?

Apparently so.

14
Arab Nationalism[1]

Facets of Arab Nationalism, by Hans E. Tütsch. Detroit: Wayne State University Press. 1965. 157 pp. Bibliog. Index. (*Political Science, WB 16.*)

The Arab Cold War 1958-1964: A Study of Ideology in Politics, by Malcolm Kerr. London, New York, Toronto: Oxford University Press for the Royal Institute of International Affairs. 1965. 139 pp. (*Chatham House Essays: 10.*)

On Arab Nationalism, by Abdul Rahman al-Bazzaz. Trans. by Edward Atiyah. Introductory notes by Hazim T. Mushtak. London: Embassy of the Republic of Iraq. 1965. 92 pp.

Herr Tütsch, a Swiss journalist with several years' experience of the Arab world, has undertaken an inquiry into the nature of Arab nationalism in a spirit which is refreshingly different from the heavily committed approach of so many Western writers to the subject. Fair, thoughtful and dispassionate, he surveys with a cool but not unfriendly eye the various manifestations of the restlessness which has characterised the Arab world for half a century now, and to which the term 'Arab nationalism' is all too often glibly applied. There is, Herr Tütsch points out, no single phenomenon to which this label can be attached, but a variety of nationalist movements, possessing some features in common but differing in oth-

---

[1] Source: *International Affairs* (Royal Institute of International Affairs 1944-), Vol. 42, No. 2, Britain East of Suez: Special Issue (Apr., 1966), pp. 314-317.

ers. He sees the remarkable insistence upon unity which permeates Arab thought and expression as deriving more from Islam than from the other unifying elements usually invoked—race, language and history. The transference was a natural one, since Islam was, and is, a faith propagated by political as well as religious means. 'Arab nationalism', he writes (p. 26), 'draws more sustenance from religious fountains than Western nationalism has ever done, and this provides it with a particular character. Arab nationalism receives from religion universalist aspirations which carry with them a devaluation of reality and hide the lack of social content.'

Far from being an aid to unity, Herr Tütsch suggests, the Arabic language may well be an impediment. The sense of frustration engendered in the Arab mind by the gap between the large and misty visions of the Arab nation conjured up by politicians and propagandists and the unhappy reality of spite, dissension and suspicion among the Arab states only deepens the more the goal is talked about, until near-frenzy and hysteria result. The Arab is saved from utter disillusionment by the satisfaction which he derives from the words themselves: lulled by the cadences of his language, and exhausted by indulgence to excess in it, he feels no need for action after the bout is over. Words themselves are reality enough.

Can the Arab nationalist movement, in the last analysis, be divorced from Islam? Herr Tütsch thinks not, despite the number of Christian Arabs in its ranks. Although Arab nationalism does not seek to re-establish religious unity and dominance it is by no means a wholly secular movement. Real nationalism demands loyalty to the nation above all, and even, if necessary, at the cost of loyalty to religion. Yet Islam is a universal, proselytising religion, appealing to, and addressing itself to, the individual. As such, it should find itself at loggerheads with nationalism. Nationalism, however, is not logical, and modern Arab nationalists do not concern themselves greatly with contradictions, syllogistic or otherwise. Islam's success, moreover, has only been assured when it has succeeded politically, that is, has created a state. Nowadays Islam is rapidly losing its force in the advanced Arab states as a consequence of Westernisation, and, more especially, of the introduction of Roman-Germanic concepts of law, which has reduced the Shari'ah to a peripheral, even vestigial, role. What remains to be seen is whether the idea of Arab unity can survive the decline of Islam.

One of the features of modern Arab nationalist theory and practice which disturbs Herr Tütsch is the lack of concern for personal liberty. Even the Ba'ath Party, which in its constitution guarantees individual rights, gives short shrift to ethnic or religious minorities. 'Whoever agitates on behalf of, or is connected with, a racial group opposed to the Arabs,' it declares, 'or whoever immigrates into the Arab homeland, for the purpose of colonization, will be expelled from the Arab homeland' (p. 104).

The Ba'ath's leaders, and Gamal 'Abdul Nasser, are the *dramatis personae* of Professor Kerr's essay on the formation and break-up of the union of Syria and Egypt, and the subsequent relations of the two countries down to 1964. Like Herr Tütsch, Professor Kerr is able to stand off from the events, persons and passions he describes, and to deal with them calmly and realistically. From his pages the Ba'athist leaders, Salah al-Din al-Bitar, Michel 'Aflaq, Akram al-Hawrani *et al.*, emerge in an unflattering light as opportunists and incompetents. 'The Ba'th was an ideological party,' remarks Professor Kerr (p. 16), 'and its leaders suffered the common illusion of ideologues everywhere that they possessed a unique vision of the Truth, which was somehow indispensable for effective political action and which could somehow be converted into political power.'

Professor Kerr suggests that they were propelled into seeking union with Egypt in 1958, not by the imminent danger of a Communist *coup d'état* in Syria, which was the explanation widely circulated afterwards, but by the fear of increasing pressure from Iraq, Jordan, Turkey and their Western allies, consequent upon the obvious incapacity, becoming more marked every day, of the Syrians to govern themselves. The Ba'ath cherished the thoroughly unrealistic notion that they could, by entering into political union with Egypt, use Nasser's prestige to overawe their rivals in Syria, while at the same time they could stand up to him themselves and treat with him on an equal footing. Subsequent events would suggest that they might profitably have spent some of the time which they had devoted in preceding years to churning out manifestos in reading Aesop's *Fables*.

This first experiment in Arab unity foundered in 1961 on the rivalry for leadership between Nasser and the Ba'ath. Furthermore, as Professor Kerr observes, it demonstrated that Nasser's personality was not enough on which to build a union, and, even more important, that the real task to which the Ba'ath should have applied themselves was to put their own Syrian house in order. But no sooner had they come to power again in Syria in March 1963 (and in Iraq a month earlier), after a period in the wilderness while Syria floundered along under one inept regime after another, than they set out hotfoot for Cairo to try to persuade Nasser to give union a second chance. 'It was', comments Professor Kerr (p. 63), 'their own ideologically motivated compulsion to ignore domestic affairs (except the elimination of their rivals) and to stumble into an absurd venture for unity with a man they distrusted, and seeking terms that he was bound to refuse, that had brought about the struggle.' A struggle was what the tripartite talks on unity among Syria, Egypt and Iraq in Cairo in March and April 1963 became, and Nasser's outwitting of the Ba'ath forms the heart of Professor Kerr's illuminating account of the talks, based on the transcript later released by the Egyptian Government and upon his own interviews with the Syrian participants.

As in 1958, the Ba'ath's aim was to secure recognition from Nasser of the legitimacy of their rule, and to use the prestige of his name to overawe their opponents at home but without allowing his supporters in Syria any share of political power. They had no chance of succeeding: Nasser outmanoeuvred them at every stage. If there was to be a union, it would be on his terms. 'The Ba'th must come to Nasir as his clients; he would not unite at their convenience' (p. 67). Nasser was not going to be placed, as he put it himself, between the 'hammer' of Syria and the 'anvil' of Iraq. Perhaps the strongest conclusion that emerges from Professor Kerr's account of the unity negotiations is that the Egyptian president will brook no rivals for the leadership of the Arab world. If there is to be unity, it will be through his instrumentality: otherwise there will be no unity.

The selection from the writings of Professor al-Bazzaz, the present (December 1965) Prime Minister of Iraq, on Arab nationalism, translated by the late Edward Atiyah and issued by the Iraqi Embassy in London, reads rather like the script of a play which the actors have decided to throw away in favour of free expression. Of the half a dozen 'occasional' pieces presented here the most interesting is one entitled 'Islam and Arab Nationalism', which has been described by Sylvia G. Haim, who was the first to publish an English translation of it,[2] as 'the best expression so far of the Arab nationalist's view of his position towards Islam'.

Professor al-Bazzaz's view is pretty uncompromising: Islam is the very essence of Arab nationalism; the real Islam is the Islam of the Arabs, and all Arabs, Christians included, should venerate the Prophet and understand Islam. Professor al-Bazzaz has no time for regional nationalism in the Arab world, and he is particularly bitter about Syrian nationalism. His impatience is understandable, but whether it is fully warranted is another matter. As Herr Tütsch notes (p. 41), in a quotation from Ibn Khaldun, 'Every Arab regards himself as worthy to rule, and it is rare to find one of them submitting willingly to another, be it his father, or his brother, or the

---

[2] English translation of *Al-Islam wa'l-quamiyya al-Arabiyya*, by Abd al-Rahman al-Bazzaz: Baghdad 1952, first appeared in *Die Welt des Islams*, n.s., III, Nos. 3-4. Leiden. 1954. Also reprinted in *Arab Nationalism: An Anthology*. Ed. by Sylvia Haim. Berkeley, Los Angeles: University of California Press; London: Cambridge University Press. 1962, pp. 172-188. Reviewed in *International Affairs*, April 1963, p. 296.

head of his clan, but only grudgingly'.

15
The USA in the Arab World

The United States and the Arab World, by William R. Polk. Foreword by Crane Brinton. Cambridge, Mass.: Harvard University Press; London: Oxford University Press. 1965. 320 pp. Bibliog. Index. (The American Foreign Policy Library.)

It is difficult to know what audience this book is aimed at. In the Foreword, Professor Crane Brinton, the editor of the American Foreign Policy Library, states that the Library was designed 'primarily as a series of handbooks directed towards formation and guidance of an enlightened public opinion on important and difficult problems of American relations with specific countries or areas'. Yet only 30-odd pages of Professor Polk's book deal with American relations with the Arab world: the rest consists of a 'potted' history of the region since pre-Islamic times, but more particularly since the 18th century, and its level and style are those of a school textbook.

Textbooks, of course, have their uses, of which the principal is the furnishing of reliable, factual information. There is too much hasty and slipshod work in Professor Polk's book to make it of much value as a textbook, too many misspellings and mistakes, too much repetition. There are also instances of what seems to be becoming a vogue nowadays, the omission of accents from French words, a practice which is all the more regrettable in a work from a distinguished university press. Professor Polk's publishers, however, cannot be held to blame for the misinformation he

---

1 Source: *International Affairs* (*Royal Institute of International Affairs* 1944-), Vol. 42, No. 3 (Jul.,1966), pp. 524-525.

supplies. From him we learn, for instance, that the first 'exclusive' agreements with the Trucial States were made in 1869 and with Qatar in 1891 (p. 98), that the British agreement with Kuwait in 1899 came about because 'the Russians intended to establish a logistics base there' (p. 158), and that it was Disraeli who remarked at the end of the First World War that 'the Allies floated to victory on a wave of oil' (p. 99).

Professor Polk defines the purpose of his book as setting down 'the essential facts, ideas, emotions, and guesses which one needs to understand the relations between the United States and the Arab World' (p. ix). The blurb says his book is 'comprehensive, penetrating'. It is neither of these things. Although its author's career to date (he was educated at Harvard and Oxford and at three Middle Eastern Universities, he taught Middle Eastern history at Harvard before leaving there in 1961 to become a member of the Policy Planning Council of the State Department, and has lately returned to academic life at the University of Chicago) has been of the kind which customarily moves reviewers to remark that he is 'exceptionally well qualified to perform the task he has set himself', it is doubtful whether American readers will gain from his book much real understanding of the nature of the regimes which have ruled Syria, Egypt and Iraq in recent years, or of the United States involvement in the politics of the Arab world. British readers will gain even less.

There is a curiously bland air about the whole of Professor Polk's treatment of American policy and actions in the Middle East in the last 20 years, which makes them appear more logical and consistent than they were in reality. He skirts all the thorny questions, such as the United States failure to try to forge something constructive from the wreck of the Suez intervention, the part played by internal Lebanese politics in persuading the United States to land troops in the Lebanon in 1958, and its hasty decision to recognise the revolutionary regime in the Yemen in 1962, a decision taken when Professor Polk was in the State Department. Although he expresses regret that Arab governments spend so much of their limited resources on armaments, he is silent about the Egyptian campaign in the Yemen, a campaign made possible, in part, by the supply of American foodstuffs to Egypt. On this and other critical issues in the Arab world all that he has to offer are such banalities as, 'Following the advent of the new administration in 1961 the United States reassessed its policies in the Middle East and decided to assist more actively in the growth process of the several countries and, diplomatically, to establish much closer contacts with the Arab governments; in some instances, notably in Yemen, the United States attempted to work out a formula to end inter-Arab quarrels and has tried to foster a slow-down of the arms race between the Arab states and Israel' (p. 291). It is hardly the stuff from which 'an enlightened public opinion' can be fashioned.

16
Saudi Arabia in the Nineteenth Century[1]

Saudi Arabia in the Nineteenth Century, by R. Bayly Winder.
xiv 4- 312 pp. Maps, illustrations, appendix, bibliography, index, London: Macmillan/St. Martin's Press: New York.

It is curious how books on Saudi Arabia and the Saudi dynasty are so often pervaded by an air of piety and reverence towards their subject. The fashion presumably began with the late H. St. J. B. Philby and it has been continued and developed, in particular, by the Arabian-American Oil Company (ARAMCO). Self-interest probably played a smaller part in determining Philby's attitude to the Al Sa'ud than did his personal devotion to the late King 'Abdul 'Aziz; but with ARAMCO self-interest must have been, as it still is, the dominant consideration. As a foreign commercial company, drawing substantial earnings from its investment in Saudi Arabia, and constituting the largest single industrial undertaking in the country, it could not but be alert to the susceptibilities of the host government and to the need to maintain amicable relations with them. As a consequence, it has felt obliged in its publications to exhibit a respectful, not to say flattering, attitude towards the Al Sa'ud and towards the history of Saudi Arabia in general. On these grounds ARAMCO might be forgiven for resorting to such unctuous and frequently cloying language as it does in its publications. What is less easy to forgive is the effect which this policy has had upon the study of Saudi Arabia by Western, and particularly American, scholars. For it has virtually decreed a sympathetic, not to say sycophantic, approach to the history of the Al Sa'ud to be a *sine qua non*,

---
[1] Source: *Middle Eastern Studies*, Vol. 3, No. 1 (Oct., 1966), pp. 91-101.

and it has had a correspondingly deleterious effect upon the work of ARAMCO scholars published in learned journals. More than once what has appeared at first sight to be an authoritative article by a reputable scholar has been found, on closer examination, to have been vitiated by the presence of elements of propaganda.

Dr Winder, a Princeton Arabist, makes effusive acknowledgement in the preface of his book and in various footnotes of the help he has received from ARAMCO, from ARAMCO publications, from Dr George Rentz, from Philby, from articles in the new *Encyclopaedia of Islam* by ARAMCO or ex-ARAMCO employees, from the Saudi Government, and from the memorial presented by that government to the Buraimi arbitration tribunal in 1955. Even without this explicit acknowledgement his debt to these various agencies and individuals is patent throughout much of his book and especially in the opinions he offers. Nor is this the limit of his indebtedness: he has also, to some extent, picked up ARAMCO's 'house style', a type of 'homespun' prose evolved to fit the subject matter of its publications, *viz.*, the pastoral simplicity of the lives of the inhabitants of central and eastern Arabia, their devotion to the Wahhabi profession of Islam, their steadfast loyalty to the Al Sa'ud, and their excellent relations with the Arabian-American Oil Company. Thus Dr Winder writes of 'stolid townsmen', of 'the sturdy folk of the southern oases', and of bringing 'the good news of Wahhabism' to outlying towns, all of which smacks more of the Wild West and the days of the circuit-rider than it does of Arabia at the time of the Wahhabi conquests. Perhaps buried somewhere here may lie the explanation of that strange love affair between some Americans, citizens of the world's most advanced and democratic country, and the most repressive and backward-looking Islamic movement of modern times. Perhaps they see in Saudi Arabia a mirror of the Old West, a vast, unfenced land. where nature is unsubdued, where the law of the gun prevails, and where religious belief is fundamentalist and simple. For them the Arabian desert may be America's last frontier.

Dr Winder defines the scope of his book as the history of Saudi Arabia from 1818 to 1891, that is to say, from the destruction of Dara'iya, the old Saudi capital, by Ibrahim Pasha to the defeat and exile of the Al Sa'ud from their homeland by Ibn Rashid. He defines these seventy-odd years (p. 7) 'as a kind of holding action by the House of Saud in preparation for the prodigious events of the third phase', which began with the capture of Riyad by Ibn Sa'ud in 1902. What Dr Winder has written, however, is not a history but a chronicle-cum-panegyric of the Al Sa'ud. For this his reliance for much of his information upon the chroniclers Ibn Bishr and

Dari ibn Rashid, and upon the Saudi Memorial of 1955 and ARAMCO publications, may be partly responsible. It may also account for the fact that he apparently feels called upon to insert little homilies of his own in his narrative, to point the moral of a story, or to voice his approval of the words or actions of a past ruler of Najd; *e.g.* (p. 86), 'Such words, reminiscent of the orthodox caliphs, would be impressive from any statesman and are in full accord with Wahhabi doctrine on the subject'; and (p. 198) 'This campaign, beginning with a rout but ending in a victory, well illustrates that steadfastness of purpose which has traditionally characterised the Wahhabis and which set their policies apart from the ephemeral combinations so often observable among other Arabians.'

What Ibn Bishr, ARAMCO and the Saudi Memorial cannot be held accountable for, however, is the poor organization of his book, its repetitiousness, the numerous anticipatory excursions, the tiresome proliferation of sub-headings, and the careless and inelegant writing. There seems to be little reason for the sub-division of every chapter into sections, sometimes as many as three to a page, and even less for the nature of some of the sub-headings, *e.g.* 'The Bedouin Put in Place'; 'New Muscle beyond Nejd'; 'Necrology Continued'; and 'Death of a Cleric'. This last is bewildering in more ways than one, for the paragraph which follows it (p. 58) records the death of a man described as 'one of the best-known religious leaders of Nejd,... a godly, learned and unselfish person,' who would seem from the text to have possessed no historical significance whatever. The writing is of a piece with the organization of the book: the syntax is tortured, solecisms are far from rare, and slang and colloquialisms abound. The last have a flavour which may be due to the confusion with Western frontier days: 'a Turkish attempt to move in on his town' (p. 60); 'the imam made a getaway' (p. 109); 'most important of his fence-mending operations was with 'Abd Allah Ibn Rashid' (p. 117); 'first appearing in Buraimi in 1821 as a semi-independent operator' (p. 198). Others defy explanation: 'The invocation of the Sublime Porte did not, however, incline the British ear' (p. 189); 'Asir, as has been pointed out, proved to be an unpluckable thorn from Muhammad 'Ali's point of view' (p. 69); 'the chiefly virgins rode in the forefront of the Bedouin host' (p. 171). Early in his book Dr Winder quotes a passage from a Ph. D. thesis by one of his students, upon which he draws for some of his material, and notes a spelling error with a prim 'sic'. He should look again at page 89 of his own book where he will find three spelling mistakes in one paragraph, not all of which can be ascribed to the typographer's carelessness.

Dr Winder has drawn for his material, apart from the sources already mentioned, mainly upon British official publications, in particular, J. G. Lorimer's *Gazetteer of the Persian Gulf, Oman and Central Arabia*, upon contemporary works of travel by Europeans, and upon a number of Arabic works. His bibliography lists several items which do not appear to have been greatly used. The origin of the half-dozen maps which accompany the book is not stated, but the draughtsmanship is reminiscent of that of ARAMCO maps, and there is a certain familiarity about the oddities in the tribal map of Arabia on page 22. A sketch map of the Buraimi Oasis on page 196 is said to be 'adapted from' the map in the Saudi Memorial of 1955. It is certainly a little more accurate.

The real faults in Dr Winder's work, however, are much more serious. The chief one is that, for a work of history, it is singularly lacking in historical perspective and judgement. Dr Winder makes no real attempt to set events in the Arabian peninsula, not all of which occurred in isolation from the outside world, in their historical context. He accords only one paragraph (on p. 121) to the great Eastern Question, and his understanding of it is on the same scale. He shows a faint glimmering of appreciation (on p. 123) of Mehemet 'Ali's purposes in undertaking the subjugation of Najd for a second time in 1838, although he seems to swallow the Viceroy's explanation that a major object of the campaign was to procure camels for use in the Yemen. He is puzzled by the rapidity with which the Najdi tribes deserted the Amir Faisal ibn Turki and joined the Egyptians, and it is quite understandable that he should be; for nowhere in his account of Faisal's reign up to this time does he even hint that the Amir's position in Najd was unstable. Many of its inhabitants disliked Wahhabi intolerance and had no love for the Al Sa'ud, and they, as well as Faisal's followers, were not exactly inspired by the Amir's example on the approach of the Egyptians when he fled to Hasa—as Dr Winder himself relates. Casting about for reasons for the Wahhabi collapse, Dr Winder is reduced to concluding that it was because of 'the lack of anything like modern nationalism in nineteenth-century Arabia' (p. 111).

It is in his treatment of successive Wahhabi Amirs that Dr Winder particularly shows his inadequacy as a historian. To him all the Saudi rulers were wise and good, none was foolish or cruel (unless he was a usurper), one or two might have erred occasionally, although he finds this a matter for regret rather than censure. He is hotly engaged in every petty squabble or *bouleversement* in Najd, distributing praise or obloquy with profligate ease, the touchstone of his judgements usually being whether or not the participants were partisans of the ruling Amir. This is not only bad history but it is unjust to the rulers concerned, most of whom were shrewd, capable and ruthless men, as rulers of Arabia had to be, and one of whom, Faisal ibn Turki, was a great ruler by any standards. But even he had his moments of weakness and inconstancy, which it serves no good purpose to disguise, and his son and successor, 'Abdullah, though beloved of the Wahhabi *'ulama*, was an unscrupulous and treacherous man who sold himself and his country into bondage to the Turks. Hagiography, as Dr Winder's book demonstrates only too well, often calls for the bending of the facts, or even their suppression. A case in point is his treatment of Turki ibn 'Abdullah's re-conquest of Hasa in 1830. Basing his account primarily upon Ibn Bishr and Lorimer, Dr Winder extols Turki's moderation in dealing with the inhabitants of the conquered province and holds it up as an example of his wisdom. Yet the same pages of Ibn Bishr to which Dr Winder refers describe the brutalities and bloodshed which accompanied the Wahhabis' suppression of opposition in Hasa, and which called forth reproaches from Ibn Bishr himself.

A further illustration of Dr Winder's selectivity in handling his material is his account of the visit of Colonel Lewis Pelly, the British Political Resident in the Persian Gulf, to Riyad in 1865. Dr Winder relates (pp. 218-19) that the Amir Faisal's secretary complained to the Resident about British attacks upon Arab slavers in the Gulf, and then went on to offer, on Faisal's behalf, 'an exchange Treaty binding him to prevent the Arabs of Oman and the Gulf from committing depredation (by sea) or injuring our telegraph establishments.' The quotation is from Pelly's report, and Dr Winder uses a further quotation from the report to explain why the offer was rejected, *viz.*, that Pelly found the secretary's manner 'somewhat familiar'. This was not the reason at all, as Pelly himself makes clear in the very pages of his report that Dr Winder quotes. The treaty was offered in exchange for an undertaking on Pelly's part that the British Government would cease their interference with the Arab slave trade in the Gulf.

It may be, of course, that Dr Winder finds difficulty in correlating evidence, or even of interpreting a piece of evidence correctly. On page 73 of his book he describes the fortunes of some mutineers from the Egyptian army in the Hijaz who seized Mocha in 1833 and were expelled from there at the end of the year by Yemeni tribesmen. An eyewitness of the expulsion was, in Dr Winder's words, 'Wellsted, the British explorer, who was at this time in the harbour of Mocha on a ship.' A few lines later Dr Winder relates that some of the Egyptian survivors of the attack 'gained the protection of a British warship, *Tiger*, in the harbour.' Is it possible that the ship from which Wellsted witnessed the attack and 'the British warship, *Tiger*' were one and the same vessel? It would seem so, since Wellsted at this time was not an 'explorer' but a lieutenant in the Indian Navy. And the ship on which he was serving at Mocha was not 'the British warship, *Tiger*' but the Indian Navy brig, *Tigris*.

A good deal of Dr Winder's book is taken up with relations between the Saudi state and the British Government in the nineteenth century, and more especially with the competition between them for influence over the littoral states of the Gulf. According to Dr Winder, the Amir Faisal several times expressed his readiness to co-operate with the British in keeping the peace at sea, and he resented British interference with his control over the coastal tribes. But whatever Dr Winder may say Faisal did not control the coastal tribes, so that his offers of co-operation, even if genuine, were worthless. Maritime irregularities occurred frequently and Faisal did nothing to prevent them or suppress them. The facts of the situation are against Dr Winder's contention: Faisal had not the power to prevent or put down disturbances at sea. The coastal rulers defied him whenever they felt so inclined, and except on one or two occasions he was incapable of coercing them. To say, as Dr Winder does (on p. 209), that Faisal did not develop a navy of his own because 'he relied on the naval support of coastal tributaries like Bahrain' is to make nonsense of historical reality. The Al Khalifah of Bahrain relied upon their naval resources to prevent Faisal from conquering the island: they would never have placed their ships at his disposal. On the contrary, they often used them to harry his ports on the Hasa coast. So far as the Trucial Coast and Oman were concerned, Faisal's power was limited to occasional forays in search of plunder or tribute, and to keeping a garrison at the Buraimi Oasis to extort money from the Sultan of Muscat. What Dr Winder fails to see is that British and Saudi interests on the Gulf coast were basically incompatible. Faisal's offers of co-operation were never rejected outright, even though they were regarded with scepticism. They were usually accepted but he failed to live up to them. Dr Winder himself relates the outcome of one of them, that made to Colonel Pelly on his visit to Riyad in March 1865. Five months later Faisal's forces raided Oman, looted a coastal town, and killed a British Indian subject.

That Dr Winder does not understand the nature of British policy towards the Gulf states and the Saudi Amirate of Najd is made abundantly clear by his repeated assertions that non-interference in the internal affairs of Arabia was a cornerstone of that policy. On the surface this would appear to be a valid statement, until one reflects that non-interference is hardly an object of policy: it is merely a concomitant of it, or an adjunct to it. The objects of British policy in the Gulf were the maintenance of maritime peace in the interests of trade, and the exclusion of other powers from the area for the sake of the security of British India. Whenever it appeared to the British Government that the achievement of either object was endangered by internal political developments in Arabia, and particularly by the spread of Wahhabi influence to the coast, they were prepared to, and did, interfere in the peninsula's internal affairs. Why Dr Winder feels it necessary to assert otherwise it is difficult to understand, but his insistence upon his theme bears a strong resemblance to the manner in which the compilers of the *Saudi Memorial* of 1955 harped upon the same theme in an effort to bolster up Saudi Arabia's claim to a 'manifest destiny' to rule the whole Arabian peninsula.

Dr Winder most clearly reveals his acceptance of the Saudi-ARAMCO interpretation of Arabian history in the nineteenth century, as well as his own inability to assess the relative reliability of his sources, in his account of British and Saudi relations with Oman in this period, which occupies a considerable portion of his book. Although he disclaims (p. 31) any partiality in the recent dispute over the sovereignty of the Buraimi Oasis and the areas to the west of it, he has, in fact, absorbed much of the special pleading put forward in the guise of historical information in the *Saudi Memorial* of 1955, and by ARAMCO in two of the publications listed in his bibliography. In part, this is due to his tendency to take material direct from the *Saudi Memorial* and the ARAMCO publications instead of going himself to the sources from which they obtained the material in the first place, sources which are included in his bibliography. Much of the information which he has obtained from the *Memorial*, and which he accepts as valid historical evidence, underwent some surprising changes in the course of its transposition from its original source to the *Memorial*, changes designed to harmonize it with the *Memorial's* argument that Saudi Arabia was entitled to the sovereignty of the disputed areas. Dr Winder also makes use of a manuscript history of Saudi activities in Oman in the last century entitled *'Uqud al-Juman*, which first made its appearance in the *Saudi Memorial* and which is said to have been written by an inhabitant of one of the Trucial Shaikhdoms. Considering that the manuscript was written in 1955, in time to be used in the *Memorial*, and that its whereabouts today is still a mystery (Dr Winder merely says, in a note on page 36, that it 'ended up in Saudi hands'), it would seem that such a source should be treated with caution, not to say scepticism. Dr Winder says something to this effect ('one is inclined to be wary in accepting information based only on *'Uqud al-Juman'*), but he then goes on to declare that 'the bare facts adduced from it seem generally in accord with what is known from other sources' (*loc. cit.*). One of the 'bare facts' which he, like the compilers of the *Saudi Memorial*, adduces (pp. 35-36) from the *'Uqud al-Juman* is that the Wahhabis first occupied Buraimi in 1795. A few lines later he quotes Lorimer as saying that the Wahhabis first occupied Buraimi in 1800, the date generally given by every reputable authority for the history of southeastern Arabia. How Dr Winder can reconcile these two statements it is difficult to see. As it happens, he does not attempt to do so, nor does he cite any other source to corroborate the dubious contention he has taken from the *'Uqud al-Juman*.

The compilers of the *Saudi Memorial* had a purpose in assigning the date 1795 to the first Wahhabi occupation of Buraimi, which was to make the period for which the oasis was in Wahhabi hands in the nineteenth century appear to be of longer duration than it actually was. For the same reason they tried to make out that the Wahhabis regained possession of the oasis (after their garrison there had been forced to surrender to the ruler of Muscat in 1819) in 1828, rather than in 1833, the date given by most authorities. Dr Winder, using the same source as the compilers of the *Memorial*, viz., Ibn Bishr, Vol. II, p. 33, says that Buraimi was re-occupied in 1828 by 'Umar ibn Muhammad bin 'Ufaisan, who was sent there as governor by the Amir Turki ibn 'Abdullah. He does not state explicitly that the occupation continued after that year, although he gives the impression that it did by remarking (p. 80): 'Once again Buraimi became an important part of the Saudi outer defence line and a pressure point for probing beyond.' Three paragraphs later, however, he writes: 'In 1832 he [the Amir Turki] appointed Sa'd ibn Muhammad ibn Mu'aiqil as the new amir of Buraimi and the surrounding regions and sent a military force to back him up. In addition, he ordered 'Umar ibn Muhammad Ibn 'Ufaisan to mobilise the troops of the Eastern Province, where he was amir and, as commander-in-chief of the united Saudi army, to proceed to Buraimi.'

These statements raise a number of questions with respect both to their factual content and to Dr Winder's historical method. If 'Umar ibn Muhammad ibn 'Ufaisan had been sent to Buraimi as governor in 1828, when was he recalled to become governor of the Eastern Province (Hasa)? If he was recalled from Buraimi (Dr Winder does not say that he was), was anyone appointed to succeed him before Sa'd ibn Muhammad ibn Mu'aiqil's appointment in 1832? In effect, did the Wahhabi occupation of Buraimi actually continue after 1828 or was the 'occupation' of that year merely a raid in force? The answers to these questions, as it happens, are to be found in Dr Winder's principal source, Ibn Bishr's *Tarikh Najd*. Ibn Bishr states, on the page cited by Dr Winder, that it was not 'Umar ibn 'Ufaisan who was appointed governor of Buraimi in 1828 but an 'Abdullah ibn Sa'ud. He was accompanied to the oasis by 'Umar ibn 'Ufaisan with a force. By the beginning of A. H. 1245 (July 1829), as Ibn Bishr relates a few pages further on, 'Umar ibn 'Ufaisan was back in Hasa, fighting on Turki's behalf, and after the final subjugation of that province in Ramadan 1245 (March-April 1830) he was made governor over it. Ibn Bishr says nothing in his account of the years 1245-1247 (July 1829-May 1832) to suggest that the Wahhabis remained in occupation of Buraimi after 1828, and there is no indication from any other source that they did. Indeed, it would have been remarkable if they had established themselves at Buraimi, over 500 miles to the east of Najd, two years before they conquered Hasa.

What Ibn Bishr does say (Vol. II, p. 62), however, is that 'his [Turki's] governor over... 'Oman was Sultan ibn Saqr, the chief of the Qawasim,' which accords with a statement by Lorimer (quoted by Dr Winder on page 80), based upon a letter from Turki, that the Amir regarded 'the Saiyid of Masqat and the Shaikh of Sharjah as the two heads of the tribes of 'Oman.' Why Dr Winder does not accept Lorimer's date, 1833, for 'Umar ibn 'Ufaisan's second expedition to Buraimi, in company with Sa'd ibn Muhammad ibn Mu'aiqil, is not clear. He gives no reference for his own date, 1832, but he presumably derived it from Ibn Bishr's account of the year 1248 which states (Vol. II, p. 44): 'So he [Faisal, son of Turki] came back and encamped at the village of al-Majura', where he spent some days equipping an army for 'Oman. He appointed as its commander Sa'd ibn Muhammad ibn Mu'aiqil, and wrote to 'Umar ibn Muhammad ibn 'Ufaisan, amir of al-Hasa, to get ready to lead his men from al-Hasa to 'Oman and become commander of the whole expedition. So they marched to 'Oman and raided some towns there and overcame some Bedouin tribes.' Ibn Bishr does not say at which point in the year 1248 (May 1832-May 1833) the expedition took place, but reports from the Gulf at the time state that it left Hasa in mid-January 1833 and arrived at Buraimi on 18 February.

Such instances of a failure to assess and correlate historical evidence occur frequently in Dr Winder's book, with the result that not only is the greater part of his account of Saudi activities in eastern Arabia beyond Hasa in the nineteenth century unreliable (it cleaves to the version given in the *Saudi Memorial*), but what he has to say about Saudi, British and Omani relations in general is distorted or inaccurate. Nor is it his historical method alone that is at fault: his knowledge even of commonplace facts is open to question. He seems, for instance, to be unsure of what the Court of Directors of the East India Company was, for he puts the term in quotation marks (p. 82), and he is under the impression that New Delhi was the capital of British India in 1871 (p. 252). Errors such as these apart, the principal deficiencies in his work may be attributed to his habit, already noted, of taking his conclusions ready-made from others, instead of forming them himself from the sources they used.

This is apparent not only in the case of the *Saudi Memorial* but also in that of a thesis by one of his former students, Dr Robert G. Landen, which Dr Winder cites in several places. Some of the generalizations advanced by Dr Landen and repeated by Dr Winder (*e.g.* those on pp. 33-35) are of doubtful validity: Dr Winder would have done better to have gone for his conclusions to Lorimer directly, or to one of the other authorities mentioned in his bibliography. In this context it is rather strange to find Dr Winder, in Chapter VII of his book, deriding Palgrave as unreliable, and citing Philby's attack on him in *Heart of Arabia* as supporting evidence, despite Philby's well-known jealousy of other travellers in Arabia. Neither Philby's criticism of Palgrave nor that of others, including Dr Winder's, is sufficiently conclusive to justify Dr Winder's confident assertion on page 222 that 'the sum total of them is enough to destroy Palgrave's credibility.'

A final doubt regarding Dr Winder's qualities as a historian is raised by his quotation, on page 247 of his book, of a translation, taken from Dr Landen's thesis, of a letter from the Amir 'Abdullah ibn Faisal to the ruler of Muscat, 'Azzan ibn Qais, in 1869. As given here (and presumably in Dr Landen's thesis), it begins: 'From 'Abdullah ibn-Faysal Imam of the Muslims to Sayyid 'Azzan ibn-Qays Imam of the Robbers.' The reference given by Dr Winder for the letter is: "Abd Allah to 'Azzan, enclosure in Disbrowe to Gonne, no. 465 (Masqat) (August 21, 1869), India Office Records (2), L, quoted in Landen, p. 269.' As a reference this makes little sense. One realises that Colonel Disbrowe was the British Political Agent at Muscat and that Gonne was the Political Secretary to Government, Bombay; but what does 'India Office Records (2), L' mean? Which series? Which volume? One can only assume that Dr Landen, in the interests of conserving space, had devised a system of referring to series of records by numbers or abbreviations, leaving it to the reader to determine the origin of any particular reference in his thesis by consulting the list of abbreviations. Dr Winder, it would seem, failed to take this into account in taking the quotation from the thesis. The omission is not perhaps a serious one, but there is another aspect to this quotation of greater significance, and that is the form in which it appears here. The source cited by both Dr Winder and Dr Landen is not the Amir 'Abdullah's original letter but the translation of it made by Disbrowe and sent by him to Bombay. Disbrowe's translation, however, runs (in the relevant portion): 'From Abdoolla bin Fysul, Imam of the Musselmen, to Syud Azan bin Ghes Imam of the robbers.' It might be argued that no harm has been done by altering Disbrowe's transliteration of Arabic names to that current today, that such an alteration is an improvement upon Disbrowe's 'old-fashioned' spelling, and that the meaning of the quotation has not thereby been changed. But to argue thus is to beg the question: a historical document is a historical document, and if it is to be quoted it should be quoted as it is, warts and all. To do otherwise is to open the door to a very dangerous practice. Any historical document might be 'improved' by changing its spelling or punctuation, but even if so much as a comma is omitted or inserted the sense may well be altered, too. Doubtless it would be highly convenient to governments and other parties involved in disputes today to be able to 'revise' historical documents bearing on those disputes, and to 'clarify' their meaning, if it happened also to suit their interests. It is not a practice to which historians, or those who would become historians, should lend their countenance.

A considerable danger exists today that the study of modern Arabian history will become caught up in current disputes and rivalries in the peninsula, if it has not already become so. For this state of affairs, as remarked at the beginning of this review, ARAMCO bears a certain responsibility, since the committed approach to the subject which it has fostered in its own publications and in those of some of its employees and ex-employees has, in recent years, taken root in more than one American academic institution. But ARAMCO alone is not to blame for the slide into hagiolatry in the study of Saudi Arabian history, still less for the ideological compulsions which too often nowadays shape political studies of the Middle East. There is no good reason why independent scholars should be swayed by modern political shibboleths or by the policies of governments and commercial companies. If Dr Winder, as an independent scholar, feels moved to write a prose idyll of the Al Sa'ud it can only be because he feels that it is called for. He should not, however, expect it to be accepted as history.

17
The Future in Arabia[1]

Divination is a difficult art, made more so by the limitations and predispositions of the diviner. Much that has been written about Arabia in the last two or three years reveals more of the preoccupations of the writers themselves than it does of the state of the peninsula, and it is rare to encounter such sober and sensible assessments of the realities of Arabian politics as are to be found in Harold Ingrams' *The Yemen*[2] and, more recently, in David Holden's admirable *Farewell to Arabia*.[3] Too often Arabia is viewed only in the context of arguments over British defence policy or of exercises in what might be called the 'new realism' or the 'new logic', which holds that certain tendencies in the modern world are inevitable—in the case of Arabia they are the triumph of revolutionary nationalism and of modernisation—that because they are inevitable they are *ipso facto* desirable, and that because they are both inevitable and desirable it is foolish, if not downright perverse, to do other than to welcome and cherish them. All of this has little to do with Arabia, for the peninsula will go its own way, according to its own lights, and in its own time, and not according to the ideological dictates of those who have constituted themselves the augurs of political progress.

* * *

---

[1] Source: *International Affairs (Royal Institute of International Affairs 1944-)*, Vol. 42, No. 4 (Oct., 1966), pp. 619-640.
[2] London: John Murray. 1963.
[3] London: Faber and Faber. 1966.

Fighting the Retreat from Arabia and the Gulf

Four years ago the brightest hope for the political future of Arabia was seen by many to lie in the revolution which broke out in the Yemen on the death of the old Imam, Ahmad ibn Yahia, in September 1962. For what more exhilarating a portent could there be than that the most backward state in the peninsula, sunk for centuries in a squalid medievalism, should be the first to bring off, if not the proletarian, at least the Praetorian revolution? No longer, it was said, would a Zaidi Imam rule in Sana'a or in Ta'iz, the southern capital, holding in thrall the Sunni population of the lowlands with the aid of the Shi'i tribes of the mountains, especially the two great tribal confederations of the north, the Hashid and the Bakil, known from old as the 'Wings of the Imamate'. Instead, a democratic and enlightened central government, supported by Egypt and other progressive states, would confer upon the Yemen and its people the benefits of modernisation, and enable them to join in fraternal union with the rest of the Arab world. After four years of civil war and foreign invasion these hopes have vanished, and the Yemen is rent far worse and bleeds more profusely than ever it did in the days of Imam Ahmad and his father. The most conspicuous contribution which modernisation has made to this wretched land has been to replace the executioner's block with the firing squad.

Nasser's purpose in invading the Yemen under cover of supporting the republican revolution was plain to see. For some years past he had been trying to carry out the design originally conceived by Mehemet 'Ali more than a century ago, of carving out an empire in the Arab world and of sustaining it with the financial and commercial benefits which his control of the principal trade routes between Europe and Asia would bring. Nowadays the main shipping route to the East is through the Suez Canal and the Red Sea, while the principal air route lies across the Syrian desert, through the valleys of the Euphrates and Tigris, and down the Persian Gulf. The Gulf, moreover, contains the greatest proven reserves of oil in the world. The possession of Egypt and ownership of the Canal after 1956 gave Nasser his grip upon the northern end of the Red Sea route. The union with Syria in 1958 placed him at one end of the northern route, and the revolution in Iraq later in the year led him confidently to anticipate the eventual opening of the road to Baghdad and the Gulf. Though his hopes in this direction were later disappointed by the defection of Syria from the United Arab Republic and by the tergiversations of successive governments in Iraq, he did not abandon his dream, but, taking another leaf from Mehemet 'Ali's book, he switched his attention to Arabia, fixing upon the Yemen as a *point d'appui* from which to reach out to the Gulf oil-fields and down to Aden, and thus attain two ends of his design.

At first he thought of making his lodgement through the agency of Muhammad al-Badr, who had been proclaimed heir apparent by his father, the Imam Ahmad, in 1955, and who at this time and for some years afterwards saw himself as a liberal reformer and Nasser as an exemplar, whose policies, and especially that of drawing to his side Russia and other Communist states, he admired and wished to emulate. Badr himself has since testified that when he visited Nasser and President Tito in Syria in March 1958, to effect that curious union with Syria and Egypt which became known as 'the Arab United States', they discussed how best to carry out both Badr's ambitions and Nasser's plans. There would be a close alliance between the Yemen and Egypt, and from the Yemen Egyptian agents would conduct a political and military campaign against Saudi Arabia and the Aden Protectorates, aimed at subverting the governments of those countries, at weakening the British position in the Gulf, and ultimately at placing in Nasser's hands the oil revenues which he needed to underwrite his Arab empire.

They seem far away now, those confident, cheerful days of 1958, when Badr courted Nasser for the help he might afford him in defeating backwardness in his own country and Nasser flattered Badr to his face while secretly preparing to use him as his dupe. Well before the Imam Ahmad's death the Egyptian president had decided upon a full-scale revolution as the only secure means of executing his plans, and when the moment for action came, in September 1962, he threw over Badr altogether and set out to turn the Yemen into an Egyptian province. Today, after four years, he is almost as far from his goal as he was at the beginning.

More than anything else Nasser has been defeated by the nature of the Yemen itself and of its people. A barbarous land of malevolent beauty, riven by tribal and religious factionalism, medieval in its society, its politics and its economy, brutal in its physical aspect, the Yemen has proved too much for the bureaucrats of Cairo and the Egyptian army. To have succeeded in his gamble Nasser would have had to bring off, at one and the same time, three strokes—military conquest, political revolution and economic progress. He has failed to achieve even the first of these: indeed, in believing in the first place that he could subdue the Yemen with the Egyptian army he showed little of the acumen with which his followers are wont to credit him; for he has become so accustomed to judging his army by its performance of its civil role in Egypt that he seems to have forgotten that it has been defeated on every occasion on which it has taken the field since 1945. Nasser has also been let down by the men he had intended to use as the instruments of annexation, the Yemeni revolutionary leaders, and in particular by Abdullah al-Sallal, the truant president, who appears reluctant to have greatness thrust upon him. That Nasser should have placed any reliance upon al-Sallal, in view of his known character and past, is again indicative of a lack of acumen on the part of the Egyptian president.

As the Egyptians cannot win the war in the Yemen, they will have to withdraw one day and leave the Yemenis to work out their future for themselves. Why, it might be asked, do they not leave now, especially as Britain has given a lead by declaring her intention to quit Aden in 1968? The answer to the question lies in that very factor and less in any considerations of face-saving on Nasser's part; for the vision of his grand design still lures him on, and only its realisation would justify the expense of spirit and the waste of shame which is the story of Egypt's intervention in the Yemen in the past four years.

* * *

Britain's policy in the last few years of uniting Aden Colony with the states of the Western Protectorate in the Federation of South Arabia has come under fire from many quarters, not least from the Anti-Colonialism Committee of the United Nations, which, with characteristic inaccuracy, has labelled Britain's long and patient efforts to persuade the colony and the states to unite as a policy of 'divide and rule'. Federation came about in whirligig fashion. Before 1958 there was little interest in federation on the side of the protectorate rulers, and none at all on that of Aden's politicians. But the spasmodic promotion by Britain of the idea of federation, coupled with the increasing pacification and administration of the protectorates, began to alarm the Imam Ahmad of the Yemen, and was the principal reason why he allied himself with the newly-created United Arab Republic in 1958. Following this union he stepped up his frontier war against the protectorates, and this in turn alarmed the protectorate rulers and led them to take more interest in the idea of federation as a means of resisting the Imam. Although the menace of the Imam was really a chimera, it now became the *raison d'etre* of the Federation of South Arabia, and by an ironical turn of fortune it was the Egyptian invasion of the Yemen which gave substance to the chimera and thus to the case for federation.

Much of the criticism of the Federation has been directed against what is regarded to be the unnatural union of Aden Colony with the politically and economically backward protectorates, which took place in January 1963. Not only, say the critics, will the Federation drag Aden down to the level of the protectorates, submerge the port's prosperity in

The Future in Arabia

the poverty of the hinterland, and permanently retard its progress at all levels, but it was, and still is, actively opposed by the majority of the colony's inhabitants, and in particular by the Arab nationalists among them, who see federation simply as an imperialist device to frustrate their desire for closer relations with the rest of the Arab world. Britain's refusal to allow elections to precede the merger is said to have only hardened their opposition, driving them to violent and extreme measures to register their disapproval. Whether the nationalists realised it or not, however, the merger meant life or death at the time to the protectorate states. As Sir Charles Johnston, the last governor of Aden and the first high commissioner, who brought off the merger, has since pointed out, the refusal of the colony to unite with the protectorates would have cut them off from the sea and forced them into the arms of the Yemen, 'a gloomy enough prospect under the Imam, and a desperate one under the distraught Republic'.[4] Moreover, as Johnston has also remarked, 'it would have been a strange misapplication of our principles to insist that the Adenese, being urban and relatively sophisticated, should be allowed to decide the question of merger by their own vote, while the inhabitants of the original Federation, although five times as numerous and no less vitally concerned, should not be consulted at all—presumably on the theory that as illiterate rifle-carrying tribesmen they somehow counted as second-class human beings'.[5]

The Aden Trades Union Congress and its political arm, the People's Socialist Party, had demanded that the arrangements made since the introduction of the Aden constitution in 1958 should be scrapped, and that elections, based upon a franchise which would include all the Yemenis resident in the colony—slightly more in number than there were native-born Arabs—should be held before any move was made to incorporate the colony in the Federation. To have acquiesced in these demands—from men who had been displaying their devotion to the principle of free elections by boycotting every one that had taken place since 1959—would have been to place the future of the colony and the Federation in the hands of transient Yemeni labourers who enjoyed, and still enjoy, no comparable political rights in their own country. The folly, if any, of Britain's policy in Arabia has been to try to introduce into an Arab colony institutions which have their roots in British and European history. Nowhere is this more clearly demonstrated than in the case of trades unions, whose transplanting to the colonies was the inspiration of Sidney Webb in 1930, during his brief tenure of office as Colonial Secretary. In Aden, where there was

---

4 *The View from Steamer Point*, London: Collins. 1964, p. 195.
5 *Ibid.*

no factory proletariat but a fluctuating labour force composed largely of temporary peasant immigrants from the Yemen, trades unions served no useful purpose but merely provided Nasser and his followers with a ready-made network for subversion in later years.

Will the Federation survive the departure of the British? It seems highly unlikely: it has too many enemies. If in the next two years Britain bows to the will of the United Nations, as expressed in the General Assembly's resolution of December 1963—which called for elections in South Arabia on the basis of universal adult suffrage, the release of all political detainees and the return of all political exiles, and introduces a constitution embodying the first of these conditions, she will have yielded the field, in Aden, at least, to the extreme nationalists. For if the Yemenis are enfranchised they will provide the nationalists with the bloc vote they need to gain power. Even if the Yemenis are not enfranchised, if they are required to meet certain residential qualifications, and even if the elections are held under British supervision, the nationalists will still gain, simply by boycotting the elections on the grounds that they cannot accept that their Yemeni Arab brothers should be debarred from voting while possessors of a despised British nationality are granted the privilege.

Whatever happens in the elections will ultimately be of little consequence: once the British leave a struggle for power will be waged between the nationalists on the one side and the federal rulers and the moderate Aden politicians on the other. It is by no means certain that the nationalists would win such a struggle; what is more certain is that, realising this, they will call in the Egyptians, if they are still in the Yemen, or even if they are not, to help them. The experience of the last 20 years and more has shown beyond any doubt that a constitution on the Western model has little chance of survival in the Arab world. It will be surprising if the Federation of South Arabia, as it now stands, will last 12 months after the British have gone.

* * *

Taking the Federation and the Yemen together, it is clear that what will happen to them after 1968 will depend largely upon whether or not the Egyptians remain in the Yemen in the interval. If they remain, commanding as they now do the sea-coast and the lowlands, as well as the twin capitals of Sana'a and Ta'iz, they may well try to expand southwards into the Western Protectorate, down to Aden State. Whether they come at the invitation of the Adeni nationalists or not, their advance will not be unopposed, for the protectorate tribes, however much they might enjoy the spectacle of Nasser tweaking the noses of the assorted sultans, amirs and naibs of the protectorates, in the way that he has been tweaking Britain's nose for the past 12 years, will view the Egyptians in the same light as the Yemenis do at present, that is, as foreigners and foes. For while much was said at the beginning of Nasser's adventure in the Yemen about the Shafi'i tribes of the coastal plain welcoming the Egyptians as Sunni allies against their hereditary overlords, the Zaidi Shi'is of the uplands, it has been evident now for some time that a state of mutual rancour and distaste exists between the Egyptians and the Yemenis, with the Egyptians looking upon the Yemen and its people with fear and loathing and the Yemenis despising the Egyptians for their arrogance and military ineptitude. There is no obvious reason why the Shafi'i tribes of the Aden protectorates should respond in a different way.

Another probability is the emergence of a rump, royalist Yemen in the north and east of the country, which might well extend its sway southwards, sectarian differences notwithstanding, over the present protectorate border into Beihan and the Upper Aulaqi sultanate and shaikhdom. A union or league of the present Yemeni Arab Republic with Aden and the Western Protectorate may be attempted, with or without Egyptian patronage. (Of course, Nasser may prefer to exercise control by a policy of 'divide and rule'.) If the Egyptians should depart, political change could be even more violent, as Imamate Yemen descends upon the Yemeni Arab Republic and puts it to the sword, before sweeping on into the Aden Protectorates.

Any economic development which may take place in the region, which under the conditions foreseen here is questionable, will probably be to the benefit of the Yemeni ports of Mocha and Hodeida and to the detriment of Aden. In past centuries Aden generally has flourished while Mocha and Hodeida were in decline, and the converse has also been true. The Yemeni republicans are pledged to resuscitate Mocha and Hodeida, and the Russians and the Chinese have set them on their way to doing so, the former by building a new port at Hodeida, the latter by improving the road from Hodeida to Sana'a. The Americans have also made their contribution by constructing a new road from Mocha to Ta'iz.

If Aden were to be united to either a republican or a royalist Yemen at their present stage of political development, the result might well be fatal for it. One quarter of Aden's population and many of its leading merchants are non-Arab—Indians, Pakistanis, Somalis, Jews, Europeans—and they would be the first to suffer under an Arab nationalist government of the kind that can be expected. Aden itself, in the view of Sir Charles Johnston, would suffer even more. 'From its present proud status as a great international communications centre and as the biggest bunkering port in the world, it would be brought down to the level of a sleepy provincial harbour in an underdeveloped country, a sort of poor man's Hodeida. All the prosperity built up since the British occupation of Aden in 1839 would be lost, and the present easy-going international co-operation would be replaced by Arab nationalism in its narrowest form'.[6]

* * *

If the Yemeni revolution and civil war have shown anything it is that, in the present semi-civilised state of that country, the only suitable form of government for it is one on autocratic or monarchical lines, whether it is of a theocratic character, as with the Zaidi Imamate, or not. The only alternative is military administration by means of a series of garrison towns, rather like the Roman *coloniae*. What is true of the Yemen is true also of the greater part of the Arabian peninsula, and of Saudi Arabia and Muscat and Oman, in particular. Monarchical rule, under a sovereign of the calibre of the late King Abdul Aziz ibn Saud, or of the present ruler, his son, King Faisal, is undoubtedly the only feasible and workable system of government for Saudi Arabia in the foreseeable future. Here, as in the Yemen, religion occupies an overriding place in the social and political structure of the country: it is the curb by which society is kept in check, it is the sanction for the ruler's office and his right to rule. All too often it is ignored or overlooked that the Saudi ruler is *imam* of his people, the Wahhabiya, and that they constitute the majority of the population of Saudi Arabia.

For at least 10 years now some observers of the Arabian scene have been saying that Saudi Arabia is ripe, indeed over-ripe, for revolution. The pervasive appeal of Arab nationalism, the discontents and ambitions engendered by better communication with the outside world and by modernisation, the rise of a new technological elite in the oil-fields of Hasa, in the government ministries in Riyadh and Jiddah, and in the army and air force—all, it is said, will combine sooner or later to bring about the overthrow of the Saudi ruling house and its replacement by a dynamic, popularly-based, and liberally-inclined régime. The argument reminds one of Harold Ingrams' observation about the influence of *qat* on Yemeni politics. 'It [*qat*] clears your head, say the addicts, and you then feel you can settle every problem. It is important to remember that anyone who is anyone in the Yemen towns chews *qat* and that all politics are discussed under

---

6 *The View from Steamer Point*, pp. 152-153.

its influence'.[7] One suspects that the politically-inspired yearnings of the prophets of revolution in Saudi Arabia have had a comparable narcotic effect upon their predictions. They tend to over-estimate greatly the importance of the Western-educated and technically qualified elite, just as they overrate the drawing power of Arab nationalism in Saudi Arabia. At the same time they under-estimate the staying power of the Saudi royal house, its grip upon its people, and the tribal and regional bases of its strength. Above all, they underrate the capabilities of Faisal himself, who, as David Holden has perceptively pointed out,[8] is a radical conservative, both astute enough to capture any incipient revolution and realistic enough to yield only the trappings of power while retaining its substance.

If a revolution should break out in Saudi Arabia under the leadership of those who are seen at present as its potential protagonists, the effect would be rather different from what is usually forecast. For one thing, it would not lead to the institution of a liberal, reforming régime but would merely replace one authoritarian form of government, suited to the needs of the country, with another entirely unsuited to them. For another, it would probably lead to the break-up of the Saudi state. Saudi Arabia is not Egypt, where a docile population, crammed into the delta of the Nile, can be cowed and subdued from Cairo. The size of Saudi Arabia alone, the nature of the land, the great distances between its settled areas, the diversity and stubborn individuality of its tribes and towns, the ramifications of the Al Saud's marital alliances, the network of the Wahhabi *ulema*—all would ensure that if revolution occurred it would not run its course peacefully. A revolt raised in Jiddah or Riyadh or Dammam, or even in all three, simultaneously or in succession, would produce violent disruption. Hijaz would split off from Qasim, Qasim from Najd, Najd from Hasa: any or all three of these secessions could take place. Hasa might survive for a while on its oil revenues as a revolutionary *enclave*, but past experience is against its withstanding for long domination by Najd.

Egyptian intervention in support of the revolutionaries would not alter the final outcome, particularly as the Egyptian army is likely to suffer defeat if it ventures into the interior of Arabia. Ibrahim Pasha's conquest of central and eastern Arabia in 1818, or Khurshid Pasha's 20 years later, is not a good guide to the fortunes of an Egyptian army in Arabia today. More than half of Ibrahim's force was composed of non-Egyptians and many of his officers were Europeans. In any case, neither he nor Khurshid Pasha was able to keep what he had conquered. A military foray into

---

7 *The Yemen*, p. 14.
8 See *Farewell to Arabia*, p. 134.

Arabia could well lead to Nasser's downfall. While he confines himself to Egypt the Arabs of the peninsula are prepared to accept him as an Arab leader (though not necessarily as their leader); but, as his intervention in the Yemen has shown, the moment that he sets foot in Arabia he becomes in the eyes of inhabitants a Pharaonic figure, a tangible reminder of the fact that Egypt has always been the invader and conqueror in Arabia, while Arabia, except for the brief interval of the Madinan Caliphate, has never dominated Egypt.

This consideration has direct relevance to any estimate of the nature and depth of the appeal that Arab nationalism has to the Arabs of the peninsula today. While Cairo Radio may lend the same enchantment to the discussion of politics in Saudi Arabia, Aden and the Gulf states as *qat* does in the Yemen, it is far from certain that the basic doctrines which it expounds are widely understood or accepted in these countries, still less that their inhabitants are prepared to subscribe to Arab unity at the price of Egyptian hegemony. To succeed in Arabia nationalism has to appeal with effect to loyalties over and above those to self, to family, to tribe, to tribal leader and to tradition. As Arabian society is constituted today, the only way in which it can be appealed to is by stressing the elemental attributes of Arab nationalism—blood, race, language and religion, above all, religion.

If Islam is to be used, however, as a means of converting the peninsular Arabs to the cause of Arab nationalism and unity, its exclusive elements will have to be emphasised at the cost of its universal, if any impression is to be made upon their primitive theological consciences. For some time past, Arab nationalism has been able to feed upon the suspicion, resentment and even hatred of the West which exist in many quarters of the Arab world. To make any reasonable headway in Arabia it will have to capitalise on these feelings where they are present, and to create them where they are absent, by harping upon the indivisible nature of the bond between Islam and the Arab race, and upon the antipathy which a true Muslim feels for men of other creeds.

Yet the apostles and augurs of revolution in Saudi Arabia hold as a doctrinal *sine qua non* that a republican régime will break the hold that Islam has upon the people of that country, as an essential first step towards leading them to the sunny uplands of material progress, and they point to the way in which Islam has been subordinated to progress and the needs of the state in Egypt as a foretaste of what will come to pass in Arabia. They would be better advised to take the Yemen as a guide. There Islam has proved neither a unifying force to be exploited nor an irrelevance to be dismissed. On the contrary, it has both inspired the Shi'i tribes in their resistance to the Egyptians, and reinforced the Sunni tribes in their dislike of them. It would be a supreme irony if Arabia, the cradle of Islam, were to prove the grave of modern Arab nationalism.

* * *

Ironies and contradictions abound in the Arabian landscape. While President Nasser is doing his best to destroy the Zaidi Imamate in the Yemen he is also trying to revive the Ibadi Imamate in Oman—and says he is doing both in the name of progress and enlightenment. Egyptian support of the Ibadi Imamate movement goes back to 1954, when the death of the incumbent Imam and the election of a more pliant successor seemed to offer the Egyptian revolutionary government a chance to make fruitful contact with this distant corner of Arabia.

To understand the nature of the Ibadi Imamate, and to assess its place in Omani life today, one must look first at the country and its people. The greater part of Oman's population, which is said to number perhaps half-a-million, dwells in the valleys of the Hajar Mountains and along the coastal plain, the Batinah, which faces the Gulf of Oman. Most of the tribes are settled, although some of the major ones are still nomadic. There are dozens of large tribes and scores, possibly hundreds, of smaller ones. Every tribe considers itself as belonging to one or the other of two political factions in the country,—the Hinawi and the Ghafiri, although in many cases the alignment is a casual one. This division may be traced back to the original settlement of the country, first, by immigrants from southwestern Arabia (the Hinawi or Yemeni tribes), and later by immigrants from central Arabia (the Ghafiri or Nizari tribes), although it acquired its present more definite outlines in the 18th century, as a consequence of a series of civil wars fought between the partisans of two contestants for the Imamate, one from the Bani Hina tribe, the other from the Bani Ghafir.

Roughly over half the tribes of Oman belong to the Ibadi sect of Islam; the remainder are Sunni Muslims. Ibadi doctrine holds that while an Imam is not essential to the Muslim community, if one is desired then he should be chosen both for his theological attainments and his qualities as a ruler, and he should be appointed by a process of election and acclamation. For the greater part of its history since the eighth century A.D. Oman has been ruled by an Imam, who wielded power not only over the Ibadiya but over the Sunni tribes as well. In the late 18th century the Imamate as an institution fell into disrepute, partly as a result of the debasement of the office during the civil wars fought earlier in the century, partly as a consequence of the accession to power of the Al Bu Sa'id dynasty, which still rules Oman today. Whereas the first two Al Bu Sa'id rulers were elected Imam, their successors had little use for either the office or the title, preferring to style themselves simply *'saiyids'*, or 'lords', while by Europeans they were called 'sultans'.

The Ibadi Imamate fell into desuetude in the 19th century, and it was not revived—except for a fleeting instant in the late 1860s—until the second decade of this century. The impetus for its revival came from two sources: from the discontent of some of the tribes with certain features of Al Bu Sa'id rule, and from the ambitions of two of the most powerful chieftains of the interior, the *tamimahs*, or paramount shaikhs, of the Bani Riyam and Al Hirth tribes, leaders respectively of the Ghafiri and Hinawi factions. The tribes' discontent arose from the neglect of the affairs of the interior by the reigning Al Bu Sa'id Sultan and his predecessor, from their laxity in enforcing the stricter provisions of the Shari'ah law in Muscat, from their cultivation of foreigners and foreign ways, from the tolerance they extended to foreigners, and especially non-Muslims, living in Muscat and the other coastal towns, but most of all from their prohibiting the slave trade and the arms traffic, at the insistence of the British Government, and from their imposing customs duties upon goods passing from the interior to Muscat.

As an expression of their sense of grievance the, tribes concerned, led by the *tamimahs* of the Bani Riyam and the Al Hirth elected an Imam in 1913, and afterwards proceeded to make war upon the Sultan. The fighting went on until 1920 when it was ended by a settlement (later termed somewhat erroneously 'the Treaty of Sib') in which the Sultan recognised the jurisdiction of the Imam and his *qadis* (judges) over certain tribes of the interior in matters of law and custom, and also promised to remove the restrictive duties on the movement of goods from the interior. There was in the agreement, contrary to what some commentators have since read into it, no mention of sovereignty or any reference to the Sultan's right to rule over the whole of Oman. What it amounted to was the grant of a measure of autonomy to the tribes involved in the ordering of their own affairs and to have their disputes settled by an Imam of their choosing, according to Ibadi law and custom.

The Imam elected in 1913 died in 1920, and the new Imam elected to replace him, Muhammad ibn Abdullah al-Khalili, was again sponsored by the *tamimahs* of the Bani Riyam and the Al Hirth, the real arbiters of the politics of inner Oman. Up to the day of his death in 1954 Muhammad ibn Abdullah al-Khalili was never a territorial sovereign in Oman, although his spiritual influence over much of the interior was very great. His temporal power, however, was circumscribed by that of the Bani Riyam and Al Hirth chiefs, and they, however much they might have resented or even flouted the authority of the Al Bu Sa'id Sultan at Muscat, never questioned the legitimacy of his rule over the interior. They only began to do so in 1954, after they, like their fathers before them, had contrived the election of a new Imam subservient to their wishes, Ghalib ibn Ali of the Bani Hina.

Behind the supine figure of the Imam Ghalib, the chiefs in question, Sulaiman ibn Himyar and Salih ibn Isa, plotted with his brother Talib to set up an independent state in inner Oman, separate from the Sultanate. Their immediate object was to gain control over the stony steppes which stretch westwards from the Hajar Mountains towards the Rub al-Khali, where, as the presence of British oil-prospecting parties indicated, oil might be found to lie. With arms and money from Saudi Arabia and Egypt, who for their own reasons wanted the dissidents' plan to succeed, they broke out in open rebellion against the Sultan in 1957. The Sultan called upon the British Government for help and the rebellion was suppressed within a few weeks, although a hard core of rebels held out in the high valleys of the Jabal Akhdhar, the cluster of peaks in the centre of the Hajar, for another 18 months. By that time Ghalib, Talib, and Sulaiman ibn Himyar had long since slipped out of Oman to find refuge in a succession of Arab capitals.

However much Nasser and others might still wish to exploit this discredited trio's hankerings after power, and any sentiment that might exist in Oman for the Imamate, it is fairly safe to assume that the Imamate movement is now a dead issue. There never was a case for creating a separate, land-locked state in the middle of Oman, for the interior and the coast have always lived in a symbiotic relationship. Oman's need, now as much as in the past, is for a strong central government, capable of handling the tribes justly and firmly, of maintaining peace and stability throughout the country, and of introducing and enforcing social and economic reforms. The Imamate, in the form in which it has been revived in this century, is irrelevant to these needs. It is repressive, xenophobic, narrow and bigoted, harking back to a stern observance of Islam according to the Ibadi confession, such as has kept the Ibadiya in ignorance, poverty, ill-health and spiritual servitude to the present day.

Whatever the faults and omissions of the Al Bu Sa'id line, and they have been many, they have at least been aware of the outside world, and they have, within their limited means, tried to develop trade and other contacts with it. Now that oil has been found in commercially exploitable quantities in Oman, these contacts will increase and they cannot fail to affect the lives of Oman's people. The oil company's operations, the construction of a pipeline through the Hajar Mountains to the Batinah Coast, the constant passage of men and *matériel* through the country, and the presence of a European community, will all open the eyes of the tribes and arouse their expectations.

Whether the present Sultan, Sa'id ibn Taimur, will be able to satisfy these expectations will depend largely upon his willingness to use his increased revenues intelligently to develop his country's resources. There is hardly a single aspect of Omani life that is not in need of remedy or improvement, whether it be administration or communication or agriculture or the health of its people or their level of knowledge and literacy. The foundations of such an improvement have been laid by the pacification of the country by the Sultan's armed forces, under British and Pakistani officers, and a few agricultural projects, schools and medical dispensaries have been opened. Oman has about as far to go along the road to the 20th century as the Yemen has, and she is confronted by much the same obstacles along the way, including a religious schism between her people, although she has so far been spared the ordeal of foreign invasion.

What the Sultan fears is that if he embarks upon the regeneration of his country he will be forced to bring in Arabs from the more advanced states, and that they will bring with them ideas and attitudes which will disturb his people and endanger his rule. Such a fear of outside interference lies behind his refusal to join the United Nations or the Arab League, and his use of his connection with Britain to shelter him from the insults and buffets of a rude world. While his reluctance to admit foreign influence, and particularly Arab nationalism as preached by Cairo, Damascus and Baghdad, is understandable, he cannot evade the consequences of his new oil wealth and the responsibility it imposes upon him to help his people. Nor can he keep Oman secluded from the world for long. He will have to come to terms with the 20th century as his fellow-rulers in Arabia have had to do.

The British Government, who have upheld the independence of Oman against its enemies and underwritten the rule of the Al Bu Said line for more than a century now, have a right and a duty to demand that Sa'id ibn Taimur should respond to the opportunities and obligations laid upon him by his new wealth. They might persuade him, for a start, to take a step which would have more than symbolic benefit, and that would be

The Future in Arabia

to remove his court from the distant and languid confines of Salalah, on the southern coast, to the ancient capital of Nizwa, in the heart of Oman. There he would be seen to rule over his people, instead of delegating responsibility—though not authority—as he has done in the past, and, confronted by their condition, he might be moved to do more for them than he has done to date. Time is running out for him, but he may yet live to earn as high a reputation as a benefactor of his people as the late ruler of Kuwait earned in his time.

* * *

Among the states of eastern Arabia Kuwait is *sui generis*. It is also now, by its own definition, *sui juris*. For the explanation of Kuwait's singularity one must look to its history as much as to its wealth from oil. The 250 years of Kuwait's existence have been in the main peaceful, so that it has avoided decline and stagnation from the later 19th century onwards, such as war and civil strife have brought to Oman. Moreover, since the end of the 19th century it has had the benefit of British protection, which has stood it in good stead against occasional attempts upon its independence by Iraq and Saudi Arabia. Whether that protection, which is still present in latent form despite the ending of the formal relationship in 1961, will serve it as well in the future is open to question. Internal subversion is probably a greater potential threat to Kuwait's continued existence as a state than external aggression, and its political stability, in turn, is very much bound up with the future of the ruling house, the Al Sabah.

How long the Al Sabah will continue to rule is a difficult question to answer. Among native-born Kuwaitis today there is a generation which has grown to maturity without any memory, or very little, of the poor and placid days before the oil boom. Educated, wealthy and young, and with the confidence which these qualities confer, they will as surely demand a share of political power as their fathers were content to leave its exercise to the Al Sabah.

The political situation in Kuwait, however, at least as far as the question of any form of elective representation is concerned, is complicated by the existence of a large *Uitlander* population, exceeding in number the native-born Kuwaitis. Most of these *Uitlanders*, and especially the ex-Palestinians, Lebanese, Syrians, Egyptians and Iraqis among them, are possessed of skills and education superior to those of the bulk of Kuwait's native population whose needs they serve. Many of them are ardent Arab nationalists—though some are refugees from the régimes in power in their own countries—and it is not likely that their political appetites have become dulled by the material rewards of working in Kuwait.

The Al Sabah have recognised the danger inherent in the presence of a large body of foreigners within the state, and they have effectively debarred them from engaging in legitimate political activity for some time to come by laying down stringent residential requirements for Kuwaiti citizenship. The problem posed by the foreign population is similar to that which has faced the British in Aden with respect to the Yemenis there, yet critics of Britain's refusal to enfranchise the Yemenis do not seem to be similarly exercised over the lot of politically more sophisticated Arabs in Kuwait. At heart the problem is the same—control of the state by outsiders.

The late ruler of Kuwait, Shaikh Abdullah al-Sabah, promulgated a constitution in November 1962, setting up a national assembly of 50 members, elected by popular vote and vested with legislative powers. The constitution and the assembly simply function to provide some of the native Kuwaitis with a more-or-less harmless outlet for their political energies. Real power still resides with the ruler and his council of Ministers, which is composed of members or adherents of the Al Sabah. Apart from the consideration that political institutions on the Western model do not work in Arabia, it is unlikely that the constitution and the assembly will satisfy the more ambitious Kuwaitis for long. They do nothing at all to satisfy the *Uitlanders*. A putsch of some kind seems destined to come in Kuwait, although at the moment the necessary ingredients for one either on the classic Saljuq or *mamluk* model, or on the modern Egyptian pattern, *i.e.*, a disaffected military elite with or without the backing of a 'Street', seem to be absent. They may develop, and even without them a *coup d'état* might be attempted.

If a revolutionary junta were to seize power in Kuwait it could hardly expect to continue to govern without outside help. If help were to come from Egypt or Iraq, or both in concert, it would have to be preceded by some kind of understanding between the two, especially if Egypt were to use Iraqi territory, as she would have to, as a base. But it is one thing to intervene in a country, another to remain there. Even if Egypt were to intervene in force in Kuwait, which in view of the incapacity shown by the Egyptian general staff in the Yemen would be a hazardous undertaking, she would be hard put to it to keep up the occupation. Logistics alone would defeat her. Iraq is better placed to make the attempt, provided that her army is not tied down fighting the Kurds.

Saudi Arabia would not submit idly to an Egyptian or Iraqi occupation of Kuwait, whether overtly or under cover of supporting a revolutionary régime, and one assumes that Britain might play a part in determining the outcome of such a move. Most probably, if Kuwait were to be attacked, the eventual result would depend upon the attitudes taken by the United States and Russia, who, according to the state of their mutual relations and their estimates of their respective self-interest at the time, would either impose a standstill agreement or take sides in the contest. Whatever happened, Kuwait's prosperity would be dealt a terrible blow.

Bahrain is also confronted, though on a smaller scale, by the dual problem of maintaining her independence and her internal stability. She is less of a prize for outsiders, however, and she possesses, in addition, the still not inconsiderable advantage of being an island. There is also Persia's dormant claim to her sovereignty, which, while it poses no real threat to her at present, would doubtless be activated if an Arab state were to lay hands on the shaikhdom. The Shah, it might be noted, has recently taken measures designed eventually to strengthen his naval forces in the Gulf. Nor should the British guarantee of protection be overlooked for as long as it lasts. The greatest danger, in fact, in which Bahrain stands in the future is that a revolutionary government, if it came to power, would be rash enough to abrogate the treaties embodying that guarantee. The chances of insurrection are perhaps higher in Bahrain than they are in Kuwait, if only because the proportion of educated and politically-minded inhabitants is larger, and because they lack the opportunities for material solace that their fellow intellectual *sans-culottes* enjoy in Kuwait.

Much of the comment and speculation that has appeared of late concerning future political development in the Gulf states is postulated upon the emergence of this educated, ambitious intelligentsia, and the inevitable challenge that it offers to shaikhly rule. Much of the criticism, too, of Britain's role in the Gulf springs from a fear that she is being committed to the preservation of that rule, a course which carries with it the danger that she will be drawn in to support unpopular rulers against their disloyal subjects. Thus, the defence correspondent of *The Times*, writing a year ago, spoke disparagingly of shaikhly rule and went on to remark: 'ideally, British involvement should be with institutions rather than specific governments.'[9] There are a number of assumptions underlying criticisms of this kind which deserve closer study. The first is that shaikhly rule is *per se* arbitrary, unenlightened and repressive. Of its nature it is not necessarily any of these things, although individual rulers may be incompetent, oppressive and cruel, just as they may also be wise and benevolent, like the late Shaikh Abdullah of Kuwait. It is vital to keep a sense of proportion

9 *The Times*, October 13, 1965.

when judging the rulers of the Gulf states. Several of them have been, and are, capable, just and generous by the standards of their own societies, and even by the standards of others, and the worst of them have never displayed the brutality and contempt for human decency exhibited by the leaders and acolytes of some of the popular revolutionary movements of our day. Shaikhly rule in a tribal or semi-tribal society is subject to checks and balances: the shaikh has a need to conciliate his subjects, and he cannot ride rough-shod over tradition, custom, the Shari'ah, the *qadis*, or the merchant classes. It would be surprising if the rulers of Kuwait and Bahrain, sprung from a line of merchant princes, were to ignore the interests or advice of their own merchants.

An even larger assumption is that rule by a newly-emerged group of detribalised young intellectuals, nationalist and socialist by inclination, would be preferable to hereditary rule by shaikhly families. Looking elsewhere in the Arab world one is not heartened by the spectacle of life under the revolutionary régimes which have sprung up. In Egypt, Syria and Iraq all the checks and balances which operated to restrain the despotic tendencies of the old régimes have been swept away, so that nowadays there is little defence for the individual against the abuse of power by the state. What is more, the introduction of Western technical aids and administrative techniques has made the functioning of the bureaucracy more efficient than ever before. Again, since shaikhly rule is the only political institution which has evolved in the Gulf, it is difficult to see how Britain can dissociate herself from individual rulers and at the same time identify herself with institutions.

It is worth noting that when it comes to visualising the political framework which will replace shaikhly rule most of the critics lose their confidence and take refuge behind hazy proposals about conciliar forms of government. In the Gulf today the alternative to dynastic rule, which at least has the sanction of usage and tradition, is government by a self-appointed revolutionary elite, with a spurious claim to popular support but which is unrestrained by any of the existing curbs on sovereign power. It might be added as an after-thought that it is scarcely logical to assume that intellectual and merchant classes cannot co-exist with autocratic governments, but must necessarily overthrow them. They have managed so to co-exist in many parts of the world up to date, and they have done so in the Middle East throughout its history.

* * *

The Future in Arabia

While predictions of revolutionary change may have some relevance to Kuwait and Bahrain, they have none to the Trucial Coast and Qatar. There is no credible alternative to shaikhly rule visible in the lower Gulf, and none will make its appearance for another generation yet, and probably not even then. There are groups of *Uitlanders* in Qatar, Dubai and Abu Dhabi, though their numbers are not large and they consist largely of Persians, Indians and Pakistanis, with only a sprinkling of Arabs from the more advanced Arab states. Whatever the discontents, nationalist leanings, or political hopes of the last group—and not all of them, by any means, are weighed down by them—they will not be in any position to satisfy them because they lack any basis of power in the shaikhdoms. Power still belongs to the ruling families, who keep a sharp watch on whoever enters their territories and on what they do while in them.

Even if against all odds the young educated men of Qatar and Dubai, who are seen by some observers as potential revolutionaries, were to seize power in these shaikhdoms, and, an even more questionable assumption, they were to hold it afterwards, what would be the nature of the rule they would inaugurate? The still uncivilised state of Trucial Oman, as in the greater part of Arabia, demands strong rule. A young, inexperienced and insecure régime, however progressive it might consider itself, and might even be, would soon prove incapable of controlling the tribes under its nominal command, and would be driven as a consequence either to employing coercive measures far more severe than those resorted to by traditional rulers, or to calling in outside help. If they chose the first course it would bring its own retribution; if they chose the latter, it would lead to international complications with what results it is impossible to foresee.

* * *

As Britain is still a power in Arabia any consideration of the peninsula's future must take that fact into account. For some time now one school of thought in England has been insisting that Britain does no good to herself or to others by remaining in Arabia, and that it is high time that she declared her intention of leaving the peninsula altogether as she has already announced her decision to withdraw from Aden.[10] While the argu-

---

[10] See, for instance, Kenneth Younger, 'Reflections on the Defence Review', *Political Quarterly*, July 1966; Alastair Buchan, 'Britain in the Indian Ocean', *International Affairs*, April 1966; Gillian King, *Imperial Outpost-Aden: its Place in British Strategic Policy*, Chatham House Essays, London: O.U.P. for R.I.I.A., 1964; and Elizabeth Monroe, 'Kuwayt and Aden, a Contrast in British Policies', *Middle East Journal*, Winter 1964.

ments with which this proposition is buttressed do not require detailed consideration here, since they are not really concerned with Arabia but are rather doctrinaire affirmations of political conviction, their general tone illustrates the unreality with which Britain's vital interests in the peninsula, i.e., her oil investments in the Gulf states and her obligations to these states and to her allies, are all too often discussed. According to the advocates of a British withdrawal from Arabia, the presence of British political and military power there not only does little to protect British and Western oil interests but it positively endangers them, by placing a strain upon the relationship of the oil companies with the local governments and by affronting Arab nationalism. The Arabs, it is said, will continue to permit access to the oilfields out of self-interest, and even if the worst were to happen and they were to nationalise the companies' operations in their territories, they would still have to sell their oil because they could do nothing else with it.

Whether the oil companies share this confidence concerning their safety, and particularly that of their employees working in the wilder parts of Arabia, is open to conjecture. Kuwait, Bahrain, Hasa and even Qatar, where the companies work in comparative security, so far as the lives of their personnel are concerned, are not Oman, the Trucial Coast or the Hadhramaut. It would not be merely speculative to say that the companies working in these regions, with memories of the upheavals that have taken place in them still fresh, would feel a sense of uneasiness if there were no British forces at hand to deal with emergencies which might arise, beyond the capacity of the local ruler to handle, such as the Oman rebellion of 1957. The presence of British forces in the Gulf does not dismay the rulers of Kuwait, Bahrain, Qatar, the Trucial Shaikhdoms, and Muscat and Oman. Nor does it disturb King Faisal or the Shah. The only Gulf state that it offends is Iraq, and that is because it makes it more difficult for her to lend clandestine aid to the scattered supporters of the Imamate movement in Oman. No doubt the proximity of British troops offends local Arab nationalists, just as it offends those of Cairo, but it would be impossible for Britain not to offend them whatever she did.

The companion argument about continued access to the oilfields, either under existing arrangements or after possible nationalisation, begs the question. For the real point, as a correspondent in *The World Today* pointed out more than two years ago,[11] is not access but the profits which arise from oil investment, and this is the very point which is ignored by the opponents of Britain's continued presence in Arabia. It is the profits

---

11 July 1964, p. 305.

from production which finance all the 'downstream' activities of the oil companies—transport, refining, marketing, etc.—as well as exploration and research. As the correspondent in *The World Today* remarked: 'There is more at stake here than some nice, and largely irrelevant, calculation of cost of armed forces against contributions to balance of payments; more than a sleepless night or two for the U.K. Treasury at the thought of sterling balances withdrawn; more, certainly, than the mere well-being of oil companies. What is at stake is the uninterrupted flow of vital supplies to the whole of the non-communist world.'

Britain's defensive obligations to the littoral states of eastern Arabia arose from the conditions which prevailed in the Gulf in the 19th century, but they are equally relevant to conditions in the area today, where the absence of defined frontiers and the ambitions of powerful neighbours still threaten the independence of these states. While Saudi Arabia and Kuwait have now agreed to partition the neutral zone between them, and the maritime frontier of Bahrain with Saudi Arabia has been settled, the frontier problem which has been the source of the greatest trouble in the last 20 years, that between Saudi Arabia on the one side and Abu Dhabi and Muscat and Oman on the other, is still no nearer solution. The blithe propositions which are sometimes made about the federation of the Trucial States (usually by those who oppose federation in the Aden protectorates), or their eventual absorption in Saudi Arabia, ignore the very real differences which divide these states from one another and from Saudi Arabia. It is not Britain's place to barter away their sovereignties, however quaint, irritating or anomalous their condition may seem. Again, while Britain has done a great deal to persuade the Gulf states to reach agreement on their maritime frontiers, an agreement which is essential to the proper functioning of off-shore oil concessionary agreements, and has gone a long way towards helping them to formulate a median line down the Gulf for the same purpose, there is still much to be done before an ordered frontier pattern prevails. It would be of little advantage to anyone if Britain were to leave uncompleted what may well be the last of the many services she has rendered the Gulf's inhabitants in the past century and a half.

Those who wish to see Britain withdraw from the Gulf argue that the protection which she at present affords the littoral states could equally be provided by an agreement among the major Gulf states—Saudi Arabia, Iraq and Persia—to maintain the *status quo*. It is scarcely a realistic proposal, since these three states are committed, by past word and action, to upset the *status quo* at the first feasible opportunity. The United States tried to work out a *status quo* agreement over the Yemen in November 1962, on

Fighting the Retreat from Arabia and the Gulf

the basis that President Nasser should withdraw his troops from that country, that King Saud and King Husain should cease supporting the Imam Badr, and that President Sallal should declare his interests limited to the then boundaries of the Yemen. Although none of the parties approached displayed any enthusiasm for the plan, the United States Government were led to believe that Nasser and Sallal were disposed to accede to the requirements affecting them, and accordingly, the United States recognised the Yemeni Arab Republic in December 1962. Immediately, Nasser began pouring more troops into the Yemen.

However awkward Britain's obligations to uphold the integrity and independence of the littoral states of eastern Arabia may be, they are still obligations, and no country earns credit in the eyes of the civilised world by abandoning its obligations. If stability is to be maintained in the Gulf there is no foreseeable alternative at present to Britain's remaining there. This may be a cause of regret to some but it is nonetheless true. What happens in Arabia in the next 10 years or so will depend as much upon what happens in London, Washington and Moscow as it will upon events in the northern Arab capitals. There is little hope that expedients such as the Islamic alliance which King Faisal is now proposing to his fellow monarchs will, of themselves, save the rest of Arabia from the same disasters as those which have overtaken the Yemen. There are too many parties interested in bringing about a breakdown of the old order in Arabia for its passage through the years ahead to be a calm one. To judge from what has come to pass in the world in the last 20 years, an Orwellian vision of the peninsula's future is better justified than Pollyanna's.

18
An Arab View of T.E. Lawrence[1]

T. E. Lawrence: An Arab View, by Suleiman Mousa. Trans. by Albert Butros. London, New York, Toronto: Oxford University Press. 1966. 301pp. Bibliog. Index.

Anyone who sets out to write a book on T. E. Lawrence is undertaking a task akin to the labours of Hercules. If he succeeds in disentangling the tendrils of fact from the thickets of fiction, he has next to surmount the Lawrentian Shield, that political-literary coterie which stands guard over the sanctuary to block the approach of the impious. Should he seek to circumvent this obstruction by going direct to the utterances of the Pythian Apollo himself, he will find that they merely throw a veil of obscurities, evasions and contradictions over the mystery within. Alas, Mr. Suleiman Mousa, who works in the Press and Information Department of the Government of Jordan, has got no further than any of the other brave souls who have ventured, sword in hand, to storm the battlements of legend, and not as far as that quixotic gladiator, Richard Aldington. For Mr. Mousa's book, which was published in Arabic four years ago and which now appears in an English version, has appended to it a 'Comment' by Professor A. W. Lawrence, T. E.'s brother, which denies the truth of much of what he says and takes him to task for his impieties. It is a most curious device for a respectable university publisher to employ, and one can only wonder where the initiative for it came from.

According to Mr. Mousa, his object in writing his book was not to denigrate Lawrence personally but to restore perspective to the story of the

---

[1] Source: *International Affairs*, Vol. 43, No. 1, Jan. 1967, pp.108-110.

Arab Revolt, and, in particular, to show how much greater was the Arabs' part in it than Western writers and Lawrence's admirers have generally allowed. Be that as it may, the method that Mr. Mousa has chosen is to prove Lawrence, at best, a liar and, at worst, a knave. His main target is the *Seven Pillars*, and his ammunition is taken from the more-or-less standard books in English and Arabic on the Arab Revolt, and from interviews with some of the surviving Arab participants. But while he rightly throws doubt upon the accuracy of Lawrence's version of events, and the versions of other British writers with a case to make, he fails to apply the same critical judgment to his Arabic sources, written or verbal. By far the most valuable service that his book performs is to draw attention to the major part played in the desert campaign by the Arab regular soldiers and officers, among them Nuri al-Sa'id and Ja'afar al-Askari, and by the other British officers involved—Joyce, Newcombe, Young, Kirkbride, *inter alios*. A proper tribute to their efforts is long overdue, and one of the many charges that can be laid against the guardians of the Lawrence legend is that by exalting their hero they have disparaged worthier men.

Some of the questions which Mr. Mousa raises, such as whether Lawrence really made a secret journey to within three miles of Damascus in June 1917, or whether the incident at Dera'a actually occurred, may never be satisfactorily answered for want of corroborative evidence. There is a better chance that we may one day find out the truth of what happened at Aqaba in July 1917, and what part Lawrence played in its capture. The capture of Aqaba was crucial to the whole Arab Revolt and to Lawrence's subsequent career, for on the strength of it he was able to persuade Allenby to increase his aid to the Sharif Husain and to give him, Lawrence, his chance to strut and fret his hour upon the Arabian stage. It is not unlikely that he embroidered his account of the episode to Allenby, just as he embroidered other exploits. '... I always thought he was a mischievous little imp and this mischievousness was undoubtedly a flaw in his fine character', Sir Hubert Young, who served with him, wrote later. 'Another small failing was the vanity which led him to pose, and tortured the better side of his nature. His attitude to publicity was that of Brer Rabbit to the briar-bush... .'[2] 'Mischievous' seems little too indulgent an adjective to describe some of Lawrence's behaviour.

The capture of Damascus in October 1918 is a case in point. Mr. Mousa's account of it differs from Lawrence's but it is hardly more accurate. If Mr. Mousa is only concerned, as he claims in his Preface to be,

---

2 *The Essential T. E. Lawrence,* selected by David Garnett, London: Jonathan Cape, 1951, p. 19.

An Arab View of T.E. Lawrence

to give credit where it is due, why does he not state that the city fell, not to the Sharifian forces, but the 3rd Australian Light Horse Brigade? Until this fact was given publicity recently by Professor Elie Kedourie,[3] an offensive and perverted version of the taking of Damascus had been allowed to circulate for 40 years: offensive because it deprived the Australians of their rightful due and compared their sense of discipline unfavourably with that of the Sharifian forces; perverted because it served the political purposes of an interested few to the detriment of the honour of many. That such a deception was allowed to continue for so long is a disgrace; not to quash it when one has the opportunity to do so is to behave no better than Lawrence did in the *Seven Pillars*, when he made his cheap gibes at Sir Harry Chauvel, the commander of the Australian Mounted Division. Mr. Mousa also perpetuates, on page 181 of his book, the myth that Sharif Husain and his son Faisal did not know of the existence of the Sykes-Picot Agreements until the Russians revealed them at the close of 1917. Yet on page 66 he notes that both Sykes and Picot visited Husain and Faisal at Jeddah in May 1917. If he had put two and two together, or, better still, had read Professor Kedourie's work on the subject,[4] he would have realised that the contents of the agreements were communicated to the Sharif and his son at that meeting.

The hagiographers have had a good innings and it is high time that a realistic assessment of Lawrence's achievements and the importance of the Arab Revolt in general was made. Thanks to the recent opening to public inspection of the British official records down to 1923 such an assessment is now practicable. Even without the opening of the records it has been possible, if one so desired, to reach a rough conclusion about the relative value of Lawrence's activities. Unconsciously perhaps—for he seems to be under the impression that the Palestine campaign was fought to assist the Arab Revolt—Mr. Mousa has indicated the form which such a conclusion might take; for at the close of a chapter in which he describes and derides Lawrence's dashings to and fro in southern Syria between September and December 1917, he casually mentions that in these months Allenby's army took Beersheba, Gaza and Jerusalem.

---

3 See 'The Capture of Damascus, 1 October 1918', *Middle Eastern Studies*, October 1964, pp. 66-83.

4 *England and the Middle East*. London: Bowes & Bowes, 1956, pp. 37-38 and 97-98 (reviewed in *International Affairs*, October 1956, p. 511), and 'Cairo and Khartoum on the Arab Question, 1915-18', *The Historical Journal*, VII, 2 (1964), 280-297.

19
Southern Arabia[1]

Farewell to Arabia, by David Holden. London: Faber & Faber. 1966. 268 pp. Bibliog. Index.
Arabia and the Isles. 3rd ed. by Harold Ingrams. Foreword by Sir Bernard Reilly. London: John Murray. 1966. 400 pp. Index.

Part I

For the past 10 years David Holden has been reporting on Arabia as Middle East correspondent successively of *The Times*, *The Guardian*, and *The Sunday Times*. He has now distilled the experience of these years into a gracefully-written and eminently sensible book on the present condition of the peninsula and what has been happening there in recent times. Some of his descriptions are brilliant, for example, his account of his interview with the late Imam Ahmad on his first visit to the Yemen in 1957, and his judgments on men and events are both penetrating and balanced. He is witty and abrasive about the Egyptians in the Yemen, cool towards the Sultan of Muscat in his self-imposed seclusion, sympathetic to King Faisal and the British in their respective—and sometimes mutual—difficulties. The old Arabia, Holden acknowledges, is passing and must pass, and on the whole he finds the prospect neither alarming nor dispiriting. But having seen at first hand some of the uglier manifestations of alien influence in the peninsula, whether in the shape of

---

[1] Source: Part I - *International Affairs* (*Royal Institute of International Affairs* 1944-), Vol. 43, No. 2 (Apr.,1967), pp. 373-374.
Part II - *Middle Eastern Studies*, Vol. 5, No. 3 (Oct., 1969), pp. 267-269.

the scabrous blight which oil wealth has laid upon the Gulf coast or the convulsions which an envenomed nationalism has produced in the Yemen and Aden, he cannot help feeling affection and nostalgia for the Arabia of other and simpler days.

Regret rises almost to a threnody in the lengthy introduction which Harold Ingrams has added to his *Arabia and the Isles*, and which distinguishes this third edition of his book from the second, published in 1952.[2] Whereas Holden believes that British policy in Aden and the Protectorates in the last 15 years has been a qualified success, Ingrams finds little to commend in it. The Federation of South Arabia, he says, was a mistake, though not for the reasons which most critics offer—that it looked too much like a colonialist device to frustrate Arab unity and to retard the separate political development of Aden Colony along Western lines. As Ingrams sees it, the folly lay in the act of destroying the independence of the Protectorate states and in thinking that Western political ideas and institutions have any place in the Arab world. An even greater folly, he believes, was to take any notice of the Anti-Colonialism Committee of the United Nations. But then, as he sadly reflects (p. 66), 'the British no longer have the will even to show power and, on the political side, feel bound to follow the line of general self-deception and accept world opinion, United Nations version, as ordaining that the proper line is to grant self-government "more quickly than immediate" on the basis of "one man, one vote"'. There is much pithy comment along similar lines throughout the introduction, which is well worth reading and pondering upon, and the original book itself is still one of the best ever written on Arabia, the record of a fine achievement in bringing to an end the brutal anarchy which prevailed in the Eastern Protectorate before Ingrams went there.

Part II

The third edition of Harold Ingrams's *Arabia and the Isles* is distinguished from the second edition, published in 1952, by the addition of a lengthy introduction, which is made up partly of an exegesis of the first edition, and partly of reflections on what has been taking place in Aden and the Protectorates during the past fifteen years. Ingrams's great achievement, related in the first edition of *Arabia and the Isles* in 1942, was in bringing peace and order to the tribes and rulers of the Eastern Protectorate in the late nineteen-thirties. The *modus vivendi* which he prescribed

---

2 Same publishers.

for them then has lasted, with surprisingly few interruptions, down to the present day, and his story of how that achievement came to pass has worn just as well.

'Ingrams' Peace', as it came to be known, performed for the States and tribes of the Hadhramaut the same service as the trucial system had performed for the principalities and peoples of the Persian Gulf a century earlier, and like its precursor it was brought about, not by intimidation or domination, but by persuasion and mediation. There were other similarities between the two systems. Like the first maritime truce in the Gulf in 1835, the first Hadhrami truce concluded in 1937 had only a limited duration, and this condition, as the experience of the maritime truces had shown, was essential to the operation, in its initial stages, of the system. For the contumacy and turbulence of the Arabian tribes could only be held in check if the prospect were extended to them of being free to settle their rancorous feuds and disputes by their customary sanguinary methods at the end of a stipulated period of time. When the truce negotiated by Ingrams expired in 1940 the tribes and their rulers had to decide for themselves whether or not to forgo the advantages to be derived from a renewal and prolongation of the truce in favour of the delights of blood-letting which would follow its demise. They decided in favour of 'Ingrams' Peace', and the truce was renewed for a term of ten years, by the end of which time its purpose had been accomplished.

While much of the success of Ingrams's work in the Hadhramaut was due to the character and abilities of Ingrams himself, it owed something also to the fact that the policy pursued in the Protectorate in those days was laid down by the Government of India, and was derived from that government's long experience of Arabia and its inhabitants. The knowledge of Arabian affairs possessed by the Indian Political Service, and the suitability of its administrative methods to Arabian conditions, are both emphasized by Ingrams in his new introduction. He believes that a great mistake was committed in Aden and the Protectorates after 1945 by the introduction of the traditional Colonial Office policy, evolved in the African dependencies and having its roots in an Imperial policy stretching back for more than a century, of fostering the growth of British political institutions and ideas in a dependent territory with the ultimate aim of having it develop along Western lines. Western political forms, Ingrams maintains, have no relevance to Arabia, and he believes that it would have been far better for all concerned if the Protectorate States of South Arabia had been left to fashion their own system of government, advised by political residents on the Indian model, instead of being guided by district commissioners along traditional colonial lines. It is hard to disagree with these conclusions, or with Ingrams's general contention that too few people with knowledge of Arabia have decided British policy there in recent years. He is, however, a little inconsistent in the way in which he arrives at some of his conclusions, and not everyone will share his regard for T. E. Lawrence's perspicacity in Arab affairs or his satisfaction with the proceedings and outcome of the Cairo Conference in 1921. The Government of India, whose greater experience and judgement in Arabian politics Ingrams more than once applauds, were under-represented at that conference, and their views were accorded even less respect.

For the Federation of South Arabia Ingrams feels little warmth, and he is pessimistic about its future. His opposition to the Federation, however, is not based upon the objections usually advanced by its critics, *viz.*, that it retards Aden's progress by tying it to the politically backward Protectorates and serves as an imperialist device to frustrate unity in the Arab world, but derives from his argument that by destroying the independence of the several Protectorate States it has deprived them of their chance to work out their political future for themselves. If some kind of unified State is necessary for the survival of all, it should be brought about, he contends, not by the imposition of an unsuitable Western constitutional framework, but by the extension of the trucial system which he introduced thirty years ago. As he remarks with some acerbity, it would be a new and salutary experience for the urban politicians of Aden, dazed from over-long contemplation of the future through a bright haze of nationalist exhortation and United Nations' resolutions, to have to sit on the ground and argue things out with a group of Bedouin tribesmen—and the Bedouin, after all, form the preponderating majority of the Protectorates' population. The experience might well shatter the said politicians' euphoric belief that they will be able to rule the tribes after 1968 by Pharaonic fiat from Aden.

A less gloomy view of the state of affairs in the Federation and of the legacy of British rule in South Arabia is taken by David Holden, who for the past ten years has been reporting on the Middle East, first, for *The Times*, and later for *The Guardian* and *The Sunday Times* in succession. His *Farewell to Arabia* takes a nostalgic look at the old Arabia that is passing and assesses with sympathy and understanding the prospects and pitfalls which lie ahead of the new. Despite some doubts about the way in which Britain has governed Aden and the Protectorates in the past decade, he is, on the whole, satisfied with the outcome. 'Nowhere else in Arabia, after all,' he observes (p. 67), 'does the victory of modern nationalism seem as imminent now as in Aden and the Federation, because nowhere else has a colonial power been at work with anything like true colonial authority to act as the catalyst of nationhood.' Yet Holden, like Ingrams, is guilty of some inconsistency in his reasoning, for only a couple of pages earlier he writes: 'I do not see the men of Upper Yafai, or Radfan, or many another tribal territory, becoming law-abiding, democratic citizens of a united South Arabian state anywhere this side of the twenty-first century—which is now, after all, only a couple of generations away.' By the twenty-first century? It is highly unlikely that the tribesmen of South Arabia will have become even Arab nationalists by then, let alone democratic citizens. Besides, what grounds are there for identifying the one with the other, or even of seeing any correlation between the two in the Arab world today? On the contrary, to judge from the type of nationalism in vogue in Egypt, Syria and Iraq, and the nature of the regimes which rule them, the two would seem to be mutually exclusive.

Holden exhibits a similar confusion in assessing the reasons for the weakness of the position of the various Federal rulers. While his stricture on the characters of some of them are merited, he errs in ascribing the feeble authority which they exercise over their subjects primarily to their supineness and political ignorance, and even more so when he assumes that nationalist politicians, educated in the northern Arab capitals, will hold more appeal for the tribes. The real reason for the Federal rulers' lack of power lies in the individualism of every tribe, clan and tribesman, in their almost anarchical sense of independence, and in their absolute refusal to bow to the will of another, indeed to do more than associate with him voluntarily for a specific purpose and for a fixed length of time. It is doubtful whether the modern nationalist politician, however forward-looking he may be, will succeed where the traditional rulers have failed.

Such criticism, however, does not detract from the general value of Holden's book. He has much to say that is sensible and shrewd about what has happened in Aden and the Yemen in the past few years, about the efforts which King Faisal is making to undo the damage done by his brother's misrule to the Saudi kingdom, and about the caprices and contortions produced by oil wealth in the Gulf States. Some of Holden's descriptions are brilliant, and he has a good eye for the revealing detail or the telling slip. Because he is a good reporter, and because he has no ideological axe to grind, he can see things for what they really are—the Egyptian campaign in the Yemen as an inept and squalid war of conquest; the government of King Faisal as a genuine if belated bid to reform the Saudi State; and Britain's presence in the Gulf as beneficent and necessary. He refuses to pontificate about the path Arabia should take, and he knows the peninsula too well to fall into the vulgar error of supposing that its ills will be cured by the application of the fashionable economic and political specifics of our day. Arabia has resisted the world for a long time, and if it has to succumb eventually to the world's insistent clamour, it will not succumb easily.

20
Salisbury, Curzon and the Kuwait Agreement of 1899[1]

When the government of Iraq, under the late Major-General 'Abdul Karim Qasim, laid claim to sovereignty over Kuwait in June 1961, its action not only precipitated a crisis which engaged the attention of a restless world for several days but it also brought a fleeting prominence to two half-forgotten episodes in Kuwait's past—the conclusion of the agreement of 23 January 1899 with Britain, and the shaikhdom's obscure relationship with the former Ottoman Empire. For it was the abrogation of the 1899 agreement by Britain and Kuwait on 19 June 1961[2] which emboldened General Qasim to advance his claim, and it was Kuwait's juridical status half a century earlier as a *qaza*, or district, of the *vilayet* of Basra which led him to base his claim upon Iraq's residual rights of sovereignty as a successor state of the Ottoman Empire. Although much was said and written at the time of the Kuwait crisis about the 1899 agreement and its origins, and although it has frequently been referred to in passing by historians writing on the diplomacy of the period before 1914, especially in the context of British, Russian and German rivalry in the Middle East, comparatively little attention has been paid to the circumstances in which the agreement came about. These, when looked at more closely, prove to be more complicated than is generally assumed.

---

[1] Source: D.C. Watt and K. Bourne, *Studies in International History* (London, 1967), pp. 249-291.
[2] See Cmnd 1409, 'Exchange of Notes regarding relations between the United Kingdom of Great Britain and Northern Ireland and the State of Kuwait', June 1961, *Kuwait No. 1* (1961).

In May 1896 the ruler of Kuwait, Shaikh Muhammad ibn Sabah, was murdered, along with his brother Jarrah, by his half-brother, Mubarak. The slain ruler's sons and those of Jarrah ibn Sabah fled to Turkish Iraq, where they found refuge with a maternal relative, Yusuf ibn Ibrahim, a wealthy merchant and landowner residing at Dorah, on the lower Shatt al-Arab. Soon afterwards they petitioned the Ottoman sultan, 'Abdul Hamid, for Mubarak's deposition and punishment, and they also asked that he should be compelled to restore to them the family estates of the Al Sabah which he had seized. The estates were located in the vicinity of Fao, at the mouth of the Shatt al-Arab, and Mubarak had seized them in order to forestall their possible sequestration by the Turkish authorities at Basra. This same concern for his own well-being had also led him, even before his nephews petitioned the sultan, to seek investiture from 'Abdul Hamid as ruler and *qaim-maqam* (or governor) of Kuwait. In so doing he was simply following a precedent set by the two previous generations of Al Sabah shaikhs, who had likewise sought to safeguard their property on the Shatt al-Arab, from which they derived the major part of their income, from interference by the Turks by allowing the sultan to confer upon them the title of *pasha* and the rank of *qaim-maqam*.[3]

Two months after Mubarak's seizure of power H.M.S. *Sphinx* visited Kuwait with the senior naval officer, Persian Gulf, Commander C.J. Baker, on board. Baker found the atmosphere in the town unsettled. 'Kuwait is nominally an independent Arab territory,' he wrote in his report, 'but in reality the Turks exercise great influence over it, more especially since the new Chief acceded to power, he finds it necessary to play into their hands. I paid him a visit, but he would not come off to the ship; I also noticed that he flew the Turkish flag, and taxed him with it, but could not get any satisfactory answer from him.'[4] Mubarak was in no position to give a satisfactory answer. While he had been lavishing bribes upon officials in Baghdad and Constantinople—including the Shaikh al-Islam and the Shaikh 'Abdul Huda, one of the influential coterie of religious shaikhs around 'Abdul Hamid[5]—in an effort to secure recognition from the Sublime Porte,

---

3 See Memo. By Stavrides (Legal Adviser to British Embassy, Constantinople), 30 June 1896, enclosed in M. H. Herbert (*chargé d'affaires*) to Salisbury, Therapia, 6 July 1896 (no.526). [Public Record Office], F.O. 78/5113. For a summary of the evidence of Kuwait's connexion with the Porte over the previous forty years, see Political and Secret Department Memoranda, no. C 239, 'Précis of Koweit Affairs, 1896-1904', I[ndia] O[ffice Records, Commonwealth Relations Office].

4 Baker to Euan Macgregor (secretary to admiralty), 4 August 1896, no. 8, passed to foreign office, 16 October 1897, F.O. 78/5113.

5 See Memo. By Capt. J.F. Whyte, Pera, 22 March 1897, enclosed in Sir P. Currie (am-

the *vali* of Basra, Hamdi Pasha, had adopted the cause of the late ruler's sons and was urging the Porte to exploit the opening offered it to impose its authority upon Kuwait. The Porte was undecided what to do, particularly as it was somewhat bewildered by a report which had reached it that Mubarak, in murdering his half-brothers and usurping power, had acted with the connivance of the British political resident in the Persian Gulf. According to the tale which had reached the ears of the sultan's ministers, and which caused some agitation in the *serai*, the resident was attempting to create 'an Arabic confederation', independent of the Porte if not actually hostile to it, and consisting of the principalities of Jabal Shammar, Najd, Qatar, Bahrain and Kuwait. When Muhammad ibn Sabah and his brother Jarrah refused to have anything to do with the scheme, so the story went, Mubarak, who had been living for a month as a resident's guest at Bushire, crossed to Kuwait and murdered his half-brothers.[6]

The story had no foundation, but the very fact that it had been concocted and had received even partial credence at Constantinople was indicative of the hostility with which the Turks viewed the British presence in the Gulf. Over the preceding three-quarters of a century Britain had built up in the Gulf a predominant position, based upon her treaties with Bahrain and the Trucial Shaikhdoms and backed by British naval power. The Turks had challenged this position in 1871 when they occupied Hasa and extended their nominal authority over the Qatar peninsula, farther south, by securing the allegiance of the ruler of Dauhah, its principal town. To their annoyance, however, the British government refused to curtail their maritime surveillance of the Gulf, which took in the coasts of Hasa and Qatar as well as the waters around Bahrain and off the Trucial coast. Not only did the Royal Navy continue to police the waters off Hasa but the British government also refused to recognize any rights of sovereignty on the part of Turkey over Qatar, or, for that matter, over any part of the Arabian coastline south of Qatif, however much the Al Thani ruler of Dauhah might profess his loyalty to the Ottoman sultan. For the point at issue, so far as the British government were concerned, was not abstract questions of *meum* and *tuum* in the Gulf, but the security of shipping and commerce, and they had no intention of abating their maritime protectorate simply to humour Turkish pretensions, especially as the Turks themselves were incapable of keeping order off their own coasts or of constraining the maritime tribes who were their nominal subjects to keep the peace at sea. Indeed, it was this very consideration which had induced the ruler of

---

bassador, Constantinople) to secretary of state, 24 March 1897 (no. 203), F.O. 78/5113.
6 Memo. by Stavrides, 30 June 1896, *op. cit.*

Qatar, Jasim al-Thani, to acknowledge Turkish suzerainty and to accept appointment as *qaim-maqam* of Dauhah.

In the last decade of the century the Turks' endeavours to make their power felt in the Gulf were concentrated upon the head of the Gulf and upon the delta of the Shatt al-Arab, in particular. A military post was established at Fao and British Indian vessels proceeding up-river were forcibly halted there and made to pay quarantine charges, even when they were not bound for Turkish ports. The outbreak of plague in India in 1896, and the subsequent convening of an international conference at Venice in 1897 to devise measures to prevent the plague from spreading, presented the Porte with further opportunities for aggrandizement. It was agreed at the conference that two quarantine stations should be established in the Gulf, one near its entrance and the other at Basra. Britain and Persia ratified the convention embodying this decision but the Turks did not. Instead, they insisted that the proposed *lazaret* at Basra should be moved to Fao, that the number of quarantine stations in the Gulf should be increased, with stations in Bahrain, Qatar, Hasa and Kuwait, and that they all should be placed under the control of the international board of health at Constantinople. Britain opposed the establishment of stations under Turkish control in Bahrain and Qatar, which she regarded as independent shaikhdoms, and she was doubtful of the Porte's right to locate one at Kuwait. Shaikh Mubarak evidently shared this feeling, for when in February 1897 a Turkish quarantine official arrived at Kuwait with the intention of taking up duty there, Mubarak sent a hasty message to the political resident at Bushire, asking to be granted an interview with him.

The request was relayed to London through both the government of India and the British embassy at Constantinople. In passing it on, the ambassador, Sir Philip Currie, remarked that he was himself unsure of Mubarak's actual status *vis-à-vis* the Porte. He had earlier been given to understand that the sheikh was 'in reality an independent potentate and only nominally subject to the Sultan,'[7] but he had recently been told by the British assistant political agent and consul at Basra, Captain J. F. Whyte, who passed through Constantinople on his way to England on leave in March 1897, that the ruler of Kuwait was usually regarded as an Ottoman dependant.

> The acceptance by the Shaikh of an appointment from the Sultan as Kaim Makam [Whyte explained] precludes the possibility of any foreign power recognizing under present conditions

---

[7] Currie to Salisbury, 24 November 1896 (no. 972), F.O. 78/5113.

his independence. The present Shaikh, Shaikh Mubarak, when at Fao in November last officially visited the Turkish Mudir of that place, a proceeding hardly consonant with the dignity of an independent Arab Chief...... Shaikh Mubarak has since his usurpation been employing his late brothers' wealth to secure his recognition as Shaikh, and his appointment as Kaimmakam of Koweit by the Sublime Porte.[8]

The foreign office was no more able to make up its mind on the question than Currie. From an examination of the files it was discovered that in 1889, and again in 1893, the embassy at Constantinople had acknowledged, at least by implication, the existence of Turkish sovereignty down the Arabian coast of the Gulf from Basra as far south as Qatif.[9] Although on neither occasion had Kuwait been alluded to by name, or specifically included among the places admitted to be under Turkish jurisdiction, the fact that a general acknowledgement of sovereignty had been made seemed to preclude any categorical statement of Kuwait's independence now being made to the Porte. Before accepting his conclusion the foreign office decided to refer the question to the India office. The disposition there was to view the matter more from a practical than from a legal standpoint. A number of piracies had lately been committed in the Shatt al-Arab on foreign shipping, including some British Indian vessels, and investigations had revealed that some of the pirates involved were subjects of Mubarak. The government of India had consequently recommended that 'there might be advantage in fixing upon the Turkish Government the responsibility for the Sheikh of Koweit's actions,' and that 'a state of affairs in which he can shelter himself under a nominal subjection to the Porte, while the Porte can disclaim at will any responsibility, is in the last degree

---

8 Memo. By Whyte, Pera, 22 March 1897, enclosed in Currie to Salisbury, 24 March 1897 (no. 203), F.O. 78/5113.

9 The principal acknowledgement had been made by the oriental secretary of the embassy in a conversation with the grand vizir in July 1889 about the measures which the Porte was supposed to be taking to suppress piracy along the Hasa coast. 'I pointed out to H.H.', the oriental secretary reported, 'by means of a tracing on a flying paper the position of El Katr [Qatar] and the considerable distance intervening between El Katif and that locality, adding that want of security prevailed between Busra and El Katif and not between the latter and El Katr. I also took the opportunity of mentioning to H.H. the considerations which made it very desirable for the Turkish Government not to extend its military action South of El Katif'. (A. Sandison to Sir Wm. White (ambassador, Constantinople), enclosed in Sir N. O'Conor to Salisbury, Constantinople, 22 December 1898, no. 667 secret, F.O. 78/5113).

unsatisfactory.'[10] On the other hand the India Office itself thought that there was little, if anything, to justify a Turkish claim to sovereignty over Kuwait. It therefore hedged in its reply to the foreign office, saying that if the latter were disposed to recognize Turkish sovereignty over Kuwait, a demand might be preferred upon the Porte both for the payment of an indemnity for the piracies committed on British Indian shipping and for assurances regarding the future good behaviour of Shaikh Mubarak. Alternatively, the India office suggested, it might be preferable to treat Mubarak as independent, and 'to convey to him a serious warning, and inform him that his responsibility will be enforced if his subjects are not restrained from repeating such attacks upon British Indian Baghlas in future.'[11]

The foreign office wanted time to consider the question further, so on 2 April 1897 it instructed Currie to avoid, if possible, any discussion with the Turks on Mubarak's status. Currie was also informed that, if the meeting which Mubarak had requested with the political resident in the Gulf took place, he would be given a serious warning about his responsibility for his subjects' behaviour at sea, on the lines suggested by the India office.[12] A few days after these instructions were sent Captain Whyte arrived in London from Constantinople. He told Sir Thomas Sanderson, the permanent under-secretary at the Foreign Office, that before he left Basra at the beginning of March he had learned that Mubarak's object in seeking an interview with the resident was to ask for the extension of a British protectorate over Kuwait.[13] Sanderson was not at all attracted by the prospect, and he said so when he reported Whyte's news to Salisbury. 'Bahrein gives us trouble enough, but it is an island; but to have constant squabbles with the Turks about the adjoining coast tribes would be intolerable, unless we were prepared to establish a military post there.'[14] The prime minister agreed but he was reluctant not to turn Mubarak's approach to some good use. 'Might we not obtain from him', he asked Sanderson, 'a promise not to accept any other protectorate – we only giving him an assurance in return that we will not encroach on his independence, but will treat him in

---

10 Governor-general in Council to secretary of state, 24 February 1897, no. 27 secret external, [I.O.] Political and Secret Letters from India, vol. 90. See also under-secretary, India office, to under-secretary, foreign office, 12 February 1897. *ibid.*

11 Under-secretary, India office to under-secretary, foreign office, 24 March 1897, F.O. 78/5113. A baghlah is a large *dhow*.

12 Draft to Currie, 2 April 1897 (no. 96), F.O. 78/5113.

13 Note by W. Lee Warner (secretary in political and secret department), 6 April 1897, [I.O.] Political and Secret Home Correspondence, vol. 170.

14 Minute by Sanderson, 8 April 1897, F.O. 78/5113.

a friendly manner?'[15]

Sanderson passed the suggestion to the India office where it aroused little enthusiasm. Sir W. Lee Warner, the secretary in the political and secret department, who had been handling the Kuwait question, thought it was now probably too late to send further instructions to the political resident regarding his meeting with Mubarak, and that, in any case, if Mubarak should raise the subject of protection or of Kuwait's independence, the resident would be bound to refer for instructions before replying. It would be better, therefore, Lee Warner concluded, not to supplement the resident's existing orders at this stage. Sanderson, on reflection, thought so too, and on 26 April he suggested to Sir Arthur Godley, the permanent under-secretary at the India office, that any contact with Mubarak should be strictly limited to conveying to him the warning about piracy.[16]

While the British government were trying to make up their minds whether or not he was independent, Mubarak was persisting in his efforts to persuade 'Abdul Hamid to recognize him as ruler of Kuwait and invest him with the rank of *qaim-maqam*. Despite the expenditure of large sums of money at Constantinople and Baghdad, he had no success up to the closing weeks of 1897. In June his nephews had made an effort to unseat him, and although the attempt came to nothing it prompted Currie to ask the foreign office for guidance on what his attitude should be if a similar attempt were to be made in the future. He was told to stay clear of all disputes over the succession at Kuwait. 'Unless.... The Chiefs in the Gulf under engagements with us intervene in the struggles at Koweit so as to disturb the general peace of the Gulf, we do not see that the matter calls for action or enquiry on our part. We have never acknowledged Koweit to be under Turkish protection. But it seems doubtful whether we could deny that in fact it is under Turkish influence.'[17]

In July 1897, a Turkish corvette visited Kuwait, and several hundred inhabitants of the Turkish frontier town of Zubair, near Basra, probably at the instigation of Mubarak's nephews, or of their relative, Yusuf ibn Ibrahim, petitioned the Porte for Mubarak's removal.[18] Alarmed by these manoeuvres, Mubarak sent a messenger to Bahrain to tell the residency

---

15 Minute by Salisbury, n.d. (8 April 1897?), F.O. 78/5113.
16 Lee Warner to C. A. Hopgood, foreign office, 14 April 1897, and Sanderson to Godley, 26 April 1897, F.O. 78/5113.
17 Draft telegrams to Currie, 17 July 1897, nos. 306 and 307, F.O. 78/5113. See also Currie to secretary of state, 16 July 1896, tels., nos. 465 and 467, cypher, *ibid*.
18 Currie to secretary of state, 21 July 1897, (tel. no. 476 cypher), passed to India office, 22 July 1897, [I.O.] Political and Secret Home Correspondence, vol. 172.

agent there that he had certain proposals which he wished to lay before the political resident as soon as possible. The resident, Lieutenant-Colonel M. J. Meade, in reporting the approach to the government of India, recommended that he should be permitted to receive Mubarak's messenger, especially as it would give him an opportunity to deliver the warning about the shaikh's responsibility for his subjects' conduct at sea. The permission was granted but at the last moment Mubarak's messenger declined to accompany the residency agent from Bahrain to Bushire and left instead for Kuwait. Before he went, however, he told the residency agent that the object of Mubarak's overture was to canvass the idea of a British protectorate over Kuwait, to the exclusion of Turkish influence there.[19]

A letter from Mubarak himself arrived at Bushire in the latter part of August, saying that he had no one sufficiently intelligent to send to the residency to discuss what he had in mind, and asking Meade to send someone to him instead. In the first week of September Meade sent his assistant resident, J. C. Gaskin, to Kuwait in the residency steamer, R.I.M.S. *Lawrence*, with orders to find out what Mubarak wanted and to deliver to him the warning about piracy.[20] Gaskin reached Kuwait on 5 September. Mubarak refused to come on board *Lawrence*, lest he compromise himself with the Turks, so Gaskin went ashore to see him. When he handed the warning on piracy to Mubarak, the sheikh denied that any of his subjects had misbehaved themselves at sea, although he admitted that some of the people employed in his date gardens on the Shatt al-Arab occasionally attacked vessels passing up the river. Most of the people involved, however, he said, lived on the other side of the Gulf, and they had often attacked and plundered Kuwait vessels. Whenever he had complained to the Turkish authorities at Basra about these attacks and asked for protection, the only result had been to subject his own people to extortion at the hands of the Turkish officers and soldiers sent to investigate his complaints. He would be willing, he told Gaskin, to co-operate with the British government in the suppression of piracy, and he promised both to pass on any information which he received about piracies and to assist in the pursuit and capture of pirates.

Gaskin then raised the question of Mubarak's quarrel with his neph-

---

19 'Précis of Koweit Affairs, 1896-1904', political resident, Persian Gulf to foreign secretary, Simla, 21, 27 and 31 July 1897, tells., [I.O] Political and Secret Department Memoranda no. C 239.
20 Political resident, Persian Gulf, to foreign secretary, Simla, 22 August 1897, tel., and foreign secretary, Simla, to political resident, Persian Gulf, 29 August 1897, tel no. 1367 E.A., *ibid*.

ews, and suggested that he should accept the offer which reputedly had recently been made by the sheikh of Bahrain, 'Isa ibn 'Ali, to arbitrate in the dispute. Mubarak replied that while he was quite ready to accept Shaikh 'Isa's mediation, and to come to terms with his nephews, he was not prepared to allow them to return to Kuwait. The conversation now turned to Mubarak's approaches to the political resident. The sheikh had no hesitation in revealing their purpose. He wished, he said, 'to be placed under British protection such as is enjoyed by Bahrain and the Trucial Chiefs. If the British Government will extend its protection to him, ... he is prepared to assist the British in maintaining law and order in that part of the Gulf [Kuwait and its vicinity] with the full force at his disposal, which .... Amounts to 25,000 tribesmen.'[21] He and his people, Mubarak went on, found the Turks grasping and unreliable, and he suspected them strongly of planning to absorb Kuwait entirely in the near future. It was to prevent this happening that he was now applying for admission to the trucial system.[22]

Meade's first reaction to Mubarak's request, when Gaskin reported it, was to treat it simply as a stratagem by Mubarak to bring pressure upon the Porte to recognize him as ruler of Kuwait. Most of the petty chieftains along the Arabian coast of the Gulf were ready to invoke British or Turkish protection whenever it suited their interest to do so, and Meade doubted whether Mubarak would have made any advances to the British government if the Porte had not hesitated to recognize him. However, in reporting the results of Gaskin's visit, Meade pointed out to his superiors that, regardless of what his motives might be, Mubarak's approach offered an opportunity to extend British influence to the head of the Gulf, which would be extremely advantageous to British interests in the region as a whole.

> Koweit possesses an excellent harbour, and will, under our protection, undoubtedly become one of the most important places in the Persian Gulf. Apart from the chances of its being the sea-port for the projected railway from Port Said, which is under consideration and which the possession of Koweit would enable us to protect, the trade with the interior is already considerable, and will greatly increase. At present, in spite of the

---

21 Meade to foreign secretary, Simla, 25 September 1897 (no. 90 confidential), enclosed in foreign secret letter 147 (external) of 21 October 1897 (passed to foreign office, 18 November 1897), F.O. 78/5113.
22 *Ibid.*

Sheikh's assertions, it is regarded as a centre for piratical expeditions, and, therefore, endangers our trade with the Shat-el-Arab. Finally, it is said that it is a great slave emporium, and that our efforts to put a stop to the slave trade are more or less barren of results as long as slaves can be marched across Arabia, and shipped at Koweit for Turkey and Persia.[23]

Meade concluded:

As far then as we are concerned, it seems advisable to fall in with Sheikh Mubarak's views, and to extend to Koweit and its ruler the protection enjoyed by Bahrein and other places on the Arab coast; but I am aware that the Turkish Government claims a certain amount of influence in the place, the Sheikh, for instance, flies a Turkish flag over his own residence, and his predecessor had the title of Kaim-Makam conferred on him by the Porte. These facts, however, do not, I think, constitute an insurmountable obstacle to the extension of our influence. We have never admitted Turkish authority in Koweit, and the Turks, as far as I am aware, have never entered into formal agreement with the Sheikh, nor have they ever exercised sovereign rights at the place.[24]

There was little inclination in London to accede to Mubarak's request for trucial status. Lord George Hamilton, the secretary of state for India, telegraphed to the viceroy, the Earl of Elgin, on 13 October: 'Her Majesty's Government are not disposed to interfere more than necessary for maintenance of general peace of Persian Gulf or to bring Koweit under protection.'[25] But the matter could not be dealt with as simply as this. On 27 October a telegram arrived from Elgin to say that a fresh attack on Kuwait by Mubarak's nephews and their supporters was expected to take place on or about 6 November, and that Meade had asked whether he should despatch a gunboat to watch events.[26] Hamilton passed the viceroy's enquiry to the foreign office, where Salisbury decided that it would do no harm to send a gunboat, provided that it did not interfere except

---

23 *Ibid.*
24 *Ibid.*
25 [I.O] Political and Secret Home Correspondence, vol. 173.
26 Viceroy to secretary of state, Simla, 27 October 1897, tel., no. 1656 E.A., For., Sec., [I.O] Political and Secret Letters from India, vol. 96.

to protect British interests.[27] On the morning of 6 November H.M.S. *Pigeon* dropped anchor off Kuwait town. There was no sign anywhere of any hostile forces, and when *Pigeon's* commander went ashore he was told by Mubarak that none were expected. Nor did he fear them, the sheikh said, if they should appear, for his enemies could raise only 3,000 fighting men while he had 16,000 armed tribesmen at his command. However, he added, he would still like to be taken under British protection, more especially as his kinsman, Shaikh 'Isa of Bahrain, had lately impressed upon him the advantages to be derived from it. Mubarak also spoke bitterly of the Turks, saying that he wished to be rid of all connection with them.[28]

Although this latest turn of events led Hamilton to look again at Colonel Meade's arguments in favour of extending a protectorate over Kuwait, it did not in the end lead him to alter his decision of 13 October. As he explained to Salisbury, *à propos* of Meade's report.

> No sufficient case is made out for the extension of the British Protectorate to a point so far north of the limit of the existing responsibilities of the Government of India. On the other hand, there appears to be nothing in the political situation of Koweit that need hamper British naval officers in the repression of piracy in case it should be found necessary to bring home to the Shaikh responsibility for acts of that character.[29]

Salisbury accepted the argument and Elgin was informed accordingly on 9 December.[30]

Events immediately afterwards seemed to confirm the correctness of the decision. Northern Arabia had been disturbed by the death of the amir of Jabal Shammar, Muhammad ibn Rashid, and by the simultaneous movement of Turkish troops southwards from Baghdad into the *vilayet* of Basra. Hamdi Pasha, the late *vali* of Basra and an old enemy of Mubarak's, had been at Constantinople, urging the Porte to place a permanent garrison in Kuwait, and it was believed that the troops collecting at Basra were

---

27 Under-secretary, foreign office, to under-secretary, India Office, 29 October 1897, immediate, confidential, [I.O] Political and Secret Home Correspondence, vol. 173.

28 Lieut.-Commander Mowbray to Meade, H.M.S. Pigeon, Bushire, 7 November 1897, no covering letter, [I.O] Political and Secret Letters from India, vol. 98.

29 Under-secretary, India office to under-secretary, foreign office, 18 November 1897, F.O. 78/5513.

30 Under-secretary, foreign office, to under-secretary, India office, 25 November 1897, and draft telegram, cypher, to viceroy, 9 December 1897, [I.O] Political and Secret Home Correspondence, vol. 174.

destined for the invasion of Kuwait.³¹ Mubarak was unperturbed by the apparent threats, and with good reason. His efforts of the previous eighteen months were now bearing fruit, and towards the end of December 1897 the *vali* of Basra was informed that an imperial *iradé* (decree) had been issued, appointing Mubarak *qaim-maqam* of Kuwait with the title of pasha. Thereafter his name appeared in the official almanac of the Basra *vilayet*, and Kuwait was formally classified by the Porte as a *qaza* of the *sanjaq* of Najd in the *vilayet* of Basra.³²

There, so far as the British government were concerned, the whole question of Kuwait's status might have rested, had it not become linked to considerations of a wider nature to which the British government's attention was drawn in the early months of 1898. These were first raised by Lieutenant-Colonel William Loch, the consul-general at Baghdad, after he had visited Basra in December 1897 to investigate the reasons for the movement of additional troops into the *vilayet*. Writing to the foreign secretary of the government of India after his return to Baghdad, Loch said that he was convinced that the troop movements and other activities, such as the appointment of a new *vali* to Basra and the renewed attempt by the Porte to establish a quarantine post at Fao, were designed to extend and consolidate Turkish control not only over the delta of the Shatt al-Arab but also over Kuwait.

> The occupation or protection by the Porte of Koweit [Loch warned] would be a standing menace to our trade interests in Turkish Arabia. Scarcely a day passes but attempts are made to hamper our trade, sometimes by vexatious quarantine regulations, at others by some move on the part of the Turkish authorities to gain complete control over the mouth of the Shattul Arab at Fao, and it is from here that they must be watched and their actions checked.³³

The Turks, however, were not the only ones in Loch's view whose activities at the head of the Gulf deserved watching.

---

31 Various telegrams from Currie between 17 December 1897 and 3 March 1898, [I.O] Political and Secret Home Correspondence, vols. 174 and 175.

32 For Kuwait's designation, see under-secretary, foreign office, to under-secretary, India office, 21 April 1899, Secret, enclosing A. C. Wratislaw, Consul, Basra, to Sir N. O'Conor, 25 February 1899, no. 10, [I.O] Political and Secret Home Correspondence, vol. 182.

33 Loch to foreign secretary, government of India, 22 December 1897, no. 659, [I.O] Political and Secret Home Correspondence, vol. 175.

For some months [he told the foreign secretary at Simla] vague rumours have been afloat that Russia and her Agents were working in the Gulf, and I would invite your reference to my letter No. 616 dated 15th ultimo in which I forwarded a copy of an Embassy despatch from Constantinople with enclosures, bringing to my notice that Russia was seeking to acquire a coaling station in that quarter, which confirms to a certain extent these rumours. Moreover, from hints I have received it is Koweit on which Russia's eyes are fixed.[34]

The dispatch to which Loch referred was one from Currie, enclosing a letter from John Dickson, the consul at Jerusalem, dated 21 September 1897, and reporting that M. Krouglov, the acting Russian consul-general at Jerusalem, who had lately been appointed consul-general at Baghdad, where he had been vice-consul some years earlier, had left for Russia on his way to take up his new post. 'I am informed confidentially', Dickson wrote, 'that Monsieur Krouglow has been instructed to report, on his arrival at Bagdad, on the much desired scheme of securing for Russia a Coaling Station in the Persian Gulf, though I have not been able to ascertain whether any particular place, outside Persian territory, has been fixed upon.'[35] Krouglov did not, in the end, go to Baghdad, but Loch was fairly certain that the Russians would push the question of a coaling station at Kuwait, if only because their consul-general at Baghdad was 'an intense Anglophobe and extremely active in intrigue.'[36] Loch also found it significant that Shaikh Mubarak had observed to the commanding officer of H.M.S. *Pigeon*, when she was at Kuwait in the first week of November, that he had heard that there was talk of a projected railway to the head of the Gulf, and he had added that, for his part, he would be glad to see it become a reality.[37]

There were other signs of a Russian interest in the upper Gulf in 1897 and 1898. On the pretext that they wished to study the effects of plague at Bushire the Russian government had sent two doctors there in 1897, although at that time there were no signs of the plague at the port. Two more doctors followed in 1898, and they, like their predecessors, vis-

---

34 *Ibid.*
35 Dickson to Currie, 21 September 1897, no. 47 confidential, enclosed in Currie to Salisbury, 1 October 1897, no. 675 confidential, F.O. 78/4808.
36 Loch to foreign secretary, government of India, 22 December 1897, no. 659, above.
37 See Lieut.-Commander Mowbray to Meade, 7 November 1897, no covering letter, [I.O] Political and Secret Letters from India, vol. 98.

ited the entrance of the Gulf. The two earlier doctors had also toured the head of the Gulf in August 1897 before going on to Baghdad. It seemed fairly clear that the Russian plan was to use the possibility or incidence of plague in southern Persia to extend their influence there, much as they had extended it in eastern Persia by sending Cossacks to establish a plague cordon in Seistan. There might even have been some connexion between the doctors' investigations and the Russian government's plans to construct a railway through Persia. They had successfully blocked any similar plans which the British government might have had by securing a decree from the shah in 1890 forbidding the construction of railways in Persia for ten years, by the end of which time, they hoped, the line that they were building through the Caucasus would have reached the Persian border.[38]

A copy of Loch's report reached the foreign office via Currie at Constantinople at the beginning of February 1898. It was read with considerable interest by George Curzon, the parliamentary under-secretary of state, who drew Salisbury's attention to it and particularly to Kuwait's place in the rumoured Russian designs.

> I think we should keep our eye on the place. It is not a Turkish port, *i.e.* the Turks have never, I believe, occupied or administered it, though they have had some flirtations with the local Sheikhs, which are going on at this moment. Sheikh Mubarak having, it is alleged, applied for their aid. Successive Sheikhs have frequently asked the Brit. Govt. to extend their protectorate over it but we have always declined. A time may come, however, when a Protectorate may be the most useful method of anticipating acquisition by another Power. I imagine that under no circ. should we admit of a Russian position in the Persian Gulf. Is it worthwhile to call the attention of the Indian Govt. to the contingency indicated by Col. Loch and to ask their opinion concerning it?[39]

Salisbury thought the inquiry worth making and a telegram was sent to the viceroy on 7 February. Elgin replied two days later to say that he had no confirmation of the rumours of Russian intentions towards Kuwait, although Colonel Meade had learned that the two Russian doctors who

---

38 It did not, in fact, reach there until 1904. Russia, however, had meanwhile provided for this contingency by obtaining from the shah in 1899 a ten-year extension of the ban.

39 Curzon to prime minister, 4 February 1898, F.O. 78/5113.

had toured the head of the Gulf in 1897 had been accompanied by a third Russian who was not a medical man.[40]

Hamilton took the opportunity of relaying the viceroy's reply to Salisbury to ask whether, in the light of the current rumours, the policy of non-interference in the affairs of Kuwait laid down the previous October should be altered.[41] Salisbury referred to Sanderson for his opinion. The permanent under-secretary, although he did not believe that the rumours had any foundation, thought it best to pass the inquiry to the director of naval intelligence, Admiral L.A. Beaumont, for his opinion on the strategic aspects of the question. Beaumont replied:

> The anchorage off the town of Koweit is a good one and could well be made into a coaling station, but it is on the way to nowhere and I cannot conceive why the Russians should desire to have it! If, however, Russia ever descends through Persia to establish herself on the shores of the Gulf, Koweit would be the natural port for any ships she might get into the Gulf.[42]

Though Beaumont's reply largely confirmed Sanderson's scepticism about Russia's supposed interest in Kuwait ('I should have thought it myself an unlikely and inconvenient place for the Russians to choose', he told Lee Warner of the India office[43]), there was just a sufficient element of doubt in it to lead him to think that it might be prudent to allow Hamilton's inquiry to stand over for the time being. Consequently no official answer was returned to it, and the subject did not come up again for discussion until the closing months of 1898, when a complicated set of diplomatic circumstances invested it with an urgency which it had not before possessed.

The year 1898 was an unhappy one for Britain in foreign affairs. It opened with a crisis over China which had begun with the German seizure of Kiaochow in November 1897 and reached its climax in February 1898, when Russia occupied Talienwan and Port Arthur and refused to evacuate them. Not only was Britain powerless to prevent Russian expansion in the Far East but she was equally hard put to it to contain it in central Asia, and

---

40 Viceroy to secretary of state, 9 February 1898, Tel. [I.O] Political and Secret Letters from India, vol. 99.
41 Under-secretary, India office, to under-secretary, foreign office, 11 February 1898. F.O. 78/5113.
42 Beaumont to Sanderson, 18 February 1898, confidential, *ibid.*
43 Sanderson to Lee Warner, 7 February 1898, demi-official, *ibid.*

particularly in Persia. The misgovernment and incapacity of the new shah, Muzaffar ud-Din, had brought widespread unrest and near bankruptcy to his country, making it more vulnerable than ever to Russian penetration. In India, disaffection in the north-west frontier tribal districts had erupted into open revolt in 1897, and the uprising was proving all the more difficult to suppress because of the flow of arms which came to the insurgents through Bandar 'Abbas, in southern Persia, and through ports on the Makran Coast. The centre of the Gulf arms traffic was Muscat, and there British efforts to curb the traffic were frustrated both by the unhappy state of relations with the ruling sultan and by the intrigues of Russia's ally, France. The French had for some time been trying to exert a quasi-protectorate over eastern Oman, and at the height of the Fashoda crisis in October 1898 news was received from Muscat that the French consul there had induced the sultan to grant a site for a naval coaling station about five miles from Muscat. The grant was a direct violation of an undertaking which the sultan had given to the Government of India in March 1891 that he would never alienate any portion of his territory to any power other than Britain.

Nor were France and Russia the only powers whose expansionist activities in Asia seemed, in British eyes, to threaten the security of India. Germany was now assuming in the councils of the Ottoman Empire the place which Britain had once held and which Russia had long aspired to hold. The kaiser's visit to Constantinople in October 1898 and his subsequent exuberant portrayal of himself at Jerusalem as a champion of Islam were the outward signs of a more intimate German involvement in Turkish affairs than there had ever been before. One practical expression of this involvement was the effort being made by the Anatolian Railway Company during the closing months of 1898 to secure permission from the Porte to extend its existing railway system, which then ran from Haidar Pasha, near Scutari, to Ankara and Konia. The immediate aim of the company was to construct a line southwards from the Konia spur to Dinair, but it had also expressed, although guardedly, an ambition to build a line to Baghdad.[44]

Ostensibly, however, it was not the Anatolian Railway Company which was making the running in this direction in the latter months of 1898 but a syndicate nominally headed by Count Vladimir Ivanovitch Kapnist, who described himself as a nephew of the Russian ambassador at Vienna. In June 1898 Kapnist had submitted a petition to the Porte[45]

---

44 For reports of the various railway projects being mooted at Constantinople at this time, see F.O. 78/5102, *passim*.
45 It was dated 'Heidelberg, 9/21 June 1898'.

applying for the grant of a concession to build a railway to the head of the Persian Gulf. The proposed line was to run through Aleppo and Homs to Meyadin on the Euphrates, and thence to Najaf. From Najaf a branch line would run north to Karbala and Musaiyib, across the Euphrates to Baghdad, and on to Khanaqin, on the Persian frontier. The main line would continue south from Najaf to Basra and terminate at Kuwait. Preferential rights would be reserved for the construction of a line from Baghdad north to Mosul and on to Diyarbekir. Kapnist also asked in his petition for the right to construct ports at Tripoli, on the Syrian coast, and at Kuwait; for the right to drain and irrigate land in the neighbourhood of the Tigris, Euphrates and Shatt al-Arab; and for the right to make whatever improvements were necessary to these waterways and to navigate them freely.[46]

A copy of his petition was obtained by the British embassy in Constantinople and forwarded to the foreign office at the beginning of August 1898. At first it excited no comment, possibly because of the disorganized state of the foreign office during that month. Salisbury having fallen ill and gone off to the south of France to recuperate, leaving Arthur Balfour in charge. During August Balfour was deep in the negotiations with Germany over the future of the Portuguese colonies in Africa, and Curzon, who would certainly have taken more interest than most in Kapnist's project, was no longer parliamentary under-secretary of state. He had resigned his seat in the Commons on his appointment as viceroy and was taken up with preliminary arrangements for his departure. When at length, a few weeks later, he learned of Kapnist's application to the Porte he lost little time in warning Salisbury of the dangers he saw in it.

> My views on the E.V.R. [Euphrates Valley Railway] and other Trunk Railways in Asia Minor [he wrote], were stated at length in a chapter on Railways in my book on Persia. They remain substantially the same. I think that railway communication is certain someday to be established via Baghdad to the head of the Persian Gulf. If the proposed railway is to end at Koweit it may be remarked that Koweit is not in Turkish but in independent Arab possession; and that such a step could be guarded against by declaring a British Protectorate over Koweit.
>
> I do not myself believe that such a railway, if built, will be of advantage to British interests or that it will be greatly used

---

46 M. de Bunsen, *chargé d'affaires*, Constantinople, to Salisbury, 1 August 1898, no. 426 confidential, enclosing copy of petition, F.O. 78 5102.

in communication with India. On the contrary it would be likely to create other and rival interests in Mesopotamia. The construction therefore of such a line by German or Russian or indeed by any alien concessionaries is to be deprecated. But I see no early likelihood of this being done: nor if there were, does it follow that we should encourage the construction of the line ourselves.

British interests in that part of the world will be best protected by a firm policy on both shores of the Persian Gulf, by a proper police of its waters, and by allowing no other Power to obtain an outlet in that sea.[47]

Much the same view was taken by Sir Nicolas O'Conor, the new ambassador at Constantinople, when he returned to his post from leave in early October. If Kapnist's scheme became reality, O'Conor believed, it would seriously affect British influence and interests in the Asiatic provinces of Turkey, not only because it would hamper the growth of British trade in those regions but also because it would conflict with plans which had already been put forward for the construction of a railway from the Mediterranean to the Euphrates and the Gulf, plans, such as that to extend the Haifa railway to Damascus and across the Syrian desert to Baghdad and Basra, which were not only British-backed but were also better suited to British strategic needs. It was highly undesirable, to say the least, O'Conor argued, to leave the construction of a railway to the Gulf 'to be carried out by a Russian company which leans on its own Government, who would reap the political advantages, for support, but seeks the necessary capital in England.'[48] Kapnist was said to be hopeful of raising the majority of capital for his project from British financiers, but O'Conor could see little to attract them in it. He had been told that between £12 million and £20 million would be required to carry it out, and that the Porte was resolutely opposed to granting any further kilometric guarantees. For this reason, if for no other, he was inclined to suspect that those who were pushing the scheme might not be entirely serious about it but might have other objects in view. In short, 'its promoters would perhaps be satisfied if it attained the political result of keeping British companies out of the field.'[49]

---

47 Curzon to Salisbury, 5 October 1898.
48 O'Conor to Salisbury, 6 October 1898, *ibid*, no. 525, F.O. 78/4919.
49 *Ibid*.

But who were its promoters? The only persons apart from Kapnist whom O'Conor had been able to discover as being associated with the scheme were a firm of London stockbrokers, Williams, Meyer and Company. On the receipt of O'Conor's dispatch, in the last week of October, the senior partner in the firm, Gerald Walton Williams, was called to the foreign office and asked to explain his part in the project. Williams said that he had originally been put in touch with Kapnist by mutual friends, and that his partner, Augustus Meyer, had agreed to help raise the necessary capital for the scheme by floating a company for a capital of £5 million. Kapnist had stipulated that half the share capital was to be reserved for issue in Russia, and that half the directors should be Russian. He or his partner, Williams went on, would be leaving shortly for Constantinople to help the venture along. It was expected that an imperial *iradé* would be granted to Kapnist in the near future, although not before a sum of money had been lodged in trust for those Ottoman officials who had helped to secure the decree. Williams concluded by saying that he would let the foreign office have a copy of the original petition, and that he hoped the venture would not be opposed by the British government.[50]

William's explanation only made the whole affair more odd in Salisbury's eyes, so in the first week of November he asked Sir Charles Scott, the ambassador at St Petersburg, to find out what he could about it. Scott replied a fortnight later to say that Kapnist had been in St Petersburg some weeks earlier, trying to interest the Russian government in his scheme.

> I have subsequently learned [Scott wrote] that Count Kapnist, who has, I understand, been put forward as ostensible concessionaire on account of his nationality and name, is only very distantly connected with the Russian Ambassador at Vienna, that he has no private means of his own, or personal influence in this country, and that, although the Russian Foreign Office has made enquiries from the Russian Embassy at Constantinople respecting his concession, they have not evinced any disposition as yet to regard it as seriously meriting official support.[51]

Augustus Meyer had arrived in Constantinople in the first week of November and had called upon O'Conor to try to enlist his help in securing the desired concession from the Porte. He told the ambassador that

---

50 Williams, Meyer and Company to foreign office, 25 October 1898, re-capitulating details of interview and enclosing copy of petition, F.O. 78/5102.
51 Scott to Salisbury, 17 November 1898, no. 372 confidential, *ibid*.

Kapnist was 'a mere figurehead', that the capital for the proposed railway company would be provided by English financiers, and that Kapnist had undertaken, as soon as he had secured a concession to prospect and survey a route, to make it over to an Ottoman limited liability company, the shares of which would be held in London. Meyer laid particular emphasis upon this last point. While Russian capitalists, he said, would continue to be interested in the enterprise, and while it would receive the backing of the Russian minister of finance, Sergei Witte, the bulk of the capital would nevertheless be raised in England. O'Conor was not impressed by Meyer's arguments. 'His story was incoherent,' he reported to Salisbury, 'and I could not make out that any security really existed against Count Kapnist refusing to allow himself to be set aside after the issue of the Sultan's Irade.'[52] As for the scheme itself, O'Conor's dislike of it had in no way been altered by Meyer's advocacy. He saw it simply as a plan 'to engage British capital in an enterprise of very questionable financial profit while leaving to the Russians the possible political advantages to be derived from it.'[53]

By now Salisbury's interest in the Kapnist affair had been fully aroused, and in the last week of November he instructed Sanderson to send the papers concerning it to the director of military intelligence, Major-General Sir J. C. Ardagh, for his opinion. Ardagh was as unconvinced as O'Conor was of the financial soundness of the venture. He estimated that it would cost nearer to £30 million than £15 million to build the railway, which made it an unattractive investment for British capital. Ardagh was not certain, however, that the aim of the promoters was to secure predominantly British financial backing. 'From the analogy of the other instances of a like nature,' he told Sanderson, 'it may be inferred that Count Kapnist's reservation [of half the share capital for issue in Russia] was not intended to furnish a field for the surplus capital of private persons in Russia; but rather to create an opportunity for the State financiers of that country to acquire predominant influence in the basins of the Euphrates and Tigris, with a view to their eventual inheritance.'[54] Unless provision could be made that British directors would form a majority on the board of the company, the undertaking, Ardagh believed, would become 'essentially a Russian monopoly,' and as such inimical to British interests in Asia. Under Russian direction, the scheme, and especially that part of it which

---

52 O'Conor to Salisbury, 8 November 1898, no. 585, *ibid.*

53 *Ibid.*

54 Memo. By Ardagh, 28 November 1898, secret, enclosed in Ardagh to Sanderson, war office, 29 November 1898, F.O. 78/5102.

provided for drainage and irrigation rights in the basins of the Euphrates and Tigris, might well lead to 'so vast an accretion of territory to that Empire [Russia] as to disturb most materially the balance of power in Asia.'[55]

The same argument was put to Salisbury with even more force by Curzon in a lengthy memorandum which he gave to the prime minister in late November, on the eve of his departure for India. The first part of the memorandum dealt with Russia's influence in Persia, which Curzon saw as constantly on the increase, mainly because of Britain's failure to take any steps to counteract it. The second, and longer, portion of the memorandum was concerned with the British position in the Persian Gulf, and with the various schemes—Kapnist's in particular—which had been put forward to construct a railway to the Gulf from the Mediterranean. Curzon feared that Britain's paramountcy in the Gulf was threatened, not only by France's intrigues at Muscat but also by the commercial activities of other powers in the area.

> Commercial interests are the familiar precursor to political claims [he wrote]. Germany is the Power that is now pushing her way into the Gulf. In November 1897 she established a Consul at Bushire to safeguard the interests of six German subjects in the entire Gulf. She is making a determined bid to get hold of the Bussorah trade, and these considerations, coupled with the German Emperor's recent evidence of particular interest in the Asiatic dominions of the Sultan, point to the likelihood of increased German activity in the Gulf, and even to the possible appearance of German claims there in the future. Germany so far has the largest railway interest in Asia Minor; and there can be little doubt that one or other of those lines will ultimately be protracted to the Euphrates or Tigris, and will finally descend from Mesopotamia towards the Gulf.[56]

For the moment, however, it was Kapnist's scheme which most engaged Curzon's attention. Like Scott and O'Conor, he doubted whether the capital for it could be raised in Russia; consequently the only possible interest that the Russian government could have in it would be to use it as a means of blocking similar projects by others. Curzon found particularly

---

55 *Ibid.*
56 Memo. By Curzon, 19 November 1898, confidential, printed for the use of the foreign office, 26 November 1898, [I.O.] Political and Secret Home Correspondence, vol. 180.

Salisbury, Curzon and the Kuwait Agreement of 1899

disturbing the proposal that the projected line should terminate at Kuwait. 'The asking of a concession from Turkey for a railway with a terminus at Koweit, and, still more, the granting of it involve the assumption that Koweit is under Turkish sovereignty, which it certainly is not, or under Turkish control, which it equally cannot be said to be.'[57] To acknowledge Turkish jurisdiction over Kuwait, even tacitly, Curzon firmly believed, would be to jeopardize Britain's whole position in the Gulf.

> For even though Turkey did not assert her authority, she could (and is very likely even now negotiating to) part with her assumed rights to other parties or Powers; and the experience of Talienwan and Port Arthur is a recent reminder of the views that are apt to be taken by Foreign Powers of the way in which the maritime terminus of a great railway, though situated in the country of another Power, is capable of being treated. A Russian railway ending at Koweit would be in the highest degree injurious to British interests. A German railway to Koweit would be scarcely less so – even a Turkish railway to Koweit would be unwelcome. Any one of these would challenge our hitherto uncontested supremacy in the Gulf, and would turn those waters into a sort of mid-Asian Gulf of Pechili.[58]

There was only one sure way, in Curzon's view, of averting such a contingency and that was to declare a British protectorate over Kuwait.

> The responsibilities entailed would be these. We should not interfere with the internal politics of the place; but a gunboat would require occasionally to visit it. We should insist upon the suppression of piracy. We should prevent the raising of any other flag. And in the last resort, should the Turks march to attack it – which they are not at all likely to do – we should have to prevent them from taking it.

> The risks are almost infinitesimal, but the trouble they would be instrumental in avoiding might, in the future, be great.

---

57 *Ibid.* Curzon had reached this conclusion both from his own investigations and from a summary of the arguments for and against the fact of Turkish sovereignty over Kuwait which had been drawn up for him the previous June by Lee Warner of the India office. A copy of the summary is appended to his memorandum.
58 *Ibid.*

Above all it seems to me important that the Persian Gulf should not be allowed to become an arena of international rivalry. For though the actual advantages of interference to other Powers might for a time be small, until they had consolidated their land connections, yet the injury they could do us would be serious and lasting.[59]

Salisbury was not fully convinced of the dangers implicit in the Kapnist scheme, still less of the need to take prompt action to avert them. Events were forcing him, however, to take more notice of Curzon's arguments than he might otherwise have done. A few days before he received Curzon's memorandum news had arrived from the British consul-general at Baghdad that the *vali* of Basra, with the sanction of the Porte, had appointed a commission to investigate the various complaints which had been lodged against Shaikh Mubarak by his nephews and others over the preceding two years. The commission had already had a meeting with Mubarak at Fao, and it was due to have a further meeting with him shortly at Kuwait.[60] On learning this, the India office expressed the view to the prime minister that it was high time that he considered seriously whether or not to modify the policy of non-interference in the affairs of Kuwait which had been followed so far. In reply, on 5 December 1898, Salisbury gave cautious approval to the declaration of a protectorate over the sheikhdom.

How far he had been converted to Curzon's views in the time between receiving his memorandum and giving the India office its answer it is difficult to judge. Sanderson, who, unlike some of the senior officials at the India office, notably Lee Warner, was not persuaded of the desirability or necessity for a protectorate, told a member of the India Council a day or two after Salisbury had made his decision that the prime minister 'attached little or no importance to the Koweit project', while he himself believed that it would lead to trouble with the Turks.[61] Salisbury himself certainly qualified his approval in his letter of 5 December; for while, on the one hand, he strengthened the draft of the reply which Sanderson had drawn up, so as to make it quite clear that he accepted the conclusion that a pro-

---

59 *Ibid.*
60 Major P. J. Melvill to O'Conor, 6 October 1898, no. 491/73, passed to India office, 15 November 1898, [I.O.] Political and Secret Home Correspondence, vol. 180.
61 Sir A.C. Lyall to Godley, n.d. (6/7 December 1898), [I.O.] Political and Secret Home Correspondence, vol. 180. Lyall had at one time been foreign secretary of the government of India.

tectorate was virtually unavoidable, on the other hand he wrote:

> The question of establishing a protectorate over Koweit and the responsibilities such a protectorate would entail is a matter primarily for the consideration of the Government of India, as on that Government would fall the duty of undertaking the arrangements to be made for the assertion and maintenance of the Protectorate and the control of the Sheikh that would be entailed by it. If the Government of India is of the opinion that the Protectorate can be undertaken without difficulty or inconvenient extension of the duties of police already exercised in the Persian Gulf, Lord Salisbury would approve such a step and would be prepared to acquiesce in the establishment of such protectorate and to support it diplomatically in case the Porte should raise counter-claims. It does not appear that there is any foundation in fact for a Turkish claim of sovereignty or control over the district.[62]

O'Conor was notified of the proposed change of policy a week later and asked for his opinion on what the Porte's reaction to it was likely to be. He replied on 22 December, advising the government to handle the contemplated protectorate as quietly and cautiously as possible, and adding, 'any formal declaration to this effect at the present moment would be considered little short of a hostile act by Turkey, and in any case it would be sure to produce very serious diplomatic complications not only with this Government but probably also with Russia.'[63] On the same day he also wrote privately to Sanderson to say that rumour had it that Witte had withdrawn any support that he might have been prepared to give to Kapnist's scheme as a consequence of being informed that British capital was to be predominant in it. This made the scheme no less dangerous than it had been before, in O'Conor's eyes, for it had now to be viewed, he said, in conjunction with the determination recently expressed by the Porte to push the German Anatolian Railway through to Iraq.

> The German line is bound by its contract as soon as traffic receipts equal its guarantee to extend itself towards Diarbekir,

---

62 Under-secretary, foreign office, to under-secretary, India office, 5 December 1898, *ibid*.

63 O'Conor to Salisbury, 22 December 1898 (no. 667 secret), passed to India office, 30 December 1898, *ibid*.

and it is not likely that any other line will be allowed to compete. Thus it is probable that if the Kapnist Company commenced operations at the two extremities of the projected route it would not be allowed to complete the connection from sea to sea; with the result that far from creating a shorter route to India the Company would end by building a line from the Persian Gulf Northwards which Russia would utilize when the line through Western Persia is completed.[64]

Barely had O'Conor's warning been received than Williams, Meyer and Company informed the foreign office that an imperial *iradé* had been issued to Kapnist at Constantinople. The *iradé* was dated 24 December and it invited Kapnist to attend at the Ministry of Public Works to discuss the bases of the concession. O'Conor telegraphed on 30 December, confirming the news, and adding that, although he had not seen a copy of the *iradé*, he doubted whether it guaranteed controlling British participation in the concession.[65] 'I wish that we had secured Koweit a year ago,' Lee Warner commented ruefully when he heard the news.[66] What Salisbury now had to balance against each other were O'Conor's warning of what the Porte's reaction to the declaration of a protectorate was likely to be (with its attendant possibility that the Russians might exploit the Turks' resentment for their own purposes), and the ambassador's second warning that Kapnist's negotiations, if carried through to a successful conclusion in the shape of the granting of a railway concession, might well result in the advancement of a territorial claim to Kuwait by Russia at some future date. Faced by these alternatives, Salisbury decided that he, or rather Curzon, would have to settle for something less than a full protectorate, perhaps in the form of an undertaking from Shaikh Mubarak that he would not alienate any of his territory to a foreign power.[67]

The government of India had not been informed of Salisbury's earlier willingness to consider a protectorate over Kuwait until 24 December, when they had been asked to report both upon the existing situation in the sheikhdom and upon the measures they could take to make the protectorate, if actually assumed, effective. The telegram had been deliberately

---

64 O'Conor to Sanderson, 22 December 1898, private, F.O. 78/5102.
65 O'Conor to Salisbury, 30 December 1898, tel. no. 234, cypher, passed to India office, 31 December 1898, [I.O.] Political and Secret Home Correspondence, vol. 180.
66 Minute by Lee Warner, n.d. (6 January 1898?), *ibid*.
67 See under-secretary, foreign office, to under-secretary, India office, 4 January 1899, immediate and secret, [I.O] Political and Secret Home Correspondence, vol. 181.

held back until this time so as to prevent any action from being taken upon it in India until Curzon had arrived and assumed the viceroyalty.[68] Elgin, it was known, did not attach much significance to the Kuwait question, and would be reluctant to commit the government of India to any new responsibilities just as he was relinquishing office. Now, on 4 January 1899, Salisbury proposed to the India office that the idea of a protectorate should be dropped and 'that steps should be taken at once to obtain from the Sheikh of Koweit an engagement that he will not cede, lease, mortgage or otherwise alienate any portion of his territories to the Government or subjects of any other Power, without previously obtaining the consent of Her Majesty's Government.'[69] If the government of India had any doubts about their ability to secure the undertaking 'secretly and speedily' through the agency of the political resident in the Gulf and the naval force at his disposal, Salisbury was prepared to ask the admiralty to send a warship to the Gulf for the purpose. He was also prepared to pay Mubarak the sum of £4,000 or £5,000 as an inducement to subscribe to the engagement, the sum to be advanced from the Indian treasury pending a decision about its ultimate incidence.[70] 'Lord Salisbury is very emphatic on the necessity of secrecy and rapidity,' Sanderson wrote to Lee Warner the same day. 'The wording of the arrangement should be made as comprehensive as possible. Lord Salisbury adds that if it is necessary to give as high a price as £10,000 we will arrange to find one half of the amount.'[71]

The secretary of state, Hamilton, was away from the India office at the time, and the draft instructions to India had to be taken to him at Sheffield by special messenger. He telegraphed his approval on 5 January. Earlier that day the government of India had been informed by telegram of O'Conor's dual warning about the need to observe caution and secrecy in any dealings with Mubarak and about the Porte's probable reaction to the assertion of a protectorate. On 6 January Salisbury's instructions to secure the non-alienation bond were telegraphed to India. It was the day on which Curzon formally assumed the viceroyalty.

Curzon's view of what was both desirable and possible in the nature

---

68 See Godley to Curzon, 22 December 1898 [I.O] European MSS. F. 111/142 (Curzon Papers): 'On the 24th we are going to telegraph for an opinion about Koweit. We have kept the telegram back till then, in order that the subject may not be disposed of without being brought before you personally.'
69 Ibid.
70 Ibid.
71 Sanderson to Lee Warner, 4 January 1899, demi-official, secret, [I.O] Political and Secret Home Correspondence, vol. 181.

of a British connexion with Kuwait had differed from Salisbury's almost from the moment that the subject was first raised. The prime minister's view was summed up by Godley, the permanent under-secretary at the India office, in a private letter to Curzon at the time of sending him the instructions of 6 January. 'We don't want Koweit, but we don't want anyone else to have it. This sounds rather bad, when it is baldly stated: but it is the true explanation of a good deal of our diplomacy, and it is not really as bad as it sounds.'[72] It sounded bad enough to Curzon, though not in the sense that Godley had in mind, and he lost no time on receiving Salisbury's instructions in trying to get the prime minister to change his mind and revert to his earlier decision to declare a protectorate. On 9 January he telegraphed to say that he had asked the political resident in the Gulf to report on how he intended to carry out the negotiation, adding, 'Proposed negotiations, if successful, seemed to involve ultimate protectorate.'[73] A day later he telegraphed again, this time to forward a suggestion by the resident, Colonel Meade, that he should be given authority to promise Mubarak a yearly payment of £1,000 instead of a lump sum, and to assure him of the good offices of the British government as long as he adhered to the agreement. Meade also recommended that the agreement should be made binding upon Mubarak's successors.[74] While Curzon himself, as he informed the India office on 14 January, thought that an annual subsidy on this scale was excessive, he was not opposed on principle to the idea of a recurrent subsidy versus a single fixed payment. Furthermore, he thought that the engagement taken from the trucial shaikhs in 1892 might prove a better model for the proposed agreement than the Muscat non-alienation bond of 1891, which had been suggested by the India office.[75]

The exclusive agreements with the trucial shaikhs of March 1892 had gone much further to bind them to the British government than the proposed engagement with Shaikh Mubarak would have bound him. Those agreements, moreover, were a natural consequence of the intimate relationship which had grown up between the trucial shaikhs and the British government during the previous century, a relationship concretely expressed in the series of treaties which had been concluded with the shaikhs

---

72 Godley to Curzon, 6 January 1899, [I.O.] European MSS. F. 111/142.
73 Viceroy to secretary of state, 9 January 1899, tel., [I.O.] Political and Secret Letters from India, vol. III.
74 Viceroy to secretary of state, 10 January 1899, tel., passed to foreign office, 11 January 1899, F.O. 78/5113.
75 Viceroy to secretary of state, 14 January 1899, tel. P. For. Sec., no. 68 E.A., passed to foreign office same day, *ibid.*

concerning piracy, the slave trade, and maritime warfare. No similar agreements—in fact, no agreement of any kind—had been concluded with Kuwait up to this time. Curzon was now seeking to remedy this omission at one stroke, by bringing the sheikhdom, if not wholly into the trucial system, at least into a dependent relationship with the British government comparable to that which the exclusive agreements of 1892 had created for the trucial shaikhs. The agreements which they had signed had bound them, their heirs and their successors, to refrain from entering into any engagements, or even correspondence, with any government other than the British, to refuse to allow the agent of any other government to reside in their territories without British consent, and never to alienate any portion of their territories except to the British government.[76] Curzon believed that unless similar obligations could be imposed upon the sheikh of Kuwait there was every chance that the non-alienation bond could be rendered worthless, either by the murder or deposition of Mubarak and the refusal of his successor to adhere to the bond, or by the Porte's simply ignoring it (if it came to know of its existence) and ceding territory in the sheikhdom to another power. The viceroy confided his fears on this score to Hamilton in a private letter on 12 January.

> If we intend, as I think we ought to do, to prevent the Turks asserting their authority over Koweit in any form, we should have to resist any such step on their part [as a cession of territory] and should be compelled to translate the proposed agreement into a more formal protectorate. It is of course for the Foreign Office to say when the moment for any such step will arrive, but I do not think that we should expect the action at present proposed materially to relieve our anxieties about the matter.[77]

The secretary of state had anticipated his arguments, knowing full well what they would be as surely as he had known that Curzon would try to widen the scope of the proposed agreement with Mubarak. Two days after receiving the viceroy's telegram of 9 January, with its allusion to an 'ultimate protectorate,' he had gone to see Salisbury to ask for a final decision on the protectorate issue. Unlike Curzon, he himself, he told Salisbury, was against the assumption of a protectorate because it would

---

76 See C. U. Aitchison, *A collection of treaties, engagements and sanads relating to India and neighbouring countries*, 5th ed., 14 vols., vol. XI, pp. 256-57.
77 Curzon to Hamilton, 12 January 1899, [I.O] European MSS. D. 510/1 (Hamilton Papers).

involve the government of India in responsibility for the defence of Kuwait, as Salisbury himself had made clear in his letter of 5 December 1898. At that time, however, Hamilton went on, the alternative of a non-alienation bond had not been considered. What he wished to know now was whether the Indian authorities were still free to make up their own minds on the protectorate question, as Salisbury had stated on 5 December that they were, or were they simply expected to acquiesce in the assumption of a protectorate should the foreign office decide at the last moment that a non-alienation bond would not suffice for the object in mind. In the latter case, Hamilton told the prime minister, he would have to point out that whilst the government of India would be willing to act as his agents in concluding the agreement with Mubarak, they could not undertake to send troops to defend Kuwait in an emergency.[78]

Salisbury replied by assuring Hamilton that the decision to secure the non-alienation bond from Mubarak in no way implied the assumption of a protectorate over Kuwait. The two questions were entirely separate. The arrangement which he contemplated did not constitute, nor was it intended to constitute, a protectorate. The power to decide upon a protectorate still lay with the India office and the government of India, having regard to their ability to defend and maintain the protectorate afterwards. All that he had intended in asking for their assistance was to use their officers, who were on the spot, to effect the arrangement which he desired. The affording of such assistance did not pledge the government of India, 'in the slightest degree.... To take any action, or to accept any liability, under any circumstances that might arise in the future.'[79]

So far as Hamilton was concerned this meant that the protectorate issue was not dead, whatever Curzon might say, and he turned to deal with the other points which the viceroy had raised. Opinion at both the India office and the foreign office was that the trucial shaikhs' agreements of 1892 went beyond what was required in the case of Kuwait, and that the Muscat non-alienation bond of 1891 should remain the model. It was similarly agreed that the proposed agreement should be made binding upon Mubarak's successors, and it was thought surprising that Curzon should not have taken this for granted. Meade's suggestion that he be given discretion to promise Mubarak an annual subsidy instead of a lump sum in payment was less easily dealt with. Lee Warner was in favour of a subsidy

---

78 Hamilton to Curzon, 24 January 1899, [I.O.] European MSS. C. 126/1 (Hamilton Papers).
79 Under-secretary, foreign office, to under-secretary, India office, 18 January 1899, F.O. 78/5113. See also, Hamilton to Curzon, 24 January 1899, above.

(though not on the scale that Meade had proposed), not only because it was more in line with traditional practice in the East and provided a regular reminder of the obligations incurred by the recipients, but also because it was economical: 'If we are disappointed in the fulfilment of the treaty we stop our subsidy.'[80] Salisbury, in contrast, thought a lump sum both a more practical method of payment and more advantageous diplomatically: 'There seems to me a great objection to making the payment for Koweit annual. It makes the transaction less permanent. Instead of buying the neutrality of the Sheikh we are only hiring it.'[81] He was prepared, however, to concede that the matter should be left to Curzon's discretion, although he stipulated that, if a subsidy were decided upon, it should not exceed £200 *per annum*.[82]

The telegram embodying these decisions was sent to Curzon on 17 January, and in a private telegram on the same day Hamilton informed the viceroy of the understanding he had reached with Salisbury on the protectorate question.[83] Curzon telegraphed his orders to Meade on the 18th. The only precaution which he urged upon him was that he should make sure that Mubarak was in a stable position, and that he was not in imminent danger of attack by his nephews or the Turks before taking the engagement from him.[84] Meade had let it be known at Bushire, after receiving the first intimation of the contemplated agreement, that he intended visiting Kuwait shortly to discuss the arms traffic with Mubarak. He had also arranged to go shooting on the island of Kharaq, off Bushire, before he left, so as to be able to slip away quietly at night in the residency steamer when he wished. On the night of 20-21 January he sailed from Kharaq in the *Lawrence* and he raised Kuwait before noon on the 21st. A

---

80 Minute by Lee Warner, 16 January 1899, [I.O] Political and Secret Letters from India, vol. III.

81 Minute by Salisbury, n.d., quoted in Sanderson to Lee Warner, 16 January 1899, confidential, *ibid.*

82 Note by Salisbury on draft telegram of 14 January 1899, *ibid.* Cf. Sanderson to Lee Warner, above, quoting Salisbury: 'Meade should be told to do it as cheap as he can, a sum down is better for our purposes than a stipend.'

83 See secretary of state to viceroy, 17 January 1899, tel, For Sec. passed to foreign office, 18 January 1899, F.O. 78 5113; and secretary of state to viceroy, 17 January 1899, tel, priv., [I.O.] European MSS.D. 508 (Hamilton Papers). On Lee Warner's covering letter of 18 January Sanderson noted: 'These telegrams had better not be printed in any series.' They were printed for the use of the cabinet but they are not to be found in the relevant confidential print (F.O. 406, Eastern Affairs, or F.O. 424, Turkey).

84 Foreign secretary, Calcutta, to political resident, Persian Gulf, 18 January 1899, (Tel. P. no. 85 E.A.), enclosed in viceroy to secretary of state, same date (Tel., foreign secret, cypher), [I.O.] Political and Secret Letters from India, vol. III.

Turkish corvette was in the harbour but she sailed on the afternoon of the 22nd. Meade's assistant, Gaskin, went ashore soon afterwards, and found Mubarak pleased with the resident's visit but unwilling to go on board the *Lawrence* to see him lest news of it should reach the Turks. Instead, he deputed his brother Hamad, to convey his greetings to the resident and to hear what he had to say.

Meade began his conversation with Hamad ibn Sabah by saying that his brother's request to be brought within the sphere of the British influence had been considered by the British government, and that they were prepared to reach a secret understanding with him. The resident then explained the provisions of the proposed arrangement. Shaikh Hamad, in reply, said that he was sure that his brother would accept the arrangement, although if he offended the Turks he might find that his family's estates in Turkish Iraq would be endangered. Would the British government be prepared, Hamad asked, to help protect these estates as a condition of Mubarak's signing the agreement? Meade said that he could give no guarantee on this head until he had referred the question to India. The interview ended with Hamad promising to convey the resident's proposals to his brother.[85]

Gaskin had meanwhile ascertained that Mubarak's position seemed to be quite secure and that there was little likelihood of his being attacked by the Turks or his nephews in the near future. He had also learned that Mubarak's price for consenting to the non-alienation bond would probably be Rs 15,000 (about £1,000) and a written assurance of support in the future. On 23 January Meade went ashore, taking with him a draft agreement which he had drawn up on the basis of his instructions. Mubarak, when he read it, raised no objections to its terms, but he expressed the same anxiety as his brother had done about the possible threat to his estates at Fao if he signed the agreement, and he also pressed Meade for a written guarantee that the British government would protect them. Although Meade could give him no more definite assurance on this score than he had given his brother, he pointed out that the general promise of good offices which he was empowered to give would probably cover the contingency which Mubarak feared. At this Mubarak declared himself satisfied and proceeded to sign the agreement.[86]

Although Meade had been instructed to use the Muscat non-alienation bond of 1891 as his model, the agreement which he presented to

---

85 Meade to foreign secretary, government of India, 30 January 1899, no. 10 confidential, enclosed in foreign secret letter 35, external of 23 February 1899, *ibid*.
86 *Ibid*.

Mubarak began by requiring the sheikh, his heirs and successors, 'not to receive the Agent or Representative of any Power or Government at Koweit, or at any other place within the limits of his territory, without the previous sanction of the British Government'. Meade's reason for departing from his instructions, as he afterwards explained, was that Gaskin had been told by Mubarak that he had recently received overtures from the French government, which he did not welcome because he did not want foreign agents residing at Kuwait. The same concern to close any loopholes through which other European powers might penetrate Kuwait led Meade to make a further departure from his instructions. After requiring Mubarak to pledge himself, his heirs and successors, 'not to cede, sell, lease, mortgage, or give for occupation or for any other purpose any portion of his territory to the Government or subjects of any other Power without the previous consent of Her Majesty's Government for these purposes', Meade also stipulated that the undertaking should extend to 'any portion of the territory of the said Sheikh Mubarak, which may now be in the possession of the subjects of any other Government.' Meade pointed out later that this condition was designed to prevent the transfer of houses at Kuwait, belonging to Turkish subjects, to Russians or other foreigners.[87]

The assurance of the good offices of the British government was incorporated in a letter from Meade to Mubarak which accompanied the agreement. It stated that these good offices would be furnished only on condition that the agreement was scrupulously and faithfully observed. The letter also promised that when the agreement had been ratified by the governor-general in council, and ratifications had been exchanged, Mubarak would receive the sum of Rs 15,000. He was warned that an essential condition of the agreement was that its existence should be kept secret and was not to be divulged without the previous consent of the British government.[88]

The principal risk of disclosure, Meade thought, lay in the discontent which Mubarak's two brothers had expressed with the agreement because

---

87 *Ibid.*, enclosing text of agreement, dated 10 Ramadan 1316/23 January 1899. See also Meade to foreign secretary, government of India, 19 February 1899 (Tel., confidential), [I.O.] Political and Secret Home Correspondence, vol. 182, and Meade to foreign secretary, government of India, 21 May 1899 (no. 70, confidential), enclosed in foreign secret letter 109, external of 8 June 1899, Political and Secret Letters from India, vol. 114. The agreement is printed in Aitchison, Treaties, vol. XI, p. 262, and in Cmnd 1409 (Kuwait no. 1), London, 1961.

88 Meade to Mubarak, 23 January 1899, secret, enclosed in Meade to foreign secretary, government of India, 30 January 1899, no. 10 confidential, above. See also, Aitchison, *loc. cit.*

it failed to give a specific guarantee of protection to the family estates at Fao. They had signified their disapproval by refusing to sign the agreement, and although Mubarak had assured Meade that their signatures were not necessary to make the agreement valid and binding on his successors, the resident felt that the brothers' resentment might lead them to reveal the agreement's existence to the Turks. Their chief fear was that, in the event of the agreement's being transformed later into a treaty of protection, the Porte might retaliate by enforcing the law which prohibited aliens from possessing landed property in the Ottoman Empire, and confiscate the estates, which were the Al Sabah's principal source of revenue. Meade tried to convince the brothers that the estates would come under the general protection of the promise of good offices, but they were not persuaded. In his report, therefore, Meade emphasized the need for some kind of reassurance to be given the Al Sabah shaikhs, and suggested that it should take the form of the specific undertaking which Mubarak's brothers wanted. There was little doubt in Meade's mind that the Turks' suspicions would be aroused by his visit to Kuwait: if they suspected that he had reached any kind of understanding with Mubarak they might react in the way that the shaikh's brothers feared. They would be less likely, Meade thought, to try conclusions with Mubarak direct: he was too well entrenched at Kuwait and he had, besides, formed alliances with several of the Bedouin tribes in the interior.[89]

Meade sailed from Kuwait to Fao to engage in a few days' shooting in the hope of disarming any suspicions the Turks might have about the reason for his visit to the head of the Gulf. He returned to Bushire on 28 January and telegraphed the news of the conclusion of the agreement to Calcutta. Shortly afterwards he sailed for Muscat to deal with the crisis which had arisen with the sultan over his grant of a coaling station to the French in defiance of his non-alienation bond of 1891. Meade's impetuous and often ill-considered actions at Muscat in the next two weeks led to a clamorous exchange of telegrams between Calcutta and London, in the midst of which the Kuwait agreement was virtually lost to sight. It was not until the India office telegraphed on 10 February, asking to be informed of its terms, that Curzon thought fit to send a summary of Meade's report to London. The viceroy himself was quite pleased with the agreement. '[It] carries us quite as far as I gather Lord Salisbury wished to go,' he wrote to Hamilton, 'although not so far as, in my opinion, we may require to

---

89 Meade to foreign secretary, government of India, 30 January 1899, no. 10 confidential, above.

go before long ... Meade has, I think, done his work pretty well.'⁹⁰ This was hardly the reaction in London. Lee Warner, when he read the viceroy's summary, exclaimed, 'Altogether the engagement is not what we authorized or asked for, and it is lucky that we telegraphed for it before it was ratified!'⁹¹ Salisbury was equally displeased. 'He is a good deal annoyed,' Hamilton wrote to Curzon, 'and I think justly, with the manner in which Meade has on two separate occasions [at Kuwait and Muscat] outrun his instructions.'⁹²

Salisbury's displeasure was mainly provoked by the clause in the agreement forbidding Mubarak to correspond with, or to receive the representatives of, other governments. As Lee Warner put it:

> The 'no-correspondence' clause made the Trucial Chiefs' agreement practically a protectorate agreement which we did not want. Now this Koweit agreement binds the Chief not to receive a Foreign Representative, and we had no authority to introduce that clause .... Its introduction seems to me to run the risk of shutting us out of the benefits of Lord Salisbury's promise .... that no liability would attach to India for a non-alienation treaty.⁹³

The second provision inserted by Meade, that the engagement should also extend to any Kuwait territory in the possession of subjects of foreign governments, was even less to Lee Warner's liking. 'We care for the seaport of Koweit, not for territories held by subjects of foreign powers.'⁹⁴ There was, of course, a reason for Meade's insertion of this clause, but it was set out in his full report of his proceedings which had not yet reached London. Even if it had it is doubtful whether it would have altered the generally unfavourable verdict which was passed upon his handling of the negotiation, nor would it have softened the strictures which Salisbury passed upon his conduct at both Kuwait and Muscat. 'His disposition', Hamilton wrote ruefully to Curzon of the prime minister, 'has always been to attri-

---

90 Curzon to Hamilton, 16 February 1899, private, [I.O.] European MSS. D. 510/1.
91 Minute by Lee Warner on viceroy's telegram of 12 February 1899, [I.O.] Political and Secret Letters from India, vol. III.
92 Hamilton to Curzon, 16 February 1899, private, [I.O] European MSS. F. 111/142 (Curzon Papers).
93 Minute by Lee Warner on viceroy's telegram of 12 February 1899, [I.O.] Political and Secret Letters from India, vol. 111.
94 Ibid.

bute high-handedness and harshness to Indian Politicals in their dealings with Native Princes, and what has recently passed will I fear confirm him in that view.'[95]

For all this, however, Salisbury was not prepared to disown the agreement or to insist upon its amendment before ratification. Moreover, he was even willing to approve Meade's suggestion that a hope should be held out to Mubarak and the British government would do what they could to protect his family estates at Fao.[96] The Prime Minister's approval was telegraphed to India on 14 February, and the agreement was ratified by the governor-general in council on the 16th. Half the cost of the Rs 15,000 later paid to Mubarak was borne by the imperial treasury, and the balance was charged to Indian revenues.

Some reaction by the Turks to Meade's visit to Kuwait was only to be expected, and so it came as no surprise when the consul at Basra, A. C. Wratislaw, reported early in February that the *vali* there had questioned him closely about the reason for the visit. What was a little more disturbing was a further report from Wratislaw that two Russians had arrived at Basra from Baghdad at the beginning of the month with letters of introduction from the *vali* of Baghdad. They had gone on to Kuwait after being given a letter of recommendation to Shaikh Mubarak by the *vali* of Basra. Although as far as Wratislaw could discover, the Russians—who were also, as was found later, Muslims—were interested only in trade, O'Conor at Constantinople leapt to the conclusion that they were visiting Kuwait in connexion with Kapnsist's railway scheme, and he informed the foreign office to this effect in the third week of February.[97] There was a spate of rumours concerning the activities of foreign powers in and around Kuwait in the second half of February and the early part of March. A German warship was said to be expected shortly in the Gulf, a French agent was reported to be on his way to Kuwait, the Porte was reputedly thinking of stationing a high official permanently in the sheikhdom, significant military preparations were under way at Basra, one of the Russians visiting Kuwait had gone on to Qatar, presumably for some sinister purpose, and a third Russian, of Armenian extraction, had passed through Basra from

---

95 Hamilton to Curzon, 10 March 1899, private, [I.O.] European MSS.F. 111/142.
96 Under-secretary, foreign office, to under-secretary, India office, 14 February 1899, immediate and secret, F.O. 78/5113.
97 O'Conor to Salisbury, 17 February 1899, tel., no. 8, cypher, passed to India office same day, [I.O.] Political and Secret Home Correspondence, vol. 181. For Wratislaw's reports, see same series, vol. 182.

Baghdad on his way to Kuwait, ostensibly to buy lambskins.[98]

Many of these rumours were accepted by Curzon at face value, and he several times pressed Salisbury to ask the admiralty to strengthen the naval force in the Gulf and to order the commander-in-chief, East Indies, to keep a ship constantly on station off the bar of the Shatt al-Arab to prevent the movement of troop transports from the river to Kuwait. Salisbury refused to be stampeded into giving such orders: he could discern no positive threat to Kuwait's security in anything that had occurred so far, and if any hostile move were to be made against the sheikhdom by the Turks, he preferred to trust to diplomatic protest at Constantinople to halt it rather than to hasty and ill-considered naval action.[99] Annoyed that the prime minister did not view the situation in the Gulf in the same light as he did, Curzon wrote to him in mid-March:

> I doubt if I have sufficiently represented to you my belief that France's action in the Persian Gulf – at Muscat, Koweit, and elsewhere – is taken in deliberate conjunction with Russia, and is subsidiary not so much to French as to Russian ends. We have just heard that the French Consul is about to be appointed to represent Russia (who has not a subject or a ship in the Gulf) at Bushire. Other plots will presently unroll: and I doubt not that we are in [the] presence of a systematic attempt to contest our position in the Persian Gulf.[100]

Salisbury still refused to be swayed from his preference for diplomatic over naval action, even when Curzon warned him that Kuwait could be overrun by the Turks before news of it reached India.[101] The best policy

---

98 For these various rumours, see [I.O.] Political and Secret Home Correspondence, vols. 181 and 182, *passim*.
99 For the correspondence concerned, see [I.O.] Political and Secret Letters from India, vol. 111, especially secretary of state to viceroy, 15 February 1899 (Tel., foreign secret), viceroy to secretary of state, 3 February and 2 March 1899 (Tels., foreign secret); viceroy to secretary of state, 16 March 1899 (Tel., foreign secret), ibid., vol. 112; under-secretary, foreign office, to under-secretary, India office, 16 February and 6 March 1899 (immediate and secret), Political and Secret Home Correspondence, vol. 181; and under-secretary, foreign office, to under-secretary, India office, 11 March 1899 (immediate and secret), *ibid.*, vol. 182.
100 Curzon to Salisbury, 16 March 1899 (copy), [I.O.] European MSS. D. 510/1 (Hamilton Papers).
101 Viceroy to secretary of state, 16 March 1899, tel., foreign secret, [I.O.] Political and Secret Letters from India, vol. 112.

now, in Salisbury's opinion, was to let the whole question of Kuwait slip quietly from view. With this in mind he took no notice officially of a half-hearted protest made by the Porte to the British member of the Constantinople board of health that Meade and his part, on their visit to Kuwait, had contravened Turkish quarantine regulations by going ashore despite the objections of the quarantine official there to their landing.[102] The Turks did not carry the protest any further, and Curzon was undoubtedly right when he characterized the objections of the quarantine official, who was not a Turk but a local Arab, as 'illegal and frivolous.'[103]

Of much more moment than the rumours current in the Gulf about Russians and Frenchmen bent on mysterious errands was what was happening at Constantinople over railway concessions, and over the Kapnist project, in particular. In the third week of April Ernest Weakley, the commercial attaché at the British embassy, learned that Kapnist had been induced to give up his part in the project, and that his place had been taken by an Austrian named Rechnitzer. Furthermore, Augustus Meyer had retired from the firm of Williams, Meyer and Company, which had been reconstituted as Williams, de Broe and Company and was engaged in setting up a syndicate for the promotion of the Kapnist scheme. A number of London merchant houses were participating in the syndicate and financial support was said to have said to have been enlisted from a number of European banking houses.[104] It seems fairly likely that Kapnist's retirement from the project was foreordained. At least, this is the impression which emerges from the account of the project's origins which Rechnitzer gave to Weakley later in April. He told him:

> The scheme was first brought forward under Count Kapnist's name, with a view to prevent Russian opposition, and with the idea of obtaining powerful influence, both in St Petersburg and in Constantinople, for the furtherance of the project. With this end in view, Count Kapnist had been successful in obtaining the support of Count Mouraview and M. de Witte on the con-

---

102 See O'Conor to Salisbury, 15 and 16 February 1899, nos. 52 and 59 secret, passed to India office 25 February 1899, [I.O.] Political and Secret Home Correspondence, vol. 181.

103 Governor-general in council to secretary of state, 1 June 1899, no. 102 external, secret, [I.O.] Political and Secret Letters from India, vol. 114.

104 Memo. By Weakley, 18 April 1899, enclosed in O'Conor to Salisbury, 20 April 1899, no. 194 confidential, F.O. 78/5102.

Salisbury, Curzon and the Kuwait Agreement of 1899

dition that a portion of the capital necessary for the construction of the line was to be raised on the Russian market. The scheme was however from the outset very strongly opposed by Prince Oukhtomsky, and M. Tatischeff, Financial adviser to the Russian Embassy in London, considered that Russian support should only be given to Count Kapnist in the event of the project he was interested in being entirely placed under Russian control. M. Tatischeff was even of the opinion that under such circumstances the Russian Government scheme of extending the Central Asia railway into Afghanistan might be abandoned. In the course of subsequent negotiations Messrs. De Witte and Romanoff stipulated that a small Share capital of 10,000,000 Francs should be raised, of which 6,000,000 Francs was to be held in Russia, and that a Debenture capital of 250,000,000 Francs should be obtained in England. These conditions could not be accepted by the London syndicate, as they would place the line entirely under Russian control, and further negotiations being impossible, it was considered undesirable that Count Kapnist should, under the circumstances, continue to take an active part in the matter.[105]

Seeing that Salisbury had known since late November 1898, when Scott had reported the fact from St Petersburg, that the Russian government were not backing Kapnist's scheme, and since he also shared Curzon's view that if the Russians ever tried to push a railway through to the head of the Gulf they would build it through Persia, it may be asked why he troubled to take the non-alienation bond from Shaikh Mubarak in January 1899. One possible answer is that he was simply being pushed by Curzon to conclude some kind of agreement with Kuwait, preferably, from the viceroy's point of view, a treaty of protection, and that, having no decided opinion of his own on the question, he allowed himself to be persuaded by Curzon's arguments, even though he suspected that there was no real cause to fear anything from the Russians. But this explanation runs counter to Salisbury's well-known caution in foreign affairs, and his reluctance to enter into engagements, or to assume responsibilities, which were not strictly necessary. He must have felt the Kuwait agreement to be unavoidable to have sanctioned it; and if his suspicions of Russian intentions were not sufficiently strong to convince him of the need for the agreement, some other

---

105 Memo. By Weakley, 21 April 1899, enclosed in O'Conor to Salisbury, 27 April 1899, no. 207 confidential, *ibid*.

consideration must have tipped the scales in his mind. That other consideration was probably German activities at Constantinople in the closing months of 1898. It was they, and not the Russians, who were the principal railway concession-hunters at this time, and it was their efforts which were eventually rewarded when the Porte confirmed the grant of preferential rights previously awarded to the Anatolian Railway Company to extend its system to the Gulf. It was they, in short, as much as the Russians, whom Salisbury sought to check at Kuwait with the agreement with Mubarak.

How early the German concessionaires had settled upon Kuwait as a logical terminus for their railway cannot be determined with any certainty, but it is significant that they lost little time after the confirmation of their preferential rights in exploring its possibilities for this purpose. Late in 1899 a German technical commission, led by the German consul-general at Constantinople, travelled the proposed alignment of the railway to Kuwait, and on arrival there in January 1900 its members tried to persuade Mubarak to sell or cede land for a terminus. It is a far from remote possibility that the whole Kapnist project was nothing more than an elaborate stalking-horse to divert both British and Russian attention from the negotiations which were quietly proceeding between the Anatolian Railway Company and the Porte in the latter half of 1898. Evidence to support this supposition can be found in O'Conor's remark in October 1898 that 'its promoters would perhaps be satisfied if it attained the political result of keeping British Companies out of the field,'[106] a result which could hardly have been looked for if the promoters had been serious in their efforts to secure a majority of British capital for the venture; and they would have had to secure a majority of British or other capital because the necessary amount, or even half of it, could not have been raised in Russia. There is also Scott's report that Kapnist had been put forward as the ostensible concessionaire 'on account of his nationality and name,'[107] which points less to a desire on the part of the promoters to attract Russian financial support, since little was available, than to an attempt to lull any suspicions which the Russian government might have had about the scheme and its backers – or the activities it was designed to cloak.

Kapnist's scheme disappeared from sight once it had served its purpose. The Kuwait agreement remained, and its usefulness was demonstrated again and again in the years that followed. Despite Salisbury's initial

---

106 See above, page 257, paragraph beginning, "Much the same view was taken by Sir Nicolas O'Conor..." (footnote 48).

107 See above, page 258, paragraph beginning, "But who were its promoters?..." (footnote 50).

misgivings about the clause inserted by Meade, forbidding the reception of foreign agents and correspondence with foreign governments, it proved to be one of the most valuable features of the agreement. Salisbury had all along been opposed to entering into a protectorate relationship with Kuwait because of the difficulties it would produce with the Turks and possibly the Russians. He was also opposed on principle to the extension of Britain's responsibilities in the Gulf. Yet he could not ignore the case for some kind of agreement with Kuwait which would prevent other powers, either alone or as a consequence of the assertion of Turkish authority over the sheikhdom, from effecting a lodgement there. He had in the end to concede the necessity for an agreement, but even then he tried to evade the consequences of it by thrusting the responsibility for declaring and maintaining a protectorate on to the government of India, and he grasped eagerly at O'Conor's warning about the Porte's probable reaction as an excuse to retreat from the protectorate to a non-alienation bond, which was as much as he had wanted from the start. Even a non-alienation bond, however, carried with it implicit responsibilities for Kuwait's well-being, as Hamilton had pointed out to him in their interview of 11 January 1899, when he asked whether an ultimate protectorate was envisaged. Reluctant though he was to commit himself finally, Salisbury could prevaricate no longer: he wanted the non-alienation bond, there would be no protectorate, and the government of India were relieved of responsibility on this head. Curzon, in contrast, knew what he wanted all along, *viz.*, the extension of Britain's maritime protectorate in the Gulf to its natural limits in the northern shore, a move which, he was convinced, should not be delayed any longer. His judgement, on this occasion, was sounder than Salisbury's. If the Kuwait agreement had not been concluded when it was, it might have been impossible a year later.

21
Saudi Arabia and Islam[1]

Le Royaume d'Arabie Saoudite face a l'Islam Revolutionnaire, 1953-1964, by G. Jean-Louis Soulie and Lucien Champenois. Paris: Armand Colin. 1966. 135 pp. Bibliog. (Cahiers de la Fondation Nationale des Sciences Politiques, 145.)

Faisal: King of Saudi Arabia, by Gerald de Gaury. London: Arthur Barker. 1966. 191 pp. Bibliog. Index.

Cairo and Riyadh are today the two extreme poles of revolutionary Islam and traditionalist Islam,' write Messrs. Soulie and Champenois (p. 10). 'But the differences which separate them are not merely of a doctrinal order. They are part also of a secular antagonism between what it is convenient to call the sedentary and the nomadic, the civilization of the city and the civilization of the desert.' Just how deep this antagonism goes today is brought out fully by these two authors in their admirable survey of Saudi Arabia since the death of Ibn Saud. The gulf between King Faisal and President Nasser, they say, is fundamental and unbridgeable: while the one takes his stand upon the inseparability of Islam and the state ('our constitution is the Koran'), the other has dispensed with the religious sanction for government and draws for his inspiration and sustenance upon a creed alien to the Islamic world—revolutionary Marxism. Faisal flung down the gauntlet to Nasser shortly after he had assumed power from his ailing brother, Saud, in the wake of the crisis which followed the Egyptian

---

[1] *International Affairs* (Royal Institute of International Affairs 1944-), Vol. 43, No. 3 (July, 1967), pp. 591-592.

invasion of the Yemen in September 1962. With revolutionary socialism militarily established in the Arabian peninsula it was no time, Faisal decided, for quibbling or dissembling, if the kingdom of his fathers was to be saved and the faith of his people preserved. Declaring that the Arab people were being led astray by propaganda, slogans and the ambitions of self-appointed rulers, he publicly reaffirmed that the only true unity was the unity of Islam, and that the only true basis of Arab nationalism lay not in theories or doctrines but in race, blood, language and birth. Not content merely to deny thus Nasser's claim to leadership of the Arab world—and even his right to call himself an Arab—Faisal has set out in the intervening years to prove that a state based upon the prescriptions of Islam is better attuned to the needs of the Arab people, especially those of the Arabian peninsula, than the Pharaonic dictatorship which holds sway in the delta of the Nile. The task which confronts him is lucidly and intelligently presented by Messrs. Soulie and Champenois in their survey of the social, political and economic structure of the Saudi kingdom. They have packed a great deal of valuable information into a small compass, and their account of the strengths and weaknesses of the country is the most thoughtful and dispassionate which has appeared to date. On balance, they believe that Faisal has a good chance of succeeding with his reforms, always provided that he is allowed time in which to implement them. Whether he will be must depend largely upon whether his enemies in the Arab world, who are 'greedy to build their own future upon the ruins of traditionalist Islam' (p. 27), are kept at bay by his friends in the Muslim world and the West. After the cool and reflective approach of Messrs. Soulie and Champenois to Faisal and his problems, Colonel de Gaury's brief biography seems rather superficial, having been put together, it would appear, from press clippings and a few well-known books on Arabia and the Al Saud. But it contains a few interesting anecdotes, and it also prints extracts from some of Faisal's speeches as an appendix. For the rest, however, it simply traverses well-worn ground in an unremarkable manner.

22
T.E. Lawrence and His Friends[1]

In a volume of reminiscences published last year (*Acquaintances*,1967) Arnold Toynbee devotes a chapter to recollections of his acquaintanceship with Colonel T.E. Lawrence, at the close of which he states his conviction that the reason why Lawrence turned his back on public life and fame and entered the R.A.F. under an assumed name was that he was tormented by feelings of disgust and guilt at the British Government's betrayal of the Arabs and of the revolt which he had raised and led during the First World War. 'I fancy that Lawrence's conscience reproached him,' Toynbee writes, 'for having promised to the Arabs, in the United Kingdom Government's name, an independence that, in the event, had been withheld from them; and, if this charge had been addressed, not to Lawrence himself, but to his principals, there would have been some substance in it . . . The British undertaking to King Husayn [Toynbee goes on] to recognise and uphold the independence of the Arabs within certain territorial limits . . . had been unconditional. The British authorities had not told King Husayn—and, without being told, he could not have guessed—that, in a subsequent agreement with France, they were going to interpret 'independence' for the Arabs to mean a substitution of British and French for Turkish political control over them . . . . I believe [Toynbee concludes] that Lawrence could not bear to profit personally from a wartime career of his which had ended with the betrayal of his Arab comrades in the field in which he had achieved his fame. This will have

---

1 This essay is from an unpublished draft manuscript. It is possible that it served as JBK's inaugural lecture in 1968 after becoming Professor of British Imperial History at the University of Wisconsin-Madison. The draft was without footnotes. I have managed to find most of the sources but a few have eluded me. SBK.

282

been unbearable to him if he believed that he himself had been an instrument, even unknowingly, in the perpetration of the Anglo-French fraud at the Arabs' expense.'²

At another place in the same chapter Toynbee speaks of the 'strain of impishness' in Lawrence's make-up, which he then proceeds to illustrate by describing an incident which occurred when he and Lawrence were on their way to a meeting at the Treasury in London after the end of the war. '. . . . We were walking along a corridor,' Toynbee relates,

> when we passed the door of a Treasury official's office. The door was open, and the official was visible, busy writing at his desk. Lawrence walked into the room, whipped out a dagger from under his robes, and held up the handle under the Treasury man's face as the harassed man looked up from his work. "Guess what this is," Lawrence said. "I have no idea," said the Treasury man. He looked uneasy. When one was under attack from Lawrence, one never knew what was coming next. Lawrence gave the Treasury man the answer to his riddle: "A hundred and fifty of your sovereigns." To see that Treasury man wince, you might have thought that, instead of just dangling the handle of the gold dagger in front of his nose, Lawrence had thrust the steel blade between the poor fellow's ribs.³

The two passages may be seen as exhibiting two characteristic attitudes or attributes of the Arabophile school in British political and intellectual circles: one, the steadfast adherence, as though to a sublime revelation of divine truth, to the doctrine of the great betrayal of the Arab cause by the British Government; the other, the ungenerosity towards their own country and countrymen, and for the sacrifices which they made in blood and treasure to defeat the Turkish Empire between 1914 and 1918. 'Betrayal' is a word accorded more than its mere alphabetical precedence in their lexicon: it is the ark and the covenant of their faith, and it is freely employed against all who do not subscribe to its narrow tenets. Nowhere in the passage quoted about Lawrence's burden of guilt for Britain's betrayal of his Arab comrades in the field does Toynbee make the slightest allusion to the possibility that Lawrence may have been guilty of betraying the trust placed in him and of treating his British comrades with contu-

---

2 Arnold J. Toynbee, *Acquaintances* (London, OUP, 1967) pp. 196-7.
3 *Ibid.* p. 189.

mely. Still less, in the midst of all his disingenuous flim-flam about the 'Anglo-French fraud and deception' does Toynbee allow any hint to drop of the frauds and deceptions practised by Lawrence in *Seven Pillars of Wisdom*. Along with other guardians who tend the sacred flame of Lawrence's reputation Toynbee is roused to indignation only by doubts cast upon its brilliance. He and they are strangely blind to the slurs and calumnies cast by their paladin upon other and worthier men. 'Betrayal' is a word which the British Arabophiles would be well advised to use sparingly, especially in the light of what has passed in recent years and of what is now known to have passed fifty years ago.

As we have seen, Toynbee places the blame for the past betrayal of the Arabs upon Lawrence's superiors, and not upon the man, or men, on the spot. The villains of his drama are Lloyd George's coalition Cabinet, the French, the India Office, and, to only slightly lesser extent, the Foreign Office—all, of course, in Zionist pay, and all conspiring to renege on their promises to the Arabs and to cheat them of their rightful heritage. It is more than merely odd that a man who spent the war years as a temporary official in the Eastern Department of the Foreign Office, who worked in the British Secretariat at the Peace Conference, and who, as Director of Research at Chatham House in the years to come, was to know scores of politicians and officials and to have almost limitless access to information on foreign affairs, should not have known the nature of the British commitments and reservations made to Sharif Husain by Sir Henry MacMahon in 1915 and 1916, whether or not the Sharif had been informed of the nature of the Sykes-Picot agreement [he had been, by Sykes and Picot themselves on a visit to Jeddah in May 1917, and he had raised no objection to it], and whether or not the terms of that agreement were incompatible with the commitments to Sharif Husain [they were not: we have this on the authority of D.G. Hogarth the head of the Arab Bureau in Cairo, who wrote ten years after the event: 'Neither to him nor to any other Arab did we ever explicitly guarantee or even promise anything beyond liberation from the Turk. We are guiltless, therefore, of any betrayal of King Husain. The sole condition of his action—that he be freed from his Ottoman overlords and recognised as an independent sovereign—has been fulfilled.' Toynbee, it might be added, worked with Hogarth at the Peace Conference on the Arab question, and Hogarth's remarks just quoted were published in 1925 in the *Journal* of Chatham House. Finally, to believe that a man in Toynbee's position would be ignorant (and remain ignorant to this day) of the fact that many of the hopes and promises held out to the Arabs, and whose sad fate he now tenderly laments, were largely the creation of the men on the spot, the projection of *their* dreams and delusions, and not of the as-a-rule cool and sceptical minds of the permanent officials of the India Office and Foreign Office. All that the India Office, in particular, was guilty of was an attempt to introduce a sense of reality into the *Arabian Nights* fantasy played out between 1915 and 1918 in the Hijaz and Syria, a fantasy which still warms the hearts of the British Arabophiles as they sat amid the detritus of withered hopes, faded dreams, and stale passions, which, together with an almost insupportable sense of bewilderment, constitute Britain's legacy from the Middle East.

Throughout the war with Turkey the India Office and the Government of India were greatly concerned with Muslim sentiment, both within and beyond the Indian Empire. They were inclined, therefore, to look with some scepticism and a measure of apprehension upon the negotiations which went on with Sharif Husain and the comings and goings between Cairo and Jeddah. The flutterings which these exchanges aroused in Arab and British breasts awakened no echoes in Delhi. Lord Curzon, the former Viceroy and a member of Asquith's Cabinet in 1915, observed in April of that year that it was too early in the war to begin talking about independent Arab states after it, and that it would be foolish for Britain to promise Basra and Baghdad 'to a people who are at this moment fighting against us as hard as they can and known to be in the pay of the Germans'. He thought it even more foolish to hold out to Sharif Husain the prospect of the revival of an Arabian Caliphate in his person. In fact, from the point of view of the India Office and the Government of India there was nothing objectionable in principle to the idea of the Arab provinces of the Ottoman Empire remaining under Turkish rule after the war. In a memorandum submitted to the Foreign Office in June 1916, a week after the Arab revolt had broken out and a month after the Sykes-Picot agreement had been signed, the permanent under-secretary at the India Office, Sir Thomas Holderness, wrote:

> It might be better for the world at large that the Turkish Empire should perish root and branch and its territories distributed among the Allies under conditions that would give indigenous peoples a chance of a more prosperous existence. But if this is not attainable, or is thought to be attended with more than counter-balancing dangers and disadvantages, a less radical adjustment of the map of the Near East need not necessarily be a standing menace to the Indian Empire and Christian Powers that have to deal with large masses of Muhammadan subjects.

Later in the memorandum he made the point again:

> The expulsion of the Turks from Europe, and the transfer of Constantinople and the Straits to strong hands which may be relied on to keep this territory out of the reach of the Central Powers, is essential. That, and a satisfactory settlement of the conflicting ambitions of the Balkan States are the primary requisites of peace, so far as the Indian interests are concerned. The disposal of the territories of the Turk in Asia is, compared with those essentials, a matter of more or less expediency.[4]

But the India Office—or even the Foreign Office, for that matter—wielded less influence in the making of the vital decisions of 1916-1918 regarding the Middle East than did individuals like Mark Sykes and the members of the Cairo school, the men on the spot in the Arab Bureau set up in 1916 as the political arm of the Egyptian Expeditionary force—men like Gilbert Clayton, Kinahan Cornwallis, Philip Graves, D.G. Hogarth, and of course, Lawrence. They were busily engaged by the latter half of 1916 in erecting what had been conceived of as a diversionary movement against the Turkish forces in the Hijaz into a full-scale Arab revolution having as its goal the establishment of a unified Arab kingdom stretching from the borders of the Yemen to the Taurus Mountains. In short, they were absorbed in a plan of their own for the political settlement of the Middle East after the war which differed considerably from that envisaged by their own government in its engagements with France and its other allies. Ronald Storrs, the Oriental secretary of the Residency in Cairo, who to some extent shared their ideas, was less doctrinaire than they were over the prospects for Arab unity and a Sharifian kingdom under Husain, who, as Storrs put it, had pretensions to 'a general mandate as King of the Arabs

> for a spiritual Pan-Araby, to which he knew better than we that he could lay no kind of genuine claim. Of the great Arab peoples of North Africa some must repudiate his Sunni claims to the Caliphate: others, like Egypt and the Sudan, vastly prefer their own superior civilization. The Christians of the Lebanon could never acknowledge him, Mesopotamia was mainly Shia, regarding his Islam about as benevolently as Alva did the Protestantism of the Low Countries; to the south the Imam Yahya

---

4 The National Archives (TNA), Kew, London, FO 371/2778, 'The War with Turkey.' Note by the Under Secretary, India Office, 13 June 1916.

(of the Yemen) recognized him as nothing at all, whilst with Ibn Saud on his immediate east he had long been on the terms which were to lead to his final ruin and exile.[5]

It is to be regretted that the Indian Government was not represented more strongly in the councils of Cairo at this time, for the great virtue of the Indian viewpoint on Arab affairs was its hard-headedness and realism. Perhaps it was because it had had much greater and longer experience of the Arabs than officials from other British services, like the Foreign Office, whose experience was largely confined to Turkey and the Levant, to the peculiar and singular world of the cities of Asia Minor, Syria and Egypt, a world which was hardly that of the Hijaz, Yemen, Najd, Hasa, Oman, the Tigris-Euphrates basin, or the Syrian steppe. The outstanding feature of the war-time Cairo school was its sentimental attachment to the idea of the noble Bedouin and sturdy cultivator of these desert, mountain, and riverain areas, a conceit which was shared by the political amateur and ci-Levant archaeologist, the experienced official of upper and lower Egypt, and the professional diplomatist alike. Nor was this the limit of their romanticizing, for deep within their hearts and minds dwelt a more intoxicating conceit, a resplendent vision of the resurrection of the glories of the Umayyad and Abbasid Caliphates embodied in a far-reaching union of the Arab peoples. It was a conceit, as Christopher Sykes has remarked, 'of the kind only open to learned men, and in this dangerous pass in human affairs, at this Asiatic crossroads where history really was at least half bunk, the more learned the man, the more heinous sometimes his errors'.[6]

Where did it originate, this fancy, and, more important how did it come to dominate official British thinking about the Arab world from 1916 onwards, thus influencing decisively the settlement that followed the First World War, a settlement whose mournful echoes still reverberate in our day?

The romantic notions of English travellers and scholars in the Middle East, from Lady Hester Stanhope onwards, are too well known to require reiteration here. Of themselves they were harmless, especially when exhibited by perennial adolescents like Lawrence, and even absurd when indulged in by middle-aged officials and scholars. But they became something less than harmless in the fevered atmosphere of war, when in a welter of disillusion, weariness, and propaganda about a new world a-coming they were taken up by a literary-political clique that expounded them at

---

5 Ronald Storrs, *Orientations* (Ivor Nicolson & Watson, 1937), p. 178.
6 Christopher Sykes, *Cross Roads to Israel* (Collins, London, 1965), p. 31.

the dinner tables of politicians if not in the corridors of Whitehall. (That was to come later, with increasingly disastrous results.) Even more important, however, in the formulation of policy in the Middle East after 1916 were the measured opinions (or what were taken to be the measured opinions) of the 'experts', the down-to-earth and practical-minded men of the political service in Egypt and the Sudan. It was they who were listened to and it was their estimates, judgements, and recommendations which bulked large in the political decisions taken, judgements to which the amateurs and romantics in Cairo and England readily adjusted themselves, since beneath the veneer of practicality in the political officers' make-up there was a wide streak of sentimentality which matched their own.

In the case of officers of the Sudan Civil Service much of this sentimentality arose from the nature of the service itself, its physical isolation from the currents which flowed through the Levant states before 1914, from the tumults and passions of Levantine politics and European political rivalries, an isolation which was matched in another sense by the Sudan's separation from the colonial service and from the Empire at large, its administrative control being vested in the F.O. [Foreign Office], not the C.O. [Colonial Office]. In the laboratory of the Sudan—for it was a laboratory in which a select group of keen young officers could evolve new methods of administration, adapt old ways to new purposes, and generally vindicate the theories of trusteeship in the government of subject peoples which were then the vogue in enlightened circles—in the Sudan, which was not a Crown colony or a protectorate but a condominium (with Egypt), it was considered more important than ever that indigenous religious and social institutions should not be tampered with but should be preserved in full working order under a political directorate imbued with high moral standards and staffed by well-chosen officials. The study of Islamic institutions, of the Arabic language, and of Muslim customs and traditions was not only an essential part of the training and working life of the Sudan Civil Service but with many of its members it became a passion. The memory of the Mahdist movement was too recent for the power and influence of Islam to be discounted, and such a view was in itself a perfectly sensible and sober one to take. What was more difficult to justify was the exaggerated and undiscriminating respect which this attitude engendered among many officials for Muslim institutions as a whole, a respect which led them to accept unquestioningly their relevance to contemporary conditions. A case in point was the Caliphate, which Sir Reginald Wingate, the Governor-General of the Sudan, himself believed to be not only an institution of far greater consequence in the Muslim world in the first and second decades of this century than it actually was, but also one which should rightly be embodied in the person of an Arab ruler and not in that of the Ottoman Sultan. Writing to Lord Hardinge, the Viceroy of India, in August 1915, Wingate declared that pan-Arabism would be an effective check to the pan-Islamism of the Ottoman Empire. He admitted that there would be difficulties in bringing such a union to pass, but, he told Hardinge, 'I conceive it to be not impossible that in the dim future a federation of semi-independent Arab states might exist under European guidance and supervision, linked together by racial and linguistic bonds, owing spiritual allegiance to a single Arab Primate, and looking to Great Britain as its patron and protector'.[7]

This reverence for Muslim institutions went hand in hand, among British Middle Eastern officials of the sentimental school, with a pronounced preference for Arabs over Turks. When Turkey entered the war on the side of the Central powers, Wingate recalled later, 'I joined more vehemently perhaps than others in the hue and cry against them. I had to govern a country in which the very name of "Turk" stinks in the nostrils of the people. They have been ground under the heel of the Turk and Egyptian (to them the names are synonymous) and were in close proximity to the Arabs of Arabia, who entertain very similar feelings to their own in regard to their Turkish masters. For these reasons, I—who so warmly supported the Turk on utilitarian grounds—now espoused the Arab cause with still greater warmth and with more real sympathy.'[8]

Ideas such as these were taken to Cairo by Wingate at the end of 1916, when he succeeded MacMahon as British High Commissioner in Egypt. But they had already been circulating there, in Residency and other official circles, since before the war, when Gilbert Clayton, the Sudan Government's agent in Cairo, made them fashionable. They were, as I have already indicated, particularly to the taste of the amateurs recruited into the war-time Arab Bureau, men who had already succumbed to the spell woven by the magisterial and semi-mystical pages of Doughty. Among them was Lawrence, a temporary subaltern, unknown and undistinguished, but harbouring large ambitions in a small frame, a yearning, as he himself put it in the *Seven Pillars*, 'to do a thing of himself, . . . a thing so clean as to be his own'. Lawrence found his 'thing' in the Arab revolt, and from the moment that he was fortuitously dispatched to the Hijaz on a minor errand

---

7 TNA, FO 371/2486/121174, Wingate to Grey, 14 August 1915.
8 Quoted in Elie Kedourie, *The Chatham House Version and other Middle Eastern Studies* (Weidenfeld & Nicolson,1970), p.15. This is from an article 'Cairo and Khartoum on the Arab Question' which had first appeared in a journal in the early 1960s.

he bent the whole of his energies and all of his peculiar talents towards making the revolt his own. Since he could not make it that—there were too many other, and weightier figures involved—he used his genius for self-advertisement to make it *seem* his own, being reckless of, and even taking a perverted satisfaction in, the injustice he was doing other British and Arab officers who fought with the Sharifian forces. And while Lawrence postured and intrigued on his Arabian stage, flattered and indulged by his masters and mentors in Cairo, Clayton was assiduously pursuing the more serious goal of converting Allenby, to whom he had been appointed chief political officer in 1917, to the cause of the great Arab kingdom.

To turn now to the figure of Lawrence himself, to the Lawrence legend, and to the guardians of the legend, who stand sentinel over the shrine to deter the approach of the impious. The lengths to which the Cairo school were prepared to go to gain their way, to impose their views on what future British policy in the Arab provinces of the Ottoman Empire should be, are well illustrated both by the propagation of the legend and the strenuous efforts that followed to keep its lustre undimmed. Take, for instance the capture of Damascus on 1 October 1918, the climax of the Palestine campaign and indeed of the war against Turkey. To Clayton, Wingate and the Arab Bureau the capture of the city by the Sharifian forces under Faisal and Lawrence was, from every point of view, desirable, even vital, for the attainment of their dream of an Arab kingdom encompassing Syria and western Arabia. The symbolic value of such a stroke was obvious but the practical benefit was just as great, for it would render virtually impossible the execution of that part of the Sykes-Picot agreement which allotted Syria west of the line Damascus-Homs-Hama-Aleppo to France and gave her a veiled protectorate over the land to the east. Lawrence coyly recalls in *Seven Pillars of Wisdom* that in September 1918 he made a 'saucy threat' to Allenby that he would take Damascus without waiting for permission to do so. The only drawback to what Lawrence considered of as an engaging piece of impudence was that the Sharifian forces were incapable of taking Damascus. The Turkish army stood in the way and the road to Damascus was not opened until Allenby defeated the Turks at Megiddo on 18 September. Even then General Barrow's Indian division still had to roll up the remnants of the fourth army east of the Jordan. At this juncture Allenby was persuaded to delay the entry of his troops into Damascus so that the distinction of taking the city could be claimed by the Sharifian forces. But the exigencies of war disrupted the smooth working of the plan: the third Australian Light Horse Brigade, assigned to cut off the Turkish retreat to Homs, found that it could not reach the Homs road without passing through Damascus. So early on the morning of 1 October they galloped through the city, pausing only long enough in the main square for their commander to receive its surrender from the group of Arab notables who had taken over the administration when the Turks left. Later that day the Sharifian forces entered in triumphant procession, Lawrence has left a lyrical description in *Seven Pillars*.

Now the process of the suppression of the truth began, and worse. Not content with blurring and misshaping the story in *Seven Pillars*, Lawrence proceeded to calumniate the Australians, saying that he had begged Sir Harry Chauvel, the commander of the mounted division, to keep his men outside the city that night, 'because tonight would see such carnival as the town had not held for six hundred years, and its hospitality might pervert their discipline'.[9] He then displayed his pique that Chauvel would not salute the Sharifian flag, now flying over the town hall ('I wanted to make faces at his folly'), and at Chauvel's proclaimed intention to 'march through' and not 'enter' the city. 'It meant', Lawrence writes, in a tone which he thinks of as schoolboy merriment but which emerges as mere petulance, 'that instead of going in the middle he would go at the head, or instead of the head, the middle. I forgot, or did not well hear, which: for I should not have cared if he had crawled under or flown over his troops, or split himself to march both sides.'[10] In the next few pages Lawrence casts reflection upon the Australians' conduct, discipline, and humanity, dwells upon his own tireless efforts to restore the amenities of Damascus, enlarges upon the tenderness with which he ministered to the wounded Turkish prisoners, and casually, mentions, *en passant*, that a little fighting broke out. With a scornful rebuke for the press correspondents for sending alarming reports of the disorder to Allenby, he laughingly tells how he accepted—not that they were needed—an offer of troops from Chauvel. How the truth of all this is very different. The Sharifian forces had been fighting with the adherents of Faisal's rivals among the Syrian politicians, Turkish prisoners were being butchered, the Bedouin were looting, and Lawrence, for all his claimed spiritual affinity with them, for all his prowess and courage of which they were said to stand in awe, could exert no control over them. It is doubtful if he even tried to do so: Sir Alec Kirkbride, who is now the sole survivor of the band of officers who fought with the Sharifian army, has recounted how Lawrence seemed to have gone into a trance, incapable of word or deed, while Kirkbride himself stalked the

---

9 T.E. Lawrence, *Seven Pillars of Wisdom: a Triumph* (Jonathan Cape, London, 1940 edition) p. 668.
10 *Ibid*. pg. 669.

streets of Damascus with the Australians, revolver in hand, shooting looters. Sir Hubert Young who was also there, has told much the same story.

It is the measure of the influence of Lawrence's friends that his version of the capture of Damascus gained immediate circulation, not merely after the *Seven Pillars* was made public in 1935 but almost immediately after the event. It could not have gone on unchallenged as long as it did— for forty years—had not the creation of the myth served the purposes of others. (One must recall the period when Lawrenciana was at its height: the late thirties Palestine). It is equally the measure of their determination and unscrupulousness that the perpetuators of the myth, public and private, were quite prepared that this offensive and perverted version should continue to circulate as long as it did—offensive because it besmirched the character of the Australians, perverted because it subordinated the honour of the many to the cheap glorification of the few.

As an example of the ruthlessness with which the protectors of Lawrence are prepared to deal with anyone bold enough to question his character and achievement, one may cite the case of the writer, Somerset de Chair, who in 1943 published a book entitled *The Golden Carpet*, which described the adventures of Paiforce, the British column sent eastwards from Palestine in the spring of 1941 to put down the Rashid Ali revolt in Iraq. At Baghdad the column linked up with an Indian brigade, sent up from Basra, and though it was successful in suppressing the revolt it failed to save the Jewish population of Baghdad from pillage and massacre at the hands of Rashid Ali's irregular supporters. One of the senior officers with the Indian brigade, Colonel W.G. Elphinston, commented to de Chair that the tragedy underlined the importance of properly policing a newly captured Arab city until its normal administration could be restored, and he went on to describe what he had witnessed in Damascus twenty-three years earlier, when, as a young subaltern in command of a squadron of Indian cavalry, he had ridden through the city on the day after it was taken. Passing the Turkish hospital, he saw 'a considerable number of naked corpses piled in the courtyard in heaps, five or six feet high, apparently – from their condition – comparatively recently dead and thrown from the windows of the upper storey.'[11]

Somerset de Chair related the tale in the preface to *The Golden Carpet* in the form: 'Lawrence had begged Allenby's permission for the Beduin to occupy Damascus, but they massacred the occupants of the Turkish hospital and hurled the bodies through the windows. Allenby arrived, saw the

---

11 *Royal Central Asian Society Journal*, Vol. XXXL, 1944, pp. 107-8.

sickening pile of corpses, said "Enough," and Lawrence was given a single ticket home.'[12] The publication of this impiety—nay, this blasphemy—brought a majestic howl from the Lawrence establishment, who turned upon this irreverent wretch and rent him limb from limb, in the pages of the Royal Central Asian Society's *Journal*. A shaken de Chair was forced to make a public recantation of his heresy and to promise abjectly that he would expunge the offensive passage from his book. Colonel Elphinston was also called upon publicly to deny that he knew for a fact what transpired between Allenby and Lawrence as a consequence of the butchery at the Turkish hospital, and he did so in a letter to the *R.C.A.S. Journal*. But he refused to retract the story of the massacre itself, and he repeated that Allenby was exceedingly angry about it and that several people at the time drew a connexion between Allenby's disgust and Lawrence's abrupt departure from Damascus for England.

Lawrence himself, as with so many of the incidents in which he was involved, is the worst of witnesses, as a consequence of his habit of blurring the sharp and uncomfortable outlines of reality with swirling gusts of flaccid prose. The account of his meeting with Allenby in Damascus comes on the penultimate page of the *Seven Pillars*: 'Mistily I realized that the harsh days of my solitary battling had passed. The lone hand had won against the world's odds, and I might let my limbs relax in this dreamlike confidence and decision and kindness which were Allenby.'[13]

There follows a cursory description of Allenby's meeting with Faisal and then suddenly, as sudden as Lawrence's departure from Damascus, we are at the end of the book. 'When Faisal had gone, I made to Allenby the last (and also I think the first) request I ever made him for myself—leave to go away. For a while he would not have it; but I reasoned, reminding him of his year-old promise, and pointing out how much easier the New Law would be if my spur were absent from the people. In the end he agreed; and then at once I knew how much I was sorry.'[14] There is no question here of the warrior-scholar flinging aside his pen, wearied to the point of collapse by the effort of recounting so much of that which tormented his mind and his spirit in the immediate past, of recoiling from the horror of war and things best forgotten. The book had too many literary godfathers for that; too many hands, Bernard Shaw's, Robert Graves's, David Garnett's, and others', helped shape the mannered gaucherie of its style. If the book ends abruptly it is not merely to put a merciful end to this dreary

---

12 Somerset de Chair, *The Golden Carpet* (limited edition,1943), pp. 8-9.
13 Lawrence, *op.cit.*, p. 682.
14 *Ibid.*, p. 683.

flow of disguised rodomontade. After all, its editors considered it a masterpiece, and took a justified pride in their handiwork. As Bernard Shaw said in reviewing it in *The Spectator* (and who better to say it?): 'There is a magical brilliance about it, . . . a Miltonic gloom and grandeur . . . . It is one of the great histories of the world . . . by an author who has reached the human limit of literary genius and who has packed into the forepart of his life an adventure of epic bulk and intensity.' No, if the literary editors and executors of Lawrence, men who have expended millions of windy words in praise and explanation and extenuation of him, have not seen fit to say more about the manner in which Lawrence left Damascus and Allenby, it cannot be out of a decent reticence. There are things that have to be left unsaid if the mystery is to retain its power.

To present the capture of Damascus to the rest of the world as a triumph for the Sharifian forces led by Lawrence and Faisal was crucial to the Arab Bureau's plan in 1918 to frustrate the fulfilment to France of the pledge of Syria made to her in the Sykes-Picot agreement. A secondary object was to defuse the Balfour declaration of 2 November 1917 so as to prevent it from serving any purpose in the future in British Imperial strategy. The reason for both objects was that which has been mentioned more than once already, *viz.*, to clear the way for the establishment of the Arab kingdom which was now for the Arab Bureau their Holy Grail. Even the British negotiator of the agreement with France himself, Mark Sykes, had come to regret the undertaking, and he worked himself (as it was to prove) to death to persuade Lloyd George to 'dish' the French in Syria. Who ordered Allenby to hold his troops before Damascus is still a mystery: did the order come from London or was Allenby worked upon by Clayton? Whatever the answer, the myth of the Arab capture of Damascus was established and it persists in some quarters at the present day. Thus Arnold Toynbee:

> . . . Within the few hours' interval that had elapsed between the defeated Turkish army's evacuation of Northern Palestine, the Lebanon, and Syria, and occupation of these evacuated territories by Allenby's victorious troops, the Arab flag had been hoisted everywhere to proclaim the Arabs' political aspirations while they were free to declare them.

This gives a most peculiar picture of the circumstances prevailing in northern Palestine and southern Syria during September and October 1918. It would lead one to believe that, in one marvellously co-ordinated and swift movement, the Turkish forces in these provinces whisked themselves away to Turkey, and after allowing a decent interval of a few hours Allenby's troops had marched in. Most odd.

The political manoeuvres carried out by the British against the French in Syria in 1918 make depressing reading from this distance. What makes the affair even more dismal is to see the British repeating their tactics a little more than twenty years later, when they overcame the Vichy French in Syria. The delusions fostered by the Arab Bureau died hard, and their effect in 1941 was to confirm General de Gaulle in his suspicions of *perfide Albion*. Still, as a man with a sense of history, he must have derived a wry satisfaction from the events of July 1941 before Damascus, when the British, and Australians, having fought and defeated the Vichy French, were instructed by their own government not to enter the city so that the Free French might be the ones to claim the honour of its capture.

Clayton, Lawrence and others worked equally hard against an outright British annexation of Palestine, which would have been a more intelligent revision of the Sykes-Picot agreement than trying to deprive the French of Syria. (Under Sykes-Picot Palestine was to be internationalized, Britain having direct sovereignty only over an enclave around Haifa.) Ironically enough, annexation might have served their protégées, the Arabs, better, for it might well have prevented, or at least greatly diminished, the Jewish immigration of the thirties and the greatly increased inflow of the forties—as well as all the troubles which have flowed from it. But annexation would have blocked the eventual attainment of an Arab state in Palestine, whereas internationalization would, they hoped, forward it. They were greatly helped in their aim by the confused thinking that characterized much of the peace settlement, and especially by the promulgation of the doctrine of self-determination. The achievement of their aim found concrete expression in the mandate, and in the clarifying statement issued by Churchill on 1 July 1922 that Palestine should not be a Jewish National State but, as the original declaration had said, the site of a Jewish national home. The declaration had been defused and its rational justification from a British point of view had been defeated. From now onwards it became an article of faith for those who shared the late Arab Bureau's vision to work for an independent Arab Palestine.

One such disciple was Hugh Foot, now Lord Caradon, whose autobiography, *A Start in Freedom*, is a portrait of the intellectual and emotional development of a British colonial servant in the years between the wars. Foot's first post when he joined the Colonial Service in 1929 was that of a junior assistant secretary in Palestine, and he remained there until 1938. He discovered early on, according to his own testimony, that

'Arabs are children of the desert', 'that the purest Arab characteristics are the result of the influences of the remotest deserts', but that these qualities 'have been blurred and half-forgotten in the towns', while 'the springs of Islam remain pure in the desert'.[15] These are thoughts that might have been taken whole from the pages of Renan, and might be dismissed as the romantic musings of a young man were it not for the fact that they have been recalled by a man in middle life and at the height of his career with evident approval. But Foot discovered even more about the Arabs in his early days in Palestine: he discovered that he was inferior to them. 'I have never ceased to rejoice [he declares] that I had the privilege of spending my early years in overseas service with the Arabs. I was never in any doubt that, however politely they received me and whatever trouble they took to put me at my ease, they regarded me as an inferior, an infidel.'[16] He recalls his shame, his embarrassment, his disgust, at the superior airs his British colleagues gave themselves and the condescension with which they treated their subject peoples, whether in Asia or Africa. The passage in which he describes these feelings is curiously reminiscent of one in the *Seven Pillars*, where Lawrence recalls *his* shame and embarrassment at the way British officers treated their Indian troops. 'My mind felt in the Indian rank and file something puny and confined; an air of thinking themselves mean; almost a careful, esteemed subservience, unlike the abrupt wholesomeness of Bedouin. The manner of the British officers toward their men struck horror into my Arab bodyguard, who had never seen personal inequality before.'[17] (One wonders at this last statement.)

From the feelings which he experienced among the Arabs it was but a short step for Foot to conclude that the whole Palestine problem was rooted in the Balfour Declaration and in the iniquities of British policy. 'The main responsibility,' he says, 'was ours'; the British have been guilty of 'prevarication', 'procrastination', 'fundamental dishonesty' and 'double-dealing'. It was this immorality which 'made disaster certain'.[18] It would seem that in the narrow enclaves of his mind Foot cannot conceive that evil consequences can flow from anything but evil causes, that it is perfectly possible, and has indeed occurred again and again in history, that honesty, straightforwardness, and the best of intentions can also lead to disaster and tragedy. No such doubts appear to have troubled him, and, secure in the belief of his inferiority to the people over whom he ruled,

---

15 Sir Hugh Foot, *A Start in Freedom* (Hodder & Stoughton, London, 1964), p. 86.
16 *Ibid.*, p. 87.
17 Lawrence, *op.cit*, p. 659.
18 Foot, *op.cit.*, p. 36.

he went on to serve in various posts in Cyrenaica, Nigeria, Jamaica and Cyprus. In the last he crowns his career, as he tells us, with 'a year of sheer happiness' (1959), when he negotiated the British withdrawal and the creation of the Cypriot republic. 'It was the year of agreement,' he exults, 'of reconciliation,' and in his joy he quotes Burke: 'From that moment, as by a charm, the tumults subsided, obedience was restored, peace, order and civilization followed in the train of liberty.'[19] (We who have seen what has happened since are not so sure.) All that was now required was for Foot to dispatch a telegram to Dag Hammarskjold, the Secretary-General, offering his services to the U.N. 'Have just finished my assignment as Governor of Cyprus having completed thirty years' work in Middle East Africa and West Indies Stop All the countries in which I have worked are now self-governing or about to be Stop.'[20] (One, too, is tempted to cry 'Stop'.)

Such then was the tradition that grew up among too many British officials whose careers were to be largely spent in the Arab lands of the Middle East, a tradition that they were there to serve and not to rule, a tradition of humility in the face of the Bedouin, secure in the elemental fastnesses of the desert and the pristine simplicity of his faith, or of the patient cultivator tilling the soil, sustained by the fatalistic unities of Islam. It was a most peculiar attitude to adopt towards a people long accustomed to venerate a ruler and to render passive obedience to him, and to whom it would not have occurred to regard the representative of an imperial power as an inferior—unless he happened to tell them he was. *A Start in Freedom* may not aspire to the literary pretensions of a *Seven Pillars of Wisdom*, but it is, nonetheless, its author's sincere, and personal affirmation that he, too, underwent a sublime experience on the road to Damascus.

There is a brief epilogue to the *Seven Pillars*, evidently intended as a coda to the mighty and sonorous movements which precede it, the closing lines of which run:

> There remained historical ambition, insubstantial as a motive by itself. I had dreamed, at the City School in Oxford, of hustling into form, while lived, the new Asia which time was inexorably bringing upon us. Mecca was to lead us to Damascus; Damascus to Anatolia, and afterwards to Baghdad; and then there was Yemen. Fantasies these will seem, to such as are able to call my beginning an ordinary effort.[21]

---

19 *Ibid.*, p. 181.
20 *Ibid.*, p. 188.
21 Lawrence, *op.cit.*, p. 684.

Fantasies they are no longer: the disciples of Lawrence have seen to that. The story of British relations with the Arab world in the last 20 or 25 years has been a melancholy one. Much of it, admittedly, was inevitable, the consequence of the decline of Britain's economic strength, the loss of empire, and her fallen position among the great powers. But much, too, was due to the sapping of the will to rule or to act in the world in a manner commensurate with her resources, her experience, her interests, or her historical commitment to the upholding of the rule of law in the affairs of men and nations. Over the years an unrelenting campaign has been mounted by the Arabophiles in British political and intellectual life to bring about a British withdrawal from the Arab world and to resign British interests there into the hands of the military adventurers and political charlatans who now rule much of it. For some years this pusillanimous policy summed up in the glib catch-phrase, 'Coming to terms with Arab nationalism', which enjoyed a vogue throughout the whole gamut of articulate opinion, from the naïve utterances of well-meaning progressives at Oxford and Cambridge to the carefully slanted reports published in the *Observer* from that newspaper's Middle East correspondent, Kim Philby. The campaign had all the marks of that obsessive pre-occupation with Arab virtue and British wickedness which had distinguished the efforts of the crusaders of fifty years ago, although it was now adorned with a patina of spurious realism about Britain's economic capacity, an argument designed to match the disillusionment of the age.

The Arabophiles' finest hour, of course, was the Suez crisis of 1956, and their victory on that occasion has been celebrated and commemorated in the years since in so many millions of words that the underlying issues have been obscured almost beyond recall in the public memory. I myself sat in the public gallery of the House of Lords a year ago and heard Lady Gaitskell, the widow of Hugh Gaitskell, without any apparent consciousness of irony, congratulate the Earl of Avon on the speech he had just delivered, declaring that the rule of law must be upheld in the Straits of Tiran and a stop put to Nasser's belligerency. One was tempted to remind the gracious peeress of something Eden had said ten and a half years earlier, in October 1956, which her late husband had labelled 'pure hypocrisy', *viz.*, that the object of his policy then was to 'insulate the canal from the politics of any one country'. In this Eden was being true to an older British policy in the Middle East, one which antedated the emotional and committed approach of the past 40 or 50 years. Eden's words were a distinct echo of Palmerston's in 1840, at the height of the Eastern crisis of that year, when he spoke of Mehemet Ali Pasha's being forced to retire to 'the original shell of Egypt'. (As an aside, one might say that Eden himself had for a time been a member of the pro-Arab school in British politics, even if not a charter subscriber, and the most important act of policy which he performed under the influence of its philosophy was the conclusion of the 1954 agreement with Egypt for the evacuation of the canal zone and base. With this agreement he sowed the seeds of his own destruction, for its conclusion changed the whole strategic balance in the Middle East. The removal of the British screen left nothing to prevent the Egyptian army from moving into Sinai in force to establish forward positions hard up against the Israeli frontier; and, equally, it left nothing to deter the Israelis from launching a pre-emptive war against Egypt.

Palmerston laid the foundations of Britain's political position in the Middle East just as surely as the Arabophiles and their allies in British politics have destroyed them. One might take the fate of Aden colony and protectorates (the ill-starred Federation of South Arabia) as an instance of their tactics in action. Palmerston had ordered the occupation of Aden in 1839 to prevent Mehemet 'Ali's army in the Yemen, where it had engaged in a desultory war of subjugation since 1834, from seizing the port. It was part of Palmerston's counter-strategy to Mehemet 'Ali's grand design of controlling both ends of the Red Sea, and thereby commanding what was fast becoming the principal route between the Mediterranean and the East. When President Nasser began his campaign in the Yemen in 1962 it seemed that he was after much the same objective, as well as Persian Gulf oil-fields. The consequences for Britain's position in Arabia and the Gulf of a successful conclusion to that campaign had been foreseen by Kitchener fifty years earlier, when the Turks were actively subduing the Yemeni tribes. In a meeting of the C.I.D. [Committee of Imperial Defence] on 4 May 1911 he said (and substitute 'Egyptians' for 'Turks' here): 'Turkish policy in the P.[ersian] Gulf seems very likely to depend upon events in Yemen. If the Turkish operations there prove successful, the situation in the P.[ersian] Gulf might become acute, but if the Turks were unsuccessful in Yemen there was little fear of their troubling us in the Gulf. The effect of our withdrawal from the Gulf would also have a bad effect on our relations with Persia.'

This has not been the view taken of late years by the pro-Arab school, however. Reinforced by the anti-colonial lobby in England, keen to expiate the sin of British imperialism wherever it might be found, they promulgated the thesis that it would be blind folly, if not criminal stupidity, to impede the onward march of Arab nationalism, socialism, and revolution by remaining in Aden. To do so, the argument went, would prevent not only its union with the new, republican, revolutionary regime in the Yemen, which had purged the country of its medieval and theocratic ills by overthrowing the Zaidi imamate, but it would also prevent Aden's assimilation into the body politic of the Arab world at large. The proponents of this theory accompanied their arguments along these lines with an attack upon the proposal to federate Aden colony with the protectorate states of the hinterland, on the grounds that this would deliver over this thriving centre of commerce and civilization, with its educated and enlightened nationalist leaders, to the mercy of backward shaikhs, sultans and amirs, together with their turbulent tribal followers. They echoed the demands of the Adeni nationalist leaders for the implementation forthwith of the promised constitution, the holding of elections in the colony on the basis of one man one vote to decide whether it should merge with the protectorates, and the withdrawal immediately thereafter of the British garrison, base, and administration.

It was, as Sir Charles Johnston, one of the last governors of Aden, has observed since, a most peculiar application of the principles upon which representative government in the Empire over the preceding 100 years had been based. 'The Adenis, being urban and relatively sophisticated, should be allowed to decide the question of merger by their own vote, while the inhabitants of the original federation, although five times as numerous and no less vitally concerned, should not be consulted at all—presumably on the theory that as illiterate rifle-carrying tribesmen they somehow counted as second-class human beings.'[22] Further, since more than half the population of Aden colony consisted of Yemenis who had come over the border to find work there, acquiescence in the demands of the nationalists and their supporters in Britain would have placed the future of Aden in the hands of transient Yemeni labourers who enjoyed no freedom of political expression in their own country, under either the Imamate or the Republic. Again, demands for free elections rang rather hollow in the ears when they came from men who had been demonstrating their devotion to the principle of free elections by boycotting every one which had been held in Aden since 1959.

Democratic procedures, adult suffrage, and free elections are mere cant phrases in the modern Arab world. The demand for free elections in Aden was merely a cloak for other objects: the elections would have been used as a plebiscite in favour of nationalism, as a means of attracting outside support, and as a device to end colonial rule. Once independence had

---

22 Charles Hepburn Johnston, *The View from Steamer Point* (Collins, London, 1965), pp. 195-6.

been gained, free elections, as has happened elsewhere, would disappear into a limbo from which they would not emerge. Liberalism as a political philosophy is now outmoded in the Arab world, as it has been for some time, and the essence of democracy is held to be, not the existence of a parliamentary opposition, but the creation of a programme of *soi-disant* reform and the enlistment of mass support for it. Johnston, at the close of his governorship in 1963, predicted a gloomy future for Aden if the trends then in evidence continued. 'From its present proud status as a great international communications centre and as the biggest bunkering port in the world, it would be brought down to the level of a sleepy provincial harbour in an under-developed country. All the prosperity built up since the British occupation of Aden in 1839 would be lost, and the present easy-going international co-operation would be replaced by Arab nationalism in its narrowest form.'[23]

It is unnecessary to add that his prediction has been fulfilled. The process continued as propagandists and politicians of the pro-Arab anti-colonial school went on their merry way, turning out books with facile titles like *Britain's Moment in the Middle East* [by Elizabeth Monroe, 1967] and meretricious articles in the fashionable weeklies all designed to prove that if Britain had 'kept faith with the Arabs' all would have worked out for the best. The feelings of guilt and inferiority, which for half a century have wracked the liberal sections of the British political and intellectual classes whenever they contemplated the Arab world, have been indulged to the hilt; yet the residual sensation experienced by the penitents is not one of gaiety and euphoria but rather that of overpowering bewilderment. Sinai and Palestine now lie under non-Arab rule, the Suez canal is closed, Egypt, the leader of the Arab world is bankrupt (in more senses than one), the Red Sea is a stagnant backwater, the port of Aden languishes, and the Russian military missions, there and in the Yemen next-door, prepare for the day when the canal is reopened and they can take the next step towards turning the flank of the Western world in the Persian Gulf and the Indian Ocean.

It is only a form of justice to remind the British Arabophiles, as they watch their erstwhile protégés slide heedlessly into a new alien thralldom, that the price that they would one day pay for their illusions had been foreseen, albeit unwillingly, by Lawrence forty years ago, when, in one of those rare passages in the *Seven Pillars* where he lets slip the mask, though not the stylized murkiness of his prose, he wrote:

---

23 *Ibid.*, pp. 152-3.

A man who gives himself to be a possession of aliens leads a Yahoo life, having bartered his soul to a brute-master. He is not one of them, persuade himself of a mission, batter and twist them into something which they, of their own accord, would not have been. Then he is exploiting his old environment to press them out of theirs. Or, after my model, he may imitate them so well that they spuriously imitate him back again.[24]

---

24 Lawrence, *op.cit.*, p. 29.

23
Eastern Arabia in the Eighteenth Century[1]

Ahmad Mustafa Abu Hakima: *History of eastern Arabia, 1750-1800: the rise and development of Bahrain and Kuwait.* xix, 213 pp., 6 plates. Beirut: Khayats, 1965.

Considering how few modern studies there are of the Persian Gulf in the eighteenth century, it is to be regretted that no more than a guarded welcome can be given to Dr. Abu Hakima's account of the history of Bahrain and Kuwait before 1800. Neither his claim at the outset to be the first to treat the rise of the 'Utub historically, nor his handling of his source material, inspires much confidence; for the first is manifestly unfair to J. G. Lorimer, whose *Gazetteer of the Persian Gulf, 'Oman, and central Arabia* appeared more than 50 years ago and is still the standard authority on the region, while the second is so inadequate as to impair seriously any usefulness that the book might have.

A case in point is his account of the conquest and occupation of Bahrain by the 'Utub, the most important event in 'Utubi history in the eighteenth century. The date usually assigned to it is 1783, when the Persian garrison was expelled and the island passed under the rule of the Al Khallfah branch of the 'Utub. For some reason best known to himself Dr. Abu Hakima refuses to accept this dating and attempts to put back the conquest to the previous year. He should have left well alone, for in 10 pages of tortuous argument he succeeds only in demonstrating his inability to read his sources carefully. Thus, on p. 112 he cites a report from the

---
1 Source: *Bulletin of the School of Oriental and African Studies*, University of London, Vol. 31, No. 1 (1968), pp. 152-153.

East India Company's Resident at Basra, 'early in 1782', to the effect that the governor of Bushahr was preparing an expedition to attack Zubara, in Qatar, in retaliation for a raid upon Bahrain by 'Utub from Zubara and Kuwait. But the Resident's report, which Dr. Abu Hakima prints as an appendix, is dated, not 'early in 1782' but '4 November 1782', and it is only logical to assume both that the governor of Bushahr attacked Zubara after that date and that he would scarcely have directed his attack to Zubara if Bahrain had been in 'Utub occupation.

The attack on Zubara, which took place in the late spring of 1783, was a failure, and it was followed shortly afterwards by a 'Utub descent upon Bahrain in force and the eventual capitulation of the Persian garrison on the island. Dr. Abu Hakima himself bears unwitting testimony to this sequence of events and dates on p. 116 of his book, where he cites a report reprinted in the Selections from the Records of the Bombay Government (New Series, No. 24) which states that the expelled Persian garrison arrived at Bushahr 'on the 5th August, 1782', and to which he adds the comment that this date corresponds with local Arab tradition, which places the event in the year A.E. 1197. It certainly does, but not in the way Dr. Abu Eakima has it; for the Bombay report gives '5 August 1783', not '1782', while the Muslim year 1197 ran from December 1782 to November 1783.

Carelessness of a similar order mars Dr. Abu Hakima's remarks on the trade and shipping of the Gulf in the later eighteenth century. It is simply not true to say that 'Arab traders monopolised sea-freight in the Gulf' (p. 184), or that Arab shipping 'monopolised Gulf trade' (p. 185). That Arab traders handled the greater part of the Gulf's trade, and Arab shipping carried the bulk of that trade, is true, but to say that they 'monopolised' it is to ignore the prominent part played in the Gulf's trade by the 'country' shipping of western India and by Parsi and Gujarati merchants and capitalists. Instead of venturing into such sweeping and largely unsubstantiated generalizations, Dr. Abu Hakima would have been better advised to confine himself to those areas and topics which he is undoubtedly competent to handle. By far the most worth-while sections of his book are those concerned with the fortunes of the Bam Khalid rulers of Hasa and the internal and dynastic affairs of the Al Sabah and Al Khallfah. Much of what he has to say on these subjects is of interest and value, in particular the fresh evidence which he produces of the course and character of the 'Utub's migrations in the early eighteenth century. More space allotted to the history and politics of eastern Arabia (in keeping with his book's title), and more careful editing, to remove the repetitiousness, inconsistencies, and crashing banalities which disfigure so many of his pages, would have resulted in a far better book.

24
The European Empires and Islam[1]

Islam, Europe and Empire, by Norman Daniel. (Edinburgh: University Press, 1966.)

Although Dr. Daniel states in the preface to his book that his subject is 'the movement of Western Europeans among Islamic peoples [in the nineteenth century], with the consequent creation of new attitudes in their minds', it never clearly emerges from the body of his work what it is that he is actually attempting, whether it is an apologia for Islam, a search for the ultimate roots of Arab, Turkish and Persian nationalism, an intellectual history of European imperialism in the Muslim world, a treatise on the pathology of prejudice, or a political history of British activities in the Middle East, Africa, and India in the last century. Elements of all these topics are present in his book, which ranges in time from the French expedition to Egypt to the Mahdist movement in the Sudan (with a backward look in an introductory chapter at medieval and early modern Western concepts of Islam), and which takes in along the way such diverse questions as the reform movement in the Ottoman Empire, British relations with Persia and Afghanistan, the War of Greek Independence, the French conquest of Algeria, Christianity in India and Africa, the Arab slave trade, the Bulgarian atrocities, and the British occupation of Egypt. What does emerge quite plainly from Dr. Daniel's book is that he firmly believes that the attitude of most Europeans, and the British in particular, towards Islam and the Islamic peoples was hopelessly warped—by the *odium theologicum* surviving from the Middle Ages, by the consciousness of their

[1] Source: *The English Historical Review*, Vol. 83, No. 329 (Oct., 1968), pp. 799-802.

own superiority derived from their technological achievements, and by the exigencies of their imperial role. He is oppressed by the twin demons of avuncular colonialism and anti-Muslim sentiment, and he has set himself determinedly to hound them and their worldly allies to their end, down 500 pages of labyrinthine prose.

There is no doubt that Dr. Daniel has read very widely, even indiscriminately, in contemporary works of travel, biography, poetry, fiction, politics, and history; it is equally obvious that he has been reluctant to omit from his book anything which he feels might be germane to his purpose. If this propensity tends to give his work the appearance of a pastiche, it also produces some highly original observations, such as that on page 189 that Minto's conquest of Java in 1811 was, along with Scott's *Lady of the Lake*, part and parcel of the romantic movement; to which Dr. Daniel adds the mysterious comment, 'The romantic approach refurbished alike the Orient's and Scotland's image'. Dr. Daniel openly avows that he is concerned to argue a case, in defence of Islam and against its nineteenth-century British detractors, and there is nothing to object to in this. What is open to objection is the method by which Dr. Daniel argues his case. The method is a simple one, consisting on the one hand of the selection of quotations and evidence to suit the argument, and, on the other, of the outright denial of the validity of the opinions of European observers of Islamic society where these opinions are unflattering.

Thus, Dr. Daniel denies the correctness of the commonly held British view that Oriental governments were despotic in nature, although he fails to put forward any substantial evidence that they were not. He is offended that British officials thought Asiatics were different from them and that they frequently framed their actions in accordance with that belief. He considers that the position of women in Muslim society has been grossly misrepresented by European writers, but his own assertions in rebuttal of their conclusions are unconvincing. Though he inveighs against partiality in others—of one nineteenth-century writer he says (p. 219), 'There is no moment in the whole course of his book when we do not feel the violence of his prejudice'—his own partiality is evident on every page, and it does little good for him to protest, as he does towards the close of his book (p. 479), 'Nothing I have said about imperialists should be construed as criticism of their characters. I intend neither praise nor blame, though both may be due'. He consistently holds those with whom he disagrees up to contempt and ridicule—his treatment of Sir John Malcolm is a case in point—and, what is equally objectionable, he misrepresents their thoughts and actions by a process of arbitrary selection, arrangement, and omission of evidence. The principle may be seen at work, for instance, in his account of the War of Greek Independence, where he endeavours to rehabilitate the reputation of the Turks by impugning the character of the Greeks, and by remaining silent on the atrocities in the Morea and the activities of Ibrahim Pasha, the sole reference to whom occurs in a footnote recording an admiring remark passed by Admiral Codrington.

At other places in his book Dr. Daniel is simply ill-informed. His descriptions of the Wahhabi movement in Arabia, of the East India Company's rule in India in the eighteenth century, of Wellesley's foreign policy, of the Arab slave trade, and of British relations with Persia are inaccurate or maladroit. The fallacies perpetrated in his chapter on the early British missions to Persia are almost unprecedented in writings on the subject. The claim made in chapter iv that the British emulated in India a technique of indirect rule worked out by Bonaparte during his year in Egypt can hardly be meant to be taken seriously. Dr. Daniel commends Bonaparte and the French in general for showing greater perspicacity in their dealings with Muslims than the British did, and he considers the French occupation of Egypt to have been, on the whole, beneficial. Neither in his footnotes nor in his bibliography, however, is there any reference to the standard authority on the subject, de la Jonquiere's *L'Expédition en Égypte, 1798-1801* (5 vols., Paris, 1899-1907), which gives a very different picture of the conquest.

In the Arab slave trade, Dr. Daniel runs up against perhaps the most formidable obstacle to the pursuit of his thesis that Islam was guiltless of the reproaches levelled against it by British observers in the nineteenth century. To circumvent this difficulty he engages in a certain amount of sophistry, pointing to the fact that slavery was practised by the Christian West as well as by the Muslim East, and asserting that, in any case, the conditions of Muslim slavery were less inhuman than those prevailing in the plantations of the West Indies. This is not good enough. No movement of any consequence towards abolition ever arose of its own accord in the Muslim world; it was the reproach of Muslim slavery, not Christian, that men and boys were castrated for service in the *harim*; and it was a Christian nation, Britain, which led the campaign to end the Arab slave trade and to compel Muslim rulers to forbid it to their subjects. If Dr. Daniel had read further—his bibliography does not list the works of Sir Reginald Coupland on the anti-slavery movement and the East African slave trade—he would have found that many of the British officials whose alleged hostility towards Islam he deplores were considerably more fair-minded, knowledgeable, and realistic in their attitude towards the Arab slave trade than he allows or realizes. It was they, after all, who led the Arab tribes of the Persian Gulf to cease trading in their fellow-Muslims, the Somalis.

Yet for all their understanding of the nature of Muslim slavery it is improbable that these officials would ever have tried to defend it by the type of reasoning employed by Dr. Daniel on pages 308-9 of his book, where he seeks to justify African slavery on the grounds of the social dislocation caused by its abolition in Zanzibar.

The confusion rampant in Dr. Daniel's thinking is reflected in the arrangement of his book, in the patchwork construction of his chapters, in the idiosyncratic order of his notes, and in the impenetrability and tedium of his prose. He gives little sign of having digested what he has read, but merely regurgitates it whole, with scant regard for form, content or relevance. His work reveals all the weaknesses of intellectual history when it is unaccompanied by an adequate grasp of the political background. It is, in short, a product of what a reviewer in the *Times Literary Supplement* some time ago called 'para-scholarship'. Dr. Daniel shows little understanding of the characters and qualities of the men he pillories, from Wellesley to Cromer, and less of the circumstances which led them to act as they did. He refuses to accept that they must be judged by the standards of their time, not ours. Instead, he has chosen to employ against them the currently fashionable doctrine of selective indignation, and to pursue a vendetta of his own, unhampered by the restraints of historical accuracy and unrelieved by a modicum of wit, grace or charity.

25
Religion and Rebellion in Iran[1]

Religion and Rebellion in Iran: The Tobacco Protest of 1891-1892, by Nikki R. Keddie. New York: Humanities Press, 1967. Pp. xx, 163.

When Nasir ud-din Shah granted to a British subject in March 1890 a monopoly of the production, sale, and exportation of tobacco in Persia, he provoked a reaction in his country the like of which had not been seen in a century of Qajar rule and the results of which were to contribute to his own assassination six years later. For the acts of revolt which occurred in nearly every important city in Persia in 1891 represented much more than the resentment of tobacco growers and merchants affected by the proposed *régie*; they were also a popular protest against the corruption and repression of Nasir ud-din's government, and an outburst of religious and national feeling over what seemed to many Persians to be the surrender of their country and its resources into the hands of foreigners and infidels. Hostility to the Shah and to the *régie* drew together in a curious alliance Persians of liberal outlook, who wanted to bring about reform and constitutional rule, and the ultraconservative *muftahids*, the Shi'i divines whose power within Persia was second only to that of the court. It was they, in the last measure, who prevailed, forcing the Shah at the close of 1891 to cancel the tobacco concession.

Professor Keddie in her book sees the struggle over the *régie* much as Professor Ann K. S. Lambton has done in a recent article ("The Tobacco Régie: Prelude to Revolution," *Studia Islamica*, XXII and XXIII (1965)),

---

[1] Source: *The Journal of Economic History*, Vol. 28, No. 4 (Dec., 1968), pp. 697-698.

viz., as a forerunner or harbinger of the constitutional revolution of 1905-6. She has worked from British, French, Persian, and Russian sources, published and unpublished, and what she has to tell us, particularly about the activities of the *mujtahids* and of that subtle intriguer, Jamal ud-din al-Afghani, is of considerable interest and importance. It is all the more to be regretted, therefore, that Professor Keddie did not take a little longer to reflect upon what she has uncovered and to place it in better perspective. There is too much evidence of haste in her book, too many signs of an impatience to present her material in its uncut state and have done with it. *Festina lente* is a good motto for a historian, especially in these frenetic times; by disregarding it, Professor Keddie does less than justice to her own talents and ability.

26
Islam and Imperialism[1]

An Islamic Response to Imperialism: Political and Religious Writings of Saiyid Jamal ad-Din, "al-Afghani" by Nikki R. Keddie. Berkeley: University of California Press, 1968. xii, 212 pp. Bibliography, Index.

Saiyid Jamal ad-Din al-Afghani has long been one of the cult figures of intellectual historians of Arab nationalism, who generally tend to represent him on his own terms as a devout Muslim divine and modern reformer, who strode from land to land through the Middle East in the closing decades of the nineteenth century like a politico-religious Johnny Appleseed, spreading the doctrines of revival, reform, and revolution as he went, and leaving in his wake cadres of worshipful disciples, murmurs of nationalist discontent, and the rumbles of *jihad*. The burden of his message is said to have been the necessity for Islam of resurgence and reaffirmation, of the creation of Islamic unity, and of the education of the Muslim community in modern science and technology, if the threat of Western dominance was to be met and the Christian hordes excluded from the *dar al-Islam*. Arrayed thus, Afghani endures in the pantheon of Islamic and anti-imperialist demi-gods erected by Western apologists of the collective phenomenon known as Arab nationalism. It matters little that many aspects of Afghani's life are obscure, that his writings and ideas have been transmitted at second-or third-hand, or that they have been subjected to little serious or sustained criticism. In the realm of expiatory apologists, which in too many instances nowadays passes for historical scholarship

---
[1] Source: *The Journal of Asian Studies*, Vol. 29, No. 4 (Aug. 1970), pp. 980-982.

on the West's relations with Asia and Africa, it is the image and the cause which count, not the reality.

Only in very recent years has the varnish been peeled from the familiar, authorised portrait of Afghani, most notably by the hands of Sylvia Haim, Nikki Keddie, and Elie Kedourie, and what they have revealed of his character, life, activities, and preaching bears little resemblance to the pious reformer of orthodox iconography. Professor Keddie has devoted several years now to the study of Afghani's life and works, and her present book, an examination of Afghani's political and religious thinking, accompanied by translations of his principal writings, is intended as a companion volume to the major biography of the man which is in the process of completing. What she has given us here is not only of great interest but also of considerable importance, for her book contains the first translation into English of the original, Persian version of Afghani's *chef-d'oeuvre*, "The Refutation of the Materialists" (or, more correctly, as Professor Keddie informs us, "The Truth about the Neicheri Sect and an Explanation of Neicheris"), which had hitherto been available to Western readers only in a French translation by A.M. Goichon, published in 1942. Valuable though Mlle. Goichon's work was—and she also reproduced in her book the piece for which Afghani is perhaps best known in the West, his "Answer to Renan"—it was derived from the Arabic version of the "Refutuation" composed by Afghani's Egyptian disciple, Muhammad 'Abduh, who paraphrased, with additions and glosses of his own, an oral rendering of the Persian original by Afghani's servant. If such a method of transmitting the message seems tortuous, even suspect, it is all of a piece with Afghani himself, his career, and his ideas.

For nothing about the man is as it seems. Despite his soubriquet, Jamal al-Din was not an Afghan but a Persian, from the village of Asadabad near Hamadan. He called himself a Sunni but was raised a Shi'i. As a young man he spent some time in India, on the eve of the mutiny, and this, his first sight of Muslims living under non-Muslim rule, had a severe and lasting impact upon him, breeding in him a hatred of Europeans and of the British, in particular. His first appearance in Afghanistan was in 1866, when he posed as a Turk and worked against British interest in the country, even to the extent of taking Russian money. His activities led to his expulsion from Afghanistan at the close of 1868, and some time later he appeared in Istanbul, where he passed himself off as an Afghan and a Sunni until he was forced to leave on a charge of publicly advocating heresy. He thereupon took himself off to Cairo, where he remained until 1879, cultivating a following among the intelligentsia, preaching sedition, stirring up anti-Western sentiment, and, in general, ensuring his eventual expulsion from Egypt.

Nothing in the career of the man up to this time marked him out from the ruck of Muslim malcontents, with a smattering of Western knowledge, and the usual impediments of resentment and ambition, who were a feature of Middle Eastern society in the last quarter of the nineteenth century; and it was not until he arrived in Hyderabad state, in search of refuge, in 1880 that Afghani began to transform himself from the semi-heretical and irreligious *enfant terrible* of Cairo and Istanbul into the pious defender of religion and enlightened elucidator of Koranic precepts of later hagiologic lore. (He could still trip a pretty, rationalistic measure, however, as he demonstrated during his sojourn in Paris in 1883 when he published his 'Answer to Renan.') From this time forward the figure of the reformer and modernizer is steadily eclipsed by that of the warrior of Islam, as Afghani sought to ingratiate himself with the Sultan 'Abdul Hamid by pandering to the ruler's bigotry, xenophobia, and caliphal and pan-Islamic ambitions.

How is it then that this man, who is still viewed by many Western students of Middle Eastern history as a paladin of traditional Islam, as a precursor or proponent of early nationalism, and as a passionate advocate of philosophic and scientific methods (without, apparently, any conscious appreciation of the essentially contradictory character of these roles), could in his own day appeal almost simultaneously to the prejudices of the Muslim masses and to the imaginations of progressives and nationalists? The answer (and in Afghani's mind, the justification), Professor Keddie suggests, lies in the early influence of Shi'ism upon him, and in particular of the phrases *ijtihad* (individual judgement), which enabled doctrine to be reinterpreted so as to reconcile it with modern scientific knowledge, and *taqiya* (caution or dissimulation) which allowed Afghani to adapt his arguments to differing audiences or to different members of the same audience. Surely, however, a man of Afghani's stripe had little need to invoke the sanction of religion to justify dissimulation, when dissimulation and deception were a way of life with him? Professor Keddie is kinder to him than she need be, both here and elsewhere, as when, for example, she argues (p.45) that the contradictions in his various writings can be attributed to the fact that his purpose was "pragmatic and worldly rather than religious," namely, to strengthen Islam by the adoption of science and technology, to unify it by playing down doctrinal differences amongst the sects, and to harness them to the pan-Islamic chariot which was to crush and scatter the Christian interlopers. To achieve his object Afghani had to appeal to Shi'a divines, Sunni *'ulema*, ignorant masses, progressive intellectuals, reactionary rulers, and Western sympathizers. Once Afghani is seen as essentially a political activist and not as a religious visionary, Professor Keddie argues, the contradictions in his writings and teachings are explicable. The only alternative, she says, "is to postulate a hopeless confusion of thought," which, she maintains, is unlikely in view of the impression he made at the time upon intelligent men, and especially among modernists, liberals, and revolutionaries. But to judge from the works here translated, Afghani's thinking was of a fairly primitive order, and, contradictions aside, confused to boot, perhaps not hopelessly, but certainly to a marked degree. As for the modernists, liberals, and revolutionaries of his day, they were themselves confused much of the time, and over many things, and as ready as succeeding members of their tribe have been to enthuse over trifles and to hail novelty as enlightenment.

To remark thus is no reflection upon Professor Keddie's perception and scholarship. On the contrary, it is a tribute to the stimulating nature of her essay and to her admirably clear and patient exposition of the development of Afghani's thought. One question that remains unanswered in her book is why Afghani should have nursed such a virulent hatred of the British. His life reveals that he was a man primarily moved by personal ambition and emotion—hence, his attack in "The Refutation of the Materialists," under the pretense of safeguarding the purity of Islam, upon Sir Saiyid Ahmad Khan and other Indian Islamic reformers who had befriended him and afforded him refuge but who earned his displeasure because they were rivals and because they were willing to work with the British in helping the Muslim community of India adapt to the modern world. It must have been something other than Muslim exclusiveness and dislike of infidels that made Afghani hate the British so. It cannot have been solely that they were ruling over Muslims: so also, at the time, were the French, the Russians, and the Dutch. The character of Afghani makes it almost certain that he suffered some personal humiliation or injury at the hands of the British, in India, Afghanistan, or Egypt, to breed in him such corrosive hostility. Perhaps when Professor Keddie's biography of Afghani appears we will have the answer, just as we now have the answers, in her present acute, learned, and highly valuable study, to so many other riddles about the man.

27
Britain and Russia in Persia and the Gulf[1]

Britain and the Persian Gulf, 1894-1914, by Briton Cooper Busch. Berkeley: University of California Press, 1968. Pp. xvi + 432.

Russia and Britain in Persia, 1864-1914: A Study in Imperialism, by Firuz Kazemzadeh. Yale Russian and East European Studies, number 6. New Haven, Conn.: Yale University Press, 1968. Pp. xii + 711.

For the greater part of the nineteenth century, Britain enjoyed in the Persian Gulf a political paramountcy which was unshaken by the intrusion of other European powers into the area and undisturbed by the vicissitudes of fortune which overtook the Ottoman and Persian empires along its northern shores. Beginning in the last decade of the century, however, Britain's predominance was subjected to successive challenges by France, Russia, and Germany, the result of which was not only to ruffle the imperial calm of the gulf's waters but also to drag it and its affairs into the arena of European diplomatic contention. The twenty years between 1894 and 1914 which form the subject of Professor Busch's book were probably the most complicated in the history of British relations with the gulf before the First World War; and it is no reproach to him, therefore, to observe—as he would himself doubtless concede—that he has not perhaps plumbed the period to its ultimate depths but rather has surveyed it in competent fashion, noting its principal features and commenting upon

---
[1] Source: *The Journal of Modern History*, Vol. 42, No. 2 (Jun., 1970), pp. 264-271.

them with both intelligence and good sense.

Busch sees the axis of British power in the gulf as running from Kuwait in the north to Oman in the south, and he consequently devotes the greater part of his book to tracing the growth of British influence in the former principality and its consolidation in the latter from the 1890s onward. The main outside challenge to Britain in Oman came from France, which, in 1894, the year of the conclusion of the Franco-Russian defensive alliance, appointed a consul to Muscat, the capital of the sultanate. By the time of the Fashoda crisis, four years later, the French foothold at Muscat had become so secure as to threaten Britain's commanding influence at the court of the ruling Al Bu Said sultan, which in turn led the government of India at the outset of 1899 to take drastic measures to compel the sultan to terminate his intimacy with the French. The quarrel between Britain and France in Oman dragged on for several years more, even beyond the entente of 1904; it was kept alive by the two issues of the grant of French flags to Omani *dhows* employed in the slave trade and the sale of arms by French dealers at Muscat. The suppression of the gulf arms traffic in the first decade of this century, which was undertaken by Britain to reduce the incidence and severity of fighting along the northwest frontier of India, destroyed the last shreds of French influence at Muscat and restored British supremacy in Oman.

At Kuwait, the challenge which emerged at the turn of the century was a dual one, coming both from the Ottoman Turks, who claimed suzerainty over the sheikhdom, and from the Germans, who saw it as the logical terminus for the Baghdad railway. Busch leaves no doubt at all that Kuwait was an integral part of the Ottoman Empire and that the Porte's claim to authority over it was legally justified. He also makes it clear that the ambitions of the Al Sabah ruler, Mubarak ibn Sabah, and the exigencies of British Indian defense combined to frustrate the Porte's endeavors to make its authority effective in the sheikhdom and to transform it in the fifteen years before 1914 into a quasi protectorate of Britain. The first step in this process was taken in January 1899 when the British political resident in the gulf obtained from Sheikh Mubarak a bond that he would not alienate any portion of his territory or enter into relations with a foreign power without the previous consent of the British government. Busch's account of this transaction, derived, as is the greater part of his book, from the Foreign Office and India Office records, is substantially correct, although he does not pay sufficiently close attention to the negotiations which were going on at Constantinople late in 1898 over railway concessions and which provided the impetus for the taking of the nonalienation bond, or to the finer points of the debate between the Foreign Office and the India Office over the question. Moreover, on the critical point of how Salisbury, the prime minister, reached his decision to secure the bond, he has misread a vital dispatch from Constantinople.

A tendency to overlook, to skimp, or to omit important matters of detail is, in fact, a weakness of Busch's book. Tedious though these details often are, they are nevertheless vital to such issues as sovereignty and jurisdiction, which were the subject of most of the disputes which arose between the British and Turkish governments in the gulf before 1914. There is no mention in Busch's account of the conclusion of the Anglo-Turkish convention of July 29, 1913 of the blue line, which marked the eastern boundary of the *sanjaq* of Najd and therefore the limits of Turkish sovereignty in eastern Arabia. Nor does he state specifically that the Turks renounced their claim to the Qatar peninsula, although he makes it clear earlier that such a renunciation was a *sine qua non* from the British point of view. In many of the statements he makes and the conclusions he draws about British and Turkish actions in Qatar and in the neighboring sheikhdom of Bahrain after 1894 he is handicapped by his uncertainty about what had occurred in these places earlier, an uncertainty which might have been removed by a more thorough perusal of some of the works listed in his bibliography.

Any faults which his book contains, explains Busch disarmingly in his preface, probably arise from the fact of its having been based upon a dissertation. One cannot so easily absolve oneself of one's sins. There are good and bad dissertations just as there are good and bad books, and the transformation of the one into the other depends as much upon the will and the capacity, as well as the patience, of the author as it does upon the quality of his training as a historian and the examples which have influenced him. Busch has not written a bad book; on the contrary, parts of it are very good, it is refreshingly free from the tiresome sermonizing which afflicts so many historians of Europe's relations with the Middle East, and its author is fair and just in his treatment of the men of whom he writes, while at the same time he displays a commendable assurance in the way in which he handles the complicated diplomatic background to his period. Yet his work as a whole is marred by defects which may or may not be attributable to the influence of the graduate school; they may simply be the fault of the author himself. The writing is too often slipshod, too heavily laced with colloquialisms, slang, and jargon. There is an awkwardness, presumably springing from unfamiliarity or a striving to be laconic in the use of terms and titles, for example, "Secretary for India" for "Secretary of

State for India," and the confusion over the use of "Home" to denote the United Kingdom and "Home Government" to distinguish the imperial government from the government of India. Elaborate footnotes are attached to simple statements of commonplace facts in the text, an exercise which appears to have a strictly limited usefulness, since too often they fail to prevent the commission of factual errors which could have been avoided had the author really mastered the information contained in the works he cites. Finally, Busch indulges in a certain amount of repetition, especially in chapter 8 on the general question of British policy between 1900 and 1905, while at the same time, he gives too brief and too spare an account of developments in Arabia and Persia in this period which are highly germane to his subject.

If Busch has been somewhat cursory in his treatment of British relations with Persia between 1894 and 1914, Professor Kazemzadeh, whose large volume is devoted to Anglo-Russian rivalry in Persia between 1864 and 1914, deals even more summarily with British policy in the gulf during this period. He could, of course, with justice point to the title of his book as exonerating him of the charge of neglecting the peripheries of his subject, and certainly there is enough in the tortuous history of Russian and British policies in Persia to fill several volumes of this size. Kazemzadeh has dealt at generous length with the main and subsidiary aspects of those policies and the events around which they revolved—the advance of Russia into Transcaspia and Turkestan, British efforts to shore up Persia against any further advances, the competition at Tehran between the two European powers over trade, concessions, and loans, the railway question and its strategic implications, the Persian revolution and Russian intervention, and, finally, the detente of 1907 and its aftermath. It is evident that Kazemzadeh has worked long and hard in unpublished British and Persian sources and in printed Russian documentary collections, and he has accumulated a great body of information which he has assembled into a detailed narrative of considerable interest and value, especially on the Russian side. It is all the more regrettable, in view of the achievement which his book represents in terms of scholarly labor, to have to express reservations about its ultimate merit, reservations which, in the main, are prompted by the particular cast given to the book by the author's close involvement with his subject.

"Believing that objectivity is not synonymous with indifference and that a historian must feel in order to know," writes Kazemzadeh in his preface, "I have not concealed my own reactions to persons and events described in this book." No one would deny a historian the right to respond emotionally to his material. After all, to be dispassionate is not necessarily to be virtuous. But a historian also has a duty to distinguish between sympathy and prejudice in himself and to weigh his verdict in the scales of justice before delivering it. Kazemzadeh's book is little short of an extended polemic against successive British governments for their pusillanimity and callousness in failing to save Persia from falling increasingly under Russian domination in the later nineteenth and early twentieth centuries. It is true that Kazemzadeh also makes fairly plain his condemnation of the Russians for their behavior toward Persia, but the condemnation is largely implied in his descriptions of what the Russians did, and it is expressed less frequently and less forcefully than it is in the case of the British.

The deficiencies and anomalies in British policy toward Persia in the last century are not exactly unknown, nor is criticism of them strictly of recent date. Sir Henry Rawlinson in his *England and Russia in the East* (London, 1875) wrote a scathing denunciation of his country's treatment of Persia up to that time; and Lord Curzon in 1892 characterized British policy toward Persia as being afflicted by "analogous spasms of solicitude and torpor," and he went on to declare scornfully:

> We have made treaties with Persia, imposing upon ourselves the most solemn offensive and defensive obligations. When the occasion arose for redeeming them, we have shirked the responsibility and have subsequently bought our release from the self-inflicted tie. We have courted and waged war against the same Persian sovereigns; we have both trained and routed the Persian army; we have at once pampered and neglected the Persian people. Our Persian policy in each successive stage, whether of interest or apathy, has ever been characterised by the note of exaggeration. [*Persia and the Persian Question* (London, 1892), pp. 605-6]

There would be more force to Professor Kazemzadeh's strictures if, like those of Curzon and Rawlinson, or of recent scholars like Dr. Rose L. Greaves and Professor A. P. Thornton, they were more measured. The tone of his book, unhappily, is set as early as page 24, where he categorizes as a "bit of Victorian cant" the refusal of the government of India in 1872 to second British officers for service with the Persian army on the grounds that they might be called upon to witness or participate in activities offensive to their honor. Either Kazemzadeh does not know, or he has forgotten, how the Persian army of those days comported itself, on or off the field.

At the close of the Anglo-Persian war in 1857 one of the Persian regiments which had disgraced itself in battle at Muhammarah was publicly humiliated at Tehran. Rings were passed through the noses of its officers, who were then dragged through the ranks at the end of ropes and flogged in front of their own men before being thrown into prison.

The choice of the year 1864 as the starting point for his study is explained by Kazemzadeh as the year that the Russian government decided to extend its rule over the lands to the east of the Caspian and into Turkestan. The justification offered to the other European powers for this policy of expansion was the by now familiar one of the need to pacify the turbulent frontier. Tashkent was occupied by Russian troops in 1865 and Bukhara was attacked. Kokand, beyond the Jaxartes, was annexed in 1875. The Turkomans were next to experience the "charm" (*obaianie*) of Russian arms. Khiva was taken in 1873, and the way was opened for an eventual advance southward to the Merv Oasis. British reaction to the Russian expansion in Transcaspia and Turkestan was vacillatory. A move upon Merv by the Russians would bring them uncomfortably close to Afghanistan, and Afghanistan was the last, as well as the most effective, outwork of British India. Russian penetration of the Turkoman lands also posed a threat to Khorasan, the eastern province of Persia. Obviously, Persia as well as Afghanistan would have to be strengthened if the line against a Russian march on India was to be held. The logic of the situation, so it now seems to Kazemzadeh, called for the conclusion of a firm Anglo-Persian defensive alliance against Russia, and he castigates the British government of the day for their failure to conclude such an alliance while, at the same time, they called upon Persia to defend her frontiers against Russian encroachment. What was "defenseless Persia to do," asks Kazemzadeh sarcastically (p. 55), "when mighty Britain herself had been unwilling or unable to stop Russia's advance in Asia?"

The issue of an Anglo-Persian alliance was not as simple as this, as Kazemzadeh would surely have realized if he had looked more closely at the course of Anglo-Persian relations in the first sixty years of the nineteenth century. It is a serious weakness of his book that he has virtually nothing to say at the outset about British relations with Persia before 1864, and he provides only a sketchy outline of Russian relations. Indeed, he does not even properly examine the treaty basis of these relations, with the result that he confuses real with imaginary innovations and inconsistencies in British policy in the latter part of the century. A similar confusion clouds the reasoning behind his reproaches to the British government. After chiding them for failing to conclude a Persian alliance, he goes on to concede, not once but several times, that Britain was incapable of defending Persia against Russia or of fighting a war in central Asia. Yet in the teeth of this admission he persists in ascribing Britain's refusal to ally herself militarily with Persia in the 1870s and 1880s to "the loss of nerve which would gradually affect large numbers of English statesmen when they confronted Russia" (p. 178).

Not only is this assertion palpably false, but the plain truth is that it was Britain's opposition to Russian aggression in Persia (and the threat of a general European war which was implicit in that opposition) which preserved Persia's independence as a state in the nineteenth century—or, at least, prevented her from becoming a Russian satrapy. Kazemzadeh refuses to see or to admit this, being bent rather upon pillorying Britain for allowing Persia to be intimidated in the slightest degree by Russia. His relentless pursuit of this object stands in strange contrast to his silence, for all his condemnation of the Persian government for its corruption and incompetence, on the utter failure of the Persians to make any consistent stand in defence of their country's interests. When the Russians resumed their operations against the Turkomans in 1880, the Persian government not only did nothing to oppose their march through Transcaspia but they actually supplied the Russians with provisions and baggage animals and even allowed them to establish supply bases on Persian territory. With this assistance, the Russians went on to defeat the Tekke Turkomans in 1881, capture Geok-Teppe, and annex the surrounding territory, thereby setting themselves on the road to Merv. The negotiations which followed to define the new Russo-Persian frontier in Transcaspia culminated in a treaty on December 21, 1881 which contained a secret clause providing for the passage of Russian troops through Khorasan to Afghanistan. Kazemzadeh makes no mention of this clause in his account of the events of these years (pp. 75-80), and it is not until 200 pages further on that he casually refers to it when he is describing the Russo-Persian treaty of June 8, 1893, which, among other things, abrogated the clause. The British government, ignorant of the existence of the clause, pressed the Persians in 1882 to assert their claim to authority over the Tekke Turkomans of Sarakhs and Merv, so as to bar the road to Afghanistan to Russia, and the British ambassador at Saint Petersburg took up the question directly with the Russians. But even with British backing, the Persians would not press their claim, and the Russians naturally rejected it. Early in 1884 they annexed Merv.

The struggle between Britain and Russia for political ascendancy in Persia was accompanied in the last quarter of the nineteenth century by increasing commercial rivalry between the two and, on the British side at least, by a number of attempts to open the country up to economic development. Kazemzadeh describes in some detail the principal attempts—the Reuter and Falkenhagen concessions, the Imperial Bank of Persia, the tobacco *regie*, the railway projects, and the monetary loans—and he has a great deal of interesting information to offer on them, especially on the Russian side. Here again, however, his emotional involvement with his material betrays his judgment. Indeed, his hostility to the whole idea of economic exploitation, especially by British entrepreneurs and merchants, is almost as great as that expressed by the Persian government of the day. The constant urging on the shah and his ministers by the British government of the desirability of increasing Persia's foreign trade, in particular by opening the Karun River, was, Kazemzadeh says, merely a blind, concealing political motives. (Russia's motives, in contrast, he notes almost with approval, were always political and never concealed.) But surely there was no duplicity or hypocrisy involved here? The stimulation of trade with Persia was always considered by Britain, from the beginning of the century, as an adjunct to, or a means toward, political ends—in this instance, the strengthening of Persia so that she might serve more effectively as a barrier power to British India. Increased trade—and the regeneration of the Persian economy which would follow—could only assist in the accomplishment of this object, to the benefit both of Persia and of Britain. Moreover, *pace* Professor Kazemzadeh, Britain was not seeking a monopoly, or even the lion's share, of Persia's external trade. On the contrary, she welcomed the participation of other powers in Persian commerce as adding to Persia's security, since these powers would have been reluctant to see their commercial interests and investments in Persia endangered by a Russian ascendancy or occupation. One might well contrast Britain's desire to persuade the Persian government to open the Karun River to the trade of all nations, an object which earns Britain Kazemzadeh's disapprobation, to Russia's action in 1883 in imposing heavy duties on European goods in transit across Russia to Persia and in securing for herself in 1887 a virtual power of veto over the construction of railways in Persia.

Emotional commitment also marks Kazemzadeh's comments upon the various loans to Persia which were negotiated from the last decade of the century onward. Although he himself concedes (and he quotes Sir Frank Lascelles, the British minister at Tehran, as informing the shah's ministers to the same effect in 1892) that it was far more difficult for the British government than it was for the Russian government to lend money from public funds, since the approval of Parliament had to be obtained first, he nevertheless maintains that the British government could have granted the successive loans needed to save Persia from financial subservience to Russia. The accusation has some force to it, but, as the history of the negotiations set down by Kazemzadeh himself reveals, the gravamen of the charge lies elsewhere than with Britain. The government of Muzaffar ud-Din Shah sought its first foreign loan in 1897. In July of the following year, while discussions were in train between the shah's ministers and the British-controlled Imperial Bank of Persia, his former chief minister, the Amin as-Sultan, deliberately sabotaged the negotiation and worked to secure his government's acceptance of a Russian loan instead. Nothing that Sir Mortimer Durand, the British minister at Tehran, could do could dissuade him from his course, and in January 1900 the first Russian loan was contracted, its price being the extension of the moratorium on railway building in Persia for another ten years.

When all is said and done, it was the shah himself and his ministers who sold their country into economic bondage to Russia. Kazemzadeh does not deny this, but he is determined to fix an equal share of the blame upon the British government and in particular upon Durand, largely, it would seem, because the envoy's manner was offensive to the Persians. The Amin as-Sultan, on the other hand, says Kazemzadeh (p. 374), "though selfish and venal, was doing his best to prolong the life of his country, begging and buying for her at least a few years of apparent independence. Iran was still alive, at least in name, and if it had to be kept alive at the expense of British interests, so much the worse for British interests." The logic behind this remark defies understanding. If Britain had had no interests to defend in Persia, the country would have fallen to the Russians long before 1900. Persia's independence, circumscribed and precarious though it was, survived because of Britain's interest in preserving it for the sake of the defense of India. It is simply not true, moreover, to imply, as Kazemzadeh does, that British statesmen were deaf to Persia's appeals for financial aid. Curzon, as viceroy of India, offered a loan of £500,000 from the revenues of India in 1901 to save Persia from falling more heavily into debt to Russia. The shah rejected it and contracted a second Russian loan in 1902. Kazemzadeh, who does not hesitate to denounce Curzon as an imperialist whenever opportunity offers, is silent when it comes to commenting upon his offer. In 1903 the British government, through the Imperial Bank of Persia, offered a loan of £300,000, which was accepted by the shah. It was not enough, however, and within eighteen months the shah was back seeking a new loan. Britain offered him £200,000 but Russia offered more, and the shah accepted it. How then, in the light of these facts, does Kazemzadeh justify his comment on page 472: "Once again no money was forthcoming from the British, and the Persians went, hat in hand, to the Russians."

It is when he comes to the Anglo-Russian detente of 1907 that Kazemzadeh's sense of proportion most markedly deserts him. Although he states that the background to the detente is well known, it is clear from what he writes that he himself understands it only imperfectly. He shows scant appreciation of the role of Germany in determining Britain's actions, he says nothing about Morocco and Algeciras, and he dismisses the growth of Anglo-German naval rivalry and British concern over the Turkish railway question in a few fleeting asides. The absence of reasoned comment upon the forces which shaped the 1907 agreement is hardly compensated for by a string of gratuitous insults and petulant complaints about the British—though not the Russian—statesmen who concluded it. Sir Edward Grey is portrayed as a poltroon, and Sir Arthur Nicolson, who conducted the negotiations at Saint Petersburg, is depicted as an unscrupulous and supine tool of the Russians. "With Nicolson the desire for Russian friendship became an *idee fixe*, an obsession to which he would sacrifice not only abstractions such as truth, fairness, or honor, but at times even the concrete interests of his country. It would seem that he was afflicted with the need to believe in the righteousness of one's allies and the evil of one's enemies" (pp. 482-83). When it comes to condemning the agreement itself, Kazemzadeh rallies to his side a most peculiar phalanx of contemporary critics, including not only men like Curzon and H. Blosse Lynch, whom he has earlier excoriated as imperialists and exploiters, but also such formidable organs of British opinion as "the South Place Ethical Society, the Cowdenheath Branch of the Social-Democratic Federation, the Society of Friends of Russian Freedom (forwarding a resolution adopted at a meeting in Trafalgar Square), the Wales District Council of the Social Democratic Federation, the Oxford Branch of the Independent Labour Party, the Fabian Society at Edinburgh University, and . . . the Streatham Women's Liberal Association" (pp. 504-5).

The last part of Kazemzadeh's book, which covers the years 1907-14, follows much the same pattern as the earlier part. It is marked by a depressing absence of any real effort to relate Britain's actions in Persia to the larger issues of foreign and imperial policy in these years. Little consideration is given to the views expressed by the government of India on strategic questions or to the differences with the imperial government to which these gave rise. Instead, as elsewhere, we are treated to a series of prim complaints about Britain's sins and the infamy of her collaboration with Russia in Persia. This is discussed with barely a single reference to increasing German penetration of the country before 1914. This may possibly be due to Kazemzadeh's having relied more upon Russian than upon British sources for his account of these years. Had he worked more from the Foreign Office and India Office records, he might have achieved a better understanding of British policy, as well as a deeper insight into the characters of Grey, Nicolson, and Charles Hardinge. Possibly, too, if he had not chosen to end his work as abruptly as he began it, but had paused to reflect upon the half century which he has covered, he might have imparted to his work the perspective which it now so sadly lacks.

28
Oman[1]

Oman Since 1856: Disruptive Modernization in a Traditional Arab Society, by Robert Geran Landen. Pp. xvi+488. Tables, maps, bibliography, index. Princeton, New Jersey: Princeton University Press; London: Oxford University Press.

Oman: A History, by Wendell Phillips. Pp. xiv +246. Illustrations, maps, appendices, index. London: Lougmans.

British Interests in the Persian Gulf, by Abdul Amir Amin. Pp. vi + 164. Map, appendices, bibliography. Leiden: E . J. Brill.

'Modernization' is one of the great bugaboo words now in vogue in historical studies of Asia and Africa. Social scientists of various persuasions have so infused the word with recondite qualities that those of us who thought it merely meant 'bringing up to date', or some such simple thing, are now afraid to use it, lest we be thought coarse and untutored. According to the O.E.D., 'modernize' means 'to make or render modern; to give a modern character or appearance to', and the word first appeared in print in 1770. Definitions as plain as these, however, do not satisfy the expositors of the new socio-scientific enlightenment, who have divined in 'modernization' something sublime and esoteric, which those of us who have not been vouchsafed a glimpse of the mystery cannot hope to comprehend. The veil of inscrutability is further darkened by the inability of any two practitioners of the new art to agree upon a definition of 'mod-

---

[1] Source: *Middle Eastern Studies*, Vol. 6, No. 2 (May, 1970), pp. 215-224.

ernization'. Nevertheless, the tyranny of fashion in academic life today is such that the neophyte historian of non-Western societies, if he wishes to be numbered among the elect, is required to make ritual obeisance before the unseen deity—or at least in the direction of the grove in which the deity resides. For the apostles of the new historiography insist that only by applying the nostrums of sociology, anthropology, and psychology to the decayed body of the past shall we be able to restore it to life. Without them, we are assured, we shall continue to stumble along, as we have done, in a Stygian darkness of humanism and intuition. It may well be so, and it may also be, as the proponents of the techniques of the social sciences claim, that we are on the threshold of a historiographical revolution. It may as easily be, however, that we are being asked to subscribe to a grand, academic South Sea bubble.

Stripped down to its essentials, what we are being invited to accept is at best a gross charade, at worst a debasement of scholarship—of knowledge, of thought, of logic, of coherence, of literacy, of grace, wit, and compassion—in the cause of a false egalitarianism, which holds that all literate men are capable of contributing to the sum of historical knowledge, even where the contribution requires the rejection of the canons by which the Western world of learning has lived up to this time. As one struggles through the windy pages of Dr Robert Geran Landen's *Oman Since 1856*, one can only ask wonderingly whatever possessed him to attempt to write a history of a faraway country on the edge of Arabia, only lately revealed to European eyes, in a spirit and from a viewpoint all too plainly manifest in the fashionable jargon of his sub-title, 'Disruptive Modernization in a Traditional Arab Society'. If one applies the simple definition of 'modernization' to Oman in the nineteenth and twentieth centuries, one is forced to conclude that by no stretch of the imagination can the country be said to have been 'modernized' to any discernible extent. Likewise, the disruptions which have taken place there owe their origins not primarily to 'modern' influences but to causes which reach back to the eighteenth century, and even, in some cases, to the Middle Ages. But Dr Landen is not satisfied with such obvious explanations, and has decided to treat Oman as a 'case study', intending thereby to contribute his mite to the growing body of 'modernization' doctrine by discovering some vast, imponderable principle at work behind every commonplace occurrence in Oman over the last century. The consequence is that we are treated to a series of generalizations of exquisite banality, such as this on page 7:

It is, of course, false to portray any modern society and the history it recorded as something static. Change was no less a feature of former times than it is of our own day even if movement was not as rapid or frenzied then as is more often the case now. Still, it is possible to see that events that occurred during a distinct period of time and within a particular locality often developed within an identifiable context, were restricted within definite limits, and normally flowed along certain well-developed channels. So it was with the Persian Gulf in the years before the nineteenth century, when change, although continual, was less sweeping and happenings in the region normally unfolded within an unrevolutionary cultural context which remained relatively constant.

Presumably this last sentence takes in the eighteenth century, which saw the Afghan incursions into Persia, the fall of the Safavi dynasty, the reign of Nadir Shah, the rise and fall of the Zand dynasty, the emergence of the Qajars, the siege and sack of Basra, the growth and spread of the Wahhabi movement, the demise of the Ya'ariba dynasty of Oman, the Persian invasions, and the accession of the Al Bu Sa'id dynasty.

Not content with forcing the history of Oman into a methodological straitjacket, Dr Landen claims for his book the status of a 'pioneering work', 'one based primarily upon Omani chronicles and official archival materials' (p. viii). It is neither of these things. Samuel Barrett Miles was a pioneer in Omani historiography, J. G. Lorimer was a pioneer, Arnold Wilson, Bertram Thomas, and Reginald Coupland were pioneers. Dr Landen is not, nor is his book based primarily upon Omani chronicles. (His use of British official records will be referred to later.) Even the title of his book, in keeping with much of its content, is misleading. Most of it is taken up with events between 1862 and 1903: fewer than 40 pages out of a total of over 400 are devoted to the years since 1903. It would seem, though Dr Landen makes no allusion to it, that the reason for his concentration upon the period in question is that his book is an expanded version of a Ph.D. thesis which he presented to Princeton University some time ago, and which, from the evidence of the sources cited, probably dealt with the years c. 1862 to c. 1880. Certainly there are only sporadic references elsewhere in his book to primary sources for the years outside this period. In an effort presumably to compensate for his book's failure to live up to its title, Dr Landen has felt compelled to wander all over the Persian Gulf, before and after 1856, discoursing at length on a variety of subjects, about the majority of which he displays little knowledge and less understanding

Thus we have, after an introductory survey of Oman and the Gulf from ancient times to 1856, a section entitled 'The Impact of Early Economic and Technological Modernization', which deals with economic development in the Gulf during the nineteenth century and in Oman from 1856 to 1900; another section called 'The Consolidation of British Political Paramountcy in Oman and the Persian Gulf', which purports to be an examination of the period 1862-1903 but which, apparently to demonstrate Dr Landen's versatility, also dwells at length on the first half of the century; and, finally, a section labelled 'Oman's political accommodation to a New Age', a rambling, semi-political history of the country from 1856 to 1903, to which has been tacked a hasty epilogue covering the next sixty years.

It is evident that such a system must, of itself, lead to repetition, and indeed repetitiousness is an outstanding characteristic of Dr Landen's work. But this quality is not attributable to poor organization alone, for Dr Landen seems unable to recall, from page to page, or even from paragraph to paragraph, what he has written before. For instance, on page 236 he writes of British political officers in the Gulf: 'Prior to the 1890s most personnel destined for important Gulf billets were given long periods of on-the-job training in the region as junior officials.' A paragraph later he writes (referring to the eighteen-nineties): 'During this period the Anglo-Indian government in general lacked sufficient numbers of officials who were trained in Oriental languages and who possessed intimate knowledge of the peoples whom they ruled; it was not until this century that the importance of such training was admitted.' Now it must be one or the other: either the importance of training was recognized before the eighteen nineties (as Dr Landen implies), or it was not (as Dr Landen also indicates). The truth, as he should have discovered, is that it was. Inconsistencies of this kind abound in the book, and, in combination with a wearisome profusion of gaucheries and jejune comments, not to mention a lamentable prose style, they make the reading of it an exercise in tedium. Matters are made even worse by Dr Landen's ignorance of, or refusal to use, commonly accepted geographical and political terms. So he gives us 'the around-Africa route' for the 'Cape route (or passage)', 'the Anglo-Indian government' for 'the Government of India', 'the Britain-Levant and India-Persian Gulf-Iraq route' for 'the "direct" route', and 'the India-Europe telegraph' for 'the Indo-European telegraph' (which becomes in one place 'the Europe-to-India Indo-European telegraph'!). The infelicities and solecisms are not made any more palatable by a frequent recourse to phrases which belong more to the pages of *Time* magazine than to a scholarly work from a university press, *e.g.* 'at the top level of policy determination responsible Whitehall officials' (p. 171), 'a new, soon to conquer philosophy—the "new imperialism" of the "white man's burden" subvariety'(p. 185), and 'also during the Pelly period a British image of Oman was solidified' (p. 203).

If Dr Landen's book had any merit, one would expect to find it either in his account of 'economic and technological modernization' in the Gulf between 1862 and 1903, or in his history of Oman in these years. The selection of 1862 as a critical date is justified by Dr Landen on the grounds that this was the year in which a regular steamship service to the Gulf ports was inaugurated'. . . This spread of modern technology', he goes on to say (p. 271), 'was the main cause of the eclipse of Oman's commercial and maritime vitality and of the undermining of the economic foundations that supported the political apparatus of the moderate Ibadi regime which ruled Oman's coast and which claimed overlordship over Oman's interior.' Surely the death of the great Saiyid Sa'id ibn Sultan in 1856, and the formal separation of Zanzibar from Oman five years later, were events of far greater consequence in the modern history of Oman than the advent of European steamers in the Gulf? Dr Landen makes passing mention of the loss of Zanzibar, the suppression of the slave trade, and the loss in revenue for Oman which they occasioned, but he fails to accord them their proper weight, being more concerned to construct a theory of his own about 'technological modernization'. So, he insists that the reasons for Oman's economic decline lay in Muscat's lost pre-eminence as the centre of the Gulf's trade and in the drastic reduction of her merchant fleet. But Muscat had long ceased to occupy an important place in the trade of the Gulf before 1861 or 1862, and her fleet had begun to rot at its moorings twenty years earlier. If Dr Landen's theory is correct, why did the trade and shipping of Bahrain, Kuwait, and the Persian ports not suffer comparably from the advent of steamships in the Gulf, instead of continuing to prosper?

The portrait of the economy of the Gulf and Oman drawn by Dr Landen in Part II of his book is muddled, contradictory, repetitive, and alarmingly inaccurate, a pastiche of ill-digested information, uncorrelated trade returns, and ludicrous guesswork. According to Dr Landen (p. 97), the Gulf's external trade in the eighteen-thirties 'was worth roughly £3,500,000'. It was not: the very sources which he has used indicate that its value was about £1,000,000. Again, Dr Landen states (*loc. cit.*) that the Gulf's external trade in 1866 was valued at £5,000,000. Again, it was not: the sources he has used show that it was worth less than £3,000,000. By 1869, he says (p. 107), the trade was valued at £6,000,000. The Persian Gulf Residency Annual Administration Report for 1874-75 gives the value of the Gulf's trade with India in 1869-70 as Rs. 2,77,09,647, or roughly

£2,500,000. It is highly unlikely that the trade of the Gulf with places other than India in that year was worth £3,500,000. Dr Landen has one nearly correct figure, that of £6,000,000 for the year 1899 (his source actually says £17,241,300 for the years 1895, 1896 and 1897), but the conclusion which he draws from it, viz., that it is 'proof of the general stagnation of Gulf trade and economic life' between 1869 and 1899, is sadly awry.

As the hero of his drama of 'modernization' in Oman and the Gulf Dr Landen has chosen Lieutenant-Colonel Lewis Pelly, the Political Resident in the Gulf from 1862 to 1873. 'It was the spirit of his administration—Pelly's desire that Britain should provide beacons to guide a modernizing Gulf—that was his most enduring legacy', writes Dr Landen (p. 183). '. . . He was in the vanguard of . . . the "new imperialism"—his successes multiplied as his term as resident progressed' (pp. 184-85). And, in case the reader has not grasped the full significance of this statement, Dr Landen repeats it two paragraphs later: 'Pelly was in the vanguard of the "new imperialism".' This is all very interesting but it is far from being an accurate assessment of Pelly's motives and accomplishments. An ambitious and irascible man, vindictive towards his subordinates and servile towards his superiors, Pelly's principal concern was with advancing his own career. Dr Landen is somewhat more accurate in characterizing Sir Bartle Frere, Governor of Bombay in the eighteen-sixties, as a disciple of the 'new imperialism', and it was Frere who appointed Pelly to the Gulf Residency. Dr Landen sees great significance in the appointment. Frere, he says, wanted a Resident who would carry out Britain's civilizing mission to the Gulf's rulers, would increase her influence among them, and guide but not force them to follow modern, enlightened practices. Frere also believed, however, Dr Landen continues (p. 179), that 'a good resident should not give the appearance of meddling in a prince's internal administration but should watch all that went on in a given principality'. Two pages later Dr Landen writes: 'With Pelly's appointment to the Persian Gulf residency a new period opened in Britain's connection with the region, a period marked by increasing British interference in the internal politics of the Gulf states.' Obviously something has gone wrong here: either Frere was mistaken in his man or Dr Landen is confused. The truth lies somewhere between the two. Frere had no great plan in mind when he appointed Pelly to the Gulf Residency: he merely wished to find him a suitable post. It was a simple case of patronage. Pelly's restless disposition and propensity for meddling, especially in the affairs of Oman, contributed to the increasing British involvement in the politics of the Gulf after 1862; but there were other causes, outside either Pelly's or Frere's ability to control, which forced the

British government into this position.

Dr Landen's whole account of Pelly's tenure of the Gulf Residency is marked by confusion. Because, as observed earlier, he imperfectly understands the nature of British policy in the Gulf before 1862 he credits Pelly with innovations in policy where he made none. Conversely, Dr Landen fails both to realize when Pelly departed from established policy—usually with disastrous results—and to discover his motives for doing so. He has not grasped the essential features of the British alliance with Muscat in the first half of the century, he is unaware of the limitations placed upon it by successive interpretations of its treaty basis, he is unsure of what those treaties were and of their import, he thinks that the *qaulnamah* of 1798, concluded to deny the French the use of Muscat during the Revolutionary War, was still operative in the late nineteenth century, and he does not understand why Oman was excluded from the Trucial system. With handicaps such as these it is not surprising that the core of his book, Oman from 1862 to 1903, should be riddled with misconceptions and errors. Because (as he reveals early in his book) he misunderstands the origin and character of the Hinawi-Ghafiri factionalism which dominated Omani political life, he interprets the unrest which swept Oman from the eighteen-sixties to 1920 almost wholly in terms of Ibadi particularism, paying scant attention to the personal, secular ambitions of the territorial chieftains who led the movement for a revival of the Ibadi Imamate. A similar lopsidedness characterizes his version of the Anglo-French dispute over Muscat in the late eighteen-nineties. He misjudges to a large extent the character of the Imam 'Azzan ibn Qais (1868-71), and underestimates the changes which took place in his government with the passage of time. He misconstrues many of the actions taken by the government of India in Oman, and he fails to convey—if, indeed, he realizes—the intense interest taken by the Imperial Government in Oman's affairs. At times Dr Landen seems to take an almost perverse satisfaction in reaching an arbitrary conclusion in the face of solid evidence to the contrary. He writes, for example, of 'Azzan's successor, the Sultan Turki ibn Sa'id (1871-88), that his 'pacification of Oman during the winter of 1875-76 marked the finish of the initial, chronically unstable, period of his rule' (p. 334). Yet little more than a year later Turki went through the most severe crisis of his reign, when he was besieged in Muscat by rebels who would have taken the town had it not been for British naval intervention—an episode noticed listlessly by Dr Landen in a brief paragraph.

When one might reasonably have expected to find fresh and interesting information in Dr Landen's book, *e.g.* on the restoration of the Ibadi

Imamate in 1913, there is none, even though he says he has consulted a history of the Imamate from 1913 to 1955 written by a son of the Ibadi historian and original chronicler of the Imamate movement, 'Abdullah ibn Humaid al-Salimi. In fact, Dr Landen's whole account of the history of Oman in this century is so thin as to be useless. To judge from his bibliography, he has neglected to consult Wilfred Thesiger's articles in the *Geographical Journal,* Sir Ronald Wingate's autobiography, the United Nations (de Ribbing) report of 1963, the 1951 Anglo-Muscati treaty, the 1958 agreement, and the United States treaty of 1959. These last four items, and the occasions for them, are not even mentioned in the text.

As a guide to the available sources for the modern history of Oman Dr Landen's bibliography, although it extends to twenty-seven pages, leaves much to be desired. He omits several important items and his annotations are of doubtful value. Is it really true, for instance, as he says (p. 431), that 'the collections of the Foreign Office archive are better sources for the twentieth century history of the Persian Gulf than are those in the Indian Office Library'? (One assumes that Dr Landen means the India Office Records: although they are administered jointly with the Library, the Records constitute a separate deposit.) Again, a few lines later, he states: 'The richest and most complete collection of material dealing with Persian Gulf events prior to 1947 reputedly is in the National Archives of the Government of India in New Delhi. For Persian Gulf affairs consult the "Proceedings of the Government of India in the Foreign Department". The "Proceedings" supposedly contain much material sent as enclosures that was never forwarded to London.' 'Reputedly', 'supposedly': what place is there in a critical bibliography for speculations such as these? Copies of the *Foreign Proceedings* of the Government of India were, in fact, forwarded to London in their entirety in the last century and this. Dr Landen could have consulted them, had he wished, in the India Office Records. As for the records relating to the Gulf in New Delhi, Dr Ravinder Kumar, who used them for his book, *India and the Persian Gulf Region, 1858-1907* (New York, 1965), a work of greatly superior quality to Dr Landen's, has nothing to say about their 'richness' in comparison with those in London.

Dr Landen's comments on the various *Précis* compiled in the Foreign Department of the Government of India in the first decade of this century in preparation for the *Gazetteer of the Persian Gulf, 'Oman, and Central Arabia,* are inept and misleading. Either he has not read them thoroughly or he is incapable of judging their worth and reliability. That the latter is the more likely explanation is indicated by his comments upon a number of the works listed in his bibliography, and upon two of them, in particular, *viz.*, the memorial presented by Sa'udi Arabia to the Buraimi arbitration tribunal in 1955, and a volume entitled *Oman and the Southern Shore of the Persian Gulf*, prepared by the research division of the Arabian American Oil Company in 1952. Of the memorial Dr Landen writes: 'A major source for the modern history of eastern Arabia, based on Arabic as well as European materials ... (It) contains much unique information on the economic, and social, as well as political structure, along Oman's borderlands.' It certainly does: indeed, the information is so 'unique' that it is not to be found in any other source for the history of eastern Arabia, not even those upon which the memorial is supposedly based.

Of the Aramco work Dr Landen remarks: 'One of the few really important secondary works on Oman ... Although prepared in the early 1950s when the dispute over eastern Arabia's frontiers was heating up, this book is remarkably free of bias and argumentative statements.' It is not an opinion shared by Dr Wendell Phillips, another American historian of Oman, who writes in his *Oman: A History* (pp. 175-6):

> To say the least, this volume hardly qualifies as an innocuous work of disinterested scholarship, in spite of the assertion on page ix of the preface, that 'The information contained herein will be of value to those who are actively engaged in the endeavour to settle the boundary problems that now exist; it will also serve a wider purpose in providing those interested in Arabian affairs with an opportunity to become familiar with one of the least known corners of the Peninsula.' This work was subsequently withdrawn from circulation and is available only to the Saudi Arabian government and such departments of Aramco which have been able to retain copies.

Could it be, Dr Phillips goes on to speculate, in a fine show of wide-eyed innocence, that Aramco had another purpose in mind in putting together this volume of 'entirely biased information, based on preconception, selected truths, halftruths or no truths'? Obviously Dr Landen does not think so. Perhaps some day Aramco will permit the work a wider circulation, thereby accomplishing the 'wider purpose' claimed for it by its anonymous authors?

Dr Wendell Phillips, who has achieved something of a reputation as an archaeologist, historian, philologist, oil magnate, philanthropist, economic consultant, and intrepid traveller, is a much more entertaining writer than Dr Landen, though he is hardly any more reliable as a historian—notwithstanding the engagingly extravagant claim in the preface of his book that 'he has drawn unreservedly from among the world's outstanding Near Eastern scholars, Orientalists, Arabists and Arabian military and political specialists to present in *Oman: A History* the truest, clearest and most exact picture of the events and times thus described'. There follows a list of some five dozen individuals and institutions to whom Dr Phillips professes to be indebted, some of whom no doubt will be surprised to find themselves so acknowledged. Generously, Dr Phillips also thanks his eight secretaries 'for their patience over a period of eight years in typing and re-typing this manuscript as it slowly evolved into *Oman: A History*'. Carried away by the general euphoria, his publishers go further and ecstatically declare his book to be 'authoritative in its presentation of facts, exhaustive in its documentation, and fascinating in its detail'. After all this one can only feel churlish for finding fault with a work in which so many people take so much pride. But, alas, it must be reported that what Dr Phillips has given us is not so much a history of Oman, 'authoritative and exhaustive', as an anecdotal excursion into the country's past, tricked out with gaudy bits of parascholarship.

Perhaps the most distinctive feature of the book is its utter lack of proportion. In a volume of fewer than 250 pages, which purports to relate the history of Oman over the past 2,000 years, page after page is given over to rambling discourses on a variety of unrelated topics, the only criterion for whose inclusion would seem to be that they took Dr Phillips's fancy. For example, chapter 5, on Saiyid Sa'id ibn Sultan and the slave trade, is largely composed of lengthy descriptions of the sufferings endured by the slaves on their journey to the East African coast and on the voyage to Oman, a subject which seems to hold for Dr Phillips a certain fascination. Of Saiyid Sa'id, the greatest of the Al Bu Sa'id rulers, he writes with minimal understanding, and his failure to deal with the serious and important issues of Sa'id's reign is not compensated for by the fulsome and indiscriminate praise which he lavishes upon that prince, or by the melodramatic flourishes with which he embellishes his narrative.

In addition to his addiction to digressions Dr Phillips has a fondness for Arabian proverbs of a singularly unilluminating kind, *e.g.* 'He shall take who has the power, and he shall keep who can' (p. 78); and 'Beware of cowardice, which is a base and not a noble quality' (p. 70). This same page also contains a good example of the type of portentous statement, usually at odds with the context, which occurs frequently in the book. Here, in the middle of a description of the early history of the Al Bu Sa'id dynasty, we are told: 'The identity in Islam between empire and faith was never more clearly stated than in the British [sic] East India Company's minutes of 1793 where it was written that "the sending of missionaries into our Eastern possessions is the maddest, most extravagant and most unwarrantable project that has ever been proposed by an enthusiastic lunatic".' Doubtless some awful and profound significance attaches to these juxtaposed assertions, but whatever it is it completely eludes this reviewer.

One charge that cannot be levelled against Dr Phillips is that of neglecting twentieth century Oman, as Dr Landen has done. A good third of his book is devoted to this century, most of it, regrettably, of mixed quality. The most interesting item is a description by Dr Wells Thoms, of the American medical mission at Matrah, of a visit to the late Imam Muhammad ibn 'Abdullah al-Khalili in 1941. The least valuable is Dr Phillips's own account of Oman's relations with Sa'udi Arabia and the dispute between them over their common frontier, an account which combines confusion with a certain amount of unacknowledged borrowing. Dr Phillips is not much better on the rebellion against the Sultan's rule in 1957, where his lack of a sense of proportion leads him to devote ten times as much space to describing the activities of the Sultan, who failed to suppress the revolt, as he does to those of the British, who succeeded in doing so. However, we must be thankful for the fact that even in describing the events of those desperate days Dr Phillips's penchant for the incongruous and the absurd does not desert him; for smack in the midst of the heat and smoke of battle at Nizwa comes a solemn disquisition on the cooking of *halwah*, 'in consistency (but not in flavour) reminiscent of a gumdrop'. Exactly.

Dr Phillips writes less as a historian of Oman than as a self-appointed public relations officer for the Sultanate. Perhaps this should not be wondered at. After all, he describes himself on the title page of his book as 'Economic Adviser and Representative for His Majesty the King of Oman and Dependencies', and he owes a good deal to the present Sultan, Sa'id ibn Taimur, who some years ago graciously bestowed upon him an unsolicited oil concession, an occasion which Dr Phillips touchingly recounted in his *Unknown Oman*, published in 1966. But even as a p.r.o. he does not do very well. His categorization of the rebel movement in Oman as being the work of a few ambitious chieftains and disaffected tribesmen, while correct enough in itself, would carry more weight if it were accompanied by some hint of the deficiencies in the Sultan's administration. Oman is a difficult country to govern, and needs the hand of a ruler who is strong, just and wise. Saiyid Sa'id ibn Taimur has not shown himself to be conspicuously rich in these qualities, and Dr Phillips's foolish adulation of him cannot obscure this fact. It might even be that the Sultan would welcome some judicious criticism; for as Dr Phillips himself tells us (p. 220), with the reverence accorded holy writ, the Sultan wrote to him during the 1957 rebellion, observing weightily, 'Criticism makes one the wiser'.

If Drs Landen's and Phillips's ambitions are large, Dr Abdul Amir Amin's are modest, which is perhaps why his book succeeds where theirs fail dismally. Dr Amin is concerned to trace the growth of British commercial and political interests in the Gulf from the death of Nadir Shah in 1747 to the mid-1770s, at which point his book somewhat vaguely peters out in the Persian siege and sack of Basra. He has drawn his material primarily from the India Office Records, and his account both supplements and corrects that given by J. G. Lorimer in the historical volume of the *Gazetteer of the Persian Gulf, 'Oman, and Central Arabia*. Although there is no mention of it anywhere, Dr Amin's book presumably began life as a Ph.D. thesis at the University of London, and one would judge that it appears now in substantially the same form as it was submitted for examination. It lacks both a preface and an index, and the only map it contains is a reproduction of Carsten Niebuhr's map of the Gulf in 1765, the inclusion of which in books on the Gulf published lately seems to have become mandatory.

Whatever its defects, however, Dr Amin's book is to be welcomed as a creditable work of historical scholarship. By the time of Nadir Shah's death the East India Company's position in the Gulf was fairly secure. The Portuguese had gone, the Dutch had lost their power in these seas, and the French were of little consequence. Up to this time the Company had concentrated its attention upon trade, but in the breakdown of order in the Gulf which followed Nadir Shah's death, as rival chieftains struggled for power on the Persian mainland and Arab tribes from both shores fought to inherit the Persian fleet, and with it to attain maritime supremacy in the Gulf, the Company was drawn, much against its will, into partisan relationships, military compacts, and political negotiations with successive contestants. Dr Amin believes that the Company's involvement in the politics of the Gulf was inevitable, the natural consequence of the consolidation of its power in India through territorial conquest and of the anarchical condition of the Gulf; in fact, he even suggests that the Company sought this involvement. But the very evidence which he presents belies this assertion, and he himself contradicts it at several places in his book.

It is here, in his judgments and conclusions, that the great weakness of Dr Amin's book lies; for he has the disconcerting habit of plucking a generalization from the air and then of contradicting it a short time afterwards. Thus, on page 78 he chides the Court of Directors of the Company for not having taken the opportunity to ally themselves with the Zand ruler, Karim Khan, against the brutal freebooter, Mir Mahanna of Bandar Rig; yet only a page later he writes, '. . . So long as Mir Mahanna did not attack the Company's ships they could see no reason to be involved in serious trouble with him.' Further down the same page he makes the point even more strongly: 'They [the Court] pointed out that unstable conditions in Persia made them doubt that the influence of Karim Khan would continue and therefore it was not advisable to assist him and quarrel with the Arab tribes. Furthermore, the bad experiences they had had in Persia made them desirous of avoiding any political involvement with the Persians.' Again, on page 84, writing of the increase in the Company's influence in the Pashaliq of Baghdad after 1750, he says: '. . . It did not assume political control such as it did on the Carnatic coast, partly because of the Levant Company's jealousy.' A few sentences further on, however, he writes, 'Also, the only interest other than trade which the British had in the Pashaliq of Baghdad was its position on the overland route'; and later in the same paragraph, 'Added to this, the East India Company itself was mainly interested in the trade. The interference in Company trade which was an important reason for the conflict between the British and the native princes in India did not exist in Basra. The Turks had presented no handicap to the Company's trade and so there was no reason for the Company to permit its employees to assume political control.'

The reason for these inconsistencies is not difficult to discern: Dr Amin has decided, as he puts it on page 92, that 'the early nineteenth century British policy of stabilizing the Gulf and maintaining effective British control had its conception at this very time in the eighteenth century' (*i.e.* between 1767 and 1773), and he has perforce to uphold this contention throughout, even where the facts are against him. For the truth of the matter is that the Company did not, nor did it aspire to, exert political control over the Gulf in the late eighteenth century. The real contest for supremacy during this period was waged by the maritime States of the Arabian shore—Muscat, Bahrain, and the Qasimi shaikhdoms of the Pirate Coast—with whose fortunes, as he candidly admits, Dr Amin is not concerned. So far as the East India Company was concerned, its interests remained predominantly commercial, as Dr Amin himself states in his closing chapter: 'Trade was the principal concern of the British in the Persian Gulf for their whole history there prior to 1778, and their military and political activities described in the previous chapters were mainly directed to promote and protect that trade.' Nothing could be plainer than this, yet it is at odds with Dr Amin's general thesis. Since he is too honest a scholar to shape his evidence to suit his thesis, he has no choice but to live with the anomalies to which his persistence in that thesis gives rise.

There still remains much of value in his work. He has the fullest account which has yet appeared in English of the activities of the Dutch in the Gulf, and he gives an entertaining portrayal of the idiosyncratic behaviour of the British representatives at Basra, who were ever involving themselves in quarrels with the Turkish authorities. Dr Amin also provides fresh information on the transmission of mails by the desert route, and corrects much of what has been written on the subject to date. His greatest achievement is the coherent description which he gives of the Gulf's trade, and how valuable it was to the East India Company in the 1750s and 1760s in helping to overcome the crisis caused in Bengal in those decades by the shortage of specie. As he remarks on page 134, 'Indeed, after thirty or forty years, India was able to recover by means of trade a large part of the wealth which Nadir Shah had taken from her by the sword'.

But the drain of specie from the Gulf also helped accelerate the decline in its trade which set in in the late 1770s, and which was brought on initially by the Russo-Turkish War and by the devastation wrought in Turkish Iraq by plague and the Persian capture of Basra. In the ensuing economic depression it was the Company's trade, and the private trade of its officials, which suffered, not the country trade of India and the Gulf; so that by the last decade of the century, although ships of British registers till participated in the Gulf's carrying trade, the bulk of its commerce and shipping was in the hands of Arab and Indian merchants. The Company had lost virtually all interest in the Gulf, and it might well have withdrawn completely from the area had it not been forced by Bonaparte's expedition to Egypt and by the outbreak of piracy on a massive scale on the Arabian shore to assume a political role in the Gulf such as it had never played before.

One failing which the three books under review have in common is the inability of their authors to portray in the round the British officials, soldiers and statesmen who pass through their pages. Dr Landen does not understand them at all, although he thinks that he does. Dr Phillips understands them better, but allows his own personality and his romantic predilections to get in the way of that understanding. Dr Amin does not pretend to understand them, and so they remain for him shadow figures on a blank screen. Both Dr Landen and Dr Phillips have their pretensions about the significance of their work—unlike Dr Amin—but the undercurrent of rancour and the tone of magisterial pomposity in Dr Landen's book make it the more objectionable of the two. An older generation of American scholars of British Imperial history both knew and understood the characters and nature of the men who governed and served the Empire, and they were able to convey that understanding in lucid fashion and in decent prose. The new men, among whom Dr Landen seems anxious to number himself, secure, and even arrogant, in the armour of the new learning, scorn the requirements of lucidity and grammatical English, and they appear also to scorn the historian's requirements of emotional balance, intellectual depth, and experience of men and affairs. It would do them no harm to reflect for a moment that particular qualities of mind and temperament are required to do justice to the past and to the shades of the dead. The gewgaws of indices, parameters and matrices will not suffice.

About the Author

Professor John Barrett Kelly was one of the foremost commentators on the Middle East, and noted for his independence of mind; along with Bernard Lewis, PJ Vatikiotis and Elie Kedourie he was one of the so-called "Gang of Four," pre-eminent scholars in the field who believed that Western policy towards the Arab world was distorted by sentimental illusions—notably, that it mistook the tyranny imposed by Arab nationalist regimes for progress.

As such Kelly was occasionally accused of being pro-Zionist. That was a simple error. He was critical of both Arab and Israeli actions at different times. His real admiration was for the British imperial servants, generally in the India Office, who had brought stability and genuine progress to Arabia and the Gulf. His real contempt was for the British and American governments who had appeased weak anti-imperial challengers, betraying their own diplomats, their sheikhly regional allies, and the subjects of repressive Arab rulers in turn.

Despite his distaste for Arab nationalist dictators, he was no supporter of the recent Iraq War. In fact, he was a strong critic of both the military campaign and of Tony Blair's statesmanship in general.

He took the view that the war had been embarked on almost frivolously, with neither a clear justification in terms of British or Western interests nor a clear idea of how its outcome would advance them. He saw it as an expression of a messianic thoughtlessness on Blair's part—and, in some respects, as the fitting climax to decades of Western policies based on fanciful illusions about the Arab world.

He did at various times, however, have some measure of influence over those policies; first over British strategy in the Arabian peninsula in the 1950s and 1960s, and then, after a move to Washington, over American Middle Eastern policy in the 1980s.

That influence came after Kelly, a professional historian, published his second book—*Britain and the Persian Gulf 1795-1880* (1968)—which established him as the leading academic authority on the history of the region. At that time his detailed knowledge of border disputes and maritime treaties in the Gulf led to his advice being sought both by the Foreign Office and local sheikhdoms.

But his robust belief that the Gulf benefited greatly from a stabilising British military and political presence ensured that he would exercise less and less influence over British policy as London relinquished its role east of Suez in the 1970s. For their part, however, local emirates continued to seek his advice and support and to relish his deep knowledge of their own histories.

Kelly was born in Auckland, New Zealand, on April 5 1925, the son of a chemist. When John was two years old his father died, and he was brought up by a succession of nuns and aunts while his mother worked as a hotel receptionist.

She scraped together enough money to send him to Sacred Heart College, the renowned local Catholic boys' school, where he showed early promise as a scholar. He went to University College, Auckland, aged 16, reading Geology before switching to History and Literature.

In 1943, when he was 18, Kelly tried to enlist in the Royal New Zealand Air Force, but his poor eyesight let him down. He had asked a friend to memorise the eye chart, but when he went in for his medical and reeled off the letters before him, he was pronounced unfit. The doctor had switched the chart.

Instead Kelly spent his summers during the war working on the docks in Auckland and helping to build aerodrome hangars for the American Air Force, which had bases in northern New Zealand for its island-hopping campaign in the Pacific. After the war he qualified as a schoolteacher and taught until 1951 in schools in New Zealand, Queensland, England and Egypt. It was in Alexandria that he met and married Valda Elizabeth Pitt – he was teaching at the British Boys' School and she at the English Girls' College.

His experience of Egypt at the end of King Farouk's reign sparked a lifelong interest in the Middle East. He would quote Talleyrand to describe life in postwar Alexandria—those who never experienced it had no idea of "la douceur de vivre."

Returning to England, and disillusioned with teaching, he decided to sit for a higher degree. Since the Auckland BA was not recognised by

About the Author

London University, he had to pass papers in Latin and Anglo-Saxon and Medieval History, under the stern but kindly eye of Professor Bindoff of Queen Mary's College, London, in order to qualify for a London University BA.

He was then accepted by Professor William Norton Medlicott to take an MA at the LSE. Realising Kelly's potential, Medlicott encouraged him to do a PhD on Britain and the Persian Gulf, which was to become his field of expertise.

After receiving his doctorate in 1956, Kelly became a research fellow at the Institute of Colonial Studies at Oxford University until 1958, under the guidance of Sir Reader Bullard, British Ambassador to Iran during the Second World War, and a British minister to Saudi Arabia in the 1930s. It was with the encouragement of Bullard, who was to become his mentor, that Kelly made his first trip to the Gulf in 1957.

He visited Iraq in the dying days of the Hashemite regime and then flew on to the Trucial Coast—known in the 19th century as the Pirate Coast, and now forming the United Arab Emirates. The only Europeans in Abu Dhabi at that time were either oil men, diplomats or soldiers.

The British political officer introduced him to Sheikh Shakhbut before taking him to see his brother, Sheikh Zayid. Kelly was to form a firm friendship with both men, which was to survive the political turmoil in Abu Dhabi in the following two decades.

He paid a particularly instructive visit to the Buraimi Oasis, from where British-officered Trucial Scouts had ejected an American-backed Saudi force (engaged on an oil-grabbing mission) in 1955. He and the political officer, Martin Buckmaster, soon picked up signs that the Saudis were retaliating by stirring up the tribes of inner Oman with arms and money. Kelly passed this information on to the British political resident in Bahrain, Sir Bernard Burrows, who discounted it, coming as it did from a Gulf novice.

Burrows returned on leave to London, only to be called back to the Gulf in a hurry in July 1957 when the Imamate rebellion broke out in Oman. Kelly's first publication, written for Chatham House, was a paper on the revolt.

His growing expertise on the tribes of Eastern Arabia was soon in demand by the Foreign Office, which hired him to advise on the long-disputed boundaries between the Trucial sheikhdoms, Oman and Saudi Arabia. His first book, *Eastern Arabian Frontiers* (1964), was based on this work.

In the meantime he had left Oxford, partly out of distaste at the academic milieu of the newly-founded Middle East Centre at St Antony's College. After expressing concern at a dinner about the tenor of the reports on Middle Eastern politics from Kim Philby, the spy who was then The Economist's correspondent in Beirut, Kelly was told that "he was not fit to clean Philby's boots."

He left for a series of teaching posts at Wesleyan College in Delaware, Ohio; the University of Michigan at Ann Arbor; and the University of Wisconsin at Madison, where he became Professor of Imperial History and published his magnum opus, *Britain and the Persian Gulf, 1795-1880*.

As Britain withdrew from Aden in 1967 and prepared to withdraw from the Gulf in 1971, Kelly left academia and became an adviser to Sheikh Zayid of Abu Dhabi on the issue of its disputed frontiers with Qatar and Saudi Arabia. Coming up against the increasingly pro-Saudi alignment of both Britain and America, Kelly fought hard to make the best case for Abu Dhabi's retention of the Khawr al-Udayd inlet on the marches of Qatar. This was coveted by the Saudis as an outlet to the lower Gulf. In addition, they sought to control the tract of desert south of the Liwa Oasis, which contained the newly-discovered Zarrara/Shaiba oilfield, then the largest strike in the world.

In the end Kelly was thwarted by the murky compromises of Arab and international politics. This experience left him more convinced than ever that Britain's hasty withdrawal from the Gulf had destabilised the region, leaving the smaller states prey to the territorial ambitions of their larger neighbours, Saudi Arabia, Iraq and Iran, and the West open to oil blackmail, a view later vindicated by events.

This opinion was not popular in Whitehall or the City, where eyes could appear more firmly fixed on recycling the flow of petrodollars through arms sales and lavish infrastructure projects. But it seemed to find a ready audience with Margaret Thatcher, then leader of the opposition. Further encouraged by Elie Kedourie and David Pryce-Jones, Kelly outlined his stance in his most accessible book, *Arabia, the Gulf and the West* (1980).

This publication made a great impact in Washington, where the incoming Reagan administration was searching for a new, more robust policy in the Gulf. As a visiting research fellow at the Woodrow Wilson Centre and the Heritage Foundation in Washington in the early 1980s, Kelly's advice on the region was sought by administration officials, senators, congressmen, journalists and think-tanks. He was directly involved in lobbying against the sale of AWACs early-warning aircraft to Saudi Arabia, arguing that it would further destabilise the region. But as Saudi influence

About the Author

grew in Washington with Reagan's forging of an informal alliance with the kingdom, Kelly's influence inevitably declined. His prescient warnings that Saudi money was being used to establish an international network of Muslim fundamentalists were thus largely ignored.

Subsequently, he advised the government of Oman on its disputed frontiers with Saudi Arabia and South Yemen, paying trips to inner Oman, Dhofar and the Masandam Peninsula.

When not advising governments, Kelly beavered away in the National Archives in Washington and the Public Record Office in London, collecting material for a book on Anglo-American relations with Saudi Arabia from 1926 to 1956, which he was never to complete.

Kelly left Washington in 1988 and the following year retired with his wife to south-western France. Although keeping up with events in the Middle East, and being asked on innumerable occasions to return to the Gulf and Washington, he preferred a quiet existence of reading and reflection. He kept himself fit playing tennis until his last years, despite his poor eyesight.

A man of great courtesy, he established for himself and his family a life of some style, though without extravagance, and was himself always immaculately turned out, with an unhurried manner which perfectly suited his innate conservatism. He recalled in retirement the prediction of his French Jesuit teacher in Auckland that he would end his days in France, a country that he always loved.

John Barrett Kelly died on August 29, 2009.

This volume was edited by his son, Dr Saul B. Kelly, a Reader in International History in the Defence Studies Department of King's College, London at the Joint Services Command and Staff College, which he joined in September 2001. Publications include *War and Politics in the Desert*, (Society for Libyan Studies, 2010) *The Hunt for Zerzura: The Lost Oasis and the Desert War* (John Murray, 2002); *Cold War in the Desert. Britain, the United States and the Italian Colonies, 1945 52* (Macmillan, 2000); Co-editor with A. Gorst, *Whitehall and the Suez Crisis* (Frank Cass, 2000).

Index

A

Abdul Aziz I Ibn Saud, Amir of Najd and King of Saudi Arabia, 21-22, 33-34, 37, 89, 216, 280, 287

Abu Dhabi, 18, 23, 25-26, 30, 35-39, 68-76, 78, 90, 92, 138-139, 150, 152, 161, 227, 229, 345-346

Aden, 9, 15, 17, 25, 28, 31, 77, 100, 107, 109, 127, 130-131, 142, 155, 182-189, 191, 210-216, 218, 224, 227, 229, 235-238, 299-301, 346

Aesop, 11, 89, 92, 192

Africa, 17-18, 23, 83-84, 109, 159, 236, 256, 286, 296-297, 303, 306, 308-309, 313, 327, 330, 336

Al-Afghani, Sayyid Jamal ad-Din, 312-315

Al-Dhahirah, western district of Oman, 31, 34-35, 75, 79-80, 84, 88-90

Alexandria, 13, 120, 125, 148, 166, 171, 174, 344,

Al-Hasa (Eastern Arabia), 21, 70, 89, 93, 119, 121-123, 125, 129-132, 140, 147-148, 165-168, 170-172, 175, 177, 201-203, 205-206, 216, 217, 228, 242-244, 287, 304

Al-Naim tribe, 34-39, 70, 89-90, 162

Arabian Frontiers, 14, 24, 34, 36-37, 44, 67-68, 71-72, 76-78, 187, 229, 335, 345-347

Arab nationalism, 9, 14, 91, 183, 185, 190-191, 193, 216-219, 222, 228, 281, 298-299, 301, 312

Arab Slave Trade, 18-19, 21, 23, 55, 83-88, 107, 187, 202, 220, 249, 267, 306, 308-309, 317, 31, 336

ARAMCO (Arabian-American Oil Company), 14, 99, 114, 198-201, 204, 208, 335

Arms Traffic, 93-94, 98, 151, 154, 159, 163-165, 171, 184, 186, 197, 213, 220-221, 255, 269, 285, 317, 321, 345-346

Asia, 17, 89, 109, 210, 254-257, 259-261, 277, 286-287, 292-293, 296-297, 307, 312-313, 321-322, 327

Auckland, Lord, 126-127, 129-130, 136-138, 140-143, 145-146, 153-155, 157, 163-165, 167-170, 174-176, 178

B

Ba'ath Party, 116, 191-193

Baghdad, 119-121, 124-125, 129-

130, 144-145, 148-149, 156, 177, 193, 210, 222, 241, 246, 250-253, 255-257, 262, 274-275, 285, 292, 297, 317, 339

Bahrain: Abu Dhabi, 138; al-Saud, 203, 229; Britain, 123, 138, 143-147, 152, 155, 159, 163, 165-167, 169-172, 179, 228, 242, 318, 345; Eastern Arabia, 68, 74, 242, 248, 339; Egypt, 121-122, 130-134, 137-138, 141, 143-148, 150, 154, 158, 165, 167-169, 177-178; Kuwait, 123, 225-227, 246, 303-304; Nasser, 100; oil, 99, 228; Oman, 123, 159-160, 168, 173-175; Ottoman Empire, 243, 246; Persian claim, 40-64, 101-105, 225; Persian Gulf, 113, 331; Qatar, 69, 170; Al Khalifah Shaikhs of, 69-70, 72, 121, 137, 168, 203, 248, 250

Basra, 44-45, 81, 102, 126, 131, 134, 140, 144-146, 148-150, 156, 168, 177, 240-247, 250-251, 256-257, 262, 274, 285, 292, 304, 329, 338-340

Britain: Aden, 212-213, 224, 237, 300, 346; Arab Revolt, 283, 285, 289, 295; Arab Slave Trade, 308; Arabia, 227-230; China, 254; Conservative Party, 15; East of Suez, 14, 186, 188, 190, 344; Egypt, 107, 137, 149, 151, 163, 165; Empire, 15; France, 255, 317; India, 107; Indian Ocean, 188, 227; Iraq, 116; Kuwait, 225, 240-279, 317; Labour Party, 13, 15, 325; Macaulay, 12; Mauritius,

109; Middle East, 285, 298-299, 301; Nasser, 215; Oman, 167, 222, 255, 317; Ottoman Empire, 111, 243; Palestine, 9, 106; Protestant, 12, 16; Persia, 126, 128, 134, 243, 260, 316-317, 319, 321-325; Persian Gulf, 13-15, 17-20, 22, 24-29, 39-40, 58, 64, 71, 90, 95, 99-100, 149, 160, 167, 186-187, 225-226, 228-230, 238, 242, 260-261, 279, 316, 319, 321, 323, 330, 332, 344-346; Red Sea, 9, 106-107, 109, 111; Russia, 10, 120, 254-255, 260, 316, 319, 321-325; Saudi Arabia, 30, 100; South Arabia, 167, 183, 185, 212-214; Suez, 190; United Nations, 100, 214; United States, 12; Welfare State, 13

Buraimi Oasis, 9, 14, 25, 30-39, 67, 69, 72-76, 78-79, 84, 88-93, 99-100, 139, 150-156, 158-164, 168, 172, 175-178, 199-201, 203-206, 335, 345

Bushire, 42-43, 45, 48-49, 51, 56, 102-103, 119, 126, 128-129, 131, 133, 135-136, 157, 242-243, 247, 250, 252, 260, 269, 272, 275

C

Cabinet, British, 12, 108, 126, 128, 269, 284-285

Cairo, 30-31, 91-98, 110, 119, 122-123, 130-131, 133, 137, 141, 143, 149, 151, 153-154, 163, 166, 172, 176, 183, 192-193, 211, 217-218, 222, 228, 233, 237, 284-290,

Index

313-314

Chatham House, 13, 15, 77, 182, 186, 190, 227, 284, 289, 345

China, 15, 95, 142, 157, 254

Clarendon, Lord, 57-64, 103-104

Constantinople, 34, 106, 121, 123-124, 144, 147-149, 241-246, 250, 252-253, 255-258, 264, 274-276, 278, 286, 317-318

Curzon, Lord, 240-279, 285, 320, 324-325

D
Dhufar (Oman), 22, 78-80, 90, 92-93

E
Eastern Arabia, 99-100, 107, 114, 118, 121, 131, 140, 144, 148-149, 151-152, 155, 158, 164, 166, 169, 171-172, 175-177, 199, 205-206, 217, 223, 229-230, 303-305, 318, 335, 345

East India Company, 17, 45, 103, 108, 119, 166, 206, 304, 308, 337, 338-340

Eden, Sir Anthony, 39, 298 -299, 308

Egypt, 13, 19-20, 25, 27-28, 30-32, 34-35, 42, 44-45, 50-52, 55, 83, 86, 91, 94-95, 102, 107, 114, 117-123, 125-127, 129-133, 134, 136-138, 140-179, 185, 187-188, 192-193, 196, 201-202, 210-212, 214-215, 217-219, 221, 223-224, 226, 234, 238, 280, 286-289, 299, 301, 306, 308, 313-315, 340, 344

Europe, 286, 288-289, 306-307, 309, 313, 316, 318-319, 321-323, 328, 330-331, 335, 345

F
Farouk, King, 13, 344

Foreign Office: 13-15, 48, 56, 58-59, 95-97, 101-102, 109, 124, 241, 244-246, 248-251, 253-254, 256, 258, 260, 263-264, 266-269, 275, 284-288, 317-318, 326, 334, 344-345

Fowler, H.W. and E.G., 11

H
Hajar Mountains, Oman, 66, 75, 78-80, 90, 92-93, 162, 219, 221-222

Hennell, Captain Samuel (Political Resident, Persian Gulf), 53, 123-124, 131-147, 149-154, 156-161, 163-166, 168-169, 170-175, 178-179

I
Imamate in Oman, 9, 14, 25, 28, 65, 77-79, 81-83, 85-89, 91, 93-99, 114, 210, 215-216, 219-221, 228, 300, 333-334, 345

India, 12, 17, 19, 28, 35, 45-46, 48,

351

Fighting the Retreat from Arabia and the Gulf

50-53, 55-56, 58-61, 63, 77, 80, 83-88, 98, 101-104, 108-109, 114, 119-120, 123-124, 126-129, 133, 136, 140, 142, 145, 151, 153-154, 157, 160, 163-170, 173-174, 176-178, 187-188, 203-204, 206-207, 215, 227, 236-237, 243-247, 249-255, 257, 260-276, 279, 284-287, 289-290, 292, 296, 301, 304, 306, 308, 313, 315, 317-321, 323-326, 330-334, 337-340, 343

International Affairs, 13-14, 30, 40, 67, 77-78, 115, 180, 182, 190, 195, 209, 227, 231, 233-234, 280

Iraq, 9, 15, 24-26, 28, 42-43, 83, 90, 99, 106, 113, 115-117, 119-120, 156, 190, 193, 196, 210, 223-224, 226, 228-229, 238, 240-241, 263, 270, 292, 330, 340, 343, 345-346

Iran, 10, 15, 40, 42, 101, 310-311, 324, 345-346

Islam, 10, 26, 33, 36, 65, 70, 74-75, 81-83, 111, 147, 191, 193, 195, 199, 218-219, 221, 230, 241, 255, 280-281, 286, 288-289, 296-297, 306-310, 312-315, 336

K
Kelly, John Barrett (J.B.): ANZAC, 11 Auckland, city of, 11-12, 344, 347; Auckland, University of, 11, 344; Britain, 12; Britain and the Persian Gulf, 13, 15, 316, 344-346; British Boys' School, Alexandria, 13; Bullard, Reader, 14, 345; Bunter, Billy, 11; Church of Rome, 12; Eastern Arabian Frontiers, 14, 345; Gibbon, Edward, 11-12; Glorious Revolution of 1688, 12; Haverstock Hill School, London, 13; Kelly, Jack and Maud, 11; Macaulay, Thomas Babington, 9, 11-13, 15-16; Marist Brothers, 11; New Zealand, 9, 11-16, 344; Pitt, Valda, 13, 344; Sacred Heart College, 11, 344; United States, 12, 14-15; University of London, 13, 120, 303, 338; University of Wisconsin-Madison, 15, 282, 341, 346; Von Ranke, Leopold: The History of the Popes, 12

Kharag Island (off Bushire), 53,126-128, 130-131, 135, 137, 145, 150, 155-159, 167, 169, 171, 173, 175

Khaur al-Udaid, 25, 69-72

Khurshid Pasha (Egyptian Commander), 35, 51, 123, 126, 129-133, 134, 137-138, 140-141, 143-146, 149-161, 163-166, 168, 170-172, 174-177, 217

Kurds, 9, 115-117, 224

Kuwait, 19, 22, 267; 180-181, 187-188, 196, 223-229, 240-279, 303-304, 317, 331

L
Lawrence, T.E., 10, 231-233, 237, 282-302

Index

M

Madinah, 121-123, 126, 134, 143, 156, 171-172

Mecca, 12, 35, 53, 103, 121, 123, 126, 143, 172, 297

Middle East, 234, 237, 240, 285-289, 297-299, 301, 306, 312, 314, 318, 327, 343-344, 346-347

Muhammad Ali (Mehemet Ali), Pasha of Egypt, 34-35, 44, 83, 107, 118, 125, 130, 143-144, 149, 168-169, 298

Muscat and Oman, Sultanate of, 9-10, 14, 19-23, 25, 27-28, 30-39, 42-47, 52, 55, 65-70, 73-75, 77-100, 102, 113-115, 119-120, 122-123, 125, 139, 147-148, 152-153, 159-160, 162-168, 170, 173, 175-178, 187-189, 201-207, 216, 219-223, 228-229, 234, 255, 260, 266, 268, 270, 272-273, 275, 287, 303, 317, 327-339, 341, 345, 347

N

Najd, Amirate of (see also Saudi Arabia), 19, 21, 24, 71-72, 83, 102, 119, 121-123, 125-126, 129, 131-132, 139, 143-144-149, 155, 165-166, 171-172, 175-177, 200-201, 203, 205-206, 217, 242, 251, 287, 318

Nasser, Colonel, 13,-14, 28, 31, 100, 107, 192-193, 210-212, 214-215, 218-219, 221, 230, 280-281, 298-299

O

Oil, 14-15, 17-18, 22-23, 25, 27-29, 31-32, 37, 65-66, 68, 76, 78-79, 88, 90, 92-93, 95-97, 99, 114, 116-117, 176, 181, 183, 185, 187-189, 196, 198-199, 210-211, 216-217, 221-223, 228-229, 235, 238, 293, 297, 299, 335-337, 345-346

Oxford, University of, 7, 13-15, 106, 115, 180, 182, 190, 195-196, 231, 297-298, 325, 327, 345

Ottoman Empire (Turkey), 19-21, 42, 71, 106, 111-112, 115, 117, 147, 192, 240, 242, 249, 255, 257, 261, 263, 269, 272, 285-287, 289-290, 295, 306, 317

P

Pakistan, 17, 21, 28, 215, 222, 227

Palestine, 9, 106-107, 109-111, 233, 290, 292, 294-296, 301

Palmerston, Lord, 107, 110, 118-121, 124-126, 128-131, 135-138, 141, 143-145, 148-149, 163-164, 166-172, 179, 298-299

Pearl Fisheries, 22-23, 43, 122, 133, 139, 170, 189

Pelly, Colonel Sir Lewis, 36, 38, 56-59, 202-203, 331-333

Persia, 10, 17, 19-20, 24-27, 32, 40-64, 69, 82-83, 87, 101-106, 113, 116-117; 119-120, 124, 126-130, 132, 134-136, 143-144, 147, 153,

167, 171, 177-178, 225, 227, 229, 243, 249, 252-256, 260, 264, 277, 299, 303, 304, 306, 308, 310-313, 316-326, 329-331, 338-340

Persian Gulf, 9, 13, 15, 17, 19, 21, 23, 25, 27, 29, 30-32, 35, 39, 45, 48-49, 52, 56, 61, 63, 68, 71-72, 76-77, 79, 83-84, 86-88, 92, 101, 105, 107, 113, 118-119-127, 129-133, 135, 137, 139, 141, 143-145, 147, 149, 151, 153, 155, 157, 159, 161, 163-165, 167, 169, 171, 173, 175, 177, 179, 182-183, 186, 201-202, 210, 236, 241-242, 247-249, 252-253, 256-257, 260, 262-264, 269, 275, 299, 301, 303, 309, 316, 327, 329-332, 335, 338-339, 344-346

Q
Qatar, 69-71, 73-74, 77, 90, 99, 113, 132, 138, 146, 158, 170, 188, 196, 227-228, 243-244, 274, 304, 318, 346

R
Ras al-Khaima, 18, 33, 46, 76, 138-140, 149-150, 177

Red Sea (formerly Arabian Gulf), 9, 27, 83, 106-107, 108-111, 118, 120, 124, 127, 132, 163, 167, 210, 299, 301

Russia: Afghanistan, 126, 313; China, 254; Egypt, 211; France, 254-255; Kuwait, 27, 196, 225, 252-254, 261, 271, 274, 277-279; Middle East, 18, 233, 240; Muslims, 315; Ottoman Empire, 44, 120, 166, 255, 257-261, 263-264, 276-278; Persia, 27, 44, 126, 253-254, 260, 277, 311, 316-26; Persian Gulf, 10, 27, 252-253, 258, 264, 275-277, 316-326; Yemen, 215, 301

S
Salisbury, Lord, 10, 240-279, 318

Saudi Arabia (see also Najd), 10, 15, 24-28, 30-32, 37, 39, 66-70, 72-75, 77-78, 90-95, 99-100, 113-114, 187, 198-199, 201, 203-205, 207-208, 211, 216-218, 221, 223-224, 229, 280-281, 335, 345-347

Shahs of Iran, 27, 42-45, 49-50, 52-53, 57, 61-64, 103-104, 126-128, 134-136, 147, 178, 225, 228, 253, 255, 304, 310, 323-324, 329, 338, 340

Sharjah, 33, 36, 76, 138-140, 149-150, 156, 159-161, 164, 177, 206

Shiraz, 43, 48, 49-50, 54-55, 103, 119, 134

South Arabia, 182-183, 185, 212, 214, 235-238, 299

State Department, 14, 98-99, 196

Suez Crisis, 13, 298, 347

Syria, 106-107, 117, 119-121, 125-126, 131, 148-149, 151, 156, 172, 174-175, 177, 192-193, 196, 210-

Index

211, 223, 226, 233, 238, 256-257, 285, 287, 290-291, 294-295

T
Treaties: Arabia and Gulf, 15, 22, 30-31, 68, 114, 186-187; Bahrain, 20, 22, 41, 47, 49, 57, 59, 63, 103-104, 133, 154; Kuwait, 269, 272-273, 277; Muscat and Oman, 19, 21, 25, 86-87, 95-99, 147, 167-168, 220, 333-334; Najd, 21-22, 40, 202; Persia, 126, 321-322; Qatar, 21-22; Shoa, 107; Trucial Coast, 18, 20, 55, 139;

Trucial Shaikhdoms (Pirate Coast and Trucial Oman), 14, 18, 27, 31-33, 35-36, 39, 46-47, 67, 74, 76-77, 79, 92, 95, 113, 139-140, 149-152, 157-159, 161, 166, 175, 177, 204, 227-228, 242, 339, 345

U
United States: Indian Ocean, 187-188, 334; Kuwait, 225; Middle East, 99, 195-196; Nixon Administration, 15; Oman, 95-96, 98-100; Persian Gulf, 17, 27, 99, 114, 117; Saudi Arabia, 99; Yemen, 229-230

W
Wahhabi, 36, 38-39, 44-45, 53-55, 75, 83-84, 86-87, 89, 90, 119, 121, 131, 143, 145, 147-148, 150, 153, 162, 176-178, 199-202, 204-206, 216-217, 308, 329

Western world, 236-237, 281, 301, 306, 308, 312-315, 328, 343, 346

Y
Yemen (North, Zaidi Imamate and South), 15, 28, 31, 81-82, 107, 109-110, 114, 120-122, 142, 172, 175, 184-186, 188, 196, 201-202, 209-219, 222, 224, 229-230, 234-235, 238, 281, 286-287, 297, 299-301, 347

Z
Zakat (religious tribute), 32, 34-36, 38, 53, 70, 74-75, 89, 147-148

Zanzibar, 23, 83-84, 99, 152, 159, 173-174, 309, 331

www.ingramcontent.com/pod-product-compliance
Lightning Source LLC
Chambersburg PA
CBHW022102150426
43195CB00008B/228